Praise for *Fearful Symmetry*

"A bracing, relentless argument for a 'character shift' that will release Canada from its torpor."

—William Thorsell, CEO, Royal Ontario Museum

"This book's expose of some of the sources of Canada's rush to the left of the United States; of the fact that the chief motives for it are obsolete; and its prediction of a traditional revival, make a stimulating read. The pursuit of a kinder and gentler Canada compared to the US will give way as a national mission to something more galvanizing, as did the preceding inspiration of Imperial solidarity. This excellent analysis by a distinguished and original public policy expert is a fine effort to map out the next national *raison d'être*."

—Conrad Black, *Franklin Delano Roosevelt*

"*Fearful Symmetry* is one of the most important analyses yet written of the recent history and directions of Canadian public policy. It will undoubtedly be required reading for politicians, civil servants, all possible policy wonks, students, and everyone else concerned about our country's recent past and its uncertain future."

—Michael Bliss, *Right Honourable Men*

"A blockbuster! To be Canadian once meant standing up for individual freedom and responsibility; marriage, family, and work. Today, according to Brian Crowley, we're a nation of 'rent-seekers,' political opportunists and lobbyists, ever looking for someone else to take charge, to pay the bills, to tell us what to do. How did this happen? In a compelling account of economic and political developments from the 1960s to the present, Crowley argues that big government inevitably corrupts identity and mores. But the die isn't cast. Big government isn't obligatory. Crowley's last chapters set out reasons for thinking that Canadians may yet recover their former and better selves! *Fearful Symmetry* will be an eye opener for the political scientists and sociologists who still believe that the Canadian propensity to depend on governments is bred in the bone and shaped Confederation."

—Janet Ajzenstat, *The Canadian Founding*

"A genuine *cri de coeur*…*Fearful Symmetry* provides a fascinating account of the demographic forces transforming Canada and does so with a deep appreciation of the historical trends and political forces that have shaped the Canadian nation. This is a book that is required reading for every informed citizen."

—Rudyard Griffiths, *Who We Are: A Citizen's Manifesto*

BRIAN LEE CROWLEY

fearful symmetry the fall and rise of
canada's founding values

Brian Lee Crowley

KEY PORTER BOOKS

Library and Archives Canada Cataloguing in Publication

Crowley, Brian Lee
Fearful symmetry : the fall and rise of Canada's founding values
/ Brian Lee Crowley.

ISBN 978-1-55470-188-9

1. Canada—History—1963-. 2. Public welfare—Canada—History.
3. Nationalism—Québec (Province)—History. 4. Canada—Social policy.
5. Canada—Economic policy—1945-. 6. Welfare state—Canada—History.
I. Title.

HC115.C765 2009   971.064   C2009-901422-X

ONTARIO ARTS COUNCIL
CONSEIL DES ARTS DE L'ONTARIO

The publisher gratefully acknowledges the support of the Canada Council for the Arts and the Ontario Arts Council for its publishing program. We acknowledge the support of the Government of Ontario through the Ontario Media Development Corporation's Ontario Book Initiative.

We acknowledge the financial support of the Government of Canada through the Book Publishing Industry Development Program (BPIDP) for our publishing activities.

Key Porter Books Limited
Six Adelaide Street East, Tenth Floor
Toronto, Ontario
Canada M5C 1H6

www.keyporter.com

Text design: Sonya V. Thursby
Electronic formatting: Sonya V. Thursby

Printed and bound in Canada

09 10 11 12 13 5 4 3 2 1

For Shelley, who knew I could
when I thought I couldn't

table of contents

THE TYGER

Tyger! Tyger! burning bright
In the forests of the night,
What immortal hand or eye
Could frame thy fearful symmetry?
—William Blake

I first met Brian Crowley when we were studying at the London School of Economics together, back in the 1980s. He had come over to do his Ph.D. on Friedrich Hayek, the great free-market theorist and contender, along with Friedman and Keynes, for the title of most influential economist of the twentieth century. As a good social democrat—for so he then was—Crowley had set himself the ambitious task of debunking Hayek. But in the course of his research, he had found himself at first unable to answer his arguments, and at last persuaded by them. In a word, he had become a convert.

Whatever that tells us about the power of Hayek's analysis, I think it tells us something essential about the author of this profoundly important book: his intellectual honesty; his unblinking openness to facts and reasoned arguments, even those that contradict his preconceptions; above all his fearlessness. He will go where the argument leads him, and let the chips fall where they may. And where it leads him, in the present case, is nothing less than a revolution in our way of looking at Canada, its history, and its future.

That's "revolution," in its original sense: as a turning full circle, a return to what once was. It is Crowley's contention that Canada is about to complete such a revolution—that after fifty years of ever-expanding government, spending, and taxation, we are entering an equally lengthy cycle in which all of these processes will be reversed: beneficially, necessarily, *inevitably*, as the tides. If the first part of the book is concerned with describing how the tide came in—how the all-providing, ever-encroaching state came to be, with all of its baleful effects on work, on family, on our very souls—the second is spent in happy contemplation of the departing tide, and the rediscovery of those historic virtues of limited government, hard work, and familial commitment on which the country was founded.

For in truth it is the last fifty years, he argues, that have been the aberration. Though mythologized by nationalists as the outgrowth of an inborn cultural bias toward big government that marked us apart from the Americans, Crowley argues convincingly that the growth of the state in Canada had more prosaic origins. Rather, he says, it grew out of the confluence of two separate but not unrelated trends: the explosive growth in the labour force as the "baby boom" cohort reached working age, and the growing threat of Quebec separatism. Beginning in the early 1960s, each set off a kind of panic in policy makers: the first, that the labour market would not prove able to absorb all these newcomers; the second, that the new generation of nationalist francophones in Quebec would carry the province out of the country—not least if Canada could not find work for them.

It was debatable whether either threat was as real as all that. Labour markets are marvellously adaptable things, and separation, as we have learned, is massively difficult, if not impossible to carry off. The point is that policy makers believed they were real. And through the decades that followed, events seemed to validate their concerns. Unemployment was the defining issue of economic policy for most of the period under study, while separatism seemed to reach new peaks with each wave of the political cycle—though whether either flourished in spite of or because of the policies intended to alleviate them is another matter.

What to do with all those young workers was not a preoccupation limited to Canada, of course. Across the developed world, governments wrestled with the same problem. In an age of seemingly permanent unemployment, any policy that would find jobs for the jobless seemed worth a try. And coinciding as it did with the highwater mark of faith in state solutions—memories of wartime planning were still fresh, and theories of Keynesian demand management had yet to be discredited by actual contact with the real world—the answer in almost every country was more government. Inflation, protectionism, subsidies, make-work programs or what Crowley calls "pseudo-work"—socially useless feather-bedding, usually in the public sector—all could be justified, whatever the costs, by the pressing need to mop up all that surplus labour. Or so it seemed.

But why did government grow so much faster and further in Canada than, say, the United States? If it was not because of any innate predisposition to statism in America's northern neighbour—for if so, it should surely have manifested itself in the preceding century, when Canada was the more classically liberal of the two—then what can explain it? Crowley's provocative answer: the coincident rise of Quebec nationalism, starting with the Quiet Revolution, when the Catholic Church was replaced by the secular religion of the state, the sword and shield of the francophone ascendancy.

The effect was to set off a bidding war between the governments of Quebec and Canada for the allegiance, if that is the right word, of Quebecers. It was not a strategy calculated to Canada's advantage—for whatever was wrong with

Quebec could always be blamed on the insufficiency of federal largesse, while whatever the feds did provide could always be chalked up to the efficacy of separatist blackmail. But it fit with the climate of the times. And in no time the battle spilled over into the rest of Canada: whatever programs were initiated, whatever powers were conceded, whatever money was spent in the name of wooing Quebec soon became the norm in other provinces as well.

But if work is not useful and productive, something we do for others, but something provided as a gift of government, when it is not actively penalizing it—for why encourage more work effort when there is already too much of it?—then the effect is to breed contempt for work, the more so if those who do the productive work are taxed more heavily to pay for those who do not. And if at the same time policies are enacted, fiscal or otherwise, that undercut incentives to marry and raise a family—for why would a society overrun with surplus labour want more children?—then society loses the principal means of instilling the habits of character on which productive work depends. And if the state, rather than the market, becomes the central mechanism by which resources are allocated, then lobbying government and flattering politicians will replace producing goods and services for consumers as the primary means of advancement, each seeking to harness the coercive power of the state to force others to pay for his upkeep. Or in Crowley's pithy phrase, *making* will be replaced by *taking*.

All of these effects are described in detail in the book, and all are observed in their most virulent form in Quebec, where the state ballooned to its greatest size and where the ethos of taking became the habit of mind not merely of "rent-seeking" special interests, but of an entire society—the "profitable federalism" that Quebecers have been taught to expect the rest of Canada to deliver, and that now forms the basis for what remains of their attachment to Canada.

Left at that, Crowley's analysis would be provocative enough. What truly sets his argument apart, however, and what makes this such an original contribution to the national debate, is what comes next. For the twin motors powering the rise of the state, he writes—the baby boom and Quebec nationalism—are both about to be thrown into reverse: arguably in the latter case, incontrovertibly in the former. As the baby boomers reach retirement age—beginning next year—and withdraw from the labour market, the proportion of the population of working age will contract: from a peak of five workers to every retiree not long ago, the ratio is projected to shrink to three or even two to one. The labour surplus that was the perennial obsession of policy makers will become a permanent labour shortage. And with that, he argues, everything will change.

A surplus of labour may be unpleasant for those seeking work, but can be tolerated well enough by society at large, provided the employed can be prevailed upon to pay for the unemployed (or underemployed). A labour shortage is the reverse: a boon for workers, whose pay and benefits can be expected to rise, but an absolute *crisis* for society. (If you doubt it, ask yourself which is the more acute problem: too many doctors, or too few?) Policies that might once have been at least nominally justified in the name of fighting unemployment, whether to keep people out of the labour force altogether, or to protect those with jobs from competition, or to keep people in pseudo-work via subsidies and so on, will not just become unnecessary: they will be intolerable. Everything will be directed toward freeing up every available man-hour of labour supply, to redress the chronic excess of labour demand.

Talking of labour shortage at a time of rising unemployment may seem strange, but the transitory effects of recession, Crowley argues, will soon be overtaken by the remorseless arithmetic of demography. Higher immigration will help, but can't save us on its own. Ditto raising the retirement age. The burden of paying for all those aged baby boomers will require not just that everyone who can work do so, but that they be put to productive work. It will mean cutting taxes, to improve incentives. It will mean opening ourselves further to international trade, to better make use of the productive talents of workers in other countries. It will mean having more children, which will in turn require policies that buttress the family unit—or at least do not discourage it. It will require higher rates of internal migration, meaning policies that allow people to move to where the jobs are, rather than, as with "regional development" policies, keeping people where the jobs aren't. It will transform not just our policies, but our politics, radically altering not just how we govern ourselves, but our cultural values as well.

Quebec, in particular, will come under increasing pressure, since its fiscal situation is already so dire, and since the proportion of its population in useful work is by far the lowest. Yet no matter how much it adjusts the policies that have contributed to this, the reality is that its population is likely to decline relative to Canada's, as will its share of the economy. Its clout in Confederation, already on the wane, will be diminished accordingly, opening the way to a rebalancing of federal and provincial responsibilities, free of the separatist threat, on more rational lines. Not that this will necessarily prove inimical to Quebec's desire for autonomy: with the end of the bidding war, Ottawa will no longer feel compelled to spend in areas of provincial responsibility, accepting in its place provincial acknowledgement of its exclusive power to promote the economic union. Which was, after all, one of the primary *raisons d'etre* of Confederation.

It is a complicated argument, and yet one that is both cogent and coherent.

Indeed, I know of no other work that has so comprehensively assessed the implications of the coming era of labour shortages, or that draws them together so effectively. Taken as a whole, they add up to a compelling argument for change. For the changes he describes are inevitable, whether we will it or not: the only question is how we will manage them. Part critique, part prescription, this is more than anything a prophecy—a prophecy of a future that, as it happens, will look very much like our past.

preface

When November 15, 1976, rolled around and René Lévesque was declaring to rapturous applause in the Paul Sauvé Arena, "*Je n'ai jamais été si fier d'être Québécois*," I was a parliamentary intern at the House of Commons. To a unilingual English-speaking kid from British Columbia, it was patently obvious that Quebec was where the action was. Something new and unprecedented was stirring there, and I desperately wanted both to understand it and be a part of it.

But how?

A few months later the answer became apparent when the interns took their annual trip to Quebec City to visit the National Assembly. This visit had two immediate effects on me. First, I was absolutely blown away by the vigour and eloquence of the ministers and backbenchers we met from the new government. The "*projet de société*" that, together with sovereignty, seemed to animate the PQ government was, to the eyes of a callow youth at any rate, unbelievably exciting and inspiring. Second, I learned that the new government had great plans to reform the province's political institutions, and political institutions were actually something I knew something about.

On my return to Ottawa I asked Stanley Knowles, dean of the House of Commons and a towering authority on Canadian parliamentary procedure, to write me a letter to Quebec's new minister of state for Parliamentary and Electoral Reform, Robert Burns, asking that he consider me for any jobs that might come open on his staff. Within a few days the phone was ringing and one of Burns' top aides, André Larocque, was calling. "We don't get many letters from Stanley Knowles," he said.

I was in.

There was the little matter of not speaking a word of French, but it is amazing what you can do when you are motivated. As Wordsworth said of an earlier time of hope and excitement in another French-speaking land: "Bliss was it in that dawn to be alive, but to be young was very heaven." In my blissful state I threw myself into learning the French language with all the zeal of a convert. The deal I had made with Burns was that I would work part-time for him and study part time at Laval University. As my French got better and better, I went less and less to my classes. At the end of six months I was learning so much more at work than at the university that I stopped going altogether.

It wasn't just mastering French that drove me. I wanted to be part of a new society that many of us thought we were creating, a French-speaking society committed to social justice that would make a break from the morally dubious English-speaking capitalism that had brought us Vietnam, Richard Nixon, energy crises, the CIA and so much more. And not only was Robert Burns a leading nationalist, he was also a famously left-wing trade union leader. He made René Lévesque so nervous that the new premier felt constrained to warn Burns that the new government was not going to adopt the "Cuban model" of economic and social development.

I pretty much went native.

But heart and head were not pulling together in harness, and as I grew older the head increasingly argued the heart into following its lead—especially as the heart began to have galling suspicions that it had been duped. It began with the nagging discomfort I felt with the dismissive contempt that met the legitimate aspirations of English-speakers and the unapologetic use of the state's coercive powers to push English to the back of the bus.

It was at this point, as Andrew Coyne relates in the foreword, that I went off to do graduate studies at the London School of Economics. There I came to grips, metaphorically speaking, with F.A. Hayek, the Nobel Prize–winning economist who was one of the twentieth century's most doughty defenders of liberal-capitalism. I wanted to prove him wrong; instead, the richness and breadth of his argument made me confront the shallowness of many of my own economic ideas. Scepticism about the benevolence of big government began to tinge my thinking.

Hard on the heels of my return to Canada came the era of big constitutional reform. I was a negotiator of both the Meech Lake and Charlottetown constitutional accords, and became ever more disturbed about the degree to which the country was tying itself in knots to accommodate Quebec when it was clear that Quebec's demands were more and more obviously arguments of convenience designed to maximize their bargaining power under threat of referendums to break up the country.

A fifteen-year period ensued in which I set aside my preoccupation with Quebec and its place within Canada in favour of a different project: challenging Atlantic Canadians to reject the damage that had been wrought on them and their economy by decades of well-intentioned but deeply misguided policy, including by Ottawa. An intrepid band, of which I was a member, founded a think-tank, the Atlantic Institute for Market Studies (AIMS) in Halifax, and we dug in for a long battle of attrition in the war of ideas. When we opened our doors, it was a courageous person indeed who was willing to say that, on balance, dependence on transfers from Ottawa had been a bad thing for the region. Today, that idea meets with widespread (but not universal!) acceptance, and we at AIMS had a major role to play in that evolution of attitudes.

A series of fortuitous events then occurred, which, like a catalyst in a science experiment, caused this book to begin to precipitate out of these diverse experiences.

Probably the first such event came in 2004, when I was still a columinist for La Presse in Montreal. The editor-in-chief, André Pratte, invited me to participate in a joint La Presse/Radio Canada conference in Montreal on the Quebec model of social and economic development. Tasked with presenting a talk on whether Quebec could afford the "Quebec Model," I laid the groundwork for much of what became Chapter 7. The next event was an invitation I received from Mackenzie King Visiting Professor Randall Morck to come and give the Canada Seminar at Harvard in November 2005. While the talk was ostensibly to be about what I had learned about regional policy during my time at AIMS, the prestige of the institution and the catholicity of tastes of the audience made me want to avoid a parochial talk. It was in my ruminations over what to say to the Harvard audience that the idea crystallized of the decades-long bidding war between Quebec and Ottawa for the loyalty of Quebeckers, an idea which forms a crucial part of the architecture of this book. EI, regional development policy, vast transfers to the provinces, massive pseudo-work, all of the themes in which I had been immersed within the region, now fit within a larger vision of how Canada had evolved over the last fifty years.

Michael Ignatieff, whom I already knew and respected, was a sympathetic member of the audience and was struck by both the bidding war concept as well as by the analysis of how long-term dependence had harmed the Atlantic-Canadian economy. Now that he has moved on to other responsibilities, I hope that he still remembers his initial enthusiasm for these ideas.

An invitation from my friend, UPEI Dean of Arts Richard Kurial, added fuel to the fire. Richard asked me to take part in a debate at the Institute for Public Administration of Canada's annual conference in Charlottetown in August 2006. On the other side of the debate was the redoubtable Nancy Riche of the Canadian Labour Congress, and we had it out on the theme of the role of trade unions in the public sector in Canada. I'll leave it to others to decide who got the better of the argument. The important thing to note is that the reflections that the preparations for this debate triggered form a large part of Chapter 6.

The next catalyst was another invitation from another friend, Kevin Lynch. Kevin had just been made clerk of the Privy Council by our new prime minister, Stephen Harper. Kevin was hosting a retreat for his new flock of deputy ministers at the old Ottawa City Hall, and he asked me to come and be on a panel about the chief economic challenges facing the country. I had recently been mulling over the demographic challenges facing Canada, and was particularly struck by the impact the coming labour shortages were already having on Atlantic Canada, traditionally the highest unemployment region in Canada, and so Kevin's invitation spurred me to put those first impressions into a more developed narrative. That story was later woven into this book, chiefly in Chapter 1.

My talk to the federal deputies was quickly followed by an invitation from Rob Wright, the deputy minister of finance, to come to Ottawa as the Clifford Clark Visiting Economist at Finance Canada. The Clifford Clark is a very prestigious and unusual post in Ottawa—the only way to describe it is as the one-man in-house think-tank and policy gadfly in the Department of Finance. The incumbent holds the rank of an assistant deputy minister, participates as a full member in the Executive Committee that makes all decisions at the officials' level, and gets to choose the policy areas in which he will play that gadfly role within the department and the government more generally. Given how I got there, and given the importance I was increasingly attaching to the transformative effects of population aging and labour shortages, I decided to make those my chief areas of interest. The second half of this book was largely conceived during this time.

I was blessed during my tenure at Finance to have the ready, and even enthusiastic, support of many incredibly knowledgeable colleagues who helped me think through many of the population change issues, both by supplying me data and by giving me the benefit of their own thoughts. Because being associated with this book in any way will likely not be a career-advancing move in Ottawa, I won't refer by name to the many people who gave to me so generously of their time and thoughts, but they know who they are and I want them to know I will never be able to thank them enough.

Because population change is one of those deep and far-reaching social and economic shifts that are actually quite foreseeable, I met little resistance within the department when I pressed on them the case for a more vigorous response from the federal government to the changes on the horizon. Much of the great work we did internally, however, has still not seen the light of day. Thereby hangs a tale that, alas, my oath of secrecy prevents me from telling in all its gory detail.

Suffice it to say, that the thing that struck me most forcibly on my arrival in Ottawa was the extent to which the federal government was mesmerized (and I use the word advisedly) by the provinces, and particularly the province of Quebec. Everything that Ottawa could or should do was weighed and measured by how it would influence or shape relations with the provinces, as if there was nothing more to the country than these peculiar quaint relics of colonial history and Victorian politics and technology. And the consequences of the uneven effects of population aging on different provinces, and particularly on Quebec, was just something that Ottawa was not willing to shine a spotlight on. The circle was neatly closed between my early fascination with Quebec and my more recent preoccupation with what an aging population means for Canada.

The most unexpected tributary of this book was the one that turned out to be the closest to me. No one can think about the great issues of population change without being struck by their intimate connection with the great life decisions of individuals, and most notably the decisions about marriage and family.

While I was off hobnobbing in Ottawa, my long-time partner, Shelley, was home in Halifax, running our restaurant and café, the Queen of Cups and the Queen of Cups Too. We missed each other terribly even though I was home on weekends, and I quickly began to realize that I couldn't think about Marriage and Family on a grand scale without also thinking about marriage and family for myself, and the critical things I had to say about the decisions Canadians had made in this regard over the past few decades applied just as much to me as to anyone else. I asked Shelley to marry me in February 2008, and we are about to celebrate our first anniversary as this book is being prepared for the printer in June of 2009. My only regret is that it took me so long to get around to it; my great joy is that Shelley would have me in spite of everything.

There are many other people who deserve my thanks for the part they played in making this book come to life.

Sean Speer is certainly one of the most important. Sean, a Ph.D. candidate at the University of Ottawa, is one of the brightest intellectual lights of his generation and it has been my privilege to have him as my researcher. "Researcher" doesn't really cover the extent of the partnership I enjoyed with Sean on this project, however, for it would really be more accurate to say that it was a close collaboration. I came to depend on Sean a very great deal and he not only never let me down, he consistently exceeded my expectations. Every reference was meticulously chased down and documented. Every idea was exhaustively debated. Every possible source turned upside down and shaken vigorously to extract the gems within. I know that in a few years Sean will be the one writing the books and I will be looking on admiringly.

My publisher, Key Porter, has made the painful process of creation as smooth as could be hoped for. Executive editor Jonathan Schmidt worked with me on the manuscript and forced me to raise my literary game. Marketing manager Daniel Rondeau and consultant Pat Cairns threw themselves enthusiastically into plans to get people actually to buy the book. Wendy Thomas was my able copy-editor; designer Sonya V. Thursby did great work on the cover and interior. Editor-in-chief Linda Pruessen was the one who saw the potential in my idea and first brought me into the Key Porter fold, in large part I suspect because of the recommendation of my friend, fellow author and best man, Patrick Luciani.

Few people deserve more thanks than my colleagues at AIMS. They patiently endured my absence for almost two years while I was on loan to Finance Canada, and then supported me when I came back with writing lust in my eye and holed up with my computer for months on end. They never complained and indeed made sure that I was left alone, deflecting many importunate requests for my time and attention. In particular I want to thank the three key staffers, Charles Cirtwill, Barbara Pike, and Bobby O'Keefe, as well as the board of directors and especially the chairman, John Irving, for their unfailing backing.

An awful lot of people were strong-armed by me into reading some or all of the manuscript, which they all did with alacrity and good grace. They include: Tom Flanagan, William Johnson, Janet Ajzenstat, Alan Beattie, William Gairdner, Barbara Kay, Doug Allen, Andrea Mrozek, Rebecca Walberg, John Richards, John Weissenberger, Angela Tu-Weissenberger, Brian Flemming, David Frum, Martin Masse, Daniel Dufort, Jack Granatstein, Brian Ferguson, Jason Clemens, Peter White, Richard Bastien, David MacKinnon, Drew Bethune, Paula Minnikin, and Robin Neill. Their comments, which were copious but always constructive, allowed me to avoid a lot of mistakes while tightening the argument and strengthening its defences.

Much that is good in this book is due to the kind assistance of the many friends and colleagues I have mentioned here; and while I would love to be able to blame them, the truth is that all errors, of whatever kind, are attributable solely to me.

1

introduction: symmetry's halves

Freud was once asked what he thought a normal person should be able to do well. The questioner probably expected a complicated answer. But Freud, in the curt way of his old days, is reported to have said: *"Lieben und arbeiten"* (to love and to work). It pays to ponder on this simple formula; it gets deeper as you think about it.

ERIK H. ERIKSON, *CHILDHOOD AND SOCIETY*

Forget July 1, the birthday of the Old Canada founded in 1867. The "New Canada" was born on June 22, 1960. The profound transformation that emerged so forcefully in the last five decades or so can be summarized as a Canada of expansive government and social programs, of bilingualism and multiculturalism, of the appeasement of an endless list of demands from Quebec nationalists, of the abandonment of anything but a highly sanitized history of the country, of the decline of the work ethic, of the family and of our fertility. The birth date can be fixed with such precision because that was the day that Jean Lesage led the Liberal Party of Quebec to power and unleashed the Quiet Revolution.

The gestation period of the New Canada, however, goes back a further fifteen years or so. The New Canada was being prepared in the wombs of Canadian women in the form of the post-war baby boom. Had the Province of Quebec not been awash in young French-speakers about to enter the workforce in the early sixties, and had Quebec nationalism not become the means by which those young workers were to be accommodated in our society and economy, the history of Canada would almost certainly have been profoundly different.

The election of the Lesage government in Quebec in 1960 brought to a fever pitch the expectations of an emerging French-speaking middle class and intelligentsia looking for opportunities hitherto denied them in a largely English-speaking economy. Lacking much in the way of levers over the private economy beyond completing the nationalization of electricity, the Lesage government acted by increasing those opportunities chiefly in the provincial public sector, ramping up taxpayer-funded jobs and other programs and the taxes and federal transfers to pay for them.

Simultaneously two transfers of ideological allegiance were occurring in Quebec. The first was from the Church to the State. The second was from French Canada to Quebec, an allegiance energized by the powerful symbolism of a national majority in charge of its own destiny.

These changes provoked a powerful but not always effective response from Ottawa, the most important elements of which were a determination to cede to the Quebec state neither the role of chief architect of social justice for Quebeckers, nor that of protector of the French language. Through bilingualism and the Just Society (Pierre Trudeau's 1968 campaign slogan), the federal government sought to show Quebec that its social, economic, and linguistic aspirations could be realized within Canada, whatever the cost.

Into this world of ideological ferment and massive increase in the size of both the Quebec and the federal governments marched the unsuspecting Boomers looking for work. The proportion of people of working age in the population rose from its long-term share of about 60 per cent in the mid-1960s to nearly 70 per cent today.[1] A sustained increase of nearly 10 percentage points is an economy-shaking event, one about to be mirrored by a corresponding decline now that the working-age population has peaked (in 2008),[2] and the supply of workers will start to dry up in earnest in 2011–12.[3]

A different way of thinking about what has happened is that over the last fifty years the number of workers in Canada grew more, proportionally speaking, than any other major industrialized country. From 1956 to 2006, our workforce grew by 200 per cent, and the growth in the number of young people of working age in Quebec led the pack in the early days. Even America, our nearest rival, was well behind us, growing by a relatively restrained 120 per cent or so. By contrast, in the next fifty years, it is our workforce that will grow by a paltry 11 per cent—better than many of our European counterparts, who will see shrinkage in absolute terms—but well behind America, where the number of workers will grow by nearly a third.[4] We'll return to this theme of the looming labour shortages facing our country in a moment.

In his award-winning book, *Born at the Right Time: The History of the Baby Boom Generation*, Doug Owram defines the "Boomers" as those born between 1946 and 1962, a period in which the number of children born annually never fell below 400,000. In *Boom, Bust and Echo*, renowned economic demographer David Foot argues for somewhat different dates; for him the boom started in 1947 and ended in 1966.[5] At the height of the baby boom in 1959, the number of annual births exceeded 479,000. On Owram's account, between 1946 and 1961, 6.7 million babies were born in Canada. For Foot, because the boom lasted a few years longer, it was even more pronounced, adding over 7.5 million people to the Canadian population. Whichever of these accounts one chooses, the boomer generation was to have a profound effect on Canadian economic, political, and social life.[6]

The Boomers created a lot of anxiety for the politicians of the day. Nicole Morgan[7] summed up what became the conventional description of what happened: the Canadian government needed to

> act as a social safety valve ... and open the doors of the public service to a part of the 7.5 million young Canadians of the baby boom generation. After 1960, they were hitting the labour market in wave after wave, *and certainly could never have all been absorbed by the private sector.* [Emphasis added]

Despite the conventional view that we would have been overwhelmed by Boomers had governments not hoovered them up, we will never know whether the marketplace would have absorbed the Boomers and women into the private economy; I am firmly convinced, however, that it would have done so with gusto, since a wave of available and willing workers is a massive opportunity—unless governments get in the way, as they did in the Depression, for example.[8] In fact, the closest analogue we have, the crush of workers moving into the economy following the end of World War II, gives strong confidence that worries about the economy's inability to absorb a wave of new workers are profoundly misplaced. In the United States during this period, workers from rural areas flooded the cities, with the happy consequence that they kept wage pressures low while the economy was going gangbusters. That meant profits for companies, who then reinvested in further productive capacity, pulling in yet more workers.[9]

As we will see as the story of the last fifty years unfolds, precisely this approach had been the overriding policy of a century's worth of Canadian governments, and it was a policy that had served us well. Nothing had occurred that had fundamentally shaken our confidence in what had been the traditional Canadian policy of a very light governmental hand on the economic tiller; it would quite likely have seen Canadians through the rise of the Boomers just fine. Confidence that huge expansion of government was not the only solution is further bolstered by examining the record of other Western industrialized countries with similar histories and traditions, such as the United States and Australia.[10] Both countries dealt with baby booms of considerable size while keeping the expansion of the state within much smaller bounds than Canada did and enjoying, on the whole, relatively low unemployment.

We made a different choice. The first half of this book offers a way of thinking about why we made that choice, how different it was from the choices we had traditionally made, and what consequences flowed from the new direction we chose. It lays out the case for thinking of the New Canada built since 1960 as an abandonment of our own history and the values on which Canada was founded, an abandonment whose chief result has been to reveal the enduring value of what we left behind.

Where Were You in '62?

A review of the profound changes in public policy over the sixties and seventies is like a pleasant stroll down memory lane for most Boomers, but we forget just how different the New Canada that was emerging was from its predecessor, where smaller government, fiscal rectitude, suspicion of dependence on government or charity, and a ferocious work ethic were the norm.

The minister responsible, Bryce Mackasey, and his colleagues in Pierre Trudeau's first government, liberalized unemployment insurance in 1971,[11] overnight creating the "UIC ski team," as it was affectionately known, a brilliant shorthand for a system that essentially paid people an income for most of the year in exchange for a token work effort—in fact, a very thinly disguised form of workfare. Economists widely credited the UI reform with an increase in difference between the unemployment rates in Canada and the United States of around two percentage points. This system was made especially vicious because it gave to thousands of seasonal workers the illusion of paying their own way by charging them a token "premium" and calling their welfare entitlement an "insurance benefit." But the intellectual dishonesty of this position is belied by these beneficiaries' outrage at any suggestion that the benefits they receive and the premiums they pay should bear any serious economic relationship to one another.

Other social welfare programs were liberally enriched as well. John Richards[12] and Ken Boessenkool,[13] for example, have both shown that the purchasing power of social welfare in much of the country rose significantly between the mid-1960s and the mid-1980s. Contrary to what one would normally expect, while numbers of people on welfare rose during economic downturns, there was no corresponding decline in welfare numbers when the economy started growing again. Welfare dependency was an up escalator, not a roller coaster, at least until the provinces, largely due to cuts to federal transfers, got serious about welfare reform in the mid-1990s.

Many of my friends in those heady early days of the expansion of the state benefited from programs we all remember fondly, such as Opportunities for

Youth (OFY), Local Initiatives Program (LIP), Katimavik, and so forth, programs that paid young people for being, well, young.

Soon our spending outstripped politicians' willingness to raise taxes, and we entered a long period of deficit financing. Then-finance minister Edgar Benson tabled a balanced budget in 1969. There would not be another until Paul Martin's fifth in 1997–98. In between, we ran up an impressive national debt at both the federal and provincial levels, to the point that the *Wall Street Journal* in 1995 said that the state of our public finances qualified us as an honorary Third World country.[14] Yet in earlier post-war years, thanks to controlled spending and many budget surpluses, we had retired a huge amount of debt acquired to prosecute the war.

> Net federal debt in fiscal 1968, just before Trudeau became Prime Minister, was about $18-billion, or 26 per cent of gross domestic product; by his final year in office, it had ballooned to $206-billion—at 46 per cent of GDP, nearly twice as large relative to the economy.... Only in Trudeau's first full year in power, 1969–70, was the budget actually in balance.
>
> Andrew Coyne, *Trudeau's Shadow*

There was a massive ramping up of our universities, not only in the number of institutions (callow universities with no tradition behind them and an entire faculty recruited during the radicalized Vietnam era, such as Simon Fraser, York, and UQAM [Université du Québec à Montréal], were bywords for chaos, protest, and disaffection), but also in student numbers and dumbing down of standards. The vocation of the cultivation of the mind was quickly overwhelmed by that of entertainment provider to, and warehouser of, young people we scarcely knew what to do with.

Expectations of when and how one might hope to retire were pushed sky-high as we practically begged older workers to get out of the way and let the rising generation take their place, even though there is little evidence that older workers block the rise of younger ones, given the very different economic and other roles they play. One financial institution's brilliant advertising slogan, "Freedom 55," came to denote a widespread expectation of early retirement. Moreover, it was widely regarded as code for "Freeing Slots for Workers Who Are 25." As a former member of the national political panel on *Morningside*, I well remember host Peter Gzowski's chat one day with demographer David Foot. Foot had just been expounding on some of the economic consequences of the Boomer generation, and Gzowski suddenly sat up and said, more or less, "Wait a minute. You've just made me understand something. The reason that I could be the editor of *Maclean's* magazine in my late twenties wasn't because I was brilliant, but because I had the good fortune to be born at a time when not many other babies were being born. I didn't have much competition. Now my children are lucky if, at the same age, they can be the obit editor on the paper in Swift Current, because there is a million of these kids." Compulsory retirement became official government policy, and buy-out packages a major topic of conversation in the company cafeteria. The Canada Pension Plan (CPP) gave the first generation of its beneficiaries benefits disproportionate to premiums they had paid.

It wasn't just spending programs that changed, of course. Immigration changed too, for example. I was a university student when the requirement became widespread that employers had to prove there was not a qualified Canadian available to fill a job before they would be permitted to fill it with an immigrant. This was a huge sea change compared to the comparatively liberal open-door policy we had operated for years. We also made it much harder to bring in temporary workers.

Laws affecting the workplace changed as well. Surprisingly, this was an era of trade union influence. Normally, unemployment weakens workers relative to employers. But the trade unions saw an opportunity, in a political climate of anxiety about unemployment, to get gains for their members through political action rather than collective bargaining. Minimum wages were driven up, labour standards legislation gnawed away at employer prerogatives while strengthening the hand of unions, and protections against firing became more stringent. To protect existing members' wages and existing retirees' benefits, unions threw up barriers to entry to their guilds.

In this same atmosphere, barriers to trade between Canadians and with the outside world, already significant, rose anew. Protectionism is a natural, if wrong-headed, response to growing unemployment, as those with a job organize to protect themselves from outsiders who might be able to do the same work more efficiently and less expensively. When I was young, doctors, engineers, and tradesmen from the United Kingdom, for example, were plentiful and found it easy to enter Canada and exercise their profession.

Today medical graduates from the University of Edinburgh are treated on an equal footing with those from Lower Elbonia when they try to immigrate to Canada, and engineers from India and Iran find the path to exercising their profession in this country blocked at every turn. Manufacturers of yellow margarine in provinces like Ontario or New Brunswick have only very recently earned the "right" to sell that margarine in the province of Quebec, and we finally have at least embryonic trade in electricity across provincial boundaries only because the Americans required reciprocal market access if we wanted to sell electricity to them. And let us not forget that the rise of the Boomers in the workforce coincided with the emergence of anti-free trade sentiment embodied in measures like foreign investment restrictions and government requirements that broadcasters use Canadian songs and programming on radio and TV, while barriers were thrown up to foreign (and especially American) cultural products.

Nor should we in our inventory of responses to the confluence of Quebec nationalism and the baby boom generation neglect the creation of a lot of public sector "employment" whose principal function was to give a salary to the incumbent rather than to provide any useful and productive service to the public or the economy. These were jobs in government departments, Crown corporations, and subsidized private companies, jobs that had little economic rationale but plenty of political payoff. To this phenomenon I have attached the name "pseudo-work," but the more traditional "make-work" or "featherbedding" would do just as well.

Lester Pearson, Pierre Trudeau, and their successors created whole new departments with no known function, such as the ministries of state for urban affairs, multiculturalism, science and technology; ministers were created for consumer affairs, international trade, financial institutions, sport, and other things already perfectly well looked after by existing departments.[15] Direct and indirect public employment skyrocketed.

Transfers to the provinces shot up and had the desired effect, especially in low-growth provinces: today Ontario has 67 municipal and provincial employees per thousand residents, while Newfoundland has 89 and Manitoba 105.[16]

To prevent workers from areas with few jobs from moving to areas of economic growth, and possibly undermining wage growth there through their willingness to accept jobs at lower pay, unemployment insurance and regional development policy were given starring roles. They muted the signals that the job market was trying to send to workers in economically underdeveloped parts of the country to the effect that their current industry and work could not, in the long run, provide them with a sustainable standard of living. Regional development policy came along and subsidized weak natural resource industries with low levels of investment and poor productivity, to keep jobs going long after their economic rationale had ceased to exist. The wholly predictable result was that movement of people around the country to seek out new opportunities took a nosedive. One of the traditional motors of Canadian economic growth stalled, and for decades the trend was down, down, down, until about 2003–04.

Despite (or, as some of us think, because of) all this massive effort, unemployment marched inexorably higher and rose to be the number one political preoccupation of Canadians for many years.

Our work ethic, regarded by our forefathers as one of the most ennobling distinguishing characteristics of Canadian society, was thus put under severe pressure by a state suddenly offering enticing alternatives that hadn't existed before on anything like the same scale. The pressure spread to the other institution that had been traditionally regarded as the cornerstone of Canadian life—not government but the family. Divorce and abortion rates rose, marriage and fertility rates plummeted, helped along, as I will show later, by a state that took over many traditional functions of the family but didn't perform them nearly as well.

Again because it helps us to put the change in perspective and to see how much we were changing and how quickly, the comparison with the United States is instructive. According to a recent Hoover Institution study comparing marriage and family between our two countries, from similar starting points almost thirty years ago (i.e., in 1980) our two societies' behaviour where family is concerned has diverged markedly. Whereas Canadians had 25 per cent more children than Americans, the reverse is now true; our fertility level is a quarter below that of Americans. In 1975, our marriage rate of 9 per 1,000 population was just below the U.S. rate of 10 per 1,000. Today the Canadian marriage rate is only 60 per cent of the U.S. rate, although both have declined.[17]

Speaking of divergences with the United States, the economic one was becoming increasingly troubling. And yet in 1960, the respective standards of living of our two countries had been almost indistinguishable. Since then our productivity and our standard of living have both been in long-term decline relative to our neighbour. Americans, too, allowed some growth in the size of government, but the scale and speed of their increases were dwarfed by the changes in Canada, and they recoiled before the consequences of large-scale redistribution and welfare dependence as the manifest failings of Lyndon Johnson's Great Society and its progeny came into clear focus.[18] Our unemployment, our standard of living, our productivity, all had been highly competitive with the United States, but the gap has widened in favour of our neighbours over the ensuing decades. In 1960, a difference of just 8.1 per cent in favour of the Americans separated real per capita income in the United States and Canada.[19] But by 1999 the real per capita income gap was on the order of 22 per cent in favour of the United States.[20] And while the current economic downturn has cast a temporary pall over America's economic portrait, the foundations of its better long-term performance remain intact: its entrepreneurial energy, its inventiveness, its technological prowess and its deeply ingrained work ethic, for example, have not gone away.

This account of the history of the last fifty years will seem unbelievable and even offensive to those raised with the official version of our recent history, namely that we had always been a kinder, gentler society than those laissez-faire Americans; that French-speaking Quebeckers had been discriminated against and we had to put right the historical wrongs that had been done to them; that we had to expand government because the private sector could never have absorbed all those workers flooding into the labour market. Such a use of government was merely an extension of our long-standing propensity to use the state for grand public purposes, a kind of natural deduction from Peace, Order, and Good Government.

This account, however, will not stand up under examination—it is wrong on almost every point. Only by setting the record straight will we come to have an appreciation of the real causes of many of the ills that assail us: hostility between Quebec and the rest of the country; transfer dependency by individuals and governments; the decline of both fertility and the family; and government that has become a powerful brake on our economic and social progress.

Vertigo Warning: Don't Look Down

This is not, however, a pessimistic book, although it certainly chronicles many tragically lost opportunities for Canada. I am an optimist because, fortunately, the ebbing of the flow of Boomers is about to lay bare for all to see the consequences of our mistakes of the past half century and to remind us of why the cultural, social, and economic values of our first century as a nation served us better than those we put in their place. The fearful symmetry to which the title of this book refers is nothing less than the rise of the New Canada under the impact of Boomers and Quebec nationalism over the last fifty years, and its unwinding over the next fifty years as the Boomer generation and Quebec's bargaining power within Confederation both recede.

The precursors of the change that is coming—symmetry's turning point—are there for all to see. One small wave has already washed over us. We are in the trough between the two, and the second, much bigger, wave is now towering above us.

The first wave struck us in the early eighties. According to David Foot,

the Canadian Boomers entered the labour force from the mid-1960s to the mid-1980s so over this period Canada experienced declining population growth but higher labour force growth resulting in a temporary economic dividend from demographic change. This has now evaporated....[21]

That helps to clarify how we paid for our massive expansion of the state. We borrowed, of course, and ran up an impressive national debt[22] in the process as we consumed public services for which we were unwilling to pay commensurate taxes. But just as important was the demographic dividend Foot describes.

Its evaporation coincided with our worsening fiscal position, with our need to improve productivity (which gave birth to free trade with the Americans) as well as with increasing resistance to abusive welfare policies that had allowed many people to escape working. So the first mini-wave of painful adjustment brought us trade opening, the battle to defeat the deficit at both the federal and provincial levels, and a wave of welfare reform at both the provincial[23] and federal (Employment Insurance reform and reductions in transfers to the provinces to finance welfare) level. Yet that was during a period when the labour force was still growing faster than the population in general, although the gap had already closed considerably compared to the sixties and seventies. When the next wave of demographic change hits, that first mini-wave of change will look like glory years.

We are already suffering its first early ripples, even though the big wave is still several years away. Starting in 2011, population will grow faster in Canada than the labour force, and that trend will continue for forty years. Already today, after nearly fifty years of the labour force growing by an average of 1 per cent a year every year (and often much more), we are in a period when it is growing at half that rate. By 2016, a few short years away, the number of net new workers entering the workforce will be zero and will be slightly negative for a decade after that. We are teetering on the edge of a demographic cliff, and we have one foot out in the air.[24]

Help Wanted

Labour shortages on a massive scale are so foreign to the Canadian experience that it may be hard for people to grasp what it may mean. The problem is made even more difficult by the fact that we are in the midst of an economic downturn that is squeezing employment in many parts of the country.

Yet the current slowdown, as painful as it may be, is nothing more than one of the ups and downs that all economies experience from time to time. That's why it is referred to as a cyclical downturn. Imbalances (in this case too much debt) build up and have to be fixed. But once fixed, we return to growth and almost invariably end up surpassing previous high-water marks of income, employment, and growth. There is little reason to think this downturn will be materially different.

The point here, however, is that a cyclical downturn such as we are experiencing today can temporarily mask much deeper and more profound changes. The coming labour shortages are a good example. The demographic changes that I have described are not cyclical; they are not the result of short-term ups and downs. They are deep changes in the very structure of our population, changes that will outlast downturns and upticks. In fact, population aging is likely responsible for the fact that unemployment in this downturn is actually quite mild compared to earlier recessions at the height of the Boomer wave. The unemployment rate in mid-March 2009 was 7.7 per cent. To put that in perspective, the unemployment rate for the quarter century from 1974 to 1999 was always higher (8.1 per cent in 1990 was the lowest during the period). Moreover, during a similar worldwide recession in the early 1980s, the Canadian unemployment rate was in double digits for four years (1982, 1983, 1984, and 1985), peaking in 1983 at 12.7 per cent. We haven't seen double-digit unemployment since 1994 (10.4 per cent).[25]

Prime Minister Stephen Harper has been quite forthright about the fact that the current downturn is merely masking a much more profound social transformation. In a speech in London, Ontario, on March 13, 2009, he said, "As the world struggles with the effects of global recession, we as Canadians are looking ahead. Despite the rising unemployment we see today, the demographic reality is this: as soon as this global recession ends, our country will face a long-run challenge of labour shortage."[26] Many others have made the same point, including those responsible for the Atlantic fishery, traditionally the employer of last resort in the highest unemployment region of the country.[27]

If we really want to see what the future has in store for us, we have to look back to conditions just before the downturn. We do not have to wait until 2016 to see how Canada will be changed by our new population circumstances, because those circumstances have already begun to make themselves felt, even if the change is being masked for a brief moment by the downturn.

Perhaps the newspaper reports[28] a couple of years ago of a proposal to build a new pipeline in Alberta did not catch your eye. After all, what is there new about another pipeline in Alberta? Nothing. Or at least so it appears until you realize that this pipeline is not to take oil or gas out, but to pipe a very light oil ("diluent") in. The purpose? To dilute the heavy oil extracted from the oil sands to allow it to be piped out to places where the labour force is available to build and operate the plants needed to process it. Even in this lull in Alberta's super-powered growth, oil sands giant Syncrude is having difficulties recruiting the workers that it needs and was on a major recruiting drive in Atlantic Canada in February 2009.[29] And even though unemployment has undeniably risen in Alberta, that province, along with Saskatchewan and Manitoba, continues to have the lowest unemployment rate in the country.[30]

In Brandon, Manitoba, in order to get the workers needed to operate its meat-packing plant for several shifts a day, Maple Leaf Foods imported workers from Mexico and Colombia, to whom the winters must have seemed a rude shock. In PEI, there were dozens of Russian guest workers at a fish processing plant, and there were requests for more. There is now discussion about closing down fish plants for want of workers, a trend that is set to accelerate. On current demographic trends, unemployment in Nova Scotia will, in a few short years, have fallen to 3 per cent, regardless of the recession of 2009–10.[31] In response to requests from businesses across the region, every provincial government in Atlantic Canada now has an immigration policy. Under federal-provincial nominee programs in virtually every part of the country, needed workers can be fast-tracked.

Until 2008 I was a partner in a restaurant in Halifax, and our biggest single challenge, bar none, was to find the workers we needed, an experience common to every other restaurant owner we knew. The Canadian Restaurant and Food Association projects huge labour shortages throughout the industry in the years ahead, again despite the gloom of 2009.[32] It is an industry, like many other services, that cannot be outsourced or offshored to China or India, but must be done by people right here in Canada.

The average truck driver in Canada falls into the 50- to 55-year-old range (and is as old as 70 in some regions)[33] and everyone is increasingly concerned that we will not be able to bring needed goods to consumers because we won't have the people to drive the trucks to get them where they need to go. Try to imagine an economy in which it has become impossible to move goods from factories and ports to stores and homes.

As you can see, there is no need to wait until 2016 (when the growth in the number of new workers goes to zero) to feel the effects of a tightening supply of workers. Those effects are already here, and they have already affected growth, mobility, wages, and investment. According to a 2006 PricewaterhouseCoopers survey, nearly two-thirds of Canadian private companies said that the shortage of skilled workers was already slowing the growth of their companies.[34] In Ontario, where the economy has been battered recently, nearly 57 per cent of business leaders polled that same year, a strong majority, reported that their growth was hampered by labour shortages.[35] And according to the Canadian Federation of Independent Business (CFIB), nearly 60 per cent of their members were expressly mentioning labour shortages as an issue of importance to their business.[36] And among specific industries, the CFIB's numbers were even higher. The momentum behind labour shortages has been growing across many sectors, including manufacturing, for several years, and now includes shortages of unskilled as well as skilled workers. A year or two's increase in cyclical unemployment will not change anything about this portrait of profound long-term change.

Most new workers entering the labour market will be absorbed simply to fill the jobs about to be vacated by retirements, as opposed to creating opportunities for new growth.

We don't have much time to prepare.

How the Future Will Differ from the Past

Can this really be Canada, where not so many years ago a party won one of the biggest parliamentary majorities in history on the slogan "Jobs, jobs, jobs"?

Yes, because that was then and this is now. When Brian Mulroney and his Tories swept to power in 1984, it was the year that, on David Foot's account, the last members of the Boomer generation (those born in 1966) turned eighteen and began looking for work. The entire Boomer generation was now in the workforce or was at least of working age.

Alongside that population change came huge political change, particularly in Quebec–Canada relations; this book describes how these two forces combined to produce many of the vast changes Canada has undergone in recent decades. The Quebec state, for example, was at the early stages of its efforts to prise open the province's private economy for French-speakers. That effort, combined with decades of bad policy in the province (which I describe in detail in Chapters 3 and 7) had undermined growth. Meanwhile, the patriation of the Constitution over Quebec's objections in 1982 had given the nationalist movement a new grievance with which to excoriate all things Canadian. The competition between Ottawa and Quebec City for the loyalty of Quebeckers drove a vast growth in the size of the state at all levels in Canada.

Today, while the problem of Quebec nationalism remains unresolved, one of its main props, the federal-provincial battle over the Boomers and their place in the economy, is about to enter a quite different phase.

Again we must not allow the temporary circumstances of the downturn of 2009 to obscure the long-term trends. Whether growth returns in 2009, 2010, or 2011, while it matters enormously to us in those years, is only a question of timing. The labour shortages that were so evident in 2006 to 2008 will return because they are driven by deep forces that transcend economic cycles. Unemployment before 2009 was rapidly becoming yesterday's issue, and the pace of that change will accelerate when today's downturn is only a fading memory. When that happens, plant closures and mortgage defaults will disappear from the headlines, and we will again find that newspaper accounts of labour shortages jostle for space with stories about declining student numbers in the public schools. As a legacy of the last half century's political battles, however, we will still find ourselves lumbered with a series of policies designed to mop up surplus labour at a time when we will need to ferret out every worker we can find. For example, the EI system still pays people not to work for long periods of the year, especially in seasonal industries, and thanks to the miracle of regionally extended benefits, pays them extra to move to areas of high unemployment, rather than paying them to move to places where the jobs are. It also discourages education, because students are not eligible for EI. The number of teachers in the public schools rises as student numbers fall. The part of the economy where employment is growing the fastest by some measures is still the public sector, and the pace is picking up, driven in part by stimulus packages. Pressure is rising for governments to make it easier to get welfare and EI again.

The period of falling unemployment that preceded the downturn that began in 2008 was no mere momentary economic conjuncture, a high in the economic cycle which has now turned and is dragging us down again. A period of sustained and indeed growing labour shortages is not a possibility, nor a probability, but a certainty. We will find our growth constrained by our inability to find workers. Inflation will be an ever-present danger in these tightening labour markets, and that means a vigilant Bank of Canada will keep its finger tight on the interest rate trigger. The standard of living of Canadians will be lower than it needs to be at just the time we will need to find ways to pay for the retirement of all those Boomers.[37] According to the federal Department of Finance, by around 2030 or so, annual GDP (gross domestic product) will be about 14 per cent lower than it would have been if we were to continue with the (unimpressive) per person growth rates of recent decades. That is a stunning loss of potential national wealth at a time when the claims of older Canadians, particularly on the health care and retirement security systems, will be on the rise. While our standard of living will continue to rise, that rise will be anemic compared to what it could be, and the risk is real that we will fall even further behind the long-term economic performance of our neighbours to the south, whose economic recovery is also only a matter of time. Nothing about this is set in stone, however; we have the choice to do things differently.

Labour Shortages, Gryphons, Unicorns and Other Mythical Animals

Society is rife with self-corrective mechanisms that deal with emerging problems by giving people incentives to change their behaviour. Some economists, therefore, argue that the aging of the population is not really an issue worthy of much attention; these self-corrective mechanisms will kick in and our behaviour will be adjusted automatically by social and economic forces.[38]

For example, if workers come to be in short supply because of aging and retirements, wages will rise and companies will simply adjust by substituting capital for labour (i.e., retiring workers will be replaced by machines rather than younger workers) or by enticing workers to stay on past the current retirement age.[39]

If it is impossible for us to have labour shortages, however, the reverse proposition must also be true: it must be impossible to have unemployment. After all, from an economic point of view unemployment is just a labour surplus, whatever else it may be when measured in human unhappiness and suffering. Yet the historical record of large-scale unemployment over the thirty years from roughly 1970 to 2000 is there for all to see.

I grant that it is quite likely true that if labour markets are left alone to function, unemployment and labour shortages are equally unlikely. On the other hand, that is a big "if." Much of our unemployment of decades past was not caused by the economy, but by bad decisions by politicians. And if we can create unemployment by bad policy, we can certainly create labour shortages the same way.

In the *National Post*, one could read in 2008 about how the retirement of Boomer-generation doctors was producing a nationwide shortage of physicians; the fewer physicians who were left were being reduced to gambits like holding lotteries to cull their patient lists, leaving millions of Canadians without a doctor.[40] That shortage, however, was a direct result of government policy to reduce medical school enrolments some years earlier,[41] a self-defeating scheme to reduce health care costs by reducing the supply of doctors.

If, in the face of a dwindling supply of workers, we cling to high levels of marginally useful jobs in the public sector, raise unemployment benefits and pensions in lockstep with rising wages, continue tax policies that discourage work, and keep up barriers to people moving to where the greatest opportunities are to be found, to pick just a few choice examples, we will, by our own choice, exacerbate the problem. After all, the self-corrective mechanisms that are the economist's bread and butter in this case would be things like moving underemployed public sector workers, the unemployed, and those retired but still able to work back into the workforce. Raising wages is the way to do that, enticing people out of idleness and low-value occupations. It works poorly, however, if government policy battles you every step of the way. It is entirely possible for government policy to create simultaneous labour shortages and high unemployment. I see it every day in Nova Scotia, where I live.[42]

And even where the famous self-corrective mechanisms can be seen at work, that does not mean there is no pain or dislocation. Especially where self-correction is obstructed by bad policy, there is no guarantee that the new state of affairs will be as desirable as it could have been. For example, labour and capital are not perfectly substitutable—some jobs simply cannot be done as well, or even at all, by machines, so we cannot spend a lot of money and replace all our missing teachers and hockey players and physicians and restaurant servers with robots and other types of machinery. And the adjustment mechanism can take time to work, during which time labour shortages can exercise a powerful upward pressure on wages and thence inflation.

So self-corrective mechanisms *can* produce high inflation, high interest rates, and lower growth, especially when poor government policy gets in the way. That would be a destructive combination at the best of times. It would be brutal at a time when relatively fewer workers are striving to produce enough wealth to keep their own standard of living rising while they pay for at least part of the pensions, health care, home care, and a host of other public services for a growing number of retirees. In writing this book I have tried to think about how we, both government and Canadians, might adjust our behaviour so as to improve the chances of good outcomes for all of us in the face of the challenges represented by the aging and retirement of the Boomers.

In any case the classical economists who don't believe in labour shortages and I are probably not all that far apart. I say that labour shortages will cause Canadians to change their behaviour profoundly over the next fifty years as we struggle to find ways to adjust to a precipitous fall in the numbers of new people entering the workforce. They say that tightening labour markets will produce big changes in the behaviour of Canadian firms and workers as wages rise to reflect the fewer workers that will be available.

Just remember the important point: we agree that profound changes are coming.[43] Canadians are entering a decades-long time that will be economically, culturally, and socially as different from the last half century as vinyl records are from MP3s and rotary phones are from Blackberrys.

Reports of Capitalism's Death Have Been Greatly Exaggerated

Some readers will object that the book's argument assumes that today's economic downturn is but a temporary bump in the road, and that in due course we will return to the kind of market-driven economic growth described in later chapters. Moreover, the book assumes that the United States, far from being finished as a global superpower, still has its best days ahead of it.

Our current economic difficulties have certainly unleashed a torrent of commentary to the effect that capitalism's day is done, that the downturn proves that private business is irretrievably corrupt and cannot be trusted because our woes are entirely the fault of greedy bankers and insurance companies and rating agencies and market manipulators.[44] Wise governments will henceforth need to replace this vicious system with disinterested technocratic management. Friedman is dead. Long live Keynes.[45]

No one can deny that greed led a number of managers to take outrageous risks with the institutions with which they were entrusted, or that they were richly rewarded even after their companies either failed or were bailed out at taxpayer expense. Their misjudgments were compounded by their shameless clinging to bonuses and other entitlements to which they had little moral claim, however much their employment contracts guaranteed them.[46]

But this constitutes no indictment of liberal capitalism as an economic and political system, nor does it establish that there is some clear, and clearly superior, alternative. Painful as the short-term stalling of the economy is, with all its attendant job losses, plant closures, bankruptcies, and family crises, we cannot lose sight of the tremendous economic benefits our economic system has bestowed on us over the years. More and more of the world has been drawn to this system, especially since the collapse of the Berlin Wall. Previously moribund economies in Eastern Europe, Asia, and Latin America have enjoyed robust growth by becoming more tightly bound into the world economy, and the freer movement of goods, capital, services, and people have dragged more people out of poverty than at any other time in world history.[47]

Consider the following extraordinary statistics about the performance of the world economy since 1980. World real gross domestic product grew by about 145 per cent from 1980 to 2007, or by an average of roughly 3.4 per cent a year. The so-called capitalist greed that motivated business people and ambitious workers helped hundreds of millions to climb out of grinding poverty. The role of capitalism in creating wealth is seen in the sharp rise in Chinese and Indian incomes after they introduced market-based reforms (China in the late 1970s and India in 1991). Global health, as measured by life expectancy at different ages, has also risen rapidly, especially in lower-income countries. Of course, the performance of capitalism must include this recession and other recessions along with the glory decades. Even if the recession is entirely blamed on capitalism, and it deserves a good share of the blame, the recession-induced losses pale in comparison with the great accomplishments of prior decades.[48]

In Canada and other Western countries, periodic downturns never wipe out the gains in income and economic well-being realized since the previous downturn, and once the recovery comes, we invariably move on to new economic achievements.

When the downturn is done, we will still want bankers and other financial institutions to be able to move capital from those who have more than they need to those who can only realize new economic opportunities by borrowing the capital of others. The fundamental reasons that make a system of private initiative within the framework of the rule of law superior to the government-dominated alternatives will still apply.[49] Even the Chinese, whom one might expect to be readier than most to defect from reliance on markets to power growth, have restated their commitment. According to *The Economist* magazine, "Chinese leaders have been at particular pains to avoid giving the impression that China is wavering in its commitment to market capitalism (albeit with a heavy admixture of government control)."[50] Chinese president Wen Jiabao delights in reminding people that his favourite bedtime reading these days is Adam Smith's master work, *The Theory of the Moral Sentiments.*

In any case, Manichean explanations casting the world in a comforting two-dimensional battle between good and evil are rarely much help in understanding a world composed largely of shades of grey. Those who have always opposed capitalism and economic freedom have uncritically leapt to the attractive conclusion that all that has gone wrong can be laid at the doorstep of evil capitalist plutocrats, while years of allegedly savage deregulation have prevented kindly and objective governments from stopping greed and self-interest from wreaking havoc.[51]

Yet the best book so far on the economic downturn of 2009–10, John B. Taylor's *Getting Off Track,* has as its subtitle *How Government Actions and Interventions Caused, Prolonged and Worsened the Financial Crisis.* In the book Taylor, a prominent economist, Stanford professor and adviser to central banks around the world, tells the story of how government institutions played a key role in the creation of the recession of 2008–09. In particular, he draws our attention to the close relationship between too-loose monetary policy by central banks and the housing price bubble. Had governments followed the so-called Taylor Rule for interest rates (named after John B. Taylor himself, who famously proposed this rule for guiding monetary policy in 1992), the asset price bubble likely would have been avoided, and with it the risky lending practices that have brought so much misery in their wake.

He also points out the extent to which governments directly encouraged these risky practices. Fannie Mae and Freddie Mac, both U.S.-government-sponsored agencies, were pushed by politicians to encourage home ownership, which they did by expanding and buying "mortgage-backed securities, including those formed with the risky subprime mortgages."[52] He might also have mentioned the American Community Reinvestment Act, which forced banks to make risky home loans for political reasons by requiring them to lower their lending standards,[53] as well as the 1997 tax law that increased the capital gains exemption for residential home sales, which encouraged the practice of flipping houses for short-term gain.

Taylor also demonstrates convincingly that governments misdiagnosed the causes of the crisis once it had begun and therefore took the wrong policy steps a year into the downturn, making things demonstrably worse, not better. So much for avuncular and trustworthy governments being a safe haven after the excesses of greedy markets and capitalists.

In fact the downturn has only reinforced the views of mainstream economists about how wealth and jobs are created. As economist William Easterly has written,[54] much of that consensus[55] can be summed up as follows:

> Free trade does create opportunities for firms and workers doing what they do best. The government can't forever spend money it doesn't have. Competitive markets reward innovation and efficiency and punish customer-abusing would-be monopolies. Rapid deregulation has its risks, which we have learned that financial regulators should manage carefully, but too much regulation is far worse.

A group of leading economists from across the ideological spectrum signed on to a statement underlining these important principles just before the 2009 World Economic Forum in Davos. Far from decrying deregulation, the signatories were much more worried that those countries that had not deregulated enough before the downturn would see the current circumstances as a reason to retreat. While recognizing that some modest regulatory tightening might be required, they wrote:

> Many countries in the midst of this deregulation backlash are starting from positions of already very high levels of bureaucracy, countries which furthermore have a tradition of strong government intervention. There is thus a danger that over-regulated economies may be about to become even more regulated. (This was one of the very damaging follow-on effects of the Great Depression—a closing off by many countries to international trade.)[56]

Finally, it is unclear what alternative model is being suggested to take the place of open markets, free trade, private initiative, and accountability under the rule of law. Even governments being forced by circumstances to take over failing banks in Western countries are assuring voters and investors that they will get rid of them as soon as possible. Canada, which followed with some modest enthusiasm the deregulatory fashion of the last decade, has weathered the current downturn much better than most. Russia and China, both with heavy government involvement in the economy, have been battered by the downturn. Many European banks, often held up as bulwarks of solidity and stolidity, and backed by conservative regulation, were much more heavily leveraged (i.e., carried a lot more debt relative to equity) than their American counterparts, who are singled out as the villains of the piece.

Nor is the downturn itself proof that governments need to have large powers to step in and direct the economy to avoid such crises in the future. Taylor shows in fact the opposite. It was only when governments and central banks tamed their temptation to intervene arbitrarily in markets in the early eighties that was unleashed what economists call the Great Moderation. Essentially by applying the Taylor Rule to monetary policy, an era of great stability was ushered in. "Only two recessions occurred in the 25 years from the end of the 1981–82 recessions in the United States until 2007, and those two recessions were very short and mild by historical standards.... The improvements did not occur only in the United States; similar improvements were seen in other developed countries around the world."[57] It was only when governments and central banks began to lose their bearings and abandoned discipline and clarity in monetary policy in particular that the economy went off the rails. That hardly justifies giving governments more such power in the future; rather it is a further argument for limiting their power to do harm by binding them to rules that limit their arbitrary discretion and create certainty for workers, employers, and investors.

Like it or not, this is no crisis of capitalism, the downturn has not proven the moral or financial bankruptcy of markets, and no serious proposal is on the table by any important government that would do anything but tinker with the regulatory framework for capitalism that has been established in the last half century. What this latest downturn has proven yet again is that liberal capitalism is the worst of all possible economic systems—except for all the others.

True, the United States has probably been wounded more than many economies through the combined efforts of bankers and politicians. Furthermore, the downturn coincides with the arrival in office of a Democratic president and Congress who seem determined to raise taxes, expand health care coverage, tackle the entitlement mess in social security, *and* run multi-trillion-dollar deficits to finance these changes and pay for huge stimulus and bailout packages. All of this is going to be painful. But Americans are a resourceful, irrepressible, and inventive people who have seen worse and always triumphed over adversity. I see no reason to think this time will be any different. The question is not if America will rise again from its economic difficulties, but when, and how much damage will be done by poor policy in the meantime to its economy, the greatest wealth-generating machine the world has ever seen.

2

Our Forgotten Political Tradition Vindicated

Some people are your relatives but others are your ancestors, and you choose the ones you want to have as ancestors. You create yourself out of those values.

RALPH ELLISON, *TIME* MAGAZINE

The founders of Canada had high hopes for us. They thought that Canada was a land of great promise for the generations to come, as when Sir Wilfrid Laurier so famously proclaimed that the twentieth century would belong to Canada. This was no mere rhetoric, for Canada was a society characterized by tremendous dynamism. We (i.e., metropolitan and colonial Britain together) built the Canadian Pacific Railway (CPR) , a project almost unimaginably huge at the time. We built political institutions to govern a vast and sparsely populated territory. We performed feats of military prowess far greater than our small size might have led one to expect. And we attracted vast numbers of newcomers, hosting one of the largest inflows of people relative to our local population ever seen in history. Living in the shadow of America, where everything is done on a grand scale, makes it hard sometimes to recall that, relatively speaking, we had no reason to be ashamed of what we accomplished in our half of North America and much reason to be proud.

But proud as our forebears were of the country that they were building, they were very much of the view that its success was not an accident. On the contrary, they believed that Canada and Canadians succeeded as they did because they had been endowed by history and Providence with a very specific set of institutions and behaviours. Our success was bound up with our character, and our character was formed by the right kind of experiences. We could welcome people from all over the world and we could populate this huge and sometimes stern piece of geography and make it all work because of the kind of people we were and the kind of people newcomers were expected to become.

Central to this view of the character of Canadians and their institutions was a notion of individual freedom and responsibility, a belief that each of us was endowed with a nature that required us to be responsible and accountable for our choices. The corollary was that if we deprived men and women of their freedom and responsibility for themselves, we prevented people from being fully free and fully human. Dependence on the government or on charity was therefore to be abhorred, not chiefly because of the cost it imposed on those who paid, but because of the damage it did to those who "benefited."

Our forefathers thought that human beings create themselves largely through their work. And just as our character is shaped by having to earn our way in the world, a different kind of character is formed when we make our way living off the efforts of others.

This is relevant to the story of what we have lost because out of our fear of Quebec separatism and out of our efforts to find something, *anything*, for our burgeoning labour force to do grew vast social institutions to give people the illusion of working or at least of not being unemployed. We tolerated an unemployment insurance program that paid large numbers of people *not* to work. We celebrated the emergence of schools and universities that provided a heavily subsidized, mediocre education but kept huge numbers of young people out of the workforce for a few more years. We pushed people into retirement as fast as we could. We enriched welfare to the point that, in the mid-1990s, over 12 per cent of the population of our then wealthiest province, Ontario, was claiming welfare from the province, a proportion that rose with each recession, but hardly declined again in the ensuing upturn.[1] At roughly the same time, 1994, McGill economist William Watson was observing that "counting the children of the unemployed, roughly one-fifth of Quebecers are on social assistance [including UI] of one form or another."[2] Welfare does not exhaust the many forms of dependence we created; for example, we pulled many people into various forms of public employment that produced a real income but little real value (a theme to which I return in Chapter 5).

While many people regard this as just the kinder, gentler Canadian society helping out those marginalized by the baby boom, the fact is that this was quite an innovation in Canada. Contrary to an article of faith of our revisionist age, for years one of the things that distinguished Canada from the United States was Canadians' unbreakable attachment to a demanding work ethic and a strong distaste for any kind of dependence on the public purse. In fact, one of the ways in which the founders of the Dominion thought that the new country distinguished itself from the United States was in the levels of welfare dependence to be found in the populist republic to the south. There voters could and did vote themselves benefits at the expense of the rich,[3] a danger of American populist democracy against which Alexis de Tocqueville had warned in his classic *Democracy in America*. The liberty that was taken to be a British subject's birthright was thought to be inimical to a radical democracy's temptation to pursue an equality of condition for its citizens. Such an equality could only be achieved, Canadians believed, by a destructive levelling down of the achievements of society's most successful members.

Richard Cartwright, a prominent pre- and post-Confederation politician, spoke for almost all his contemporaries when he said in the United Province of Canada legislature in 1865,

> I think every true reformer, every real friend of liberty, will agree with me in saying that if we must erect safeguards, they should be rather for the security of the individual than of the mass, and that our chiefest care must be to train the majority to respect the rights of the minority, to prevent the claims of the few from being trampled underfoot by the caprice or passion of the many. For myself, sir, I own frankly I prefer British liberty to American equality.[4]

Charles Tupper, a Father of Confederation and briefly prime minister of the new Dominion, echoed these sentiments in the Nova Scotia legislature: "It is necessary that our institutions should be placed on a stable basis, if we are to have that security for life and property and personal liberty, which is so desirable in every country."[5]

The divide that separated the "two solitudes" of French and English was bridged by a common understanding of the importance of work and the damaging nature of dependence. Étienne Parent, one of the great journalists, public intellectuals, and orators of French Canada in the first half of the nineteenth century gave a passionate speech at L'Institut canadien de Montréal in September 1847 on the theme Work and Humanity (*Du travail chez l'homme*):[6]

> You will no doubt realise that by "idleness" I don't merely mean the cessation of all work, but also this laziness of mind which prevents you from developing through your work all the potential of your intelligence, for your own benefit and that of all of humanity.[7] [author's translation]

Parent continued,

> Yes, gentlemen, early on in life make regular continuous work a habit and I predict that you will derive great pleasure from your work, that you will love

your work for itself over and beyond the personal advantages that you expect from it, just as I predict that idleness or inactivity, once satisfied our indispensable human need for rest, will become for you a source of unbearable boredom.[8] [author's translation]

And Parent issues a clarion call to action to ensure that everyone benefits from the moral advantages that work procures: "And so, gentlemen, let us ensure, through our laws, through our institutions, through our values and through our ideas, that each and every person works in our society."[9] [author's translation]

Sir Wilfrid Laurier, the first French-Canadian prime minister, reflecting those same French-Canadian roots and the influence of British political liberalism, was a staunch believer in minimalist government and personal responsibility and abhorred any form of welfare dependency. His most famous declaration about Canada's values ("Canada is free and freedom is its nationality") is far more stirring than its modern equivalent: Canada is free health care and medicare is its nationality. He once declared that "the role of government [is] ... not to force action in any one direction but to remove barriers to man's own efforts to undertake personal and social improvement.... Man must be free to seek his own improvement and be responsible for his own destiny."[10] When Australia and New Zealand began experimenting with new state-provided social programs, according to Doug Owram, Laurier was quick to denounce these innovations as inimical to traditional Canadian values: "If you remove the incentives of ambition and emulation from public enterprises," Laurier said on the subject in 1907, "you suppress progress, you condemn the community to stagnation and immobility."[11]

William Lyon Mackenzie King, who eventually succeeded Laurier as both Liberal Party leader and prime minister, agonized in his early book *Industry and Humanity* over what he foresaw as the corrosive effects on Canadians' character of the relatively activist government he was attracted to. And in fact his record as prime minister shows that he too was predominantly a traditionalist who thought that people were best left alone to resolve their own problems rather than having government play that role, although he certainly was not averse to introducing just enough minimal welfare state measures to keep the Liberals in office—welfare if necessary, but not necessarily welfare.

Mackenzie King was also surrounded by people who shared this world view. When, as Laurier's minister of labour, Mackenzie King engaged in some unwonted interventionism (he used legislation to end a railway strike), Laurier thought this a very ill-advised innovation, and the minister was lectured in Parliament by a senior Liberal MP about this departure from the sound principle that the government that governed least governed best.

Immigration in the early days did not challenge this orthodoxy in favour of freedom and personal responsibility, even though Canada at the time was admitting newcomers at a ferocious pace. As Laurier's minister of immigration, Clifford Sifton, famously remarked in 1922 of the millions of Ukrainian, Russian, Polish, and other East Europeans admitted under his supervision: "I think a stalwart peasant in sheep-skin coat, born on the soil, whose forefathers have been farmers for ten generations, with a stout wife and a half dozen children, is good quality."[12]

In other words, these were people inured to hard work and more than capable of looking after themselves. There was no question of people being admitted to fall on the public charge. Everyone, native born or immigrant, was expected to look after themselves, and unemployment was almost universally seen as a personal failure and disgrace.[13]

At about the same time, Stephen Leacock, one of the country's most influential public intellectuals, was warning,

> We are in the danger of over-government; that we are suffering from the too-great extension of the functions of the State; that it is doing already great harm to our economic life, and threatening greater still; doing a great deal to undermine the sounder principles of morality and self-reliance, and doing much to imperil the older and sterner spirit of British liberty on which our commonwealth was founded.... In my opinion we are moving towards socialism. We are moving through the mist; nearer and nearer with every bit of government ownership and government regulation, nearer and nearer through the mist to the edge of the abyss over which our civilization may be precipitated to its final catastrophe.[14]

Leacock feared that we were edging toward the abyss in 1924, when government spent about 11 per cent of GDP, roughly a quarter of what it controls today,[15] which is itself down from its peak of over one-half of GDP in 1992.[16]

This deep suspicion of government programs was not limited to men, either. Ottawa's future mayor Charlotte Whitton who, according to Dennis Guest, was Canada's most influential voice on social welfare matters in the early thirties, was determined that any state aid to those in need be subjected to stringent rules, the most important of which was that those being helped, must honestly and sincerely participate in the whole plan, which is the development of initiative and self-reliance and independence at the earliest possible date, and to such a degree and strength as to avoid future dependency.[17]

William Watson underlines that Whitton's opposition to mothers' pensions was entirely in line with the then reigning consensus.[18] Those who thought about the welfare of the most vulnerable and how they could be helped most effectively were one in thinking that the problem of one-parent families was not one of income, but of character and values. Such welfare problems were best left in the hands of local agencies that could know each of their clients and support them in a way tailored to individual needs but always with the aim of ending dependence on charity or government aid at the earliest opportunity.

While the mythology of Canadian politics has it that the Great Depression put paid to classical liberalism in this country, the record shows quite the reverse. R.B. Bennett was on his electoral deathbed when he shifted half-heartedly to imitating the early stages of Roosevelt's New Deal, much to the disgust of his predecessor as Tory leader, Arthur Meighen. His program was gutted by the courts and quietly shelved by Mackenzie King's victorious Liberals, much to King's satisfaction.[19]

This rejection of American-style interventionism wasn't limited to a few plutocrats in private clubs in Montreal and Toronto and Anglos in Ottawa either. For example, the Quebec provincial government was firmly opposed to the New Deal style of politics. The Liberal premier of Quebec at the time, Louis-Alexandre Taschereau, scathingly called Roosevelt's innovation "a socialistic venture bordering on communism."[20]

Elite opinion did not see public spending as the solution to the country's ills; rather it was the contrary. At the height of the Depression,[21] at a time when the state in Canada was spending roughly a quarter of the share of national wealth that it spends today, the *Globe and Mail* could editorialize (under the headline "Crippled by Government"):

We have been indulging in a glorious spending spree much of the time since Confederation was established, mortgaging the future, signing notes for posterity to pay, and not at any time using such prudent measures as a well-ordered business would adopt to prepare in good years for the demands of the bad.

In 1938, the famous Rowell-Sirois Report[22] was far from revelling in Canada's great advance over other nations as a provider of social welfare services. On the contrary, the commissioners deplored our slowness in getting with the program of expanding the welfare state:

> No person should be compelled by economic necessity to work or to live below a standard fixed by public policy. Canada for a number of reasons has been slower to accept this responsibility than have Great Britain, New Zealand or Australia.

While some, like James Struthers, have argued that the report served as a "blueprint for the development of the Canadian welfare state,"[23] the predominant historical view is that the report and ideas were shelved and largely forgotten in the frenetic activity of post-war prosperity.[24] Rowell-Sirois barely made a dent in Canada's obstinate attachment to limited government and individual responsibility.

Not even the heady days of what was essentially central planning of the war effort in World War II could knock the Liberals, liberals, and Canadians off course. According to William Watson, "Following the New Deal we were probably the most laissez-faire country going. [Author Bruce] Hutchison regarded it as 'the final tragedy of the war [that it] compelled a ministry devoted in theory to a minimum of government into complete and detailed control of the nation's economy.'"[25]

Hutchison need not have worried; the tragedy was short lived. After a brief flirtation with the welfare state in the form of the Marsh Report, Canada's equivalent of the Beveridge Report that led to the post-war creation of the British welfare state, Mackenzie King essentially reverted to laissez-faire form after the war, having seen off the threat of a briefly resurgent CCF with the Marsh diversion.

Economic policy in Canada during this period was dominated by the redoubtable Clarence Decatur Howe, who during the war became known as the Minister for Everything because

---

Mr. [Arthur] Meighen noted that the word "relief" had been dropped from the [Unemployment Relief] bill, replaced by "the more dignified term 'assistance.'" The feeling had grown up that claims for "assistance" were in the nature of rights, he said. With each succession of strength to that state of mind, the problem of relief became greater. "If one part of the country can say, 'We are going to live off the other part, we are going to cast all obligations away,' do you think civilization can exist on that basis?" asked Meighen.

Arthur Meighen, quoted in the *Globe and Mail*, May 18, 1938

of his role in directing the war production effort. But once the war was over, Howe couldn't get rid of his central planning powers fast enough.

> The real Liberal plan, whether by accident or design, was Howe's. It was based on optimism about the economy, and skepticism about the potentialities of planning. It would not be the economic abstractions of doctrinaire planners in Ottawa that would shape post-war Canada. That would be left to business's self-interest, guided, prodded and shaped by incentives that businessmen could understand. Post-war Canada would be a free enterprise society.[26]

Louis St-Laurent, who succeeded Mackenzie King as prime minister in 1949, was said to regard American levels of welfare dependence with distaste and typical Canadian moral superiority; he resolutely but ultimately unsuccessfully fought Jack Pickersgill's attempts to extend Canada's meagre unemployment insurance program to Pickersgill's fishermen constituents in Newfoundland on the grounds that it would not be actuarially sound to include seasonal workers such as these, and it would encourage others to seek unemployment benefits in similarly unsuitable circumstances. As Watson remarked, St-Laurent proved right on both counts.

As late as the federal election of 1957, St-Laurent was opining:

> Any ideas of non-essential interference by the Government is repugnant to the Liberal Party. We believe that the private citizen must be left to his own initiative whenever possible and that if some help is required for the individual, that which is afforded by the national government must encourage rather than replace the help which the community or the province with its municipalities can give.[27]

At the same time as St-Laurent was underlining Liberals' attachment to small government and individual liberty, so-called progressive forces, represented by figures like Keith Davey and Tom Kent, were pushing the party in a new direction, especially after the defeat of the Liberals by John Diefenbaker's Tories in 1957. Even then, however, the old roots of the Liberal Party in the founding traditions of Canada were deep and resistance to the reformists was strong. Right after the 1957 election, for example, former Saskatchewan premier and federal Liberal finance minister Charles Dunning argued against the party adopting a social welfare policy agenda. He noted that the ever-increasing number of social services created a tremendous and expensive machine to bring about redistribution of wealth by taxation, and lessening the responsibility on the part of the individual citizen, and by doing so are decreasing both the dignity and freedom of the individual person. I know it may not sound like practical politics to be flashing this kind of red light, but surely we Liberals must get back to fundamental thinking in terms of principles.[28]

Nor was the traditional political philosophy of individual responsibility and initiative that animated all our national political leaders prior to the 1960s absent on the local level. Dunning, after all, was a former Liberal premier of Saskatchewan. In 1948, Maurice Duplessis left those listening to his government's Speech from the Throne in no doubt where he stood: "We are of the opinion that state paternalism is the enemy of all progress."[29]

To pick another example, almost seventy years ago, Nova Scotia's greatest premier, Angus L. Macdonald, a Liberal, stood before a Toronto audience and gave a remarkable speech. He told that audience what his part of the country—the Maritimes—needed to overcome its underdevelopment.

The biggest obstacle to the region's development was what he called "the tariff," or the old National Policy of Canada's first prime minister, Sir John A. Macdonald. So what could Ottawa do to help?

First, he said, lower the tariffs—in other words, he called for a policy of free trade. Failing substantial reductions in tariffs, some compensation for the effects of those tariffs (such as reduced freight rates) would be a second-best policy, but better than nothing. Finally, and least satisfactory of all, he said,

THE TWO SOLITUDES RECONCILED

But the government dole will rot your soul back there in your home town.
So bid farewell to the Eastern town you never more will see.
There's self-respect and a steady cheque in this refinery.
You will miss the green and the woods and streams and the dust will fill your nose.
But you'll be free, and just like me, an idiot, I suppose.
Stan Rogers, *The Idiot*

The best way to kill a man is to prevent him from working by giving him money
...
And the best part is that your cities will be full of the walking dead.
Félix Leclerc, *100,000 façons de tuer un homme*
[author's translation]

would be the granting of subsidies from the Dominion Treasury: "Subsidies do not increase the general level of the prosperity of the people. They may make the task of government a little easier. They may render the work of balancing the budget a little less difficult, but in the last analysis they do not add to the economic advancement of the people."[30]

What about the CCF government of Tommy Douglas in Saskatchewan? While there is no denying that Douglas and his colleagues pushed the province and the country on welfare state issues such as hospital insurance and medicare, these are not programs that discourage work or the work ethic. Does the Douglas government (1944–61) disprove my contention that there was a broad social and political consensus against reliance on the state and in favour of work and a sturdy individual independence? After all, didn't he create a brand new department of social welfare? True, but in Douglas's own words, "We were not interested in paying able-bodied people merely because they weren't able to work."[31] According to his biographer, Walter Stewart, under Douglas and the CCF,

> "relief" was gone, and in its place were two classes of people eligible for "social aid." Those who were too old or too handicapped to work received support automatically, but anyone who couldn't find a job elsewhere would be put to work clearing roads, fencing pastures, installing phone lines, or working in community pastures—what is today called "workfare" and is roundly condemned by every respectable left-winger.[32]

What was reviled as socialism in those days turns out to have been pretty mild stuff. Douglas certainly used the state to build infrastructure and to provide services that the private sector had been unwilling or unable to provide, but he also ran seventeen consecutive balanced budgets, significantly repairing the province's finances. He had no interest in creating programs that would undermine people's work ethic. Looking back from today's vantage point, most observers agree that Douglas's government, far from being the Red Menace, was best described as mildly reformist.

Neither America nor Europe: Where Canada Fits In

In other words, the reigning political consensus, which was also a consensus on moral values, that characterized this country right up to the birth of the New Canada in 1960, took a quite different view of the role of the individual, of government, and of the effects of government intervention on people's character than the one that prevails today. The view that predominates today on both sides of the border is of Canadians as kinder and gentler than their American neighbours, as more willing to use the power of the state in pursuit of public goods, as more welfare-minded, more socially left wing. It is also a view that could establish itself only by defeating and then consigning to a trunk in the never-visited attic of our collective memory the older view that had defined Canada for almost the first century of its existence and for many decades prior to 1867.

This revolution in Canadians' intellectual and moral self-understanding was fed by many tributaries. We were certainly well plugged into the broad intellectual currents washing over Western civilization. For instance, the influence of Marxism, some branches of feminism, post-structuralism, and other "radical" philosophies in the universities and elsewhere helped to create fertile soil for new ideas across the West, while simultaneously demonizing the bourgeois virtues.[33] Starting in the 1960s it became fashionable in intellectual circles to believe that individuals were the creation and the prisoners of social forces over which they had little control, and that the employer-employee relationship was essentially an exploitative and purely materialist one in which all the benefits were economic, and those flowed predominantly to the owners of capital. During the decades stretching roughly between the presidencies of John F. Kennedy and Ronald Reagan, it was not clear to many which side would win the Cold War, and Western capitalism's ultimate decisive triumph as the superior economic system had not yet been satisfactorily demonstrated. The alternative collectivist models of Russia, China, Cuba, and even, incredibly, Albania exercised a peculiar

AND YOU THOUGHT MARX WAS DEAD AND GONE ...

My daughter and a friend, who were in high school, were offered a job in a fast-food restaurant. This was to be their first experience of work, and they were suitably excited and a little anxious at this new transition to adultlike responsibilities and status. The mother of the friend squashed all of that simply by observing to the children that they would be crazy to take such work, which was obviously purely exploitative, all the benefit flowing to the restaurant, and none to the workers. In the vernacular, they were simply going to be "ripped off" rather than participating in a mutually beneficial exchange of values—some moral, some economic, some social, some cultural. Disillusioned and newly suspicious, the children declined the jobs and for years afterwards had a jaundiced view of and fraught relationships with employers.
Private communication with author

fascination over many. Vietnam and the counter-culture produced a vibrant movement of protest and questioning of authority throughout the Western world, including the authority of traditional values and behaviours.

Not to be neglected in the list of ways in which Canadians' old values began to fall into desuetude was the extent to which Canada copied American innovations. As is so often the case in Canada–U.S. intellectual history, America led the way with bold social experiments that didn't really pan out. America drew back, but Canada rushed in and embraced the American innovations as the latest thing.[34] Yet once the Americans had abandoned them, Canadians then deluded themselves that their now "distinct" approach demonstrated how different they were from the people they had originally copied, whereas in reality it proved the less flattering proposition that we are slower to learn from our mistakes.

The "War on Poverty" of Lyndon Johnson was one such innovation, an innovation whose failure was later documented in exquisite detail in Charles Murray's path-breaking 1984 book, *Losing Ground: American Social Policy 1950–1980*. Even before Murray interred the remains, however, politicians in the United States had begun to back away from Johnson's faith in state action as the saviour of the poor and disenfranchised. Daniel Patrick Moynihan, social commentator and later Democratic senator, quickly saw the faults of the traditional American approach to welfare, especially as it had been expanded under Johnson. Moynihan's provocative 1965 study, *The Negro Family: The Case for National Action*, for the first time cast light on the potential social consequences of the American welfare system and the so-called War on Poverty. Richard Nixon, after becoming president, shut down the Office of Economic Opportunity, the central agency of Johnson's "unconditional war on poverty," and after Nixon's 1972 re-election, he told a reporter the sixties had been a failure because "the government threw money at the problem."[35]

Here at home, the Canadian left, far from being reflexively anti-American as it is today, drew much inspiration from such U.S. social policy, and the CCF and its successor, the NDP, were at least as inspired by American Progressivism and the Social Gospel movement[36] as by British Labourism and Fabianism. In the period that interests us, Cy Gonick, influential editor of the iconic (on the left)

> Canada is often regarded as a welfare state—particularly by its American neighbours. However, this is only a recent phenomenon. Until the 1960s the timing, extent and progression of Canadian welfare legislation lagged the US experience.
>
> Douglas A. Allen, *Welfare and the Family*

Canadian Dimension, wrote admiringly of American social policy and lamented Canada's status as laggard. "The United State has discovered poverty," Gonick wrote in May 1964; "it is curious that this subject is being ignored by Canadian counterparts."[37] Welfarism was part of the new spirit of the age and Canada had a lot of catching up to do.

We caught up with a vengeance, rapidly surpassing the United States, and were soon breathing down the necks of some of Europe's welfare states with regard to the size of our social welfare apparatus. In one of those intellectual inversions with which history is replete, we began to associate the values of Canada's first century with foreign values, American values, values that had nothing to do with us. We literally suppressed or at the very least forgot our history because it suddenly became inconvenient when faced with the need to rationalize the rapid spurt of growth in the welfare state.

So no change in the general zeitgeist of the post-war industrial world can prove a sufficient explanation for Canada's sudden embrace of the welfare state, an innovation to which Canada had so far proved remarkably resistant. Others will find the popularity of left-wing ideas, the counter-culture, feminism, effective contraception, cities and city life, the attractions of Keynesian-style demand management, rejection of tradition and the rise of relativism and hostility to authority and other ideas abroad in the West at this time to be sufficient explanation of the direction Canada took in these years.

But the very ubiquity of those ideas makes them unsatisfying as an explanation as to why Canada suddenly fell in line with them so comprehensively after having resisted their rise so energetically over previous decades. Marxists and feminists in the universities were no more common in Canada than the United States, and Keynesian acolytes and big-government apologists were no rarer in the halls of government on their side of the border than on ours.

Yes, Rowell-Sirois eventually gained some traction, and programs like equalization and regional development, old-age pensions, and family allowances and unemployment and hospital insurance all predate (some barely) 1960,[38] although these programs were tiny compared to their present-day equivalents. It is also the case that these programs on the whole were not ones that created individual dependence on the state for one's livelihood. No one ever stopped working because they got state-financed hospital care. Unemployment insurance in this period created little disincentive to work, and old-age pensions offered meagre support for those past the age where they could work. Creating individual dependence on the state, as we shall see later, was really a new feature of the Canadian state's expansion from the mid-sixties onward.

The state had been expanding on both sides of the border for years. I pointed out earlier that when Stephen Leacock warned of the impending arrival of socialism in Canada in 1924, the state in Canada was spending 11 per cent of GDP. By 1960, we were spending over 28 per cent.[39] Again, however, there was nothing in that that distinguished Canada; government was carving out a bigger role for itself everywhere. No one denies that the zeitgeist was there, no one denies that government in general and the social service state in particular were growing. What has to be explained is not the direction of change, but rather its speed and scope and timing.

And here the parallel social and economic developments of Canada and the United States over the previous century must be given their due weight. We were two societies with a similar intellectual, philosophical, and institutional endowment. We Canadians thought of ourselves as the truer guardians of the British traditions of liberty and limited government, but the Americans fought a revolution in order to vindicate what they thought of as the rights and liberties of Englishmen. The spirit of the great liberal individualist John Locke presided over America's founding debates in the eighteenth century, just as he did over the Confederation debates of the nineteenth.[40]

In most ways that matter, by 1960 we had comparable achievements and believed those achievements to be rooted in our shared heritage of limited government, individual freedom, personal responsibility, and the rule of law. Canada was not a European welfare state, we were not Sweden or France or Germany; indeed *those* were the ideas that were foreign to our history and traditional practices. We were resolutely North American, men and women, French-speakers and English-speakers, Westerners, Central Canadians, and Easterners together. Indeed, we often thought that what distinguished us from Americans was their less fervent attachment to those values that set us both apart from other peoples who had not yet understood the secrets of development, both personal and economic. We didn't think we were Americans. We thought we were the superior brand of North American.

To explain our divergence from the United States in the decades following 1960 as somehow simply the result of a more "European" character, of profoundly different cultures and values, confuses what must be explained with the explanation. It is no good to argue that we are only middle of the pack among Western democracies in social welfare provision today[41] when it is the movement to there from our very different starting point that we are trying to understand. We in effect changed teams. What must be explained is why we stopped being resolutely North American and moved so fast toward a European-style welfare state. Some of the shift is surely due to the zeitgeist of the Western world, but there is little reason to think that the zeitgeist was, of itself, so much more powerful in

Canada than, say, in the United States. There had to be something specific happening in Canada, something unique to us, that can help us to understand the *volte-face* that we performed, almost overnight.

When I began writing this book, I was drawn to the argument that the most important change in the post-war period, and what made Canada particularly vulnerable to this new ideology of social welfare, was our rapidly faltering confidence in the ability of the economy to absorb all our children. But the more I dug into it, the more I realized that this was not enough of an explanation either. Not only had we faced similar waves of job-seekers before (as in the post-war period) but we had also met and mastered depressions and bouts of high unemployment without abandoning our principles. While our Boomer generation was the largest among the industrialized countries, America was not far behind, and it too had to expand universities and schools and other new infrastructure and institutions to manage the wave of youngsters. It was their president who said "We are all Keynesians now"[42] and that same president (a Republican to boot) introduced price and wage controls well before Ottawa did. European countries that did not experience anything like North America's post-war baby boom did, however, expand the size of their governments and welfare states significantly. Clearly you could have the boom without the massive expansion of government and particularly the welfare state (Australia and the United States), and you could have the expansion of the welfare state without any real boom at all (much of Western Europe).[43]

In any case, the rapid unfolding of the expansion of the welfare state and the dependence it brought in its train from about 1968 or so didn't match closely enough the rise of the Boomers in the workforce. It didn't match the economic cycles that might have been the giveaway of a Keynesian-inspired *coup d'état*. There had to be something else that suddenly supercharged what otherwise had been a rather lazy drift to expanded government in Canada. That something else was the destructive dynamic created by Quebec nationalism that unleashed a bidding war between Ottawa and Quebec City for the loyalty of Quebeckers. That bidding war used rapidly expanding government spending as its chief weapon and had important reverberations all around the country.

The attraction of this argument is only deepened by the regional nature of the growth of government in Canada over the period in question. If we back out Quebec, most of the rest of the country has seen dependency levels that most of the time are not so very different from what we might see in those peer jurisdictions such as the United States or Australia. As I'll show in later chapters, the exceptions, places like Atlantic Canada or Manitoba, have certainly been drawn into the dysfunction and decline caused by excessive redistribution and the use of political power by organized groups to grant themselves economic and other privileges while preventing economic change. The important point to remember, however, is that they would never have been politically, economically, or demographically powerful enough to *cause* that increased redistribution and its consequences to happen in the first place. They did not drive the process, and they are only collateral damage from its effects. Quebec remains the key.

Before we talk about how we lost the political tradition I have just described, it might be valuable to take a moment and reflect on whether we should be happy to have jettisoned it. Maybe it was just tired old ballast that was weighing us down and preventing the emergence of a brighter and more compassionate future. After all, how we react to the story of the birth of the New Canada post-1960 will be conditioned by how we feel about that new country.

> WHERE FREE MONEY COMES FROM
>
> As a good friend of mine, the son of a former central bank president, once told me, while still a child he was out walking one day with his father. His father said to him casually, "If you found a $10 bill just lying on the ground with no one in sight, what would you know about who it belonged to?" The boy replied, "Nothing." He never forgot his father's reply: "You are quite wrong. You would know one thing with absolute certainty, and that is that it did NOT belong to you."
>
> Private communication with author

Sharing out the Booty

The more I think about the evolution of the New Canada over the last fifty years, the clearer it becomes that the traditional values on which Canada was founded were correct in their view of the corrupting effects of too-powerful government on human character. The difference between then and now is that we have fifty years of evidence about the relative decline of the Canadian economy (both compared to its historic growth pattern and compared to the United States) and of the changing behaviour of Canadians. We also have a burgeoning intellectual tradition that enjoys a lot of success in explaining how our poor economic performance, the growth of government, and certain changes in the behaviour of individuals (things like a declining work ethic and the weakening of the institution of the family) are closely related.

One of the lessons of the growth of the modern state is that, as it achieves a certain size and regulatory power and reach, no one can ignore it; indeed, everyone is brought within its orbit whether they wish to be or not. This happens for three chief reasons.

First, a rapidly growing and well-financed state represents spoils that must be captured and divided. This is the "free money" incentive. Whether you think the state *should* have this money or not, the fact of the matter is that the state *does* have it; it is there for the taking. If you don't get your share, others will get it instead. And since it costs you nothing (once it is in the hands of the state, it is too late; the tax burden you bear is just a sunk cost you cannot change), government money appears to be "free," like manna from heaven. Who would leave money lying on the ground?

Second, failing to "get your share" puts you at a competitive disadvantage. Even if you prefer to mind your own business and just do your own thing, you cannot. If trade unions are going to lobby the state for special powers (such as laws forbidding replacement workers), companies need to be there to make sure their interests are protected. If your competitors are going to lobby for special tax breaks or subsidies or trade barriers or tariffs or regulations, you need to get "your share" by being at the table or your taxes will be financing your competitor's advantages. If others are going to get state-financed welfare benefits or social services, if you don't get the ones you want, you will foot the bill but get little in return. Everyone is drawn to the state in unproductive activity that is essentially defensive.

Three, human beings have a visceral reaction against what they perceive as unfairness. Most of us are morally outraged if we see someone getting ahead through unfair means, by cheating on a test, or sleeping with the boss, or sycophancy or lying or bribery or exploiting family connections. Human nature being what it is, a surprising number of people, seeing such things going on, feel themselves to be morally entitled to act improperly, and the more widespread the illicit behaviour, the more people will feel that they are chumps if they do not abandon their principles and grab what they can while the going is good. Put another way, the cost of being good is low when the vast majority are good but rises rapidly as larger and larger shares of the population defect from this standard. Once some tipping point is reached, playing by the rules is simply allowing yourself to be taken advantage of, because decisions about who gets what are being taken arbitrarily and on the basis of relative power rather than merit or justice.

On the other hand, unless our character and judgments are disfigured by corrosive and unworthy emotions like envy, we have little quarrel with people getting ahead in economic terms on the basis of merit, which is the application of the principle that people should get out of the economy something closely related to what they contribute. Similarly, on a narrower range of goods (especially those provided by the state and therefore supported by compulsory taxation), generally speaking we don't quibble too much about everybody getting the same share of desired things (which is just the application of an equality rule). But when the patronage powers of the state become too large and the largesse is distributed according to the preferences of those in power, rather than by merit or the equality rule, we react very differently.

Why does all this matter in trying to understand how the growth of the Canadian state (at both the federal and provincial levels) became self-perpetuating, even though people thought that dependence on the state was a bad idea in principle? Because of the way rewards are distributed in the marketplace versus the way they are distributed by the state. Markets reward and encourage people for producing valued goods and services for each other. The state rewards and encourages people to organize politically to use the state to get the things they want based on their relative political power.

You may think that your employer determines, in his or her sole discretion, what you will be paid, but nothing is further from the truth. Your boss is constrained by the market. If he pays too little, other employers will bid away valuable employees by offering them more money. If he pays too much, his product will be overpriced in the marketplace or his return on investment will be too low and he'll go out of business. One of the critical pieces of information that employers are always chasing is what the market is paying today for the kind of employees they have and wish to keep. And ultimately the value you have to your boss is determined by the value you give, measured by your productivity. If you are more productive than the average employee in your field, you'll command a premium wage. If you give less than average value, you probably won't last long in your job.

That means that most real jobs in the real economy offer an opportunity for someone who wants to get more than they get today, and the way that they avail themselves of that opportunity is to work harder. They can then either get better pay or, if their boss doesn't want to reward superior productivity, they can find an employer who will. It is just the same with people offering services, lending money or selling widgets. In most circumstances you get ahead by providing superior value.[44] And here is the crucial point: the other party to these transactions has to agree that they are getting the value they are looking for, because transactions in the market are not compulsory, but voluntary. I don't have to hire you; you don't have to buy from me. We engage in these kinds of exchanges only when both parties see the value in doing so.

So we get ahead by creating more value (or by "making"), and we are not subject to the arbitrary will of others in our business or employment relationships because, except in very exceptional circumstances, we have choices about what we buy and sell, when and to whom. No party to the vast majority of economic transactions sets the terms of those transactions unilaterally.

This is the exact opposite of transactions with the state. The state takes its resources compulsorily from taxpayers, not as a result of a negotiation of value to which each party must agree. It then distributes them in accordance with the will of those who hold political power, whether directly or indirectly. And while people will generally acquiesce in the distribution of income and so forth by the market because that distribution is not the imposition of someone's will or preferences, they quickly grow to resent the arbitrary awarding of benefits and advantages to those close to government.

Why You Can't Just Mind Your Own Business

This phenomenon, where more and more members of society are drawn into taking rather than making, is known as "rent-seeking," an extremely ugly social science term that I try to avoid whenever I can (even though it will slip into this book from time to time).[45] It is easier to think of it as "People Using Political Power to Enrich Themselves by plundeRing You" or, if you will forgive the acronym, what I call "PUPPETRY," in the same spirit as "Fannie Mae" is understood to mean the Federal National Mortgage Association, or "Freddie Mac" the Federal Home Loan Mortgage Corporation. This idea of people winning unearned benefits at others' expense through successful political activity was first systematically described in modern terms by the American political economist Mancur Olson, most famously in his little classic *The Logic of Collective Action*. One of his students summarized his thinking:

> "The great majority of special interest organisations redistribute income rather than create it, and in ways that reduce social efficiency and output," said Olson. Groups rarely propose 'social benefits' that don't also handsomely benefit themselves.... As society becomes more and more dense with networks of interest groups, as the benefits secured by groups accumulate, the economy rigidifies, Olson argued. By locking out competition and locking in subsidies, interest groups capture resources that could be put to better use elsewhere. Entrenched interests tend to slow down the adoption of new technology and ideas by clinging to the status quo.... *At last society itself begins to change.* "The incentive to produce is diminished; the incentive to seek a larger share of what is produced increases." *The very direction of society's evolution may be deflected from productive activity and toward distributional struggle.* [Emphasis added][46]

Another way of thinking of this shift is that the character of individuals and the society that comprises them begins to change, from one of *making* to one of *taking*. This insight that the state becomes a temptation to immorality and a character-corrupting institution when it is permitted to engage in excessive redistribution was best expressed by the nineteenth-century French political economist Frédéric Bastiat.

Since, Bastiat notes, we are all asking the state to take from others and give to us, and since the state cannot give to us without taking from everyone, the state may properly be defined as "*the great fiction through which everybody endeavours to live at the expense of everybody else*" [emphasis added].[47]

In other words, when we allow the state to become an instrument of redistribution on a large scale instead of impartially administering laws that treat everyone the same, it too easily becomes the instrument of some groups imposing their will on others. When you know that political power may be used against you, from a purely defensive point of view it becomes imperative to organize and to seize that power, even if all you want is to be left alone.

PUPPETRY can take many forms. Using the state to commandeer the income of individuals to redistribute it to others is just one. That use of the state is not just limited to taxation, by the way. If the state establishes marketing boards that can set the price of milk and eggs, that action transfers income from consumers (who pay higher prices) to producers (who don't have

> The tyrant and his victim are still present, but there is an intermediate person between them, which is the State—that is, the Law itself. What can be better calculated to silence our scruples, and, which is perhaps better appreciated, to overcome all resistance? We all, therefore, put in our claim, under some pretext or other, and apply to the State. We say to it, "I am dissatisfied at the proportion between my labour and my enjoyments. I should like, for the sake of restoring the desired equilibrium, to take a part of the possessions of others. But this would be dangerous. Could not you facilitate the thing for me? Could you not find me a good place? or obstruct the industry of my competitors? or, perhaps, lend me gratuitously some capital which you may take from its possessors? Could you not bring up my children at the public expense? or grant me some prizes? or secure me a competence when I have attained my fiftieth year? By this means I shall reach my end with an easy conscience, for the law will have acted for me, and I shall have all the advantages of plunder, without its risk or its disgrace!"
>
> Frédéric Bastiat, *Government*

to face competition). If widget makers win tariff protection from foreign competitors, PUPPETRY is allowing them to get extra money from consumers who now have to pay more for their widgets than they need to. If the local municipality forces taxi owners to have medallions to operate legally and issues only a few such medallions, that requirement artificially drives up the cost of cab rides, a straight politically produced transfer of income from passengers to owners. The resulting transfers don't even have to be monetary. Language laws like Quebec's Bill 101, for example, confer benefits on the speakers of one language at the expense of others.

Every democracy has some PUPPETRY. Politics being what it is, government is inevitably involved in redistribution; even before the welfare state, it certainly helped to transfer wealth from taxpayers to railway builders during the opening of the west, for example, from taxpayers to munitions manufacturers during time of war, and from taxpayers to civil servants and politicians in every era. There is a point, however, past which it ceases to be the exception, requiring strenuous justification and causing moral anxiety, and becomes the common coin of everyday life. Ultimately everyone asks for such special dispensations, to get what they want by having the state take it from someone else.

PUPPETRY's Legacy

Let's tie this back to the earlier discussion about how Canada and the United States have diverged over the past few decades. In 1960, Canada and the United States spent very similar shares of their national wealth on government (Canada spent 28.6 per cent of GDP on government, the United States, 28.4 per cent) and had very similar standards of living (a gap of about 8 per cent in favour of the United States). Over the ensuing forty years, spending by government grew by only about 6 percentage points in the United States, but at its peak by over 20 percentage points in Canada,[48] although it has since fallen back, in large part in response to the ending of the demographic dividend of the baby boom that occurred in the mid-eighties. Over those decades U.S. per capita income grew by 222 per cent, whereas in Canada it grew by only 126 per cent.[49] Even at this relatively low level of size of government, the United States has clearly strayed into the borderlands between a making society and a taking one.[50]

Canada, by contrast, has shifted decisively to a taking state. If Marxism, feminism, Keynesianism, urbanism, and all the other -isms that so powerfully shaped the Western zeitgeist of this era were the explanation of the growth of the Canadian state in those years, we would expect similar societies to be influenced by them to roughly similar degrees. The changes in Canada over those years are so powerfully different from those in the United States, however, that we need to look elsewhere for the explanation. The rest of the first half of this book lays out in detail the mechanisms by which we have shifted from a making to a taking state.

A sad irony of this evolution toward a taking state, by the way, is that the outcomes in social equity are no better in high-spending societies than lower-spending ones and are frequently worse.[51] This underlines the vacuousness of the claim that the growth of the state in Canada has made for a fairer society, a result that might have justified our relative decline in standard of living compared to our southern neighbours. What it does reliably produce, however, is a huge flow of resources through the hands of government, resources available for plundering by those adept at PUPPETRY (rent-seeking). That no doubt helps to explain why much of the spending of governments in Canada is in fact "churning"—money taken from the middle class through taxation and then returned to that same middle class in the form of various "benefits" conferred by politicians seeking to ingratiate themselves with articulate and motivated middle-class voters.[52]

Symmetry Casts Its Shadow Ahead

Population aging and declining fertility, however, will require us to make choices. On the one hand, we have the option of a continued expansion of the state and its allied economic underperformance. On the other hand, we might choose rolling back the size of government and unleashing the productive power of Canadians to make more through taking less. This phenomenon of population aging pressing governments to reduce their take is already observable in Europe, which is farther along the curve of demographic decline than we are. For instance Sweden, the archetypal welfare state, has been forced by demographic change to reduce the take of government from the economy.[53]

In fact the decline in size of government over the last decade (of which Sweden is a striking example) is led by European economies "that are experiencing the third phase of demographic transition, lower fertility rates, which are exacerbating the problem of an aging population with higher life expectancy rates. These developments are forcing government to reduce its size."

In any case, just to maintain the current levels of public services and programs to a rapidly aging population is expensive. If we left current levels of taxation alone and current benefit entitlements unchanged, the results of aging on our federal and provincial budgets would be sobering indeed. Pierre Fortin, a Quebec economist, has looked at the cost increases (pensions, health care, etc.)

of an aging population and set them against the cost savings (e.g. lower program costs for young people, such as education) in 2020. If the conditions he projects in 2020 were to have obtained in 2008, he calculates that it would have left a hole in federal and provincial budgets combined of roughly $40 billion.[54]

As daunting as the future fiscal affordability of our past behaviour might be, however, Canadians might nevertheless prefer to keep on the same path they have been on, even at the cost of lower growth, weaker incomes, and high cost of government with little to show for it, if they think that they are getting other important benefits. This has certainly been the message of much of the political class of the last fifty years, that Canada is one of the top countries in the world, that we are nicer, kinder, and gentler than Americans, that we have shed an uptight colonial past and have entered a brave new world of equality and freedom guaranteed by big government.

Too bad this message is self-serving twaddle.

3

Quebec and Ottawa: The Bidding War Unleashed

We formed a people who were distinct and consequently unique in the world. We, that is, we French-speaking Québécois, are not French, or at least haven't been so for centuries. Observers of the French regime had recognized this fact well before the Conquest. A new continent had already forged a new and original type of man, and the small interest the Old Country showed in him only reinforced his spirit of independence ... And now we were in a position to establish that, warmed under the sun of the Quiet Revolution, the same sap that ran in his veins was feeding all kinds of expression of a true national community, one that nothing could prevent from aspiring to break its bonds to reach full realization of its potential.

RENÉ LÉVESQUE, *MEMOIRS*

What caused Canada to abandon its commitment to both small and limited government and individual liberty and responsibility, a commitment that was widely and fervently embraced by political and social leaders on both sides of the language divide? Why did a well-developed welfare state emerge only in the sixties and seventies in Canada and not much earlier if the conventional accounts are correct—that Canada is a kinder, gentler place than the United States, that we are more left wing, that we have a longer and deeper tradition of harnessing the state to democratically chosen economic projects like the CPR and the CBC, that we are more European, that the country's national minority, French Canadians, were more "progressive" and pulled us into modern welfare-state policies through efforts to accommodate their "distinctiveness"?

However satisfying these prejudices may be, they are belied by the historical record. As we saw in the previous chapter, our tradition was individualist and sceptical of the state. America, despite its rhetorical excesses about markets and individualism, was in practice more inclined to welfarism, and in both state-led economic development and the embracing of the welfare state was generally ahead of Canada, not behind it.[1] Quebec was just as committed to such a stubborn scepticism toward the state as the rest of the country.

Quebec is nevertheless just as central to our story as is the flood of the Boomer generation into the workforce because the rise of the nationalist-separatist movement in Quebec coincided almost exactly with that flood. In interesting and unforeseen ways, these were the two main tributaries of a river of change that washed over Canada, transforming out of all recognition the political, economic, and even moral landscape that had existed before. That does not mean that Quebec nationalism is a purely or even largely economic phenomenon; obviously it is not. It remains that the rise of a Quebec nationalism willing to call the country into question on the one hand and the big influx of workers into the economy on the other coincided and that that had consequences.

In fact it is quite likely that what was going on in Quebec in the sixties and seventies was the deciding factor in Canada's reaction to our huge labour force growth. The change of character Canada underwent was, as the horse breeders say, by Quebec Nationalism out of Unemployment.

It is instructive to engage in an exercise in historical imagination and to project ourselves both back in time to the Quebec of the 1960s and 70s and into the shoes of federalist and nationalist strategists to see how strategies that seemed rational at the time, pursued on each side of the linguistic/constitutional divide, ended up transforming Quebec and the rest of the country in ways that few foresaw and no one intended.

French Canada Is Dead. Long Live Quebec

Let's start with the Quebec nationalists, both federalist and separatist. Central to their strategy was a clever appeal to history. French Canadians had long seen themselves as the bearers of a sacred and historic mission: to bring Catholic culture, and especially French Catholic culture, to North America. In its origins the antipathy that characterized the divide between English and French was more importantly confessional than it was linguistic. English was the language of Protestantism and therefore perdition, French the language of Catholicism, and therefore salvation. The *rayonnement de la foi* (spreading of the faith) was at least as important as economic self-interest in motivating the spread of the *coureurs de bois* and the priests that were never far behind, reaching far into the continent to places that still bear French names, such as Des Moines, Detroit, Joliet, St-Albert, and Gravelbourg. *La Nouvelle France* was the heart of a *mission civilisatrice* (civilizing mission) to a continent.

The unforgivable sin of English-speakers was that they became the uncontested winners of the battle for the continent. First the British conquered France in North America, leaving New France cut off from its metropolitan roots. Then America broke away from Britain and became a democratic and resolutely English-speaking, largely Protestant republic. French Canadians had to content themselves with limiting their mission to the northern half of North America[2] and to contending for dominance of that half with English-speakers who were predominantly Protestant.

Being French Canadian meant continuing that civilizing mission within Canada, and in the early days that looked like a promising prospect. French-speakers represented 40 per cent or so of the new country; they dominated the second-largest province and were significant minorities in two of the three others. The next province to join, Manitoba, under the leadership of Louis Riel and the French-speaking Metis, looked as though it could easily be French-dominated. The Church led colonizing missions to take Quebec's surplus French-speaking population to underpopulated regions. Despite these promising beginnings, however, it soon became clear that Canada would be predominantly Protestant and English-speaking, and culturally and politically Quebec became relatively inward looking, adopting a defensive posture to protect itself against depredations by the increasingly strong non-Catholic and English-speaking majority.

The Quiet Revolution of 1960 marked a decisive turning point in this evolution. Slowly and tentatively at first, and then with the gathering momentum of a mountain avalanche, nationalists invited French-speakers within Quebec to abandon being "French-Canadian" in favour of being *Québécois* at the same time as they invited them to abandon a Catholicism that, it was argued, together with English domination, had kept them poor and backward.[3]

The reality was that the invitation was based to a large extent on a historical fiction from an economic point of view, as a new generation of Quebec historians is showing.[4] Contrary to the arguments of Léon Dion, Michel Brunet, Hubert Guindon, and others alleging that French Canadians in Quebec had been kept poor and backward by the Church and a rural-dominated existence, the truth was that Quebec in 1960 had participated just as much as other Western societies in the phenomena of industrialization and urbanization and their attendant economic development. If Canada were removed from the equation, in 1953 Quebec's income per person would have made it the second-richest society in the world after the United States.[5] Quebec workers showed the same propensity to join trade unions at roughly the same time as workers in the United States and elsewhere in Canada, and their willingness to go on strike to protect their rights and privileges was not significantly different than elsewhere. French Canadians were, contrary to the historical revisionism of the Quiet Revolution and its apologists, well represented in manufacturing and commerce, with vigorous French-speaking business communities throughout the province. Business people were well represented in politics and decision-making at all levels and often offered an economic and cultural counterweight to the conservative influence of the Church.

The historical record also shows that in the early days of the transition between French-Canadian nationalism and Québécois nationalism, the role of the Church was by no means settled.[6] Prior to the Quiet Revolution, nationalism and the Church frequently made common cause, through dominant figures such as *chanoine* Lionel Groulx as well as the Union Nationale, the provincial conservative party, for example, and the Church was a strong supporter of earlier changes that carried the seeds of the Quiet Revolution within them, such as the creation of Hydro-Québec, Radio-Québec, the CSN (Confédération des Syndicats Nationaux), the great French-language universities, l'Union des producteurs agricoles, and others. Even after the Quiet Revolution, Catholic elites often worked in tandem with the province's political leadership to promote many of the changes that we now associate with modern Quebec: a Jesuit priest, Jacques Couture, was the architect of much of modern Quebec's immigration policy, and the father of the Charte de la Langue Française (Bill 101) was the deeply Catholic Camille Laurin. It was the "modernizers," of both left and right, who wanted to reduce the Church's influence in favour of the state, and they were ultimately successful in having the state supplant the Church. In this effort they were helped by the modernization movement within Catholicism itself, which criticized and abandoned traditional Church practices and authoritarianism in Quebec, but ultimately ended up by undermining both Quebeckers' sense of their own history and the moral authority of Church as a possible counterweight to the all-powerful state. The alliance of the modernizers and nationalists, together with Quebec Catholicism's own internal divisions, sealed the fate of the Church as a dominant institution in Quebec. The results were not always welcome: sociologist Fernand Dumont, one of the most influential left-wing nationalist thinkers of the time, for example, was a very religious man and bemoaned the decline of the Church.[7]

Even if the nationalist economic history was not always accurate, there was lots of substance to the nationalist critique, though, especially where it concerned relations between English- and French-speakers. While it is true that French Canadians had urbanized as much as other Western societies, English-speakers in Quebec were far *more* urbanized again than French Canadians in Quebec, and they controlled far more of the levers of international and national business. French Canadians, while certainly far more present in the business world than the mythology of *la grande noirceur* would have it, were heavily concentrated in small and medium enterprises and served primarily local and regional markets within Quebec. The business elite that dealt outside the French-speaking community was overwhelmingly English-speaking,[8] as was the language of work in those industries. Being French-speaking and Catholic before 1960 clearly did not entail working the land as the only alternative to being a *notaire* or a priest. On the other hand, they clearly were not the keys to membership in the Canadian economic elite. Continued acceptance of the status of *minoritaire* within Canada seemed to many to signal an acquiescence in this unequal state of affairs.

Being Québécois, on the other hand, meant a major change in outlook and mental geography. Being French-Canadian had originally meant contending aggressively with English Canadians for domination of a newly emerging national space called Canada. When it became clear which way that battle had turned, it then meant defending gains in all parts of Canada for the French-speaking minority. This defensive posture, concentrating political power on protection of language and confessional rights, is perfectly captured in the names of some of the French-language newspapers founded in the early years of the twentieth century: Montreal's *Le Devoir* (the *duty* to be vigilant on behalf of French and Catholic culture), Ottawa's *Le Droit* (the *right* to speak and be French), Winnipeg's *La Liberté* (the *freedom* to be and to speak French).[9]

Jean Lesage's electoral slogan, "*Maîtres chez nous*," that ushered in the Quiet Revolution, however, was revolutionary in two respects. First, it proposed mastery rather than defensiveness, a renewed energy for the *mission civilisatrice* after nearly a century of defeat and rearguard defensive skirmishes. But it also proposed a new geography and new identity for these happy culture warriors: no more time and effort was to be wasted on French-speaking minorities; the rest of Canada was lost to French culture and was no longer *chez nous*. It was now definitively *chez eux*, the home of the Other. It was no longer humiliatingly to be shared with a dominant English-speaking majority on terms largely dictated by them.

There was now to be a strategic retreat to *chez nous* where French-speaking Catholics were in the majority. *Maîtrise* and *chez nous* were distinct terms, inextricably linked and equally revolutionary. But a problem presented itself. The coherence and solidarity of French Canada had been closely bound up with the notion of French-Canadian exceptionalism and its corollary, the *mission civilisatrice*. French-Canadian exceptionalism, the idea of New France as a culturally, linguistically, and religiously distinct people in North America, meant that, symbolically if not literally, *la race canadienne-française* had a divine mandate and a sacred mission. If being *maîtres chez nous* meant pushing Catholicism into the background, what could take its place as a symbolic mission that unified and energized the entire society? How could French-Canadian and Catholic exceptionalism in a Protestant and English-speaking continent be modernized? How could its institutional manifestation, the Church, be replaced? What could take the place of its sacred language, Latin? How could Quebec society continue to distinguish, metaphorically speaking, the faithful, and therefore those bound for salvation, from those not so favoured?

There is no need, in asking these questions, to commit the historical error of believing that French Canadians adhered uniformly to the Catholic ultra-montanist[10] creed that gave the Church leadership in most social and cultural fields. We know that there was a wide diversity of viewpoints on the role of the Church in secular affairs in Quebec, and the Church had had to make many compromises with its liberal critics.

One can recognize tremendous diversity of thought within French-speaking Quebec society without committing the opposite error. That error is thinking that resistance to Church domination of civil society meant the abandonment of a common identity built on the idea of French-Canadian exceptionalism, of a sense of a historical mission for Catholic French-speakers in North America, and of that identity being forged in part in opposition to the English-speaking Protestant alternative. A history characterized by struggles with English-speakers over the rebellion and the Durham Report that came in its wake, over the Jesuit Estates Act, over Louis Riel, over conscription and a host of other conflicts, had forged a political and cultural identity that transcended internal differences over the precise status of the Church. Economic liberals in the business and professional communities sang just as lustily as anyone else of the role of Canada in protecting their homes and their rights when they joined in Sir Adolphe-Basile Routhier's French-Canadian nationalist lyrics to Calixa Lavallée's "O Canada."

The question posed by the Quiet Revolution and its aftermath was, what could unite this ideologically diverse French-speaking population, still nominally Catholic and impregnated with a historical sense of great exploits achieved in the face of hostility and indifference by the English-speaking Canadian majority?

Hors de l'État, point de salut

The answer was simplicity itself. The mental template, the cultural narrative, the habits of mind of French-Canadian exceptionalism were all to be preserved, but virtually all reference to Catholicism was ultimately to be expunged. French-Canadian exceptionalism was now to be a profoundly earthbound and secular affair.

Salvation was transferred from an afterlife, where God would mete out justice, elevating the deserving and casting down the wicked, to the earthly realm. The state was deputed to distribute justice to the members of a community uniquely morally superior to the peoples who surrounded it because of their communitarian solidarity and therefore their commitment to social justice. This was the new sacred mission to which the Québécois alone were called in North America. But meting out a superior standard of justice to the members of the community required an ability to distinguish those to whom justice is due from those to whom it is not. A path to membership in the justice community was also required for those who aspired to its higher moral calling.

This was the role assumed by the struggle to preserve and promote the French language: in this world of old symbols made new French was the new sacred language that identified members of the justice community, while providing a path to those who aspired to the salvation on earth offered by this *communauté solidaire*. And the state was to be the physical and institutional manifestation of this unique mission, distributing to each according to need and desert, while taking from each according to their means.

It is vital to understand that this makes the struggle to preserve and protect the French language not merely a linguistic struggle; it is a struggle imbued with a high moral purpose, because it calls on every member of the community to preserve and protect a unique, and uniquely threatened, way of life. Individual sacrifice in pursuit of this high moral mission is part of what imbues the struggle for control of all aspects of Quebec society and economy with its distinctive and characteristic energy. Moreover, it is not just that the Québécois are being called upon to sacrifice in order to preserve what they are. They are also just as importantly being called upon to sacrifice in order to avoid becoming something else, something clearly morally inferior. For, the alternative to being Québécois is not just being English-speaking, thus losing one's linguistic identity. It is also to embrace a set of values that, in the minds of Quebec nationalists, characterize what they call "*les Anglo-Saxons.*"

Chief among these differing values is a contemptible individualism and crass materialism, originating, in their view, in the American republic and reproduced in English-speaking Canada. Léon Dion remarked, "It is impossible for Quebeckers to adhere collectively to the American creed of economic success through individual effort, because the number of the chosen is far too few to give any likelihood to such a belief."[11] Another pair of prominent social analysts opined about this aspect of the nationalist strategy that "Quebec's nationalist politicians and interest groups made up of labour unions and other left-leaning organisations that are tightly embedded in the Quebec state maintain the existence of two societies with different values."[12]

The main political dividing line within Quebec was not, then, federalism versus separatism, for virtually all French-speaking politicians are nationalists of one sort or another (although many of them have a profound attachment to Canada). French-speakers were rather divided into two clans united in a nationalist vision but riven by an essentially theological dispute over the road to "salvation." Was Quebec's progress on the road to creating a uniquely just French-speaking society in North America best served by a millenarian nationalist vision or an incrementalist one? The millenarians argue that only by shaking off the restrictions imposed by sharing political power with another people—who do not believe in this vision of salvation—can true justice be achieved in Quebec.[13] Separation will usher in a new era of enlightenment and solidarity undiluted by having to share power with those who cannot or will not be saved because their spirit has been corrupted by a materialism against which the most formidable barrier is the social justice community and its sacred language.

The incrementalists, by contrast, say that the millenarian vision is a chimera and would be hugely and unnecessarily costly to achieve. Instead Confederation provides the Quebec community unique bargaining power with the rest of Canada; that power allows Quebec to pass many of the costs of the province's social justice project on to outsiders. Many federalist politicians in Quebec, while individually bound to Canada by ties of affection and respect, believe that the political purpose of the relationship with the rest of the country is chiefly to allow them to bring home the bacon. No one summed up this view better than the master federalist strategist of Quebec politics, Robert Bourassa, who boiled it down to its essence in his election slogan in the provincial election of 1970: "*le fédéralisme rentable*" or "profitable federalism." And even though federalists will often play along with the sovereigntists' claims that Quebec is a big loser in fiscal terms within Confederation, putting in more than it gets out, this is really a case of *reculer pour mieux sauter*: a widely felt grievance, no matter what its objective merits, is often the condition for a successful new raid on the federal treasury and taxpayer. And the fact that the separatist movement may use the grievance to whip up anti-Canada sentiment in Quebec greatly increases the chances of federalists arriving home with major new bacon imports.

Federalism's principal merit to the Quebec-federalist side is thus that ultimately you can get more out of federalism than you put in, whereas the millenarian version is a risky proposition: in the era after the Second Coming of New France, freed from English domination, a newly independent Quebec state would be on its own, unable to pass the costs of its *projet de société*[14] on to others. It wasn't that the independence strategy was wrong or unacceptable; it just seemed unnecessarily risky.

Note one particularly important area of common agreement between the two kinds of nationalism in Quebec: that being outside the justice community meant that you were not entitled to justice or fair treatment, that you were seen primarily as an instrument to be used or exploited by the community in its pursuit of justice for its members. Non-French-speakers, whether living in Quebec or outside, would get only what their political bargaining power could win for them; they had no moral claims on the community because they had, by definition, not been won over as converts to the *mission civilisatrice*. Indeed, part of the concept of the social justice state centred on Quebec was that old wounds would be salved by calling to account those remnants of the English-Canadian majority suddenly transformed into a vulnerable minority within Quebec. After all, delivering justice means punishing the wicked just as much as it means rewarding the virtuous.

Quebec: The Welfare State

Quebec is not alone in this nationalist strategy linking the unique virtue of the national community to a claim for political power and financial resources. It is not hard to see why nationalist movements quickly make a link between national virtue and social policy, especially when the nationalism is that of a national minority, whether the Québécois or Basques or Scots.

Political progress for nationalist movements depends on clear differentiation from the national majority coupled with a sense that only the minority taking control of its own affairs can result in justice and fairness being done to its members. The concept of "solidarity" becomes central to the nationalist appeal.[15]

The idea of the Québécois nation, and not Canada, as the "social justice community" for those living in Quebec has been an enduring theme of the rise of the nationalist movement, whether federalist or separatist. Even before separatism became a respectable political option, and before this idea of the role of the minority state as the vehicle for social justice against the mean-spiritedness of Canada became fully articulated, Quebec was struggling to gain control of social policy. In the early 1960s, for example, Quebec opted out of the new Canada Pension Plan to create its own QPP (La régie des rentes du Québec), presaging an ever-lengthening list of social demands. Nor was this limited to the *indépendentiste* side in Quebec. Claude Ryan, then editor of *Le Devoir* and later the head of the Quebec Liberal Party and leader of the federalist forces in the 1980 Quebec referendum, opposed the Trudeau-Bourassa deal to repatriate the Constitution in 1971, largely on the grounds that it was too ambiguous on the predominant role that Quebec ought to play in social policy. He won his point when Bourassa withdrew his support for that agreement.

The Quebec national community was not merely portrayed as seeking to promote the social development of all its members, however useful that portrayal was. For this casting of the Quebec state as the fount of generosity and social solidarity allowed the federal state to be portrayed correspondingly as the obstacle to the full development of this more caring Quebec national community.

In seeking control over social policy, nationalist movements can project powerful images about how their community is different from another because it espouses distinct values. For example, Scottish nationalism, much like Québécois nationalism, features the image of Scots as more egalitarian and progressive with respect to redistribution than the English.[16]

The Quebec-as-agent-of-justice-and-solidarity theme offered a rich political vein that nationalists of all parties mined with enthusiasm. Social programs of all sorts were expanded over the last forty years, including the $7-a-day daycare, the state-run auto insurance scheme for personal injuries, an extensive network of retirement and nursing homes, as well as community clinics (the CLSCs), the lowest tuition fees in the country, very high minimum wages, a strongly progressive tax system, etc. Quebec also led not only a movement among the provinces for more autonomy in social and economic policy, but also the charge for extra resources from Ottawa's coffers, on the grounds that only Quebec could spend them in a way that was consistent with Quebec's unique values (despite the fact that the evidence from polling and other sources lent slender support to the idea of the existence of these allegedly distinctive Quebec values).

Thus Quebec was able, to choose just a few examples, to get disproportionate funding for integration of immigrants, it promoted vast expansion of the equalization program of which it is by far the largest beneficiary in absolute terms, it got large transfers of tax points not available to other provinces in the sixties,[17] and more recently it got Ottawa to pony up impressive new transfers to the provinces as a result of a fictitious but politically astute claim that a "fiscal imbalance" existed that allegedly favoured Ottawa at the provinces' expense.[18] This struggle for extra resources for the province was carried on equally aggressively and equally successfully by both federalist and separatist governments in the province. And the other provinces merely sat bemusedly by on the sidelines, looked on admiringly and waited for the booty won by Quebec from a frightened Ottawa to be spread, by the logic of federalism, to all and sundry. Michael Bliss observed, "All of the provinces speedily developed an appetite for being treated like independent principalities, their premiers like princes. Ottawa appeared to be dealing from weakness, not strength, and sharp-witted provincial politicians were happy to rake in the chips."[19]

It mattered not that there was a wide consensus that Quebec actually did little that was all that distinctive with the social policy levers it controlled[20]: what was crucial was the symbolic positioning of Ottawa as the stumbling block to a more just future.

Economically the strategy was similarly two-pronged. First, nationalism offered an attractive economic proposition for groups seeking more money and other resources they didn't actually have to earn, but that they could use the state to take from others: support us now in our struggle for jurisdiction and resources with Ottawa, nationalists of all stripes intone, and you will be rewarded with a bigger share of the enlarged pie in the hands of the Quebec state. Second, a ready-made explanation was to hand to rationalize any economic ill effects that might be occasioned by this overbearing state: mismanagement of the economy by the federal government and a voracious appetite in Ottawa for tax resources that properly belong in the hands of Quebec. Not only could nationalists offer a more just society with or without sovereignty, every economic hiccough today was proof that the Quebec state would do better in the future and every social program that had to be forgone for budgetary reasons was the fault of Ottawa's Anglo-Saxon miserliness.

By focusing economic discontent on federal actions, the nationalists of all parties distracted Quebeckers from looking at the extent to which their own redistributionist policies were at the root of the province's difficulties. In fact, any suggestion from outside the province that the "social justice state" being created in Quebec was at the root of their economic and social underperformance was simply treated as further evidence that the rest of Canada didn't share Quebec's "values." Objections from within the province were treated as an embarrassing social solecism best greeted by a sad smile and a disbelieving and therapeutic silence, most like the one used to distract you before they clap on the straitjacket.

Thus isolated from economic criticism (you were either someone who obviously "didn't get" Quebec's distinctiveness and the extent to which French was threatened with disappearance unless heroic measures were taken, or else you were blaming the innocent victims of Ottawa's mismanagement), the Quebec state in the post–Quiet Revolution period could concentrate on building alliances with powerful interest groups that shared the redistributionist agenda.[21] That would include not only the usual suspects—the civil service, the Crown corporations, the nurses and the teachers, the farmers and the trade unionists—but also the private companies looking through special pleading to be dispensed from bearing the heavy and uncompetitive burden of taxation and regulation that Quebec was now putting in place.

Sorry, I Don't Speak French

In this symbolic scheme that shapes the mental picture French-speaking Quebeckers have of their uniqueness, and what that uniqueness entitles them to, language is on an equal footing with the nationalist *projet de société* (social justice project). If justice on this earth can alone be the fruit of a community uniquely caring for and committed to the welfare of its members, there must be some way to distinguish those who are members of the community, and therefore entitled to claim justice from the other members, and those who are not so entitled. For this community is a small one in world terms; it must conserve its strength in a hostile continent and avoid wasting resources on those who do not share its goals.

In this world of symbols, the French language therefore plays an indispensable role as the sacred tie that binds. It becomes the sign of community membership and the symbol of the moral superiority of staying French as the price one must pay for salvation (resisting the siren call of contemptible Anglo-Saxon materialism), while learning French becomes the taking of instruction necessary to understanding the true path to salvation. To become English-speaking is not just to change languages, it is to abandon the higher moral calling of the community and to elevate mere individual material comforts over the moral duty one has to other members of the community both to contribute to social justice for them and to protect the sacred language by which the community identifies itself, distributes justice, and excludes the undeserving.

And what better tool for rallying the troops could there be, if your mission is to protect and promote the French language and the culture out of which it grows, than French as an endangered language? The civilizing light of the French language is flickering, and we, its guardians, have been asleep at our post. *Aux armes, citoyens!*

Thus was born a key nationalist industry in Quebec: crying that the linguistic sky is falling. Going right back to the reports of the Royal Commission on Bilingualism and Biculturalism, which sounded the alarm about the relative economic status of the two languages in Montreal, as well as the under-representation of French-speakers in the federal government, there has since been an unending series of often polemical studies about how many French-speakers there are, whether the French language is in retreat, whether it is being sufficiently protected and promoted, and so forth. These anxieties are raised to a fever pitch from time to time by language-related crises, such as the affair of *Les Gens de l'Air*, those pilots and air traffic controllers who wanted French-speakers to be able to fly in their own language within Quebec, or outraged discoveries that one could not get served in French in this or that retail establishment on *la rue Ste-Catherine*.

A quick survey of a few French-language newspapers in Montreal in the first few months of 2008 turned up the following examples of doomsday accounts of the status of French in Quebec[22]: on the front page of *La Presse*, the largest-circulation French-language daily in North America, you could have read: "*Loi 101: Le Français en péril*" (Bill 101: French Imperilled). And what did the article in question contain? The startling revelation that a reporter had found a few imported items bearing English-only labels in a Montreal store. In *Le Devoir*, newspaper of the nationalist intelligentsia, one headline was "*Québec aide les immigrants à parler l'anglais/Le gouvernement paie des cours aux francophones pour améliorer leur employabilité*" (Quebec helps immigrants to speak English/The government pays cost of French-speakers' courses to make them more employable). Another front-page *Le Devoir* story was headed "*Québec s'adresse en anglais aux trois-quarts des immigrants allophones*" (Quebec communicates in English with three-quarters of those immigrants who speak neither English nor French). And yet a third: "*Québec tait des données alarmantes; Conférence de presse de l'Office de la langue française annulée sans raison*" (Quebec hushes up alarming statistics/Press conference of the Office of the French Language cancelled without explanation).

> The key finding of the 2006 census as far as the French language is concerned is that three-quarters of all allophone immigrants (i.e., those whose mother tongue is neither English nor French) are adopting French rather than English. That is the largest share ever recorded. Forty years ago, the majority adopted English.
>
> Yves Boisvert, "L'autre secret sur le français," *La Presse*

Most egregious of all was a fifteen-page series in the *Journal de Montréal* that trumpeted over several days the message that people would not be served in French in downtown Montreal. If you scratched under the surface, however, this alarmist flame-fanning was based on this set of facts: a reporter was sent out to apply for jobs waitressing or selling in commercial establishments in downtown Montreal. She applied to ninety-five such establishments, professing her inability to speak French. Eighty of the establishments turned her down. Fifteen of the smallest were, however, willing to hire her. This prompted the headline [author's translation]:

Difficult to be served in French in Montreal,
SORRY, I DON'T SPEAK FRENCH,
Our journalist finds 15 jobs while speaking English only.

Little effort was expended finding out whether other employees or the owners might be able to serve any customers wishing to speak French, and no effort was made to determine whether there was any link between this "scandal" and an article in the *Globe and Mail* several months later that reported that employers in the province are struggling to fill many jobs: "The Quebec government is turning to welfare recipients and the unemployed to fill the huge gap in the province's labour shortage."[23]

Every numerical twitch of the census figures for the share of French-speakers in Quebec's population provokes deep bouts of angst and political crises in which the status of French is painted in such dire terms that radical and far-reaching action alone could save it from certain death and, with it, the end of the *mission civilisatrice* and Quebec's unique place on the continent. The myth of French's inability to rise from its deathbed became an article of faith, at least in certain quarters; contesting it required some intestinal fortitude. In recent years there has been more diversity of voices, especially now that it is clear that by most important objective criteria, French is in good health.[24] In fact, the 2006 census gives the best news about the place of French in Quebec in a generation.[25]

In the past, French was threatened in Quebec by another powerful linguistic competitor: English. The two languages were rivals for the affections of new arrivals who spoke neither language as their mother tongue. Forty years ago, English was the hands-down winner in that rivalry. Now, however, English is the threatened language in Quebec (because of the decline of the native-speaker population), and new immigrants are choosing to integrate predominantly into the French-speaking community. Thus even if the proportion of *native* French-speakers declines today, it is no longer relative to a large competitor language. Instead, it is relative to a pastiche of many language groups, the large majority of whom are converging on French as the common language of communication.

In fact Quebec nationalism's preoccupation with tendentious accounts of French's imminent demise reminds me of nothing so much as Algernon's imaginary friend Bunbury in Oscar Wilde's play *On the Importance of Being Earnest*. Whenever Algernon needed to escape a social obligation to his gorgon-like Aunt Augusta (Lady Bracknell), his imaginary "friend" Bunbury would fall deathly ill and call Algernon by telegram to his bedside for a last sad farewell. Aunt Augusta was ultimately driven to make the following apposite remark:

> Well, I must say, Algernon, that I think it is high time that Mr. Bunbury made up his mind whether he was going to live or to die. This shilly-shallying with the question is absurd. Nor do I in any way approve of the modern sympathy with invalids. I consider it morbid. Illness of any kind is hardly a thing to be encouraged in others. Health is the primary duty of life.

Like Algernon, however, Quebec nationalists have found Bunbury altogether too valuable to dispense with. In their view, progress in winning more autonomy for the province could be made only by solidifying and then expanding the dominance of the French language in Quebec, while simultaneously portraying the rest of the country as hostile to that language and making repeated fevered claims about its imminent demise.

Given the dominance of economic decision-making by English-speakers in Montreal, it made sense at the outset of the Quiet Revolution to use the instruments of the state, which were under the control of Quebec's French-language majority, to seize a share of economic power. This the nationalists did very successfully through means such as completing the nationalization of the Quebec electricity industry begun in the 1940s by Premier Adélard Godbout and taking over the asbestos and (at least partially) auto insurance industries, for example. They also expanded the Quebec state into many areas (such as education and social services) previously controlled by the Roman Catholic Church and acquired many kinds of industries through state action (other than outright nationalization) such as Rexfor in the forestry industry, Sidbec in steel, and the Caisse de dépôt in finance. Much of this effort to create opportunities for French-speakers was explicitly justified by the beneficial effects it would have on the survival of the French language.

Take La Société de développement industriel (SDI), created in 1971. The SDI was, according to Matthew Fisher, the most stridently nationalist Quebec Crown corporation of them all. It gave grants to companies with strict stipulations: that 50 per cent of executives had to be French-speakers within four

[The] educational reforms of the Quiet Revolution were enormously successful in creating a new body of Francophones who were fully qualified to assume managerial positions, and who could be a major source of political discontent if their ambitions were not met. Over the short term, the rapidly growing public sector could absorb many of these Francophones, but this could only be a stop-gap. With the 1970s, attention turned to the one governmental strategy not attempted during the Quiet Revolution: directly intervening in the operations of English-Canadian and American corporations to ensure greater mobility for Francophones. For many Quebec Francophones, the key to this improved mobility was to make French the primary language of work. They began to pressure the Quebec government to do so.

Kenneth McRoberts, *Quebec: Social Change and Political Crisis* years, twenty new managerial jobs had to be created for graduates of Quebec universities, and 40 per cent of the company's insurance had to be bought in Quebec. After its election in 1976, the Parti Québécois (PQ) replaced two-thirds of the SDI board and more than tripled its budget.[26] According to one former executive with the Caisse de dépôt, Pierre Arbour, "speaking very frankly, without the SDI, many Quebec corporations would now be bankrupt."[27] He goes on to point out that what he calls the "linguistic interventionism" of the Quebec state has thrust it into a role for which it is ill suited, namely the management of business enterprises, and this has led to the unfortunate transformation of Quebec taxpayers into involuntary shareholders who are now paying the costs of the Quebec state's ill-advised business ventures.[28]

> Among those who had completed only primary education [in 1965], separatism was supported by 11 per cent; the figure for those with only secondary education was the same; but among those with special or technical training, 29 percent favoured separation and for graduates of university or *collège classique* the figure was 26 percent.
>
> Charles Taylor, "Nationalism and the Political Intelligentsia"

In fact there was a very conscious policy of using the levers of state power to open up jobs for the rising educated class of French-speakers, as the Quiet Revolution had opened education to them on a massive scale just as their numbers began to rise precipitously.[29]

The drive to open up jobs to French-speakers began, though, with the creation of public sector work on a huge scale, starting with, among other things, the completion of the nationalization of the hydroelectric industry, immortalized in a brilliant phrase by Albert Breton as "not a decision about investing in electricity, but one about investing in ethnicity."[30] Already in 1965, Charles Taylor of McGill was remarking on the extent to which the rising nationalist sentiment was expressed in terms of opening up high-paying professional jobs for French-speakers and used the nationalization of Hydro-Québec as a good example.[31]

This was the point where the demographic bulge of Boomers first met and mingled with Quebec nationalism. Poor levels of education, divisions within Quebec society about the desirability of the commercial life, and to a lesser extent anti-French prejudice had kept the bulk of French-speakers out of the mainstream of national and international business life in Quebec for many years, even though they were extremely successful running small and medium-sized businesses that primarily served the local market. But the Quiet Revolution opened economic opportunity within the Quebec state to French-speakers at almost exactly the moment that this rising tide of young workers was poised to pour into the workplace. Neither Quebec City nor Ottawa could allow this to result in a large pool of politically active and disaffected young people feeling deprived of opportunity by the fact of their language.

Young people during this time were, in fact, a key political battleground. Educated, imbued with a sense of injustice that French-speakers, according to the conventional accounts, had somehow been excluded by the English-speakers' old boys' network from the economic sphere, and taught in the new educational institutions by members of the rising nationalist elite who had themselves often been frustrated by their inability to succeed in a business and institutional world dominated by English, they were both impatient and ardently in favour of new power for the province of Quebec, the only powerful political institution controlled by French-speakers.[32]

And this was before the Quiet Revolution's educational reforms had really had a chance to make much of a mark at the primary and secondary levels. Even before the Quiet Revolution, however, there had been an expansion of education in the post-secondary sector in the post-war period, and this new class of non–liberal arts graduates—people with degrees in more technical fields such as engineering, architecture, science, and so forth—had sought work in the private sector but quickly discovered that this was a place where the language of work was English. The modernization movement accelerated by the Quiet Revolution was in large part a response to the rise of this new professional middle class, seeking opportunities for itself and for its children, opportunities where language would not put them at a disadvantage.[33] This rising middle class would "effectively use a rejuvenated and modernized Quebec state to wrestle control from the Catholic Church over all health, social welfare, and educational institutions, as well as to begin to challenge the English-speaking elite's control over Quebec's economy."[34] Charles Taylor noted at the time,

> by the early 1960s, not only was the bargaining power of the French professional classes greater than it had been in the past, but many of them had discovered that nationalist agitation in itself increased this bargaining power; for example the noise made around the separatist movement made English-Canadians more ready to make concessions in matters such as bilingualism and the use of French.[35]

The nationalist movement was clearly used by a rising (both economically and demographically) French-speaking middle class as a tool by which to win benefits for itself, and its members gave their political support to the party most likely to advance their rise. The PQ and its millenarian vision was attractive for its commitment to use the state more vigorously to open opportunity for French-speakers, but as long as its central plank was independence or even sovereignty-association, the risk of such a strategy was high, leaving government in the hands of the incrementalist federalists until René Lévesque and his strategists, such as Claude Morin, hit on the referendum manoeuvre (itself described by its authors as "*étapisme*" or incrementalism). By guaranteeing that no risky constitutional strategy would

All these councils, departments, boards and enterprises provided previously unexisting [*sic*] high-prestige and high power jobs for university-trained Francophones. This is indicated, for instance, by the number of people involved in new managerial tasks in the Quebec civil service between 1964 and 1971 (economists, sociologists, social workers, psychologists): it increased by more than 400 percent, while the traditional professional personnel of the government (like doctors and engineers) increased by only 20 percent.

Marc Renaud, *Quebec since 1945*

be pursued without an explicit mandate from the population, to be decided in a referendum separate from elections for the government, the PQ and its aggressive program of expansion of the status of French was rendered safe for the middle class. The PQ was rewarded with a long stint in power, but no referendum mandate to negotiate sovereignty-association. The PQ was, however, to be the instrument of opening the private sector to the French-speaking middle class, just as the federalists who preceded them had spent the previous couple of decades opening opportunities within the state.[36]

A Very Canadian Coup

But the nationalists did much more to clear the road for native French-speaking members of the middle class who were arriving on the scene in such large, disquieting, and aggressive numbers. French-speakers were pulled in, and non-French-speakers were pushed out to make room for them. Language legislation was the spearhead of a generalized policy of an exquisitely polite and therefore very Canadian kind of ethnic cleansing. In Quebec, signals were simply sent that English-speakers and inassimilable immigrants were not welcome, chiefly because they represented both a threat to French and its dominance and a threat to the solidarity of the social justice state for French-speakers that together gave

Quebec its *mission civilisatrice*. Successive governments made sending your child to an English school progressively more difficult. English-speakers were made an endangered species in the Quebec public sector. Professionals such as physicians and engineers, no matter how badly needed, could not practise in the province unless they could pass French-language competency tests that had nothing to do with their professional skills.

Certificates of "francization" were required for all enterprises employing more than fifty people, thus more or less creating a legal requirement that no big employer could offer a working environment in a language other than French without attracting the attention of the language police. In 1984, just over a third of businesses employing more than fifty people had been awarded such certificates, meaning that they had created a French-language working environment that got the provincial government's stamp of approval. By 1994 over three-quarters of such employers had such certification.[37] Now the PQ is aggressively promoting the extension of this certificate requirement to employers with fewer than fifty employees.[38]

> At the time [1976] I was a member of the Quebec civil service, but working in Ottawa.... A few weeks earlier, a separatist party, the Parti Québécois, had been elected to form the government of Quebec. It seemed obvious that interesting and important things were about to happen in my home province, and I wanted to be involved. So I flew back to Quebec City and called on Louis Bernard, the *chef de cabinet* of the new premier of Quebec, René Lévesque. Bernard was about to become secretary to the Executive Council, the most important civil servant of the Quebec government, and I asked him to reintegrate me into the public service. His answer was surprisingly clear. He told me he thought I should resign, because there was no more place for Anglophones in the Quebec civil service.
>
> Reed Scowen, *Time to Say Goodbye*

You Are Not from Around Here, Are You?

The visible face of the bilingual, bicultural nature of Quebec society and history was simply erased. It became more and more difficult to get English-language services in the public sector outside the federal government, and eventually even historically English-dominated municipalities were amalgamated into a single greater Montreal (although some were allowed to escape partially after a change of government). English-speakers and other non-French-speakers could not even give a public face to their language, as the sign law aspect of Bill 101 (La Charte de la langue française) essentially stigmatized languages other than French as embarrassments not to be tolerated in the public space. All of this and more was presented as promotion of the ever-endangered French language, which it undoubtedly was, but it was also largely achieved through the demotion of English and other languages.

And it wasn't just the visible signs of the English language that were to be effaced. A large set of English-language institutions (schools, hospitals, universities, social services) that had been created by the English-speaking community over the course of centuries were slowly robbed of their autonomy and identity. They were drawn into dependence on provincial funding, subjected to stringent language requirements, so that professionals such as doctors and nurses who would be called on to serve a predominantly English-speaking population would be denied permission to work if they could not demonstrate competence in French, their client populations drifting out of the province. Even McGill, once the proud bulwark of the English-language community in Montreal, is now so dependent on provincial funding that it has become a meek observer of the hollowing out of the community that gave it birth. And the nationalists of all stripes bristle at this description, saying that "their" English-language minority is better treated than the French-language minorities of most other provinces, an argument ignorant of history and realities on the ground.

These signals were heard and understood by successive generations of English-speakers and members of ethnic groups that identified with the Canadian and North American English-speaking majority and economic mainstream. In a later chapter, on the consequences of Quebec City and Ottawa following through on their respective post-1960 strategies, I will document the extent of the ensuing out-migration.

For the moment suffice it to say that the result was a stunning loss of people and the rich experience, knowledge, and wealth-creating capacity they represented. Estimates vary, but it seems quite clear that these policies were at least partially responsible for a massive exodus of people, often young people with highly valuable skills, who understood that they were not wanted if they were unwilling or unable to work in French, the minority language of their country, a language, moreover, with extremely limited and declining economic value internationally or even nationally outside Quebec and Ottawa. Pierre Arbour estimates that the Quebec government gave up a minimum of $1 billion per year in tax revenues because of the "going down the road" of English-speakers and corporate head offices between 1976 and 1986 alone.[39]

So having undermined the economic value of the English language by law, having prevented by law most French-speakers and members of ethnic minorities educating their children in English, having erased, by law, much of the face of the historical English-speaking community and having neutered its institutions, the nationalist strategy also turned its sights on the other main source of ethnically and linguistically suspect population growth: immigration.

You Say Multiculturalism, I Say *Interculturalisme*

Prior to the rise of the modern nationalist movement, immigration had been a largely uncontested federal responsibility. Immigrants thought that they were immigrating to a country where English was the dominant language and that Montreal was a city where immigrants could and did participate in the mainstream of North American economic life. Thus did large-scale immigration from non-English-speaking countries, such as Italy, Greece, Portugal, and elsewhere, nevertheless result in an immigrant community that identified more with the English-speaking national majority in Canada than with the national minority concentrated in Quebec, but not overwhelmingly dominant on the island of Montreal. Unsurprisingly, the most violent protests against efforts by the Quebec government to restrict access to English schools were seen in St-Léonard, an Italian-dominated suburb of Montreal, not in Westmount or the West Island.

Political unrest in Montreal and the rise of nationalism in Quebec more generally created unease among traditional immigrant groups, many of whom were fleeing politically motivated troubles in their countries of origin. Immigration to Canada shifted decisively westward; Quebec had to forgo a major source of population renewal, but, again, the result was less competition for French-speakers in the local economy.

In response to demographic concerns, the Quebec government strove to gain control of immigration policy from Ottawa and to concentrate their recruitment efforts on the so-called *francophonisables*, on those immigrants who were likely to be inclined to assimilate into the French-speaking minority rather than the English-speaking majority of Canada.[40] That meant that Arab, African, Asian, and Caribbean countries with a French colonial history (e.g., Haiti, Algeria, Lebanon, Senegal, Vietnam, and so forth) moved up the ranking of source countries, while immigration from traditional sources that had proven more resistant to seeing Quebec become increasingly predominantly French, such as Greeks and Italians, were not solicited as keenly. And it was to be made clear to new immigrants that they were now moving, not to a majority English-speaking Canada, but to a majority French-speaking Quebec, and that participation in public life and in the economy was to be carried out in French, not English.[41]

In 1990, this previously implicit policy was made official by the government of Robert Bourassa, under the name of "*interculturalisme*." In return for relatively easy immigration to Quebec, this policy emphasized that immigrants must accept "a moral contract" to integrate into the French-speaking community by accepting the principle that Quebec "is a society which has French as the common language of public life."[42] Unlike multiculturalism, this was not a policy of "no official culture." *Au contraire.* The official culture was Québécois culture, and the language that was the glue holding it all together was the French language. In exchange, immigrants could expect a Quebec more open to dialogue between cultures, more accepting of differences. By learning the sacred language, immigrants were signalling their intention to join the social justice community and could therefore expect that community to extend to them the hand of welcome.

Immigrants willing to accept these terms were fast-tracked, but Quebec's relatively poor record at actually attracting immigrants, despite the disproportionate share of federal recruitment and integration funding they receive, shows that its attractiveness as a destination remains poor compared to other parts of Canada to the west, a theme to which I shall return later.

Quebec: The Let's-Make-a-Deal State

Continuing the survey of the nationalist strategy post-1960, relatively little attention has been paid to the way that social and economic policy affected and reinforced each other in the last forty years in Quebec, although a great deal has been said about each individually. This leaves a gap that I believe must be filled if we are to understand how the country as a whole changed in response to the coincidence of the baby boom and the rise of Quebec nationalism.

An important part of the strategy binding Quebeckers to the social justice state was the dynamic by which people's lives are increasingly entangled with the state as that state comes to commandeer a disproportionate share of society's resources, and citizens, in turn, are forced to demand "their fair share" of the booty. I described the dynamic of rent-seeking or PUPPETRY in an earlier chapter.

The PUPPETRY strategy pursued by Quebec adds a new dimension, however, to the standard rent-seeking story. In the case of Quebec under the post-1960 nationalist strategy, it isn't just that the state exploits many of its own citizens, often to the point of driving them out. It isn't just that powerful interest groups, such as farmers and trade unions and favoured corporations see no problem in using the state to transfer benefits to themselves at the expense of everyone else, and to present this as a victory of an enlightened social justice state. It is also that it has become a matter of ordinary daily business to expect transfers from people in the rest of Canada under threat of breaking up the country. In this the situation of the Quebec state is truly different from the one Bastiat described for the state in general, for there the universe of people paying was also the universe of people benefiting, guaranteeing a zero-sum game. In Quebec to the extent that transfers of various forms into Quebec exceed federal taxes paid, Quebeckers are using people in the rest of the country to pay for the costs of choices made by Quebeckers, choices often intended to damage the long-term survival and success of the country. That makes the Quebec social justice state, not the "fiction" that Bastiat foresaw, but a PUPPETRY machine par excellence. *Le fédéralisme rentable* indeed!

Taken together, all these elements of Quebec's behaviour made up a strategy that posed a potent challenge to Canada's continued survival. Quebec became the homeland of a linguistic majority imbued with the importance of its singular mission: to create a uniquely just society based on the community solidarity that joins French-speakers together, making common sacrifices for the survival and promotion of French. French, in turn, was the bulwark or barrier that separated the members of this justice community from the mere dog-eat-dog Anglo-Saxon capitalism that surrounded them. It was not just that Quebec was a tiny drop of French-speakers in an English-speaking sea (as the song has it "*On est six million—faut se parler*"); more importantly language was taken as a proxy for moral virtue or turpitude. To become English, to lose one's Frenchness, was to become an apostate and to lose access to salvation.

The very existence of Canada and the many ways in which it made its presence (and that of its non-French-speaking majority) obtrude on Quebec was the chief obstacle to the success of this sacred trust of the social justice community. Not only was Quebec therefore justified in actively trying to crowd out the federal state on as many fronts as possible, it was also justified in seeking to crowd out its own English-speaking minority. As the vanguard of the linguistic opposition, English-speakers could be expected to have a deep and enduring attachment to Canada that would be largely unaffected by the appeals to ethnic and linguistic solidarity of the nationalists.

The Quebec state was sitting astride the economy in a way that no other government in Canada was attempting, and using that dominant position to advance the cause of French-speakers. Immigration was being transformed from a buttress of the English-speaking community and of attachment to Canada into a source of renewal for the French-speaking community. And, finally, the

Quebec state was positioned as the instrument of social solidarity and justice for French-speakers and those allied with them, while the federal state was made into the chief obstacle to the realization of a more just society. That obstacle was created by Ottawa's occupation of social policy fields (thus dominated by values inimical to the alleged generosity and egalitarianism of the Québécois) and through its selfish insistence on keeping its hands on tax revenues that Quebec could spend to better effect in the pursuit of justice and fairness.

Canada's Response: Unity through Profligacy

Canada was taken by surprise by Quebec's evolution in the sixties and was constantly playing catch-up. But what the country's leadership did dimly comprehend was that the future of the country was being played out, especially once Daniel Johnson and his Union nationale party won the 1966 provincial election in Quebec on the slogan "*Égalité ou indépendence.*" Even if Johnson's clear preference was for *égalité* over *indépendence,* the separatist genie was officially out of the bottle, and the election of the UN was quickly followed in 1968 by the formation of the Parti Québécois under the leadership of a charismatic former Lesage cabinet minister and architect of the modern Hydro-Québec, René Lévesque.

The federal government's options were always constrained by the terms the nationalists had established. Ottawa could not maintain the federal government's classic reluctance to expand the welfare state without ceding all the ground to Quebec's self-portrayal as the "social justice state" for French-speakers. It could not too vigorously contest the portrayal of French as constantly teetering on the brink of disappearance, or its credibility would be destroyed with an anxious Quebec electorate whose fears were always being stoked by the nationalists. It could not be a vigorous defender of the rights of English Quebeckers and other non-French-speakers without being portrayed as the stooge of an English-language majority that was indifferent at best and actively hostile at worst to Quebec's unique mission. Any deterioration in Quebec's economic or social performance would certainly be attributed by the nationalists (of all political stripes) to Ottawa's poor management, while all successes would be claimed by the Quebec government. And the wave of young French-speaking workers pouring into the labour force in Quebec was clearly going to be the major battleground for the contending forces.

Bilingualism: A Loser's Guide

The starting point for the federal strategy was to offer the federal government as the chief agent of the older vision of Canada as a bilingual and bicultural project of English- and French-speakers, united in a rivalry to be the dominant force in a half-continental national construction project. Thus the mantle of grand defender of the older "French-Canadian" view fell on Ottawa's shoulders, but, alas, it was already too late to make any difference. In Quebec it was truly a loser's strategy, however much it may have appealed to the rest of the country as "the solution."

The original appeal of "French Canada" for French-speakers had been the prospect that French-speakers were a credible competitor in the struggle to put their stamp on the whole country. But by the time Quebec nationalists had put on the table the alternative identity of Québécois for the French-speaking majority of Quebec, it was clear to that majority that the pan-Canadian dream was dead; any defence of "French Canada" was a purely rearguard action whose chief effect would be to maintain the old defensive minority mentality, always at the mercy of a hostile English-speaking majority. Even constitutionally Quebec wants no truck or trade with the idea of French Canada: the distinct society that French-speakers may constitute is not scattered across the territory of Canada, but for nationalists is present only in the territory of Quebec, over which French-speakers have majority control.

Thus was born one of the great misunderstandings of the last half century. Ottawa's Royal Commission on Bilingualism and Biculturalism, created in reaction to the nationalist ferment of the early sixties, naturally saw the language problem in the then still-dominant framework of French Canada and proposed a French-Canadian solution: a bilingual federal state, embodied in the Official Languages Act by Pierre Trudeau and his government and followed up by an aggressive expansion of jobs for French-speakers (of which more in a moment). Unfortunately, as in so much else during this period, Ottawa was chasing events rather than leading them, and by the time the machinery of bilingualism was in place, it was no longer relevant to the French-speaking majority in Quebec, whose mental geography of citizenship and belonging had shrunk to the borders of that province.

Thus what Trudeau and his followers sold to the rest of Canada as a recipe for national harmony, a legislative and eventually constitutional enactment of the equality of French and English, was seen in Quebec as a "Canadian" affair not relevant to them. They were washing their hands of their status as "national minority" within Canada, a status that had become humiliating because it consecrated their permanent status as losers in the effort to shape Canada in their own image. Instead they were choosing the more powerful self-image of national majority in a struggle with another country to "recover" the symbols and powers of nationhood. Not only is this a more assertive, "liberating," and "anti-colonial" view, it also has the benefit of symbolically putting the French-speaking national majority of Quebec on a morally equal footing with the English-speaking national majority of Canada, since all nations are moral equals even though their resources and power may be quite disparate.

Ottawa's bilingualism ploy was too little too late. Today bilingualism is of interest chiefly in Quebec as a barometer of how well French-speaking minorities, the historical remnants of an earlier bi-national struggle, are treated by the victorious English-speaking Canadians. Through their control of language policy within their own borders, however, Quebeckers have escaped the circumstance in which the status of French is a gift dependent on the generosity of an English-speaking majority. In its place is a French-language majority deciding for itself. It is not that Quebeckers think that bilingualism is a bad policy for Canada—rather they think that either it has little to do with them, or that it accords only them the right to work and be served in French by the federal government, a result they regard as nothing more than their due if they are not to vote the country out of existence. Its absence would be a cause for grievance; its presence is no cause for gratitude or celebration.

Moreover, personal[43] and institutional bilingualism is regarded with great suspicion by many nationalists in a society where the fear is that every French-speaker who knows English already has one foot out the door of the social justice community. They may be enticed away by the higher standard of living of the rest of the continent, and therefore abandon their moral duty to build a more just society for the chosen people of Quebec. Knowledge of English is like eating of the forbidden fruit of the tree of knowledge—it puts your soul in peril by creating distance between you and the community and risks severing the connection altogether.

While recognizing the economic advantage bilingualism creates, Quebec nationalists also fear that it endangers their *projet de société* by offering a way out for those who think the price of salvation is too high. They would prefer that the exit remain firmly shut. So what was regarded by the rest of Canada as a hopeful and generous offer of full language equality was regarded with suspicion as a linguistic Trojan horse by its supposed beneficiaries.

The one-sided nature of bilingualism was made painfully clear by Ottawa's almost total indifference to the fate of English-speaking Quebeckers. The federal government spends millions on bolstering and celebrating French-speaking enclaves no matter where they may be in English-speaking Canada—St-Boniface, Gravelbourg, Maillardville, Chéticamp, Abram Village, Penetanguishene. They pressure provincial governments with tiny French-speaking minorities to offer a broad range of services in French at a minimum and even to become officially bilingual, as in Manitoba, which almost cost then-NDP premier Howard Pawley his job.[44] Ottawa subsidizes French-language minority and immersion schooling but essentially stands by while Quebec declares itself officially unilingual (except for the constitutional obligation to offer bilingual services in the legislature and the courts) and restricts the right of both immigrants and French-speakers to choose the language of instruction for their children. In 2008, the federal government intervened before the Supreme Court in support of a Quebec government appeal aiming to restrict the guarantees of access to English-language schooling in the Charter of Rights and Freedoms. The federal argument is that parents who pay to send their children to non-subsidized English-language private schools should not thereby gain the right to send them on later to publicly funded English schools, even though the Quebec Court of Appeal has found that parents do have such a right under the Charter.[45] Even Pierre Trudeau, father of the Charter, thought that it was acceptable for the French-speaking majority in Quebec that did not want English-language education for their children to have the right to oppress the French-speaking minority who did.

Given the anxiety nationalists had instilled in the population about the vulnerability of French and the way they portrayed the traditional English-speaking community as somehow insensitive interlopers rather than a centuries-old community just as legitimate in its presence as French-speakers, Ottawa decided that discretion was the better part of valour. Principles could be sacrificed if it meant the survival of the country, and a too-successful defence of the English-language community in Quebec might undermine what became one of the chief federalist claims against the nationalist movement: that Bill 101 and the rise in the economic status of French-speakers within Quebec proved that Quebec did not need to separate in order to defend the French language successfully. The province enjoyed the power to do what needed to be done within the existing constitutional arrangements. If a few "Westmount Rhodesians," as the English-speakers came increasingly and dismissively to be called, had to be sacrificed, it was a small price to be paid for the survival of the country.

The Maple Leaf Forever ... or at Least Until It's Inconvenient

Nor was bilingualism the only "compromise" that English-speakers were called upon to make in the name of making "French Canadians feel at home in Canada." The old historical symbols and associations that the Québécois linked to their historical "humiliation" as the losers in the struggle to predominate in the new country to the north of the United States had to go. Thus English-speaking Canada agreed to jettison the Red Ensign flag and Dominion Day; to stop singing "The Maple Leaf Forever" and "God Save the Queen"; to foreswear the now-deprecated idea that newcomers might be expected to give up some of their old ways and allegiances and become members of an already existing cultural, historical, and language community; and to become simultaneously forgetful and vaguely ashamed of a history now characterized as colonialist and exploitative.

It has become far easier in our public schools to learn a sanitized version of the history of pre-Columbian aboriginals in Canada or tendentious accounts of how we have ruinously exploited our environment than it is to learn about Wolfe and Montcalm, Lafontaine and Baldwin, Macdonald and Cartier, Laurier and Sifton, Passchendaele and Vimy, Confederation and the Statute of Westminster, and the many other cardinal personalities and events of this country's illustrious and honourable history.

But while we stooped, we did not conquer. At least not if conquering meant winning the hearts and minds of French-speakers in Quebec. They saw nothing of interest to them in the wiping clean of English Canada's historical memory, in the silencing of all reference to the proud symbols and traditions on which much of the country had been built. They might have felt a small frisson of triumphalism in eliminating the old symbols of a culture and history they had been unable to best on the field of contention, and so they simply pressed successfully for their erasure. In neither their hearts nor their minds did they still inhabit that country, so such changes in it could not win them over. Again, Ottawa was pursuing a loser's strategy.

The feds played a somewhat cannier game with respect to the social justice state, but even there their room for manoeuvre was severely limited and they were late to realize the good cards they held. Under Lester Pearson the government was so overcome by fear of what they saw happening in Quebec, they were in full rout. Virtually every demand for erasure of the country's national symbols, for Quebec autonomy, and for an opt-out from federal programs was granted. This was the period of the birth of the Canada Pension Plan, for example, which Quebec opted out of from the beginning. We forget now, however, how great was the retreat of Ottawa and the transfer of resources to Quebec during these early years. Claude Morin, master strategist of Quebec's federal-provincial game plan, tells the story:

> During the transition period from 1965 to 1970 in the case of most programs, and from 1965 to 1967 for some lesser ones, Ottawa's participation in hospital insurance, old age assistance, and blind and disabled persons allowances, as well as vocational training and health programs, would be replaced by a fiscal abatement of 20 points of personal income tax. Of these 20 points 14 would apply to hospital insurance, two to old age assistance as well as blindness and disability allowances, two to the welfare component of unemployment insurance, and one point each to the other programs. This fiscal equivalence was to be filled out by cash payments in such a way that tax points plus payments would be precisely equal to the sums the federal government would have authorized for Quebec in the case of no withdrawal. Certain cost-shared programs of minor importance were replaced by a simple financial equivalence, that is, involved no supplementary fiscal abatement.... The proposal was put to Quebec in a way that left it open to all provinces, in principle, as interested in pulling out of shared cost programs as was Quebec. It is hardly necessary to point out that this was not at all the case, as proven by the rest of the negotiations, but the federal government wanted to avoid the impression that Quebec was getting special treatment.[46]

When Pierre Trudeau came to power, however, Ottawa began to fight back in some measure. Where Ottawa could not win the battle on the social justice state, it beat strategic retreats, but in other areas, such as unemployment insurance, it held fast against Quebec demands for autonomy. Determined not to yield the social justice terrain to Quebec, Ottawa was nevertheless clearly and explicitly following Quebec's lead, as Morin recognized.[47] And it was during this period that Ottawa began to ramp up considerably its use of the federal spending power as well as its spending in areas under its own jurisdiction. The reasons for this are not far to seek and are central to our story.

My Government Can Spend More Than Your Government

Under Trudeau, cannier and more strategic than his predecessors and with a government with deep roots in Quebec, Ottawa quickly began to see the outlines of a strategy that was not for losers, however unattractive and even sordid it might have been.

Trudeau noticed that there was a disparity between what the government of Quebec demanded of Ottawa and the behaviour of individuals and institutions in the province. Quebec City was largely of the view that any spending by Ottawa on virtually anything outside defence and the post office was pretty much illegitimate (what Felix Leclerc, the great Quebec *chansonnier*, would have called *les gros doigts d'étrangers dans les papiers de famille*, or the fat greasy fingers of strangers pawing through the family papers). The official demand was therefore always for Ottawa's withdrawal and the transfer of the money being spent by the federal government to the provincial government, to be spent according to the latter's priorities.

But people and institutions that actually got money from Ottawa, while they might have been publicly silent or even supportive of the general autonomist orientation of Quebec, were also loath to give up Ottawa's lucre. Who knew, if the money was transferred to Quebec City, whether it would keep flowing to its current beneficiaries? The colour of Ottawa's money was just as agreeable as that of Quebec City, and a bird in the hand, etc.

Quebec City railed, but impotently. Even in the sacrosanct field of education, where Ottawa gave money to post-secondary institutions and students, Quebec could not stop the feds from using their constitutionally legitimate power to spend money wherever they liked because the province got no real support from its own institutions and citizens in this battle, and much opposition.

Interestingly, while Quebec City always deprecated in the most uncompromising terms these federal "intrusions" in its areas of jurisdiction, the truth is that it always had the means to stop it. The simple expedient of a law forbidding provincial institutions and individuals from accepting federal money would have done the trick in most cases. That, however, would have required the province to break the cardinal rule never to do anything that might drive an institution or group to feel that their future was better assured by allegiance to the federal government than to Quebec City. This rule has had to be broken occasionally, but only under extreme duress.

This struggle gave rise to a long-standing battle between Quebec City and Ottawa over the legitimacy of the spending power. But the real subtext of that battle was that the only way Quebec City could defeat the federal spending power would be by shaming or strong-arming Ottawa into giving it up or have the courts take it away as unconstitutional. It would offend against the nationalist strategy for Quebec to legislate it out of existence against the wishes of those who benefited from it within the province.

Ottawa's crucial insight was that while the government of Quebec would always want the federal government out of any direct contact with its citizens, *those citizens actually had an interest in having the two governments fighting over them.* While the hearts of Quebeckers might be with a social justice state controlled by a French-speaking majority, they were no fools. As long as Ottawa was there and had money to spend, they were going to get their share.

A classic example of this took place in the years when Trudeau and Lévesque were in power.[48] As an economic stimulus measure, the federal government wanted the provinces to cut, temporarily, their provincial sales tax. To encourage them to do so, the feds proposed to the provinces that Ottawa would make up the lost revenue from such a cut by a direct transfer. But the cut had to be done by Ottawa's rules: it had to be an across-the-board cut of several percentage points.

Jacques Parizeau, then Lévesque's minister of finance, saw an opportunity to wrong-foot Ottawa. He left the Quebec sales tax intact for most things but decided to eliminate it entirely on the so-called *secteurs mous,* or those industries that were suffering losses of sales because of high costs, poor productivity, and international competition: sectors such as clothing, textiles, shoes, and furniture. In other words, Parizeau decided to use such a sales tax cut, not as an instrument of general economic stimulus, but as an industrial policy to prop up dying industries. Parizeau demanded that Ottawa make up his revenue shortfall even though he had deliberately not respected the conditions Ottawa set for the reimbursement.[49]

Ottawa demurred. Quebec City is not playing by the rules, Finance Minister Jean Chrétien intoned, and so will not get the money. But, he went on to say, he would never penalize the citizens of Quebec for the bad behaviour of their government. Instead he sent to every Canadian taxpayer in Quebec a cheque for their share of the money he was prepared to give to Parizeau.[50]

The nationalist elite, predictably, was outraged and launched a campaign to encourage Quebeckers to simply sign their cheques over to Parizeau. Equally predictably, the campaign proved an embarrassing flop. Those cheques disappeared into Quebeckers' bank accounts faster than you can say "federal intrusion." There was some discussion of taxing the money back from Quebeckers, but that too fell flat. Parizeau ended up being too clever by half and had to eat much of the revenue shortfall he himself had created.[51]

Ottawa learned a different valuable lesson from Quebec: the state-as-instrument-of-social-justice ploy could be a powerful mechanism for the wide distribution of government cash. Two could play at that game, it reasoned, especially as it came to appreciate the political benefits of having numerous client groups dependant on federal largesse. Even though Ottawa's primary motivation was the battle for Canada's survival in Quebec, it could not limit its response to the Quebec social justice state to that province. A federal government must govern the whole country, and its programs cannot be limited to St-Jean-sur-Richelieu and Victoriaville but must extend to St. John's and Victoria as well.

No Prosperity, Please; We're Quebeckers

The Quebec social justice-state approach created another kind of opening for federal intervention and the creation of dependence on federal transfers. The redistributionist state, as I will show in detail in Chapter 7, was undermining Quebec's economy, creating economic dislocation, unemployment, and social dysfunction. With any other province, especially one representing such a big slice of the national economy, Ottawa might have used this as an occasion to pick a fight over policy and try to bring the province into line. That option was not available, not least because part of the nationalist appeal is explicitly that Quebec makes no promises of a higher individual material standard of living. That is what the alternative "Anglo-Saxon" model promises.

What Quebec promised (and continues to promise today) is moral superiority and social solidarity. The fact that this may come with an economic price tag is further proof of the moral superiority of the Quebec nation, for it is willing to make sacrifices for the greater good of social solidarity and the survival of the French language.[52]

But Ottawa, not constrained by the narrow Quebec-based social justice model, could use the increasingly superior standard of living in much of the rest of the country as an excuse for massive spending in Quebec, in effect compensating the Québécois for the destructive policies pursued by their own government. Quebec City created a demand for social spending by its counterproductive policies; wherever possible Ottawa was eager to supply that demand, even if it took the form of further transfers to the province to finance these programs. The deeper the dependence of the Quebec state, as well as of Quebeckers themselves, on Ottawa's generosity, the more vulnerable would appear the millenarian separatist version of the Quebec justice state at referendum time.

A bidding war was unleashed, pitting the government of Canada against the government of Quebec in a battle for the loyalty of Quebeckers. Both sides in this battle of the purse have taken it as axiomatic that, while emotion and sentiment would play their role, the most powerful force binding Quebeckers to one government or the other, and hence to one or the other of our competing national projects, was and is self-interest; that in turn they have defined in terms of dependence. A citizen dependent on a flow of benefits from one government will likely not vote to quit that government's jurisdiction.[53] Thus the feds ramped up EI, regional development, equalization, marketing boards, and a host of other programs, including in areas of provincial jurisdiction, and did so across the country.

In response, the government of Quebec wanted to make it appear that it could and would step into any void created by Ottawa's absence and that anyone benefiting from federal cash now could expect more generous treatment from a Quebec that could get control over both jurisdiction and money.

The other provinces took careful note of how successful Quebec was at getting resources out of Ottawa. Organized interest groups such as trade unionists, civil servants, municipalities, universities, and others in other parts of Canada noticed how solicited their counterparts were in *la belle province* by both levels of government. Into the unfolding bidding war rushed the baby boom generation looking for work.

The consequences for Quebec and Canada have been momentous.

A note to readers

The next three chapters concern themselves with understanding how the changes of the last fifty years have affected the character of Canadians. In them I try to lay bare the strength of our political and social tradition, the self-understandings that it presupposed, and the kind of civility that it made possible. I will talk about our founders' theory of happiness and how it presupposes a deep commitment to productive work and to family as the two most important wellsprings of human growth and satisfaction. I also talk, in the chapter about pseudo-work, about how the growth of the state and PUPPETRY change our behaviour in ways that are destructive of both our prosperity and our happiness. Along the way I talk about how the expansion of the welfare state has consistently drawn us away from the values of our founders and how their predictions regarding the ill effects of such a policy have been borne out in the facts on the ground.

Then in Chapter 7 I return to a detailed description of how these dynamics played out in the bidding war between Canada and Quebec, namely how the bidding war is the best explanation of the expansion of the welfare state; moreover, the concentration of the effects of the welfare state on Quebec (and incidentally economically weaker parts of the country like Atlantic Canada) has resulted in exactly the kind of social and economic dysfunction that our ancestors confidently predicted. For those of you less interested in the details of why work and family make us happy or how pseudo-work and PUPPETRY (i.e., rent-seeking) changes our character, you should skip ahead to that chapter. You can always come back and graze on these explanatory chapters later.

4

Work and the Meaning of the Content of Our Character

Toward the end of the Golden Age of Athens, democracy was weakened by paying citizens to attend the Assembly and to be jurors. There were poor people who did not have jobs but who made all their meagre income from these fees.

RANDY OLDAKER, *SOME TIDBITS ON ANCIENT ATHENS*

Therein is the secret of cheerfulness, of depending on no help from without and needing to crave from no man the boon of tranquillity. We have to stand upright ourselves, not be set up.

MARCUS AURELIUS, *MEDITATIONS*, BOOK III, SECTION 5

Dependence begets subservience and venality, suffocates the germ of virtue, and prepares fit tools for the designs of ambition.

THOMAS JEFFERSON, *NOTES ON THE STATE OF VIRGINIA*, QUERY XIX (1787)

When the New Canada was born in 1960, large-scale dependence on state benefits by individuals was virtually unknown. Social welfare, such as it was, had been provided, in general, by municipalities with modest help from the provinces or by private charitable agencies, including churches. By the early nineties, the New Canada had created vast dependence on new programs of various descriptions. More than 10 per cent of the population of Ontario, our richest province, was on social assistance. Tens of thousands of people were trapped in Atlantic Canada, eastern Quebec, and other rural areas on a destructive cycle of seasonal work and bouts of EI, and the liberalization of EI (then called UI) in 1971 had caused our unemployment rate to rise as much as two percentage points relative to the United States. We have stepped back from the highest levels of dependency as governments wrestled to bring their finances under control, but doing so was politically highly controversial, and the pressure never lets up to reverse course and restore welfare to its previous generosity, especially in the context of stimulus packages aimed at mitigating the worst effects of the current economic downturn. Government income assistance for older people helped to explain why Canada does a relatively poor job at keeping workers over fifty-five employed. Governments live in fear that the courts will declare welfare a Charter right and that judges will begin to decide what levels of support are appropriate.

Given the insistence of our forebears on the importance of work and the dangers of dependence, this state of affairs would appear to them incomprehensible. But the incomprehensibility is mutual: our ancestors' way of thinking about these issues will surely seem foreign to many Canadians raised on now-fashionable ideas such as a right to welfare, that no one should have to move to find a job, that dependence on government is a worthy alternative to being exploited by capitalist employers, or that there is no real difference between a make-work job and one that actually produces a good or service that people want to buy at a price they are willing to pay.

Indeed, if one thinks that the Canada that has emerged in the last half century under the twin impulses of the rise of the Boomer generation and Quebec nationalism is a great improvement over the "bad old days" of unenlightened welfare policy and "blaming the victim," our earlier review of how our ancestors thought about these issues will be like a tour through a mediaeval torture chamber: good chiefly for giving you goosebumps and for being glad that we moderns have left all that primitivism behind.

Here is a spooky thought, though: what if our ancestors were, on the whole, *right* and we have been, on the whole, *wrong* about the danger of allowing the state to loom too large in our lives? What if one of the unintended consequences of the bidding war between Ottawa and Quebec City has been a damaged work ethic and increasing dependence, giving rise to a self-perpetuating cycle of rent-seeking or PUPPETRY that drives the growth of government even when we don't mean to? And what if one of the other unintended consequences of the growth of the welfare state has been to crowd out to some considerable degree the role of the family, the social welfare institution par excellence?

If those propositions turned out to be true, it might cause us to pause and reflect on whether the New Canada is all that it has been cracked up to be. We might even be drawn into a humble re-examination of the wisdom of our forefathers and what they tried to teach us before we imperiously waved them off as ignorant know-nothings. And most important, if these propositions turn out to be true, the coming ebbing of the baby boom generation will soon raise enormously the cost of the mistakes of the past fifty years. We will not be able to afford the high taxes, the various forms of dependence on the state, the high degree of make-work or pseudo-employment in our economy, or the breakdown of the family that they have all brought in their train.

This chapter and the two that follow, then, will document how grossing up the state in Canada has affected who we are, has shaped our character, and has affected our behaviour as workers, as citizens, and as members of our families. The chapter after that will document how Quebec in particular has been egregiously damaged by the changes of the last half century, because it has become far more mired in the pathologies that these changes have unleashed.

Our Founders' Theory of Happiness

Let's start with the value of work, especially measured against the alternative we have expanded so mightily over the past decades: dependence on various forms of government benefit such as social welfare and unemployment insurance. In a sense it is embarrassing to have to insist on the importance and value of work and the loss of dignity and self-worth that accompanies dependence because it feels like retailing the patently obvious. Alas, however, like many forms of traditional wisdom that our grandparents understood intuitively and without their having to be explained, we have spent so much intellectual effort undermining them that they seem hardly credible to people who have been raised with a half-baked and half-understood Marxist/post-structuralist world view and a welfare state practice that has decried these values as "blaming the victim."

If we hark back for a moment to the set of ideas that characterized Canada for the first eighty-odd years of its existence, for example, we might notice something quite interesting. The founders of our society weren't trying to make themselves and their fellows miserable through unrelieved Calvinist gloom, including a mean-spirited insistence that everyone capable of working should do so. On the contrary; they had a theory about what made people happy; work was part of that theory in the sense that they believed that work fulfilled one of the deepest needs of human beings. We are not made for sloth but for productive work. Real work, work that confers benefits on us, our families, and the broader society, is one of the two key ways in which fully mature adults realize their highest purpose and greatest satisfaction. The other is by forming and nurturing a family, the subject of another chapter.

But our forebears also believed that to achieve this kind of fulfilment human beings had to overcome a natural desire to avoid work and to be looked after by others. In fact, achieving this level of self-reliance and self-respect is part of the maturation process, what distinguishes a fully developed adult from someone who remains behindhand in achieving their fully human stature.

Babies are totally needy, totally self-centred, totally dependent beings. If they progress successfully in their development, they gradually learn that they cannot remain dependent on others, but must increasingly assume responsibility for themselves, while learning to cooperate successfully with others. Progress is painful and fitful, but when children are successful they take their rightful place as fully mature adults who have learned to overmaster the childish impulse to think that others exist to serve them. They put in that impulse's place a growing mastery of their capacities and abilities, earning their way in the world by deploying those capacities for the benefit of themselves and others. This traditionally brought self-respect, reputation, honour, and livelihood from the community.

For Canada's founders, then, one of happiness's deepest sources sprang from a learned ability to discipline untutored emotions and desires. Nature pulled us in a destructive direction; culture, supportive social institutions, and self-discipline allowed us to resist that siren call. And part and parcel of this view of happiness was that we had an obligation as a society to support each other in the often difficult struggle to get our selfish impulses under control. A world in which people could too easily live from the efforts of others wasn't just a world that was expensive for those who paid the bill; it was a world that set temptation before fallible people and encouraged them not to strive to achieve the discipline and self-control by which human beings reach their greatest good. It is the moral equivalent of encouraging crime by leaving your wallet and laptop in an unlocked car, putting temptation in the path of the weak-willed.

While they might not have thought of it in these terms, in fact Laurier and Macdonald and Mackenzie King and Leacock and others too numerous to mention were of the view that the human condition, a condition of having to work in order to survive and in order to honour one's duties and commitments to family and community, was an essential condition of happiness.

Importantly, it was understood that work was not just valued for the income it produced, or else you could get the same happiness out of being given your income and your standing in the community, as opposed to having to earn them. You couldn't short-circuit the work part. It was a package deal.[1]

Even people whose temperament might have inclined them to sloth and dependence literally could not get away with it in a world in which no one offered to help you if you refused to work to support yourself. Mutual benefit was the guiding principle of social cooperation as far as those who are able to work were concerned. With the exception of the criminal classes, people got out of the economy exactly what they were willing and able to put in. Slackers got minimal charity if anything. So in normal times our experience in life helped to reinforce the moral teaching about the origins of human happiness, and vice versa.

To put this in a more modern vernacular, the reason we as a society should want to see people in real jobs and not in make-work (pseudo-work) or on welfare is not merely so that the tax bills of workers can be lowered, however welcome that might be in itself. It is chiefly because when too many people in a society live by taking rather than by making, it changes the character of the people, the character of its institutions, and it changes democracy itself. Unlike the Marxist view of work as an exploitative and purely economic relationship, our traditions teach us that work is to be valued equally for its economic *and its moral* benefits.

First and Second Natures

The idea that the actions we habitually perform shape our character is an idea as old as civilization. Aristotle perhaps said it best in his *Nicomachean Ethics*; my gloss on Aristotle is that we *become* what we habitually *do*. It is thus to Aristotle that we owe the idea of "second nature." When we do something often enough, it becomes "second nature" to us, an overlay on the inclinations and instincts that Nature implanted in us, which are our first, untutored, nature. If we habitually lie, we will become liars. If we habitually act courageously, we become courageous. If we discipline ourselves to act honourably, eventually we simply do it unthinkingly, instinctually, as part of our second nature, and become honourable. While our first nature is simply given, we can shape our second nature by essentially repeating desirable actions until they become impregnated in our mind and soul. And the great gift that parents bestow upon their children is not to indulge their first nature but to discipline them to act in accordance with the right behaviours even before they are old enough to understand why they are the right behaviours. Because while adults have some ability to discipline themselves to right living, to self-control, and to honourable behaviour, that task is made infinitely harder by a youth of indiscipline and libertinism under a regime of parental permissiveness. Another name for second nature, as you will have seen by now, is *character*.

It may sound quaint, but *work is one of those vital character-shaping activities*; in fact it (along with the responsibility, mutual commitment, and give-and-take of family life) is perhaps *the* character-forming activity *par excellence*.

It is not only philosophers like Aristotle who understood the centrality of work to the human spirit and the forming of strong, honourable, and dignified character. The Judeo-Christian tradition, on which Canada was founded, for example, celebrated work as central to both human dignity and human fulfilment.

In the Christian tradition, "work is part of the original state of man and precedes his fall; it is therefore not a punishment or a curse."[2] Work is

> an integral part of the human condition, although not the only purpose of life. No Christian, in light of the fact that he belongs to a united and fraternal community, should feel that he has the right not to work and to live at the expense of others (cf. 2 *Thes* 3:6–12). Rather, all are charged by the Apostle

Paul to make it a point of honour to work with their own hands, so as to "be dependent on nobody" (1 *Thes* 4:12), and to practise a solidarity which is also material by sharing the fruits of their labour with "those in need" (*Eph* 4:28).[3]

Many non-religious moral traditions also underscore the centrality of work not merely to life, but to the good life. Hannah Arendt remarked, "Labour assures not only individual survival, but the life of the species. Work and its product, the human artifice, bestow a measure of permanence and durability on the futility of mortal life and the fleeting character of human time."[4]

Modern psychology has also weighed in on the differing effects of work versus dependence, and the preponderance of the evidence echoes Aristotle, Western religious tradition, Canada's founders, and many modern philosophers and economists.

> By doing the acts that we do in our transactions with other men we become just or unjust, and by doing the acts that we do in the presence of danger, and by being habituated to feel fear or confidence, we become brave or cowardly. The same is true of appetites and feelings of anger; some men become temperate and good tempered, others self-indulgent and irascible, by behaving in one way or the other in the appropriate circumstances. Thus, in one word, states of character arise out of like activities. That is why the activities we exhibit must be of a certain kind; it is because the states of character correspond to the differences between these. It makes no small difference, then, whether we form habits of one kind or of another from our very youth; it makes a very great difference, or rather *all* the difference.
>
> Aristotle, *Nicomachean Ethics*

Charles Murray,[5] for example, argues that dignity, self-respect, and self-actualization arise from taking internal responsibility for oneself and that dependence on government support actually acts as a sometimes insuperable obstacle. As he puts it, "The threshold condition for self-respect is accepting responsibility for one's own life, for which the inescapable behavioral manifestation is earning one's way in the world."[6] Later he underlines the tight connection that modern social science has established between responsibility for self and human happiness and fulfilment. We are not made happy by being given the material necessities of life because those necessities do not get at more profound needs; what we need is control over our own lives, an ability to make our own decisions and take responsibility for our actions: "People who believe and act as if they are in control are happier."[7] And being in control doesn't simply mean deciding how to spend the money given to you by others, but earning the means of one's own sustenance and self-development.

The Hardest Job Is No Job

But it is not merely that work shapes character for the better, compared to not working. It is also the case that work makes us happy, although not in some trite and sentimental whistle-while-you-work sense. This might be a surprising claim to some. We are assailed daily by televised talking heads who are always decrying the extent to which work intrudes on home life. Hard on their heels come the trade unionists pushing for more leisure time for their members. Beer companies lobby governments for ever more long weekends. One might be forgiven for thinking that we work entirely too much and moreover that work makes us unhappy, that it is a burden from which we constantly seek release and escape.

> The high value Judaism sets on work can be traced throughout the biblical and rabbinic literature. If not itself a religious act, it comes close to being a condition of the religious life. "Six days shall you labour and do all your work, but the seventh day is a Sabbath to the Lord your God"—meaning that we serve God through work as well as rest. By our labours we become, in the striking rabbinic phrase, "partners with God in the work of creation."
>
> The Jewish liturgy for Saturday night—the point at which the day of rest ends—culminates in a hymn to the values of work: "when you eat of the labour of your hands, you are happy, and it shall be well with you." Work, in other words, has spiritual value, because earning our food is part of the essential dignity of the human condition. Animals find sustenance; only mankind creates it.
>
> Jonathan Sacks, Britain's Chief Rabbi

While almost all of us fantasize about being released from the unpleasant aspects of work, the reality is that work is more therapeutic than we realize. Work is more constructive than many of us care to recognize. It would not be in any way an exaggeration to say that work makes us happy in Aristotle's sense of helping to equip us to live a fully human life and to exercise our powers.

I wish in no way to diminish the truth that there are nasty bosses and poor workplaces, that some work is physically exhausting or even dangerous, just as some work is morally draining. It is true that people can work more than is good for them or their families; it is possible to have too much of a good thing. But those are all different issues from the central one here, which is that working, thought of as taking control of one's life and shouldering one's responsibility to be a productive member of the community, is essential to the kind of happiness that Aristotle thought suited human beings.

To see this truth at its most stark, we have to think less about work and managing all the issues it raises responsibly and sensibly; we have to think instead about what happens to us in the absence of work. For while we may have been fixated in recent years on the issues related to working too hard and having too much of a good thing, we have made the opposite error of forgetting that one can have too little of an essential thing. Bad jobs and employers exist, but a bad job is still more conducive to human happiness than no job at all. As Oscar Wilde so trenchantly observed, "The best way to appreciate your job is to imagine yourself without one." The point is driven home powerfully by Arthur Brooks's account of the effects of unemployment on an Austrian town called Marienthal:

> Marienthal is a small Austrian village about half an hour from Vienna by train. In the 1920s, it was dominated by one textile factory, which employed the majority of the town's residents. As the firm fell on hard economic times, it pulled the fortunes of Marienthalers down with it: by the time the factory closed in 1929, three-quarters of the town's 478 families had lost their income. The Marienthalers were not starving—Austria in those years had unemployment insurance that covered most of a factory worker's wages. But the townspeople languished nonetheless. There were no regular jobs to replace their old positions, and to qualify for unemployment support workers were strictly prohibited from taking any part-time work. One poor soul lost his benefits after he was discovered playing the harmonica on the street for money. Economic circumstance and government policy conspired to guarantee that the Marienthalers had nowhere to go and nothing to do.
>
> Marienthal had previously been an active community with social clubs and political organizations. The paradox is that, after the factory closed and people had abundant leisure, these activities withered. Villagers could not seem to find the time and energy to do much of anything. In the two years after the factory closed, the average number of volumes loaned out by the town library dropped by half. Said one woman, "It used to be magnificent in Marienthal before—just going to the factory made a change. During the summer we used to go for walks, and all those dances! Now I don't feel like going out anymore."
>
> Time seemed to warp. Men stopped wearing watches, and wives complained that their husbands were chronically late for meals—even though they were not coming from anything. Outsiders observed that it took villagers

longer and longer just to walk down the street. People slept for hours more each night than they ever had. They could not recall how they spent their days, and they whittled [*sic*] away far more time sitting at home or standing around in the street than doing any other activity.[8]

Like the Marienthalers, the absence of work, even when our material needs are looked after, makes us anxious, suspicious, and, well, miserable. This too is a key part of our founders' theory of happiness that coping with a flood of young workers and high unemployment made us forget over recent decades: work is not only a burden but, much more importantly, is one of the keys that unlocks the wellsprings of human satisfaction.

Canada was founded on the proposition that human nature is such that work makes people happy and encourages constructive behaviour, while money simply given as an alternative to work makes people unhappy and encourages destructive behaviour. And because this theory is correct, the state's increasingly frenetic efforts to put money in the hands of those "in need" doesn't just miss the point; it lessens the sum of human happiness when it results in people not working when they are capable of doing so.

When the universal example that is given to us by those around us is that people work, we learn to work ourselves, and the benefits of work flow to us almost incidentally. It is only when we enter a period when other choices are possible, such as not working and being dependent on the state, or being in phony work that can exist only because it is funded through compulsory taxes, does it become necessary to think about what we have lost through not working.

Working Your Way to Happiness

What is the evidence for this proposition that working makes us happy? Many Marxists, post-structuralists, social democrats, and even many economists assume that work is drudgery, undertaken for purely instrumental purposes to earn the means to do other more enjoyable things, and that people prefer leisure to work, so we must give people suitable rewards or they will not work.

Then how are we to understand that most people, not just a majority, but around 90 per cent of them, express great attachment to their work and this is quite independent of whether people are above or below average in income, well or poorly educated, middle class or working class, and whether they work for private companies, not-for-profits, or the public sector? In the United States, two-thirds of those surveyed by the University of Chicago's General Social Survey in 2002 said they would continue to work even if they no longer needed to (in other words even if they could have 100 per cent leisure time because they won the lottery, people still say they would prefer to work).[9] Interestingly, the proportions of people saying they would continue working are the same for those with below-average incomes as for those with above-average incomes. Poll-

> Happiness is a by-product which sneaks up on you, unsought, when you're busy at something else.
>
> Betty Jane Wylie, *Beginnings: A Book for Widows*

ster Ipsos Reid found a similar result for Canadians:[10] only 35 per cent of them would stop working altogether and retire on their lottery winnings. Over half would continue in the same job, and the rest would continue working, but in a different job, presumably one they enjoy more but that pays less. Similarly, over four-fifths of Canadians say that they would like to continue to work even if they had enough money to retire.[11]

The amount of leisure time one has is not statistically correlated with depression or sadness (in other words, more leisure time doesn't necessarily mean less sadness or depression), but being out of work does correlate with higher levels of such unhappiness.

Put simply, the causal relationship between work and happiness is firmly established in the research literature. In the past several decades, social scientists from around the world have conducted qualitative and quantitative studies showing the robust link between work and what they call "subjective well-being" and what the rest of us call "happiness."[12]

Interestingly, as Richard Easterlin concludes in his path-breaking research, happiness is not necessarily linked to rising incomes or material reward. The "Easterlin paradox," as it has come to be known, shows that there is indeed a wage threshold above which one does not become happier. Other factors, such as personal dignity, health, and family, are the primary sources of happiness. Increasing financial reward, contrary to popular conceptions, falls pretty low on the list.[13] Analogous Canadian research comes to similar conclusions: factors like family, vocation, and civic engagement, in all cases working with others to make a difference in lives shared with others, are all much more important than, say, increased income.[14]

Unhappiness isn't just related to actual job loss or unemployment either. The fear of job loss or the sense that one's work is precarious—just the possibility that one may lose one's job—makes people unhappy,[15] even when unemployment benefits are generous. That is hardly evidence that work is bad for us or that we seek to escape it whenever possible.

Does the reverse proposition hold, namely that people without a job are unhappy? In fact, the literature shows an even more profound relationship between unemployment and alcoholism, depression, dislocation, family breakdown, and suicide—in other words, unhappiness. Indeed, international research in this area is quite powerful and sobering. For instance, British social scientists have found a "strong association between being unemployed with suicide for male and female adults ... [even] after controlling for income, education, car access, deprivation, and marital status." According to their analysis, men and women aged twenty-five to forty-four who were unemployed were two to three times as likely to commit suicide as their employed peers.[16] People who experience involuntary unemployment are hugely more likely to report feeling hopeless and worthless than people with jobs. Ditto for those on welfare.[17]

Such findings are corroborated by studies in the United States. According to one such analysis, for example, "Those not working had a 48 per cent greater risk of having major depression adjusting for sex, age, and ethnicity."[18]

Canadian research in this area closely mirrors international findings. A long-term 1989 study of seventy-seven unemployed workers in Montreal's manufacturing sector noted various problems flowing from their unemployment. In results that strongly echoed the experience of the Marienthalers of Austria, the researchers found that "one of the most important aspects of the unemployment problem was the individual's loss of the social status that comes with being an employed worker. This aspect was ... manifest not only in the sense of non-identity felt by the unemployed but also in the inability to cope with the increase in free time and the decrease in time structure. This loss in status was also seen in an increase in family friction."[19] A similar study in the *Canadian Medical Association Journal* found "a strong, positive association between unemployment and many adverse health outcomes."[20]

Work gives people a sense of power over their lives because they produce things or services that others value; they feel productive and useful compared to not working and being dependent. Thus, according to survey data, the vast majority of people, in all kinds of jobs, find that their work is satisfying.[21] On the other hand, despite decades of effort to eradicate the notion that dependence is bad for us, even the dependent themselves experience it as a source of unhappiness.

Even the rich, whose children might not have to work, are aware of the problem of idleness and its destructive potential. One of the richest men in the world, Warren Buffett, is famously in favour of a stiff inheritance tax for precisely this reason. He thinks his wealth should be an enabler of his children's work, not an obstacle to it: "A very rich person should leave his kids enough to do anything but not enough to do nothing."[22] And many are the rich people who did not follow

Buffett's advice and saw their original fortune frittered away by a couple of generations of idle self-indulgence.

The same considerations that motivate Buffett's resistance to big inheritances motivated an acquaintance of mine to change the rules at his house once his son hit sixteen. His son, a champion snowboarder, had become quite used to his parents being at his beck and call to take him to competitions and training and to pick up the tab for everything, including any new equipment he wanted. His father thinks he is now old enough that he needs to understand the value of what he asks for, so it has become the son's responsibility to get a job and pay his own way in the pursuit of his snowboarding. The son has taken a job at a fast-food restaurant, beginning at minimum wage. For many people that's a crappy job. For the boy involved it has become the means by which he pursues what he cares about most in life.

Lots of well-meaning people dismiss such jobs as mean, cruel, pointless, and exploitative. But as the example I've just given shows, it is condescending and paternalistic to look just at the job and make judgments about whether its balance of hardship and rewards is acceptable or even desirable. Jobs and the plans and intentions of those who hold them are intimately linked. People in the toughest, lowest-paid jobs still gain the dignity and moral self-assurance that comes from being responsible for themselves and paying their own way. To denigrate that achievement is to say that the hopes and plans they pursue through the work available to them are unworthy of respect. Through such jobs many people have learned the basics of productive life—to show up on time, clean and sober, to start with, because your employer has legitimate expectations and can get rid of you if you don't live up to them. You get to learn the local language if you are an immigrant. Gaining knowledge of the business opens up the possibility of more responsibility and higher wages, maybe even supervisory work. When you establish a good work record and recognized skills, you can use the reputation you have gained to look for better work.

And those are just the benefits within the work world. Every person has those things they work for that make the difficulties of the job worthwhile.

> **WORK AND CHARACTER: HARRY S. TRUMAN**
>
> To go up to the Square each morning to a regular job was for a boy to be very like a man. It was to be known, to be spoken to and spoken well of if one were a bright, cheerful dependable boy like Harry Truman.... His first week's wages of three silver dollars were, in memory, "the biggest thing that ever happened to me."
>
> David McCullough, *Truman*

It can be Saturday night in the pub with your buddies, paying your way through high school evening classes or even university, saving up for a down payment on a first house, that motorcycle you've always dreamed of, or the skates your daughter longs for. All these are honourable desires, worthy of our respect because they have been earned. We can never separate the work being done from the worker doing it, and dismissing the value of the work because we wouldn't like to do it ourselves is a cruel and destructive kind of paternalism. As my father-in-law used to say, "It is the worker who confers the dignity on the work, and not the other way round."

Work connects people in a complex web of relationships of mutual interdependence and benefit. It makes us aware of the needs of others, while building a sense of our own contribution to our fellows. It creates a direct consciousness that everything we consume must be made by someone, and that if we wish to get, we must ourselves give. Finally, it breeds a sense of ownership over the fruits of one's work.

> A man who is holding down a menial job and thereby supporting a wife and children is doing something authentically important with his life. He should take deep satisfaction from that, and be praised by his community for doing so. Think of all the phrases we used to have for it: "He is a man who pulls his own weight." "He's a good provider." If that same man lives under a system that says that the children of the woman he sleeps with will be taken care of whether or not he contributes, then that status goes away. I am not describing some theoretical outcome. I am describing American neighborhoods where, once, working at a menial job to provide for his family made a man proud and gave him status in his community, and where now it doesn't. I could give a half dozen other examples. Taking the trouble out of the stuff of life strips people—already has stripped people—of major ways in which human beings look back on their lives and say, "I made a difference."
>
> Charles Murray, 2009 Irving Kristol Lecture

Not only does that engender a greater resistance to seeing them commandeered by government for the benefit of those who did not work to create them, but also a greater willingness to defend the established order, the rules and institutions that underpin your own success.

Work is deeply satisfying to us even though we don't get to decide by ourselves what work we will do. The world is full of accountants and factory workers who had to abandon their adolescent fantasies of being rock stars or captaining the Stanley Cup–winning team. We have to take account of what others want and what we can do that others most value if we want to be able to exchange what we make for things others produce. Work is not selfish but is oriented by its very nature to serve the needs of others. Because of this necessity to serve the needs and desires of others, we are all led to produce as much as we can of what others want, thus enriching both ourselves and them, just as those who are best able to innovate and better satisfy the needs of others tend to prosper more than the rest. That is why Adam Smith so wisely observed that it is not the benevolence of the butcher and the baker that gets us our supper, but their self-interest. And that self-interest feeds humanity better than any benevolence could ever hope to do.

> The highest degree of charity, exceeded by none, is that of a person who assists a poor Jew by providing him with a gift or a loan or by accepting him into a business partnership or by helping him to find employment—in a word, by putting him where he can dispense with other people's aid. With reference to such help it is said, "You shall strengthen him, be he a stranger or a settler, he shall live with you" (Leviticus 25:35), which means to strengthen him in such a manner that his falling into want is prevented.
>
> Maimonides

Each person expecting to have to work for their living nurtures another character trait: independence of mind and spirit. Earning one's way means being entitled to decide how one's earnings are to be spent without need for permission or approval from anyone (unless, of course, you are in pain and trying to buy a hip replacement in Canada, but that's another story). Your labour earns you income, which you may then spend as you please. In other words, others will meet *your* needs and desires, up to the precise point where your work *has satisfied the needs and desires of others*; giving and getting become woven together beyond unpicking.

One final observation on the benefits work confers on individuals and society: commerce, as the early French economists remarked, "*adoucit les moeurs*" (softens manners), by which they meant that a commercial society is a civil or polite society. In a world of many buyers and sellers, one can never treat one's clients and suppliers too respectfully, because they almost always have the choice of dealing with you or another. The best commercial transactions are not the ones in which the stronger party hangs the weaker out to dry, but rather those where both parties realize a real benefit. That builds goodwill and openness to future exchanges, because market relationships tend not to be unique, never-to-be-repeated events, but rather a chain of exchanges over time. Civility, mutual respect, concern for reputation, and self-control are the result.

These were the qualities that generations of Canadians prized above all others. By contrast, dependence was not merely an economic state requiring support; it was a state of moral degradation. Since by definition one who does not work cannot improve his lot by making (i.e., working), he can only do so by taking from others who have worked for their living. The link between the personal effort one furnishes and the standard of living one enjoys is broken, and respect for the effort of others is transmuted into envy for their success and a belief that it was unfairly earned while one's own dependence is undeserved and therefore must be compensated by authorities.

The welfare state adds a complex twist to this tale of the development of character, in that the charitable relationship is no longer voluntary, but compulsory, and those who are dependent can compel those who are self-supporting to pay more benefits as long as the dependants and their allies form a large enough share of the population. And since the redistribution has the imprimatur of "democracy," it is seen by the recipients, not as an act of charity or patronage, but a matter of right, an entitlement, their due as citizens.

A Funny Thing Happened on the Way to the Welfare State

While such "rights talk" about welfare has been a prominent feature of the development of the welfare state in Canada, it is a poor way of thinking about welfare and dependence. Our forefathers had the more subtle and insightful theory about human happiness, and their insights have been proven right by the damage that the rise of the welfare state has wreaked on vulnerable people. It has been the misfortune of those damaged by our indiscriminate welfare policies to have fallen onto dependence on benefits at a time when the design of those benefits was driven by a sense that large-scale Boomer-driven unemployment was a fact of life, that an inability to find work was a common and unavoidable condition, and that Quebec nationalism made limiting access to major social welfare programs an undertaking fraught with danger.

As the Boomers ease into retirement and labour supply begins to tighten, however, Canadians will almost certainly become more attuned to the fact that our experience of the last fifty years has proven our founders' theory of happiness and work to be quite correct. Already with early welfare reform in the nineties, we began to shift away from an unhelpful focus on "poverty-as-victimization" to seeing poverty as much more an outcome of the behaviours of the poor themselves. In this we are rejoining the mainstream of thinking in the Western world.

We see poverty, in other words, more and more as a matter of character. If we want to get any purchase on the problem of poverty, we must stop thinking of it in the materialist sense as an absence of income. Instead we ought to view it more as an absence of the behaviours that confer success. Harking back to Aristotle, we might think of it as a failure to acquire through habitual action the right second nature. In other words, we are beginning to fight our way back to the traditional understandings that Canada so blithely dispensed with over the past half century.

Isabel Sawhill[23] of the centre-left Brookings Institution in Washington recently summed up a great deal of the new thinking in her testimony before the Income Security and Family Support Subcommittee of the House of Representatives of the American Congress, where she stated: "I strongly believe that reducing poverty requires a focus both on what government needs to do and on what individuals need to do. We need a combination of responsible policies and responsible behavior."

> **THE DEVIL MADE ME DO IT**
> A burglar demanded to know from me why he repeatedly broke into houses and stole VCRs. He asked the question aggressively, as if "the system" had so far let him down in not supplying him with an answer; as if it were my duty as a doctor to provide him with the buried psychological secret that, once revealed, would in and of itself lead him unfailingly on the path of virtue. Until then, he would continue to break into houses and steal VCRs (when at liberty to do so), and the blame would be mine. When I refused to examine his past, he exclaimed, "But something must make me do it!" "How about greed, laziness and a thirst for excitement?" I suggested. "What about my childhood?" he asked. "Nothing to do with it," I replied firmly. He looked at me as if I had assaulted him. Actually, I thought the matter more complex than I was admitting, but I did not want him to misunderstand my main message: that he was the author of his own deeds.
> Theodore Dalrymple, *Life at the Bottom*

Thus, contrary to much political rhetoric and the claims of the welfare rights movement, poverty is not merely—or even primarily—an economic condition. It is also in many cases a cultural condition—it involves values. That means that *poverty can never be overcome by mere income support or the passive writing of cheques, but only by challenging and changing behaviour.* Poverty really is a question of character to a surprising extent, at least where people capable of working are concerned. Obviously people who are disabled, who suffer some mental illnesses, or who have addictions or other kinds of physical or mental conditions fall into a different group.

Our philosophy of social welfare has done a very great deal to undermine these cultural values, through its insistence that poverty is something that just "happens" to people, who are its powerless victims, not something from which hard work allows people to escape. Because if it is true that some people work hard and escape poverty, then many of those left behind could also have escaped, but did not—not necessarily because they are lazy but rather because they may lack the set of cultural values that make success possible.

The language that must be used to describe these changes wrought by the welfare state, that of undermining old values, of the evolution of incentives as a result of social welfare reform and so forth, implies that these changes are slow to occur. The evidence confirms this intuition: the emergence of a comprehensive welfare state does not change everything overnight but may need a generation or more to take root.[24]

So we have, over time, so gently as to be almost imperceptible, but with devastating cumulative effect, created a new set of cultural values in which work at the bottom end of the social scale is undervalued, and indeed denigrated, whether through poorly designed welfare schemes where it pays better not to work than it does to work, or through the notion that there are many kinds of low-paying work that are beneath people's dignity, and that it is preferable to remain in dependence on the state than to take these jobs.

In fact, we have created the conditions in which low-income people who actually work, who make sacrifices, who save, who believe in the dignity of work, are chumps. Incredibly, the interaction of the tax system and the total edifice of social welfare programs in Canada is such that the highest marginal tax rates in the country are paid by people earning roughly $13,000 to $20,000 a year—precisely the people trying to move from welfare dependence to better economic opportunities. This counterintuitive result arises from the fact that as one moves into employment, cash benefits are clawed back at very high rates (often dollar for dollar). In addition, one loses non-cash benefits that may include prescription drugs, transport services, child care, subsidized education, and more. Not for nothing is this phenomenon known as the "welfare wall" or the "welfare trap."

Letting Ourselves off the Hook

Except in the field of aboriginal policy, for most of Canada's history, social policy was based on the understanding that individual character was, generally speaking, what made the difference between success and failure in life, and that the state simply handing over an income with no expectations regarding character and behaviour would have a damaging effect on recipients even greater than the damage caused to society.

The last five decades, however, saw these presumptions wither as unemployment became such a powerful problem that it was preferable simply to pay vulnerable populations not to work, thus keeping them from competing with the already large numbers of workers jostling for jobs in the marketplace. It became first unfashionable and then unacceptable to draw a distinction between the deserving and the undeserving poor, since poverty came to be seen as a condition over which one had no control and into which one fell through unmerited circumstance. Similarly, it became unacceptable to expect that people living in economically declining parts of the country might move to more dynamic regions. After all, there were no jobs. The unintended consequence, however, was to inculcate in an important part of the population the idea that working was optional, and that if one didn't want to work, the state was

> Serious benefit-dependency or "learned helplessness," may emerge only in a long-run perspective. Examples of such gradual adjustments are increased tendency to apply for social assistance, less job search and greater choosiness among unemployed workers, more absence from work for alleged health reasons, more applications for (subsidized) early retirement due to alleged inability to work, and more time and effort devoted to tax avoidance and tax evasion. All this means that warning signals about disincentive effects may be considerably delayed. As the delayed effects are not usually possible to predict in advance, welfare-state policies easily "overshoot" in the sense that politicians would initially have chosen to offer less-generous welfare-state arrangements if it had been possible to anticipate from the beginning the negative long-term consequences for the national economy, inducing deteriorations in the financial position of the government itself.
>
> Assar Lindbeck, "Hazardous Welfare-State Dynamics"

only too happy to supply an income, and to do so as a matter of individual right, with no accompanying expectations of behaviour.

The outcome was that people felt released from onerous social expectations about their behaviour, expectations that cannot be ignored when one's livelihood depends on work rather than social benefits. Isabel Sawhill singles out three behaviours that, according to her work, make a huge difference:

getting a good education, not having children before you marry, and working full-time. Government should expect people to make real efforts to comply with each of these norms. When they do, then government should reward such behavior by making sure that those who play by the rules will not be poor. The analysis we have done at Brookings shows that individuals who play by these rules are much less likely to be poor than those who don't.[25]

Poverty is not a problem of lack of cash, she writes, but rather a problem of destructive behaviours, or perhaps it might be more accurate to say that the lack of cash is the effect rather than the cause of poverty. If she is correct in this analysis, it follows that the best way to reduce poverty is not to give poor people more money, but to induce them to change those self-destructive behaviours—in other words, to change their character, to get them to change the things they habitually do from vicious ones to virtuous ones.

> For any individual, moral failure is hard to live with because of the rebuke of conscience. Habitual moral failure, what used to be called vice, can be lived with only by obliterating conscience through rationalization. When we rationalize, we convince ourselves that heretofore forbidden desires are permissible. We advance the reality of the desires over the reality of the moral order to which the desires should be subordinated. In our minds we replace the reality of moral order with something more congenial to the activity we are excusing. In short, we assert that bad is good.
>
> Robert R. Reilly, "Culture of Vice," *National Review*

Sawhill and her colleagues did some statistical analysis comparing changing the behaviours of the poor with increasing their cash benefits. The results are eloquent. If all able-bodied adults in the United States worked full-time, even at the wage they currently earn (or, if unemployed, at a wage commensurate with their education), poverty in that country would plummet by 42 per cent. Getting the marriage rate back to the level seen in 1970 would reduce poverty by 27 per cent. Universal high school completion would cut poverty by 15 per cent. By contrast, *doubling* cash benefits would cut poverty by only 8 per cent.

These relationships may be, it is true, correlations and not causes, in the sense that they may mask other kinds of behaviours or factors that lead people to have higher incomes, such as a strong work ethic. But it is likely that this is a bit of a "package deal." And although this is an analysis of U.S. data and the rather different U.S. situation, it certainly squares, first, with evidence from Statistics Canada that the best way for a family to escape low income is for more family members to work more hours and, second, with some recent research from the C.D. Howe Institute to the effect that,

> in terms of the low income cut off (LICO), Canada's traditional poverty threshold measure, poverty declined significantly over the last decade.... The increases in post-transfer post-tax median incomes and decline in poverty rate have been driven primarily by the increase in employment rate.... These statistics are at an aggregate level, but they are highly suggestive: the link between Canada's higher employment rate and lower poverty rate is very strong.[26]

So it was not stupid, cruel, or ignorant to group the poor into two classes, as was routinely done prior to the sixties. The distinction was then called the deserving and the undeserving poor (a description that has come back into vogue in Britain under Gordon Brown, Tony Blair's successor as Labour prime minister). What this distinction was meant to capture, I believe, was that there is one class of low-income people that is not especially problematic for social policy; they have ingrained in them a set of behaviours and expectations, including discipline and a sense of the value of work, which allows them to move relatively easily out of low income and back into a way of life more in keeping with their expectations and abilities. The turnover in this class of the poor is just one sign of the robustness of the particular individuals that find themselves there at any particular moment. Or put another way, their success in escaping poverty is a testament to their character.

The real social policy problem *for those able to work*, then, is not the total number of people on low income at any one time, but rather that second class of the poor, those who do not or cannot hear the inner voice urging them to change their behaviour.

Increasingly, then, social policy is grappling with the problem of how to change the behaviours of this second class of the poor. In this struggle to inculcate the right cultural values that equip the poor to succeed, incentives matter hugely. We will get the kind of behaviour we want only by rewarding it and reinforcing it. And this is doubly true in the coming era, which will be characterized by an abundance of capital and knowledge but a shortage of labour.

The End of Welfare as We Know It, the Return of Character as We Knew It

To understand how a shortage of workers can help to change the behaviour and ultimately the character of people, think about a recent example. In Ontario and

Alberta, but predominantly in the United States, the technological revolution was accompanied by a huge social transformation: the end of welfare as we have known it, as U.S. president Bill Clinton liked to say. Just as huge economic opportunities were opening up, governments throughout the United States began pushing people out of the welfare trap and into labour markets. They began to demand that people get training and get into work instead of merely being warehoused as "unemployable" in the welfare system.

The result has not been impoverishment and misery but rather a jump in the number of people working or looking for work, the application of new technologies to the problem of how to make people with little education productive, and the growth in both employment and incomes of the bulk of people who had previously been virtually totally excluded from work.[27]

The application of the new technologies I mentioned is particularly apt in the context of our age's technological revolution. As the labour supply began to dry up, it became more and more necessary to find ways to put people previously thought unemployable to work, and to do so quickly. Thus, for example, the fast-food industry invested a great deal of money in designing a cash register that could be worked by people who are illiterate. And since working provides tangible and immediate rewards (paycheques, self-esteem, a sense of achievement), whereas going to school requires a faith in long-term rewards that is absent in many cases, putting people to work is often a more realistic strategy than trying to force them to go to school.

So what looked like harsh social policies in fact turned out to be hugely empowering for hundreds of thousands of people. And the fact that the U.S. labour market was able to draw so many new people into its labour pool was a big factor in its economic boom throughout the 1990s, the longest in post-war history, just as more recently Canada was able to do, reaching record highs in the share of the population working. The best social program is still a labour shortage, where people are rewarded for taking advantage of the opportunities that a labour shortage creates and where there are immediate rewards and reinforcement for the cultural values that allow people to succeed.

It is worthy of note that this has been a hugely successful *left-wing policy*. In Sweden under the Social Democrats, the United Kingdom under Labour, the United States under Clinton's Democrats, and increasingly in Germany under the Social Democrats and later the grand coalition, social policy has been designed to push people capable of work aggressively back into the labour market, into training, and into work. This is in part motivated by a realization of the problem of perverse incentives under traditional welfare state policies. Equally, however, it is motivated by a realization that every dollar spent on someone capable of working and therefore of looking after themselves is a dollar not available to be spent on someone who is incapable of working, for whatever reason, or is at least incapable of producing enough economic value to support themselves and who therefore does not face the kind of incentive problems that these other members of society do.

So welfare reform (begun in the nineties with modest reform in the provinces and EI reform in Ottawa), like the return of genuine work for all, opens at least the possibility that ultimately the character of the next generation or two will, on balance, be less self-absorbed than that of much of the Boomer era. That era's welfare system meant that one never needed to concern oneself with what others might want or need, because one's ability to get an income was divorced from one's ability to deliver real value to others. An important part of several generations was taught that there was no need to place limits on one's selfish desires, a notion completely contradicted by the qualities required to get and keep a job, find and keep a mate and raise a family.

Welfare in its many guises, however, was not the only part of the broad corruption of character of Canadians. After all, even at its height, no more than perhaps 20 per cent of our most dependent province's population was reliant on welfare in one form or another. To this kind of dependence, however, must be added another: pseudo-work, the subject of the next chapter.

5

Perverting the Course of (Social) Justice: Pseudo-work, Corporate Welfare, and Trade Unionism

The tool of politics ... is to extract resources from the general taxpayer with minimum offense and to distribute the proceeds among innumerable claimants in such a way as to maximize support at the polls. Politics, so far as mobilizing support is concerned, represents the art of calculated cheating—or more precisely how to cheat without really being caught.

JAMES R. SCHLESINGER, "SYSTEMS ANALYSIS AND THE POLITICAL PROCESS"

In 1960 a tiny minority of Canadians worked for government or had their private-sector job subsidized by the state. Yet within a decade, the level of employment in the public sector had exploded, and in the case of Quebec it eventually reached the second-highest level among industrialized countries. Transfers by government to business, mostly used to support employment either directly or indirectly, were tiny in 1960. Five decades later, those same transfers are counted in the many billions of dollars.

In other words, it wasn't enough to undermine the independence and self-respect of a large share of our most vulnerable populations by drawing them into an insidious dependence on various forms of government benefit.

In addition, we created vast amounts of what I call *pseudo-work*, work that exists only because governments in Canada, at all levels and in every part of the country, stuffed the economy with legions of federal, provincial, municipal, and Crown corporation workers, as well as workers in subsidized jobs in the private sector. These people were handed jobs that barely existed and added little to the sum of human prosperity. We provided them with the semblance of work in return for a real income, in a perverse parody of the basic principle of the Soviet economy that "we pretend to work and they pretend to pay us." The Canadian content version, alas, kept the part about pretending to work but involved real payment in return.

The growth of the bureaucratic state, then, also played a role in changing the character of Canadians. People who work in large bureaucracies, and especially those funded by the state's ability to commandeer our income, never have to worry about whether their work is actually creating value for the people who are the alleged "beneficiaries" of their efforts. When Shakespeare's melancholy prince listed the "insolence of office" as one of the plagues of the human condition, he was talking about how character is shaped by political and bureaucratic power and authority.

In our time that insolence has become chiefly the power to take from others without regard to their desires or needs and to bestow the takings on yourself and your client populations.

Pseudo-work is work that depends on precisely that kind of patron-client arrangement financed by taxpayers and enabled by the law. Groups bully and cajole governments into conferring on them privileges backed by the sanction of the law. Those privileges provide a good livelihood in exchange for going through the motions of working, or at least give a full-time wage for what is often essentially part-time work. Like the drawing of large numbers of people into dependence on various kinds of social benefit, pseudo-work changed our economy and our politics and most importantly, changed the character of Canadians. The way it worked, however, was different and more subtle than crude welfare dependency. It gave people who occupied these positions at least the semblance of real work, and that is always to be preferred to living off the goodwill of others and being expected to give nothing in return.

While the growth of pseudo-work and welfare dependency in Quebec requires separate treatment and will form the subject of another chapter, it should never be thought that these phenomena have not been present in every part of Canada over the past few decades. This chapter lays out the logic of the growth of pseudo-work, trade union power, and corporate welfare in Canada as a whole, and that will help us later to understand how these phenomena came to be even more important in Quebec over this same period.

The Scale of Pseudo-work

Pseudo-work is, by its nature, a little tricky to quantify. After all, some share of public service jobs *do* produce real value for Canadians. We need police and soldiers and judges and nurses and hospital administrators. On the other hand, we almost certainly don't need so many of at least some of them, and it is not at all clear that we need many other public-sector workers whose whole occupations are of dubious benefit. So in trying to get some sense of the size of the phenomenon we are looking at, it might be helpful to proceed by examples.

We might think, for example, that pseudo-work would be a bigger deal in high-unemployment, low-growth provinces than in the faster-growing provinces. And that is in fact what we find. Ontario gets by with 67 provincial and municipal employees per thousand people. Alberta sits at 73, just below the national average of 77. But Nova Scotia needs 82, Newfoundland and Labrador an impressive 89, and Manitoba a truly awe-inspiring 105.[1]

There is lots of scope for pseudo-work throughout the public sector, though. Recalling that the size of the state in Canada and the United States was comparable right up until about 1960, and that it was only afterwards that we ramped up the size of the Canadian state, it is worth observing that in the 1970s public-sector employment actually declined in the United States, whereas in Canada it rose by nearly a third. But it would be pretty hard to establish that Canadians got a third more valued public services. It would certainly be true, however, that public servants got a third more valued and well-paid public service jobs and public-sector union dues likely rose in tandem with this trend.

In 1960 we spent almost identical shares of our GDP on government on both sides of the Canada–U.S. border (just under 29 per cent); by 1996, our spending on the state had grown to 46.4 per cent of GDP, compared to 34.6 per cent in the United States. And that difference is not explained by medicare in Canada: governments on both sides of the border spend almost identical shares of GDP on publicly funded health care. Public-sector employment grew, again from very similar numbers in 1960 until, in 1996, about 27 per cent of the Canadian workforce was employed in government and the broader public sector (e.g., health and education). As a share of total employment, public-sector employment in Canada is about 30 per cent higher than the US and the OECD average.[2] And on this much larger public-sector base we have built a much higher trade-union density in the public sector: "a Canadian public-sector worker is more than twice as likely to be unionised as his or her US counterpart."[3] Canada's public sector is 75.7 per cent unionized.[4] Whereas public- and private-sector compensation had tracked each other nicely in Canada for many years, by the early 1970s, according to Andrew Coyne, the total pay package of the average federal employee exceeded that of a private-sector counterpart by more than 20 per cent,[5] and other research shows that this phenomenon of overpaying public employees relative to their private-sector opposite numbers is a well-established and widespread phenomenon in Canada.[6]

It is not merely that pay is elevated relative to equivalent jobs in the private sector, but also that the public sector employs far more people than it needs to accomplish its work. The theory behind why politicians might wish to employ far more people than they really need in the public service is pretty well established: "Public enterprises are inefficient because they address the objectives of politicians rather than maximise efficiency. One key objective of politicians is employment: they care about votes of the people whose jobs are in danger and, in many cases, unions have significant influence on political parties."[7]

It is well known within governments that much of the money spent on various programs that employ large numbers of people actually achieve little in the way of important public purposes. During my stint at the federal department of finance from 2006 to 2008, for example, one of the members of the senior executive team in the department, a career finance official who was a true connoisseur of government spending, said to me during budget preparation, "We all know that we could cut 40 per cent from the federal budget—it is useless and even harmful spending." And when I repeated this comment to other senior managers around the federal public service, the usual response was something like, "Gee, I don't think it is that high. I would have said about 30 per cent"! I would venture to say, therefore, that the unofficial off-the-record consensus in Ottawa was that somewhere around one-third of spending is wasteful and unnecessary. We might therefore conclude that of the current total federal employment of nearly 400,000, the equivalent of roughly one-third, or 133,000, is pseudo-work, or work for which taxpayers are paying real money but getting little in return.[8]

Crown Corporations: Affecting to Trade for the Public Interest

An interesting test case of this general proposition is offered by Crown corporations because a number of these have been privatized over recent years; the record of their post-privatization performance gives us some inkling of what happens when public-sector services are subjected to real market discipline where jobs can exist only if customers think they are getting real value. Crown corporations were an important vehicle of state employment (and a great deal of pseudo-work) as the Baby Boomers hit their labour-force stride.

There have been lots of attempts to count all the Crown corporations, but it appears that it is a tricky business. In one of the most comprehensive surveys in 1979, the comptroller general identified 464 federal Crown corporations, including 213 subsidiaries and sub-subsidiaries and 126 "associated" corporations.[9] That count came at the end of a twenty-year period when the bulk of the major federal Crown corporations were created. Additionally, two researchers identified 233 provincial Crown corporations operating in 1980.[10]

How much pseudo-work was salted away in the ranks of Crown corporations? When CN was privatized, it had a workforce of some 36,000 people. A few years later, under the leadership of CEO Paul Tellier, that number was down by half to 18,000, while profitability and efficiency were way up.[11] These improvements made it one of the most successful railways in North America, measured by its ability to deliver results for customers and shareholders. But if it was able to do all this with 18,000 fewer workers, what were those workers doing while employed by the Crown corporation before privatization? The post-privatization workforce's performance shows that they weren't necessary for railroading. That means these workers were in pseudo-work, and on a pretty massive scale.

Something similar emerged when Maurice Strong tackled the huge inefficiencies at Ontario Hydro. While preparing the company for eventual privatization and a competitive electricity market (which in fact never occurred), Ontario Hydro was broken up into several operating companies, and productivity gains were expected throughout these new companies. As a result, 7,000 workers overall were shed, out of a total of roughly 28,000.[12] Again, what were these workers doing before privatization occurred? Whatever it was, it clearly wasn't necessary to the running of a successful power business.

In a September 2007 article by Sean Silcoff in the *Financial Post* about the future of Canada Post, it was suggested that capital investment and other modernizations in a privatized post office might allow the Crown corporation to shed perhaps as many as 27,000 of its current 72,000 employees.[13] And yet they still can't offer home delivery to those new housing developments. Whatever are those workers doing?

Perhaps the most important thing they are doing is confirming, as was the case with the other examples I used, the general proposition made earlier that roughly 30 per cent of public-sector workers aren't doing anything useful from an economic point of view and therefore that some other factor must explain their employment. Just to be clear, two qualifications need to be made. First,

> These [private companies chartered by government to fulfil public tasks], though they may, perhaps, have been useful for the first introduction of some branches of commerce, by making, at their own expense, an experiment which the state might not think it prudent to make, have in the long run proved, universally, either burdensome or useless....
>
> I have never known much good done by those who affected to trade for the public good. It is an affectation, indeed, not very common among merchants, and very few words need be employed in dissuading them from it.
>
> Adam Smith, *The Wealth of Nations*

saying that Crown corporations and the public sector more generally employ too many people and pay them too much does not mean that the public gets no value from public services. What it does mean is that the public sector supplies a lot more of these services than people would choose to buy if left to their own devices. Two factors explain this phenomenon: the public sector gets to make you pay whether you want the service or not, and politicians benefit from having lots of people getting their paycheque from the public purse. The mechanisms by which this results in a steady expansion of the public sector beyond the actual demand for public services are well documented.[14]

Second, it is not necessarily the case that such superfluous and overpaid workers don't have their days fully occupied with some kind of industrious-looking activity. It is quite likely, however, that many of them could be made redundant without affecting the quality of public services through the more effective use of technology, including new management techniques, as well as getting out of activities there is little reason for government to be providing. That is, for instance, one of the chief reasons that the article cited earlier suggested a privatized Canada Post could do with so many fewer employees. This conclusion is backed by lots of solid research. To choose one example, Jim McDavid, a local government expert at the University of Victoria, did wide-ranging surveys of local government provision in Canada. He discovered that in-house garbage collection, on average, costs 50 per cent more than contracted out and that the difference was primarily due to the private operators investing more in labour-saving equipment. His research is typical of a number of studies that have reached similar conclusions.[15]

Pseudo-work in the public sector is in large part due to decades of avoiding reforms that private-sector operators would have been obliged to make to keep their productivity levels up. Unemployment was such a huge political issue that it hardly occurred to most politicians that there might be benefit in reducing levels of public employment through increased efficiencies. In the private sector in the eighties and nineties, by contrast, there was a huge shake-out of employment as economic pressures forced companies to squeeze out unnecessary levels of management, get out of marginal product lines, tighten measures of performance, and get rid of workers who weren't essential to production. The public sector got a foretaste of such change in the Chrétien-Martin fiscal reforms, but has been reversing course furiously ever since.

Fishermen and Dairy Farmers Bring Home the Bacon

If we wanted to look beyond public-service and Crown corporation jobs per se to non-government jobs that exist only because the power of the state decrees that they shall, we might look at the fishing industry. There the federal government deliberately destroyed productivity in the industry on the east coast by enforcing an increasingly artificial distinction between inshore and offshore fishing and limiting the former to relatively small boats. It restricted the gear that those boats could use to catch fish and the seasons in which fishing was allowed, thus further obstructing productivity. Finally, the provinces on the east coast made rules about the distribution of the catch among processing plants to guarantee that work would be spread around without regard for efficiency or profitability. Then Ottawa unilaterally established a two-hundred-mile limit for Canadian management of the oceans off our shores, thus increasing the fish stocks available for Canadian exploitation. The result was that thousands more people lived from the fishery (supplemented by EI) than the resource could support. This too is pseudo-work, as are similar arrangements in the forest and pulp and paper industry that spread the resource among uneconomic plants and prevent anyone from achieving economies of scale that would allow the industry to prosper in the face of international competition.

Another effusion of pseudo-work is to be found in the dairy and other agricultural producers that enjoy production quotas. These quotas, which grant an exclusive right to the holder to produce milk or eggs or other agricultural commodities, also grant the producers the right to fix the price, which they gleefully do on a regular basis, always in an upward direction. Because only quota holders may legally produce the commodity in question for sale, and because we have steep tariffs at the border to keep out foreign products, many barely profitable producers are kept in business. Without the protection that quotas and tariffs provide, the industry would quickly squeeze out such marginal producers and move to a smaller number of bigger, more efficient operations, as they strove to meet the competition offered by foreign producers. Canadian prices would come down. But like many fishermen and forestry workers and public-sector employees and others in pseudo-work, dairy producers don't need to respond to market pressures or consumer preferences. What they need to do is to organize themselves aggressively to bargain with government in order to get benefits conferred on them at the expense of hapless taxpayers and consumers.

Canadian content regulations in our media are also a form of pseudo-work generation. The effect of such regulations is to create a demand in the private sector, as well as the CBC, for the services of people who would not be employed (at least in this kind of work producing what they produce today) if we consulted only the listening and viewing choices of actual Canadian consumers. Based on viewership and listenership, the CBC is almost pure pseudo-work—CBC employees and fans use the power of the state to make the rest of us pay over $1 billion annually for a service we never actually use. Despite improbable rhetoric that paints the CBC as the bulwark of Canada's very identity and essence, based on the total lack of public outcry, or even awareness of the CBC's silence during the strike several years ago, Canadians apparently don't even notice if the service is on the air or not.

The logic of why and how pseudo-work gets pseudo-workers to band together and use aggressive bargaining and intimidation to win concessions from government is best understood by looking at the trade union movement. But the trade union example is merely the most obvious and easily understood case of what happens when economic benefits are conferred on workers and companies, not because of what they produce, but because of a politicized process of bargaining between interest groups and political authorities. Those authorities then either cut cheques at the taxpayer's expense or else force consumers to pay directly an unearned bounty to the holders of some legally conferred privilege such as a tariff or production quota.

Trade Unions and Pseudo-work: A Match Made in Heaven

The modern trade union movement in this country came of age largely in the 1970s and still bears many of the marks of its birth. The seventies, for those of us who still remember them, were a time of great ideological ferment and enthusiasms. Marx was everywhere studied in university, where many of us thought Fidel Castro was a great leader and we mourned the death of Mao Tse-Tung. America was mired in Vietnam, a war that seemed deeply illegitimate to the young. Authority was contested in every possible arena. Capitalism was clearly a conspiracy and was associated with many historical wrongs, such as racism, colonialism, and exploitation of the working class. It was an exciting time of idealism and of ideas, and trade unionism seemed to many of us an instrument of righteous struggle against capitalist and imperialist exploiters.

Anyway, that was the story we told ourselves, and it helped us understand the place of trade unionism in the world. It is a story full of powerful emotional resonances, such as appeals to class solidarity and solidarity with the oppressed around the world, including Cesar Chavez's agricultural workers in California. This story endowed trade unions and their demands with a legitimacy that few other groups or institutions could match. Membership numbers were high, leftist political parties and their trade union allies were on the march, and union-friendly legislation was being passed almost effortlessly.

Less obviously at the time, the era of trade union influence coincided with the arrival of the Boomers.

Everywhere in Canada we were using the power of the state to soak up these surplus workers. The interests of the trade union movement and a society in the grips of a painful bout of demographic indigestion co-incided, not least because the public sector is heavily unionized. And the baby boom is a far more plausible and satisfying explanation of the behaviour of workers and unions over this period than that offered by, say, Seymour Martin Lipset.[16] A famous analyst of differences between Canada and the US, Lipset sees in higher unionization rates in Canada than the United States further confirmation of his thesis that Canada has

> One [bicycle] courier, who calls himself Suicide, has a plan: organise Washington's messengers and strike for better wages. "If we could have a work stoppage ... you'd hear it around the world! This city would grind to a halt, man, just completely shut down." ... In effect, Suicide's plan is to form a union, or a labor cartel. The collective strike threat would win him and his companions better pay or benefits. On the other hand, courier service would become more expensive, and some customers would switch to fax machines or Federal Express. The end result is likely to be that couriers with jobs will earn higher wages, but fewer new couriers will be hired. Money would be redistributed to the ins at the expense of the outs, with some loss of efficiency along the way. Newcomers lose, Suicide wins.
> Jonathan Rauch, *Demosclerosis*

a different political culture than the United States, one more characterized by collective action, democratic socialism, and deference to the state.

Unfortunately for Lipset, that does not explain why the historical trends of trade union density in Canada closely followed those in the United States from the 1930s until the 1960s. One author wondered, "If underlying social attitudes are an important source [of differing rates of trade unionism], why did the Canada–US unionization differential emerge only in the past three decades? Why did the two countries display very similar trends in union density until the 1960s?"[17]

Good questions. Part of the answer is that Canadian trade unionism since 1960 has not been the fruit of a different culture. It was demographics and Quebec nationalism that changed the culture and produced a new kind of trade unionism, not a culture of long standing that simply allowed a distinctive trade unionism to flourish. If we set aside the story we all told ourselves at the time about the heroic role of trade unionism in the struggles against exploitation and capitalism and try to look at trade unions analytically, their behaviour through-out this period was shaped by perfectly rational and easily understood incentives.

Most people who sell their goods or their labour intuitively understand that competition is what limits their economic power. The obverse of that proposition is that monopoly confers huge power. That is why every producer wants a monopoly on what they supply and why Adam Smith said that every meeting of producers is liable to result in a conspiracy against the public.

Trade unions are no different. They understand that power flows to them in direct proportion to their ability to monopolize the supply of workers. Indeed, unions were illegal for many years because competition legislation treated them as conspiracies in restraint of trade. And it is precisely their objective to prevent employers from dealing with any other workers but union members. If any other economic agent tried to exercise this kind of power, it would be illegal. But unions enjoy a special dispensation.

That dispensation has conferred a lot of bargaining power on unions, but contrary to the myth that unions propagate, the benefits that flow to union members are not screwed out of *employers* by worker solidarity. The cost of the relatively high wages of union members[18] is borne, not by the companies that employ the workers, *but by the non-union workers who are prevented from competing for these jobs and by the unemployed.*

Why them and not employers? Because when unions push up wage rates through collective bargaining, companies must raise the productivity of their workers to compensate. This they do by investing more capital, giving each worker more productivity-enhancing machinery, and reducing the need for workers. Thus do unions with real bargaining power reduce the number of jobs overall by artificially inflating the cost of labour relative to capital. Their *members* may get higher wages (and the unions higher dues from their members), but only by pre-venting non-union members (including the unemployed) from competing with them for the available work. If that competition were allowed, the wages paid might be lower but more people would be employed.

That does not mean that unions enjoy unfettered power. In the private sec-tor there are still lots of constraints on the ability of a union to put the boots to an employer. There is always the possibility of bankruptcy or capital fleeing the country, causing plant closures, for example, if wage rates and labour practices become too onerous for productivity improvements to compensate. That ex-plains the hostility of many trade unions to globalization, which exposes their members to competition from workers in other countries and not just here in Canada. High unemployment in the surrounding economy can put a brake on union power too because the easy availability of replacement workers can stiffen management's spine—unless obliging governments outlaw replacement workers or legislate closed shops, thus making the trade unions' monopoly complete.

But there are other ways to maintain your near-monopoly position in the labour supply. You can, for example, support the extension of very generous social programs and high minimum wages. The effect of these is pretty clear. If you set the minimum wage at $10 an hour, as some within the labour movement are lobbying for across the country today, you are in effect decreeing that anyone who cannot produce more than $10 worth of value with an hour of their labour shall not be employed.

The nexus between trade union power and the expansion of the welfare state is one that deserves careful scrutiny. In the example I've just cited, the real effect of raising the minimum wage is to forbid, by law, all low-productivity workers from competing with higher-productivity workers. What would otherwise be an unacceptable outcome can be made socially palatable only by reasonably generous social programs. This throws a rather different light on the social demands usually associated with the trade union movement (and its traditional political allies, the New Democrats). Trade unions have tried to paint themselves as the friend of the poor and the downtrodden by promoting high levels of social programs (and coincidentally the taxes to go with them). Thus their concern with the welfare of their members is portrayed as all of a piece with a larger concern for the most vulnerable in our society.

Contrary to this touching tale, however, the economic power they exercise on behalf of their members is paid for by the very poor and downtrodden the trade unions profess to wish to defend. When unions succeed in winning artificially high wages through collective bargaining or political pressure for higher minimum wages and other labour market regulation, they can be paid for (at least in the private sector) only by raising productivity. That means fewer workers with jobs, but higher wages for the lucky few who belong to the union or who have minimum-wage jobs. Social programs clean up the damage for low-income, low-skill people but do so at the expense of trapping many of them in dependence, preventing them from acquiring the job skills that would allow them to improve their lot, and driving up the cost of government through expensive social programs whose main rationale is to relieve powerful interest groups from the consequences of their bad economic behaviour.

Even when workers at the low end of the skill and wage scale have the drive and desire to escape this dependence, the welfare wall lies in wait. And of course each time the minimum wage is raised, that gives a powerful bargaining tool to the unions, who will then call for the maintenance of "historical differentials" between the minimum wage and their own, much higher, wages.

Ironically, eliminating the monopoly bargaining power and unearned privileges of such powerful groups can be one of the fastest routes to job creation. A perfect example is to be found in the privatization of liquor stores by the Alberta government. When the liquor stores were in the hands of the provincial government, liquor store employees (who are essentially grocery clerks) were extremely well-paid unionized civil servants. When the public-sector monopoly was broken and private providers were allowed to enter the marketplace, however, wages in the sector fell by about half to a level commensurate with the skills actually needed to provide the service, with the result that employment levels in the industry were much higher.[19] Six months after privatization, there were 535 retail stores (versus 205 under the old dispensation), and employment in the industry had tripled. This is exactly what you would expect to see if my argument is correct, namely that powerful unions and analogous organizations win benefits for their narrow membership at the expense of other workers who are prevented from competing for those jobs. Nor does this contradict the CN and Ontario Hydro examples I cited earlier, where employment within those organizations was squeezed when market discipline was introduced. If you looked only at the Alberta liquor commission, its employment levels fell too after privatization, reflecting the level of pseudo-work that had been created by that organization's monopoly position.

> After slightly over a decade [of privatized telephone service in Manitoba, the former Crown corporation] MTS has twice the assets, three times the revenue, and a fifth more jobs compared to [unprivatized] SaskTel. Prices are the same and Manitoba's local telco pays more taxes.
>
> David Seymour, "Telecommunications Privatization, Services, and Provincial Well-being"

Typically what happens in such cases, when public providers lose legal monopolies or other privileges, is that while employment within those organizations shrinks, it expands within the industry overall, as more nimble and disciplined competitors with more innovative management, technology, and business plans steal business away or fill market niches that were going unserviced before. This experience has been repeated in industry after industry in places as diverse as Manitoba, New Zealand, and Sweden.[20]

It should come as no surprise, then, that the parts of the country with the least trade union density and the least divvying up of the government pie by such politically powerful bargaining groups (places like Alberta and Ontario) traditionally have had the highest levels of employment, even at the height of the Boomer wave of workers. On the other hand, those parts of the country most prone to such politically motivated carve-ups were also the ones with some of the highest levels of unemployment and social costs associated with it.

Similarly, of course, the trade union movement resists being exposed to competition from workers in other countries and so will argue for tariff and other barriers and against free trade. They will push for early and compulsory retirement, withdrawing yet more workers from the labour force. All these actions and policies (and I've just picked a few here and there) have the effect of increasing union monopoly power at the expense of other workers, whether those workers are here in Canada or in other countries.

Monopolies are by their nature unstable, however, both because there are big economic rewards for getting out from under a monopoly and because people are very clever. Put together incentives and intelligence and the outcome is usually a foregone conclusion. When Canada Post enjoyed its greatest power, it was because physically moving pieces of paper around the country in envelopes was perhaps the most important way people could stay in touch and carry on business. That meant that Canada Post's monopoly on letter mail conferred on it huge power, which the inside and outside workers' unions turned frequently to their advantage through painful and damaging national strikes.

But it was precisely this kind of abuse of monopoly power and the costs that it entailed that drove people to seek alternatives to the mail. Now with email, text messaging, faxes, private couriers, and all the other alternatives to moving information, a postal strike has lost its ability to bring the economy to its knees, even though Canada Post still technically enjoys its monopoly on letter mail below a certain level of postage. The situation might well be different, of course, if Canada Post had succeeded in its once-mooted scheme to extend its monopoly into the cyber-world and charged, in effect, a stamp duty on each and every email sent in Canada. Monopoly creates incentives for people to defeat the monopoly. The only kind of monopoly that really escapes the economy's natural ability to discipline and defeat monopoly abuse occurs when the monopoly is created by government's coercive legal power rather than by some short-term economic advantage.[21] Competition in areas outside its legal monopoly brought low Canada Post and its union barons. In telecoms something similar happened when legal bars were removed to competition against the old incumbent monopoly. Investment skyrocketed, productivity rose, competing services emerged, and the quality of telecoms rose.

In the private sector, union power is in terminal decline as work shifts away from traditional blue-collar occupations in natural resources and manufacturing to white-collar services where people have more confidence in their own abilities to represent their own on-the-job interests and are more reluctant to see a bureaucratic third party representing their interests to their employers. The growth of awareness by employees that they work in a competitive world has helped as well, as they see clearly that their solidarity needs to be with all the members of their team, including management, as they struggle to win market share and keep their jobs in a globalizing economy. Solidarity with all other workers and against all employers just doesn't make sense.

The movement to free trade has sapped a lot of union power in the private sector, as the ability of homegrown unions to keep out the fruits of workers in other countries has declined, and that trend has been exacerbated by large investments in Third World countries to equip them with the machinery to make them highly productive. Legacy unions in industries like autos and airlines and rail and steel and elsewhere have been forced to roll back wages and working practices. In some cases they (i.e. the unions) have agreed to lower wages for new union members, or even across the board, as they struggle to meet the competition from non-union manufacturers that their own intransigence (plus management incompetence, of course) helped to bring about.

Welfare reform has begun, hesitantly, to eat away at the welfare trap, pushing many thousands of people back into the workforce whence they had been excluded by perverse incentives created, in part, at the behest of unions and other analogous organizations that exist chiefly to win benefits for their members at the expense of everyone else.

Why the Public Sector Is Different

The result of all this has been a notable decline in the share of private-sector workers in trade unions. But not in the public sector. What makes the public sector different?

First, the loss of local economic dominance that hit domestic industries in the private sector has been slower to hit the public sector. That can be explained by lots of things, such as governments' reluctance to admit their mistakes and being sheltered from the competitive consequences that business would face from taking similar decisions. It took us decades and billions of dollars to extricate the public sector from Cape Breton coal and steel, long after the private sector was ready to cut its losses and close it down. Something similar could be said about the Canadian Wheat Board, dairy and egg marketing boards, and a host of other similar wheezes that suck money out of taxpayers and consumers for little or no demonstrable benefit.

Second, the public sector creates lots of opportunities for PUPPETRY (or rent-seeking) at others' expense. The costs of having too many civil servants, or keeping the coal mines open, or subsidizing the nuclear or dairy or aerospace industry are spread across the entire population. Each person may pay only a small amount for these inefficiencies, and it is hard to disentangle those costs on your tax bill from other more legitimate uses of tax dollars. The benefits, however, are highly concentrated on a few beneficiaries. There is thus created an asymmetry in which those who pay cannot be bothered to do much to reduce costs because the benefits of doing so are small and the chances of achieving the result uncertain. Beneficiaries of government largesse, by contrast, are highly motivated, easily identified, and well organized, not least because the benefits of these state schemes are highly concentrated on them. Thus the impotent rage of taxpayers in the face of coffee-drinking road crews and absurdly high dairy prices.

Third, the discipline of the bottom line is absent in the public sector. I don't mean to say that the ability of the public sector to pay is unlimited. But private companies rapidly get into difficulty if they try to spend more than their customers and investors will give them voluntarily. Governments, by contrast, have the ability to take money compulsorily from taxpayers. Given my previous point, that those who benefit from government largesse are more effective and active politically than those who pay, it is not hard to see where the convergence of interest arises between powerful and well-organized public-sector unions and political authorities who generally want peace on the labour front and are willing to pay for it.[22] No government relishes the prospect of angry taxpayers finding their hospital closed, the garbage uncollected, or their mail undelivered.

So what happens when you put together a public-sector monopoly service (say, health care or the public schools or garbage collection) without a hard budget constraint and a powerful rent-seeking public-sector union? You get hugely increased bargaining power for the public-sector union compared to its private-sector counterpart.

If the unionized auto workers go on strike at GM or Ford or Chrysler, you can still buy a car from (non-union) Honda or Hyundai or Toyota. If Air Canada goes on strike, you can still fly WestJet or Porter. But if the nurses go on strike, or the teachers, or the air traffic controllers, or the hydro workers, the service they represent is essentially withdrawn. This draws the public into public-sector labour disputes as a third party at the table in a way they hardly ever participate in private-sector negotiations. And politicians always have a nervous eye on voters' discontent. This is precisely why for years public-sector workers were not allowed to bargain collectively and their right to strike was severely qualified. The consequence of public-sector workers effectively wielding a veto power over whether public services could actually be provided was that the state restricted the damage that power could do. In the seventies, at the height of our ideological enthusiasms, we swept that away. We see now the consequences.

Seen in this light, the behaviour of public-sector unions and their analogues is entirely understandable. They resist to the death any attempt to introduce competition into the provision of public services, through privatization or contracting out. They naturally dress it up as the defence of the public good against the rapacious capitalists, but this is pretty transparent stuff.

It also gives rise to the most amusing mental contortions. My favourite runs roughly like this: our health care services are the best in the world and are higher quality and cheaper than any private provision could ever be. However, if you try even the tiniest experiment with private provision, it will spread like wildfire throughout the system and destroy it. It is never very intelligibly explained exactly how this cheap high-quality public system will be supplanted by the expensive inferior system, but it is taken as a self-evident article of faith.

Not only are such derogations from pure public monopoly fought tooth and nail, but naturally any opportunity to bring more activities into the public sector is vigorously promoted. Any attempt to bring the benefits of free trade, another monopoly buster, to public services is, of course, anathema.

The most militant, ideological, and intractable part of the trade union movement (the public sector) is also its fastest growing. The last redoubts of trade union ideology in its purest form are not the factories and the mines, where international competition long ago brought reason to the bargaining table. They are the unionized faculty clubs and white-collar workers of the public sector.

And they have won attractive benefits. In every province in Canada, the public-sector pay premium relative to the local industrial wage is significant.[23] Job security in the public sector beats that in almost any private-sector job. Have you ever tried to fire a teacher? Despite all the fashionable talk about public-sector accountability, measures of productivity and performance in the public sector remain few and controversial, leaving low-performing public-sector activities to their dogmatic slumbers. And public-sector employment levels remain very high in spite of a few forays into privatization and other forms of rationalization here and there.

While the Martin–Chrétien fiscal reforms of the mid- to late nineties pared back modestly the size of public employment (part of the first mini-wave of reforms to be triggered by the receding of the baby boom), the effects were short-lived. Federal public-sector employment peaked in 1991 at 415,387. Public-sector employment fell to its lowest number—328,186—in 1999, as the Martin reforms reached their greatest intensity. Given the current mania for stimulus programs, however, by the time this book is published a new peak will almost certainly have been reached.

Ottawa is clearly anxious to make up for lost time. Federal public-sector employment reached 388,722 in 2006, and is rising fast.[24] Similarly, combined public-sector employment (federal, provincial, and local) peaked in 1992 at 3,180,142. It fell to its lowest number—2,855,533—in 1999. It has grown ever since, reaching 3,029,285, and almost every month, it seems, StatsCan reports public-sector employment as one of if not the fastest-growing sectors.[25] If we were to apply our rule of thumb that one-third of all public-sector employment is pseudo-work of one kind or another, that's a million people we should be struggling to put into more productive occupations.

The public sector also has had a major role to play in changing the retirement behaviour of Canadians. According to the Canadian Federation of Independent Business,[26] self-employed people retired on average at age 66 in 1975, and that retirement age has remained intact over the intervening 30-plus years. Private-sector workers taken as a whole were retiring at 65 in 1976, and that had fallen to 62 by the early part of this decade. Public-sector workers, by contrast, were retiring on average at 64 in the period from 1976 to 1979, but by 2000 to 2005, that average age of retirement had fallen to 59.

The CFIB's research shows that since the late 1980s, the public sector has driven the early retirement trend. The proportion of early retirees within the public sector was around 56 per cent in the year 2005, while in the private sector it was just over 33 per cent, and for self-employed individuals it was well below the public-sector rate at only 20 per cent. Nor does this tendency toward early retirement in the public sector contradict my earlier argument that most people actually want to work. Of course some retired public servants go on to hold other jobs, but that's not the central point. Over and over again I have come back to the theme that incentives matter, and retirement behaviour is no exception. Public-sector workers on the whole have access to retirement plans more generous than private-sector workers, and for many of these workers a point is reached at which the incentives to retire outweigh the desire to keep working in their current job. We'll talk more about this in later chapters.

Taking Pseudo-work Private

These special features of public-sector employment help to explain the continued strength of unionism in the public sector in Canada even as it continues to retreat in the private sector. The benefits and rewards of militant trade unionism in the public sector are simply much greater now than in the private sector. And workers in the private sector, knowing how much their jobs depend on high productivity, flexible work practices, and satisfying their customers, find the obstructive and militant attitudes of the modern trade union movement simply incomprehensible and frightening.

Unless, of course, their "private-sector job" depends on public-sector subsidy. In that case, the discipline of private-sector constraints, consumer attitudes, competitive pressures, and bottom lines goes out the window. Using one practical example, Fred McMahon has described the mentality that grips trade unions *in the private sector* when they believe their members' jobs exist chiefly as a result of taxpayer generosity rather than private-sector efficiency:

> The Trenton rail works in Trenton, Nova Scotia, were saved by a private multinational company, which specializes in taking over defunct yards, introducing new efficiencies, and making them profitable. Its only unionized shop is in Trenton. Two things are being created that wouldn't exist without that company: profits and high-paying jobs. Despite the jobs, the union thought the company was making too much profit. It demanded more money and loudly attacked the company.
>
> Such loud attacks have worked in the past in Atlantic Canada. Labour problems are bad for government; votes could be lost. The company pays up, and government helps out. But the company operating the rail works reacted differently. It has to sell on world markets. To be efficient, it requires consistently competitive wages, not inconsistent government handouts based on politics. Instead of being intimidated, the company redirected contracts away from the Trenton yards, saying the labour situation made completion of the work uncertain there. Failure to perform on contracts would affect the company's reputation with its customers.
>
> Interestingly, the rail-works company said the language the union leaders used was a key reason it was redirecting contracts. Workers had to understand, the company believed, that they and management needed to cooperate. If not, the rail works were doomed to failure. Union leaders admitted to being shocked at the criticism of their rhetoric. This sort of language had a long tradition of grabbing the attention of politicians and leading to the translation of government money into higher pay. Ultimately, the union and management reached an agreement that reflected the economics of a market-oriented firm [although ultimately the plant was closed several years later by the parent company].
>
> Had the firm been locally owned, the story might have followed a different scenario. The company might have displayed the lack of concern about quality, costs, and good management that is typical of some Atlantic Canadian firms, firms that have come to rely on government support.... Such a firm would likely have paid off the workers and demanded more government support.[27]

There is nothing uniquely Atlantic Canadian about this behaviour. Many industries in other parts of the country, especially ones that are in decline but still employ large unionized workforces, are totally familiar with the pattern of behaviour described by McMahon. Buzz Hargrove, former head of the Canadian Auto Workers (CAW), delighted in putting the boots to the large car companies using some pretty strong anti-employer rhetoric and then looked, in concert with the companies, to Ottawa and provincial governments to bail them out of the consequences of their uncompetitive bargains. And governments tend to open the taxpayer's pocketbook in response because the idea of job losses among these politically powerful workforces is more daunting than throwing a few hundred million, or even a billion or two, into corporate coffers here and there. The Harper government came to office reluctant to continue this tradition, but given the collapsing fortunes of GM and Chrysler in the downturn, that reluctance has been overcome. Stimulus packages on both sides of the border now invariably feature various kinds of bailout for the unionized companies. Even the more successful non-unionized Japanese manufacturers have bellied up to the trough.

Out with the Old, in with the New

Demographic change in the coming decades, however, means that paying people not to work, or paying them to do phantom jobs that bear no relationship to the fiscal burden they place on taxpayers, will simply become socially unacceptable as Canadians see more and more around them the evidence that they are forgoing improvements in their own standard of living because genuine productive work is going begging.

Work will be plentiful and workers scarce, and *that will change everything*. Unlike the last forty years, when circumstance forced us to pull too many people into low-value, low-performance pseudo-work, or even squarely into dependence on various forms of welfare benefit and transfer, we will be forced by our new circumstances to pull the fewer workers we have into high-value, high-performance work. Politicians will not find it nearly so beneficial to conspire with companies to jack up their payrolls artificially.

The consequences are not hard to see: the relationship of Canadians to their work will change, and the proportion of Canadians in pseudo-work will fall dramatically, and so will the power of trade unions, of "corporate welfare," and of special interests pleading for government benefits generally. The share of the population that believes that their economic well-being rises and falls with the reach and power of the state will decline, and with that will come a more economically literate attitude toward competitiveness, productivity, and taxes.

Family and the Audacity of Love

For Goldwyn Smith, the really creative social agencies were unimpeded individual initiative and work, the family and religion. "The family," he wrote, "is more important than the State; it is a deeper source of character and happiness...." It was in the household that character was moulded and proper conceptions of duty and obligation instilled.

CARL BERGER, *THE SENSE OF POWER*

The strengthening of family life in Canada [is] the basis on which our nation's moral strength and vitality depend.

LESTER B. PEARSON, *THE EMPIRE CLUB SPEECHES, 1968-1969*

Real work, then, is a deep source of human happiness, dependence a source of sadness, shame, and dysfunction; pseudo-work is a source of lost productivity and empowerment of public-sector unions and other interest groups; and too large a state is a cause of economic decline, unemployment, and pointlessly burdensome taxation.

These propositions will be controversial enough in themselves in early-twenty-first-century Canada. We have further to go, however, for the growth of the state, the rise in welfare dependence and PUPPETRY, and the corruption of individual and institutional character they have brought in their train have deeply affected another vital traditional social institution, an institution also fitted by millennia of experience to our deepest nature: family and marriage.

Introducing a discussion of marriage and the family into this book will surprise and disappoint many people. In the widely held account of the social history of the last half century, the evolution of our attitudes about marriage is often held up as a measure of social progress. Marriage is often seen as a quaint hold-over that more enlightened people can dispense with and suffer no ill effects. In fact, the conventional wisdom now runs, marriage trapped women in relationships of dependence on men, kept them uneducated, domesticated, uninteresting, subject to the tyranny of their husbands and their children.[1] The decline of marriage therefore heralds a new era of liberation from patriarchal tradition, as an institution that served men's interests is supplanted by more free-flowing arrangements that give women more choices than they've ever had before.[2] Supplement those freer arrangements of relationship with a generous welfare state that promises a minimum income (and the higher the better) to all, and women will be free to be themselves and do what they wish.

Indeed, there is much truth in the view that the abandonment of a rigid and unbreakable definition of marriage has created, on balance, more good than harm. Who could deny that there were loveless marriages and bad and abusive spouses and parents? Who would not recognize the injustice of a system that allowed divorce only for those people with the money and connections to get a private member's bill through Parliament? Who could be indifferent to the suffering caused by the relentless squeezing of men and women into arbitrary and confining career and family goals on the grounds of their sex alone?

And yet one can recognize all the progress brought about by the

> The less soul a woman has the greater her asset as a wife, the more readily she will absorb herself in her husband. It is this slavish acquiescence to man's superiority that has kept the marriage institution seemingly intact for so long a period. Now that woman is coming into her own, now that she is actually growing aware of herself as a being outside of the master's grace, the sacred institution of marriage is gradually being undermined, and no amount of sentimental lamentation can stay it.
> Emma Goldman, 1914

> If divorce has increased by one thousand percent, don't blame the women's movement. Blame the obsolete sex roles on which our marriages were based.
> Betty Friedan, 1974

> You became a semi-nonperson when you got married.
> Gloria Steinem, 1987

progressive marginalization of marriage as an institution and still harbour reservations, doubts, and concerns. The decline of marriage and family laid out in detail in this chapter is demonstrably connected with disturbing social developments. Declining fertility, poor preparation for children to shoulder the responsibilities of adulthood, the poverty associated with lone parenthood,[3] the growing evidence that neither men, nor women, nor children are getting from non-married relationships what they want and need—all this should make us want to ponder if we have not gone too far in redefining family and marriage. There is no need to return to the *Father Knows Best* 1950s. On the other hand, the evidence from the United States, the United Kingdom, and, increasingly,

Canada, should point us toward looking to see if we might be able to achieve a better balance. What is good about the freewheeling liberation that followed the 1960s might, perhaps, be tempered by an awareness of what has been lost, and how it might be recovered without reverting to the days and ways of Peyton Place, Stepford, and Harper Valley.

Regardless, many will try to make out that this chapter calls for a return to some kind of mythical past viewed through rose-tinted spectacles, that the argument assumes all families are perfect, that there is never sadness, irretrievable breakdown, or abusive parents. They miss the point. The earlier chapter on work will be wilfully misinterpreted as saying there are no unpleasant or bad jobs, when the focus there was on what we know about how the absence of work harms people. This chapter will similarly be misinterpreted as saying all marriage is perfect when it merely asks the reader to look at the growing evidence of the effects of the disappearance of marriage, especially on particularly vulnerable parts of the population. To choose just one example, when, on the basis of comprehensive data on marriage and children in Canada, the *Globe and Mail* editorializes that "marriage is still the best framework in which to raise healthy, happy children,"[4] it is not engaging in contentious polemic. The editorial board is stating the result of a large and growing body of knowledge made possible by a long period of widespread marriage decline. Just as we need the absence of work to be able to really understand work's value, we need the absence of marriage and the breakdown of the family to assess what the value of marriage and family is.

Family: The International Experience

Unfortunately the study of marriage and family from this point of view is still rather embryonic in Canada, and this state of affairs is not helped by the fact that many sources of statistical data do not distinguish adequately between different types of family relationship (e.g., between cohabiting partners and married spouses). That is in itself an indication of the extent to which inquiry into those differences has come to be seen as an intrusion into private affairs that are nobody else's business. Before we pass to what is available from Canadian sources, however, it might be instructive to look at what the data from other, better documented societies are telling us about the effects of family breakdown and the decline of marriage, especially on society's most vulnerable, including children and those on low incomes.

The British Family

The British family has undergone a significant change in the past few decades. In 1971, seven out of ten households were couples, whether married or cohabiting. By 2001, that figure had fallen to just over one in two.[5] And within the share of households that were couples in 2001, those who were cohabiting increased rather dramatically.[6] In fact, by 2003, there were an estimated 2 million cohabiting couples in Britain, representing 10 per cent of households and 16 per cent of all couples.[7]

Lone-parent families have also become increasingly common in Britain. Before 1975 over 90 per cent of British children were born to married mothers. The number of births to unmarried mothers increased dramatically from 54,000 in 1975 to 276,000 in 2005, a fivefold rise from 9 to 43 per cent of all births. More than a quarter of all British children (almost 2.5 million children) are currently living in lone-parent households.[8]

Does any of this matter? It does when you consider the social, economic, and personal costs of these changes. For example, married people in the United Kingdom are healthier. Compared to unmarried people, the risk of mortality is significantly lower. The effect is stronger in men than women, in that the mortality risk for unmarried women is 50 per cent higher than married women; however, it is 250 per cent higher for men. Divorced individuals have higher death rates from coronary heart disease, stroke, many forms of cancer, pneumonia, and cirrhosis.

Divorce and separation are associated with increased mental illness and risk of suicide. Severe depression is three times higher among women and nine times higher among men who have been separated or divorced compared to stably married men and women.[9] Children of lone parents are also about twice as likely to have a mental problem as those with married parents.[10]

Sadly, there is a strong statistical connection between lone-parent families and crime and delinquency. More than 70 per cent of young offenders come from lone-parent families. Alcoholism, drug abuse, and other forms of bad behaviour and delinquency are also higher in children from separated families than those from intact families.[11]

Poverty is much more prevalent in lone-parent families. In the United Kingdom, lone mothers are twice as likely as two-parent families to live in poverty. Lone parents are also more than twice as likely as married couples to have no savings. Lone-parent households are over twelve times more likely to be receiving income support as married couples.[12] In 2003–04, 56 per cent of lone parents with dependent children were receiving some form of income-related benefit compared with just 10 per cent of couples with dependent children.[13]

Unemployment is closely linked to family breakdown in Britain. The country's employment rate for lone parents is 56.6 per cent, the lowest in Europe. By contrast, the employment rate for married parents is almost 75 per cent.[14] Unemployment is endemic in lone-parenthood households and cohabiting couples, particularly for women. A study by the British government found that the unemployment rate for lone-parent mothers was 2 to 4 percentage points higher than for women in cohabiting relationships and 4 to 10 percentage points higher than for married women.[15] Children from lone-parent households on average achieve poorly at school. Children from divorced families are almost twice as likely to be expelled from school as are children from intact marriages. Children of single, never-married parents are more than four times more likely to be expelled. These same children are more than twice as likely to repeat a grade when compared with children raised in intact marriages.[16]

The overall cost of family breakdown to the British taxpayer is estimated to be £20 billion to £24 billion per year, or £680 to £820 for every taxpayer. The costs include not only the direct costs of supporting lone parents, but also the indirect impacts on employment, education, health, crime, police, prisons, etc.[17]

Family in the United States

As in Britain, statistically it appears that marriage and family arrangements are becoming the main differentiators between those who succeed and fail economically in the United States. Kay Hymowitz is only the most recent author to paint a devastating portrait of what marriage breakdown has meant to America's most vulnerable.[18] She writes:

> One can't disentangle the economic from the family piece. Given that families socialize children for success—or not—and given how marriage orders lives, they are the same problem. Separate and unequal families produce separate and unequal economic fates.

Hymowitz is by no means the first author to make these connections. The American experience with family breakdown and its consequences has been well documented by scholars such as Daniel Patrick Moynihan, Gary Becker and James Q. Wilson.

In the United States—as in Britain—marriage is much less common than it was forty years ago. Between 1960 and 2004, the divorce rate more than doubled so that now roughly half of all marriages end in a courtroom. Not only are more marriages resulting in divorce, fewer Americans are even taking the plunge in the first place. Since the 1970s, cohabitation has increased by more than 1,000 per cent, with such couples now representing slightly more than 10 per cent of all couples.[19] Added together, over 1 million children experience parental divorce each year, and over 8 million children currently live with a divorced lone parent. The combined effect of divorce and out-of-wedlock child-bearing means that more than half of America's children will spend all or part of their childhood living in a lone-parent, divorced, or remarried family.[20]

Again, one might ask, does this matter? One scholar notes, "There is abundant empirical research in the United States that demonstrates the strongly negative effects of cohabitation and lone-parent families on child wellbeing."[21] The research literature in support of this proposition is extensive.

That research shows that children living in families with married parents have better outcomes than children in all other living arrangements on a broad range of measures, including economic well-being, behavioural and emotional health, and educational attainment, even when researchers control for differences in income and other characteristics.

Children and adults living in married families are healthier. The children of lone-parent families have high incidences of substance abuse, obesity, and mental illness.[22] For adults, marriage is closely associated with longevity, better physical health, and lower rates of mental illness and depression.[23]

In the United States, as in Britain, crime and delinquency go hand in hand with family breakdown. A state-by-state analysis indicates that a 10 per cent increase in the number of children living in lone-parent families typically leads to a 17 per cent increase in juvenile crime.[24]

Divorced or lone-parent families are poorer. Families with children that were not poor before a divorce see their income drop as much as one-half. Almost 50 per cent of the parents with children that are going through a divorce fall below the poverty line afterwards.[25] Children who do not live with both biological parents are roughly twice as likely to be poor.[26]

The economic consequences are particularly pronounced for lone-parent families headed by women. The economics of lone-parent family life mean that lone mothers are disproportionately represented among the poor. Among U.S. households headed by lone mothers in 1998, one-third lived below the poverty line, compared to 12 per cent of families headed by men. In 1999, 42 per cent of children living in female-headed families were poor, compared to 18 per cent in male-headed families and 8 per cent in couple-headed families.[27] Overall, women with dependent children make up two-thirds of the poor population, a phenomenon referred to as the "feminization of poverty."[28] School-age children living with both parents fare better than those who do not when measured for cognitive development, academic achievement, and impulse control. The high school dropout rate for children of lone-parent families is about twice as high as for those children living with both biological parents.[29]

Why Family Will Matter More in Canada, Too

Just like work, family and marriage were part of the bedrock social assumptions that Canada was built on in its first ninety years, as well as in the colonial era that preceded Confederation. Just like work, they were seen as part of a full human life, and without them humans were diminished, unhappy, and unfulfilled. Just like the role that work plays in life success, the life chances of children whose parents are married and those whose parents are not are distinctly different, and the health, happiness, and economic prospects of married parents are also better, to the point where one may now make the argument that race and class and education are being overtaken by these other factors as the determinants of who will succeed in the Canada of the future.

And just like work, the decline of marriage and the family is intimately tied up with the closely related phenomena of a sea of young workers; an expansive state; and a moral permissiveness and hedonistic individualism, all of which is about to become much more difficult to maintain in the face of the reversal of the baby boom and the consequent adjustments we will have to make.

Like work, family is a discipline at which our first nature chafes. But also like work, research, some of which we have just seen, is increasingly documenting the extent to which family is an institution that is indispensable to our social and economic success.[30]

Moreover, being the place where our character and values are formed, family is the place where we learn to master our selfish instincts and become valuable to others, as prospective spouses and employees and parents. It is the place where the rising generation is formed. Family thus confers benefits on both individuals and society.

That happy reciprocity, however, comes with a price. Family makes demands on us. We have to be obedient children, responsible parents, supportive spouses. The last forty years have seen a unique period, however. The discipline of the family was not so socially necessary, because we were awash in workers and didn't have enough for them to do. Surplus workers meant that failure to teach some children self-discipline and how to work hard didn't matter as much as it might have otherwise. Accompanying that development came the growth of a diverse range of state-funded ways in which one could get by in the world without really working. Thus, in some vulnerable parts of the population, family lost its power as the last refuge in times of trouble.

The need for the disciplined family unit to socialize the rising generation having declined, it became harder and harder to justify the legal, social, and institutional supports that buttressed marriage and encouraged couples to stay together even when times were hard.

> To corrupt family relations is to poison fountains; for the sources of the Commonwealth are within the households, and errors there are irretrievable....
>
> Edmund Burke, *Correspondence*, Volume III

Politicians and other opinion leaders began to define selfish behaviour down, in the sense of offering people with a guilty conscience the political cover to escape the obligations of family when those obligations became inconvenient or too burdensome. Not only was it made remarkably easy to dissolve the marriage bond, but the state stepped up to the plate to help cover the cost of the damage, at least in the short run. Just as it made it easier than it had ever been to choose not to work, it also made it easier than it had ever been to choose not to have a family or to choose to leave it once it had been started. Program after program was conceived to pick up the pieces of family breakdown, whether in support for lone mothers and their children, or income support for the elderly, or child care for parents who could not afford to stay home with their children no matter how much they wished to do so. And in its headlong rush to finance the social costs of what had traditionally been seen to be anti-social behaviour, the state pushed up the tax burden on those who were married and working, making a major contribution to the demographic bust.[31]

So "liberated," people began to abandon marriage and family in unprecedented numbers. And like the abandonment of work, this had far-reaching consequences, including a decline in trust between men and women, a rise in dependence on the state, a rise in child poverty, a decline in the birth rate and more.

Work and Marriage, Work and Marriage, Go Together Like ...

We agonize a great deal over the fate of marriage and family, but almost always in the context of the impact on children or low-income spouses after marriage breakdown. Hardly any attention is paid to the ways in which marriage, fertility, and work are intimately intertwined.

Family is the first and most important place where character is formed.[32] It is there that the struggle to civilize children and turn them into mature adults begins and is largely completed. And while later in life that struggle to reach maturity is chiefly an internal one, in childhood it is of necessity a struggle between parents and children.

The reason that family has survived and thrived throughout human history is that there is no superior substitute for two parents, committed to each other and their children, providing example, discipline, and, above all, love to their offspring. Family can, of course, take a number of forms, such as extended families characteristic of agricultural and subsistence society, or the nuclear family more familiar in modern industrialized society. The universality of "a system of primary relations among people related by blood and marriage and living together (for some part of their lives) in social and economic dependence,"[33] however, is not in any serious dispute.

On the contrary, the family has been the object of a great deal of philosophical and empirical study. Philosophers as diverse as Aristotle, Hegel, Burke, Rousseau, and Engels have described and analyzed family relations in great detail, sometimes to praise them, sometimes to condemn them, but never to deny their importance in understanding human development. Few have argued that there was any serious competitor to family as a framework for procreation and the rearing of children.

And as the rest of this chapter shows, when the family's ability to give children what they need declines, one inevitable result is that children grow up to be, on average, less well prepared to accept the responsibilities of adulthood, less able to discipline their untutored emotions, and less able to master their selfish instincts.

And while that family breakdown is a calamity for society, it is first and foremost a tragedy for the children, who are thereby deprived of those acquired character traits, or "second nature" that alone make full human happiness possible. All other possible arrangements for raising children are, on average, inferior in the preparation they give children to face the rigours of adult life, including the openness, trust, cooperativeness, and perseverance necessary to succeed at work and to create a family for themselves able to confer the same benefits on their own children. So having sound families and encouraging marriage means that the young Canadians who are shaped by such families enter the labour force better equipped to succeed there, raising their own standard of living and that of all Canadians.

No family, of course, is perfectly loving, perfectly trusting, and perfectly supporting. They don't need to be and no one is asserting the contrary. All that needs to be established is that, on the whole, intact families provide more of these features on a systematic basis than the chief alternatives, such as lone parenthood, serial live-in partners, government institutions, or some combination of all three.[34]

The second way in which marriage and family are related to the question of work is that marriage changes the behaviour of the adults just as it shapes the character of their offspring. Social anthropologist David Murray[35] has argued the behaviours that make one a good mate and parent—diligence, competence, trustworthiness—also happen to be among those that make one a valuable employee or successful entrepreneur.[36] Honouring your promises is a trait one learns by observing that behaviour in your parents, for example, even if no parent is perfectly trustworthy or truthful and even if some parents are irretrievable liars. Remember that the point of comparison we are after is not some impossible ideal no flesh-and-blood human being could fulfil. The point of comparison is a flesh-and-blood human being with all his or her failings who stays and tries to work things out versus the one who disappears and is replaced by some inferior substitute, or who was never there in the first place.[37]

Moreover, the data show that men who marry are changed by the experience. For example, they work harder than their unmarried counterparts[38] because they have responsibilities

There has been an unholy alliance between those on the left, who believe that man is endowed with rights but no duties, and libertarians on the right, who believe that consumer choice is the answer to all social questions, an idea eagerly adopted by the left in precisely those areas where it does not apply. Thus people have a right to bring forth children any way they like, and the children, of course, have the right not to be deprived of anything, at least anything material. How men and women associate and have children is merely a matter of consumer choice, of no more moral consequence than the choice between dark and milk chocolate, and the state must not discriminate among different forms of association and child rearing, even if such non-discrimination has the same effect as British and French neutrality during the Spanish Civil War. The consequences to the children and to society do not enter into the matter: for in any case it is the function of the state to ameliorate by redistributive taxation the material effects of individual irresponsibility, and to ameliorate the emotional, educational, and spiritual effects by an army of social workers, psychologists, educators, counselors, and the like, who have themselves come to form a powerful vested interest of dependence on the government.

Theodore Dalrymple, *Our Culture, What's Left of It*

and, a word one hardly hears any more, duties toward their family. So the health of our families is directly related, not only to how well our children succeed in the workforce, but to the examples our parents set for us by how hard they work and how reliable and trustworthy they are toward us as children.

In a Canada without enough workers, family will become more important for a third reason: the kinds of relationships Canadians have and how governments treat those different relationships (e.g., through taxes) tell us a great deal about why Canadians have so few children and what to do about it. After all, one of the key reasons for the decline in fertility in wealthy societies has been the far-reaching influence of the modern welfare state.[39] It has tried to crowd out other earlier forms of social relationships, and especially the family, on the grounds that they were oppressive and demeaning. One classic example was the famous "Spouse in the House" court case[40] in which the Supreme Court held it improper for the Ontario government to expect live-in partners to support their welfare-receiving "co-habitor" financially. The court did so in part on the grounds that women would find it demeaning to have to be financially dependent on a man. But not, apparently, demeaning to be financially dependent on the state, a perfect inversion of the traditional view. Yet as I will show below, being bound to one another in a healthy marriage creates for women as well as men the possibility to specialize at what each does best and for each to make the most valuable contribution to the success of the family. Having one partner specialized largely but not exclusively in earning, and another specialized largely but not exclusively in child-rearing, for example, is cooperation in pursuit of common goals that are enriching for the parents, the children, and the larger society. It is in no way analogous to dependence on the state or charity.

> Self-discipline, a sense of justice, honesty, fairness, chivalry, moderation, public spirit, respect for human dignity, firm ethical norms—all of these are things people must possess before they go to market and compete with each other. These are indispensable supports which preserve both market and competition from degeneration. Family, church, genuine communities, and tradition are their sources.
>
> William Ropke, *A Humane Economy*

What Children Learn at Home

Males who marry and males who get and keep jobs, which are circumstances of clear advantage for child rearing, share a common foundation—they keep commitments. Such men come from common environments—they had fathers who wed their mothers.[41]

Promise-keeping, David Murray tells us, is something that children learn first at home watching how their parents treat each other. The reality is that many forms of behaviour first learned at home are the cornerstone of future behaviour in both family and the workplace.[42] The reason this matters is that there is an increasingly common view among libertarians (of left and right), classical liberals and others that whether or not to have children (and whether or not to be married when doing so) is a purely private decision,[43] rather like what job you choose, what neighbourhood you live in, and what car you drive. The state and, more importantly, society, in the form of other family members, friends, and club and church members, have no business having any views about the child-bearing and child-rearing behaviour of individuals, and those people who have children have no resulting claim for help or support on their fellow citizens. Having children or not is simply a matter of personal liberty, and we as autonomous individuals may order these matters just exactly as we please. The decisions we make in this regard should be treated as much as an expression of our private beliefs and values as the clothes we wear or the books we read or the spiritual values we profess.

If we accept, however, that family is where we learn many of the behaviours that make things like economic exchange and contracts and even democracy possible, then family becomes a matter of central public importance. Promise-keeping, taking account of and even caring about the interests of others, respect for what belongs to others, trustworthiness, and self-control are just some of those behaviours.

In fact many of our economic and political freedoms are predicated on the notion of society being composed of responsible and accountable individuals who also take account of the interests of others in their actions. Self-government in a political sense and self-responsibility in an economic sense take for granted a world composed chiefly of self-governing and self-responsible individuals. The success or failure of the Canadian family is therefore of prime concern to all of us.

Of all the character traits that children learn at home, however, one deserves pride of place in this discussion, and that is self-control (what we might also call individual self-government). Self-control is the ability to contain current desires in the interest of achieving a more important good that takes time to reach fruition. Such self-discipline is the character trait that most separates those who will enjoy success in work, school, and family from those who will not.[44] And it is the character trait pre-eminently learnt at home.

The classic struggle between parents and children, the thing all parents fear and all children resent, is getting the children to restrain their appetites and think of the good of others. Children by and large want what they want right now: another's toy; the attention of their mother or father; sweets; pets; television; leisure. To begin with, they have no conception of respecting the property of others, the need to respect their mother's conversation with someone else, the fact that they will be having a meal shortly, are not ready to take on the responsibility of the care of an animal, or have household chores or homework to perform. Parents see the value for their children in acquiring the self-control to realize these important benefits, but children rarely do and come to see the value of the self-discipline they acquire only after they have acquired it.

Later, children learn to resolve their disputes through negotiation and consideration of the interests of others. They learn to be able to put off enough immediate satisfactions to succeed in school, acquire a profession or trade, be attractive to the opposite sex, avoid unwanted pregnancies and sexually transmitted diseases, save for houses and cars, and, the ultimate emotional investment in the future, have children and make sacrifices in order to equip them to succeed in life too. All these goods are more important than immediate pleasure, but they all require the ability to set aside that pleasure to realize them. Parents are the first and most important force teaching children that a successful future imposes constraints on what you can do and have in the present.[45]

At least teaching the principle of short-term pain for long-term gain is what most parents do for most children. Sometimes this essential set of character traits fails to jump the generational divide or is never there to be instilled in the first place. This can happen for a number of reasons, including the failure of parents to acquire these values themselves from their own parents. Many traditional family and community members, such as grandparents, in-laws, church leaders, teachers, sports coaches and other role models, police, and others, played and continue to play supporting roles, but the evidence is pretty clear that they can only marginally compensate for a failure to transmit these values in the home.[46] In any case, the legitimacy of these social supports has been badly undermined in recent years, just as parental authority and the ability to impose standards of behaviour within the family has been. At the same time as the state has been reducing the cost of self-destructive and anti-social behaviours (such as teen pregnancy, juvenile crime, drug use, and idleness), it has been tightening restrictions on the behaviour of parents trying to impose discipline within the home.

In one high-profile trial, American tourist David Peterson was charged for spanking his five-year-old daughter in 1995 in a London, Ontario, parking lot after she closed the car door on her brother's hand. While the parent's right to discipline his child reasonably was upheld in this case, it was upheld only after a nightmarish period during which criminal charges were pending, and it was by no means certain that Peterson would be vindicated.

In a more recent case, a Quebec father, fearing his daughter was behaving unsafely in on-line chatrooms where she was vulnerable to sexual predators, banned her from making use of them. She persisted, even using a friend's computer when access to the computer at home was restricted. After an escalating series of provocations by the daughter and disciplinary responses by the father, he barred her from a camping trip with her friends. When he refused to relent, the girl's mother went to court and got Judge Suzanne Tessier to reverse the father's decision. No one suggested the father had been abusive. He did nothing illegal. His custody agreement (he had full custody of the child) did not prevent such discipline. But a judge still thought it important to substitute her judgment for that of the child's father.[47] That judgment has recently been confirmed by a higher court on appeal.

And advocacy groups, such as the Canadian Foundation for Children, Youth and the Law, are constantly pressing the government and courts to restrict even further the latitude that parents have to establish effective limits on their children's behaviour. Too many parents and prospective parents have heard the stories of false and exaggerated accusations of child violence resulting in charges, social and economic losses, children being taken into custody by government agencies, and the virtual destruction of family life.

Given the obstacles already in the path of parents in trying to establish a calm, ordered, and safe home life, the prospect of their child not merely being able to defy their authority with impunity but being able to call in the authority of the state to prevent their parents taking the action they judge necessary for their child's welfare can make the already awesome responsibilities of parenthood seem too daunting for mere mortals.

If parents are unable to establish effective discipline, however, the consequences are not just terrible for the parents but cast a life-long shadow over the child's chances for success.

So the family is the first little culture, first little society, and first little economy we ever belong to, and it is there where we acquire the character that largely settles whether we trust one another, whether we are worthy of being trusted, whether we are honest, cooperative, honourable, industrious, and respectful of the interests of others.[48] Whether we succeed in inculcating these values and behaviours on a broad enough scale will settle to a large degree how free we can be and how rich we can be collectively. What goes on in families affects every one of us, and the parents who bring up their child successfully imbued with these values do a work of inestimable value for each of us.

The Welfare State Comes Home

It matters to our freedom and to our standard of living that people be raised in families. As we enter an era in which we cannot merely set aside those who have not acquired the sort of character one needs to participate and succeed in working, family breakdown will matter even more than before. It mattered less when we believed we didn't have enough work for everyone; faced now as we are with a scarcity of workers, everyone unable to work successfully is a tiny social as well as personal catastrophe.

Earlier I referred to the rich literature about the extent to which children learn things like trust and promise-keeping in the home. But what about work and dependence? Do the work activities of the parents leave an imprint on the character of their children?

In a particularly comprehensive look at the U.S. data, Casey Mulligan[49] showed that there is a direct link between parents getting welfare and the work habits of their children. A child's work ethic is largely determined by both his or her parents' work ethic and the amount of work the parents actually do. Mulligan finds that "the intergenerational transmission of unemployment and welfare program participation is strong."[50] Moreover, he is able to demonstrate that the transmission across the generations of the willingness to work is largely independent of income, so the key explanation here is not whether the parent or the child is well paid or not. While income has some effect on the decision to work, the actual behaviour of the parents, as observed by the child, seems to have an indispensable formative effect on the child's work ethic as an adult.

The wheels of social transformation grind exceeding slow, but the change gathers force with each generation. The changes in individual behaviour produced by the last half century's expansion of the welfare state have been slow and subtle, precisely because the state began by battling cultural values already inculcated by parents in children whose characters were formed before the rise of the easy availability of various forms of welfare benefit. More recently, however, children have been raised in a world in which the availability of such benefits is a given. Here, too, the state's good intentions have been insufficient to prevent its generosity from undermining behaviours that are vital to our success as a society.

Take a moment to think about the kind of values a parent might seek to inculcate in his or her child in the absence of a comprehensive welfare state. Among others would be the various virtues that we have seen are successful in the working world, including, pre-eminently, an appetite for work. While hard work does not always guarantee success, its absence nearly always guarantees the opposite of success. In any case, in the absence of a well-developed welfare state there is no real alternative to getting the skills one needs to work and then putting those skills to work.

Not only is this in the interests of the child, but it is also in the parents' interest. Leaving aside the shame and stigma that usually attaches to any kind of sloth or dependence within the family in a society where people are expected to work for a living, there is also direct economic self-interest. First, parents usually stand ready to help their children when they have difficulties or meet a major challenge in life. They may help them pay for higher education, they may help them out with food or even free accommodation at home in the case of some crisis, or they may offer generous gifts at a wedding or the purchase of a first home. And these are just a few examples. But while most parents stand ready to help out, they also don't want to help out more than they have to, because they might have travel or retirement or other plans for that money. So they both want to be available to help but don't want their help called on to excess. The key here, then, is to inculcate a strong work ethic in their offspring in order to keep the need for parental transfers within bounds.[51]

Similarly, parents in the absence of a comprehensive welfare state must think about their own circumstances when age or illness prevents them from being self-supporting. Family is the first source of support. Again, the interests of parents coincide with the interests of the larger society in that the sensible parent prepares their children to work hard so that, when the time comes that the parent needs to call on the child for support, that support will be forthcoming. Moreover, the two aspects of the economic relationship between parents and children are mutually reinforcing. Parents can offer both rewards and punishments even to adult children for behaviour that maximizes the chances of economic success for the children and ultimately for the parents in their old age. Parents in their prime earning years can make major contributions to their children establishing their household as young adults but might withhold some or all of that help if they think the child is making a poor career choice or living common-law (which reduces work incentives and increases the chances the relationship will fail, with consequent lost future income and assets) or having a child without a husband or any one of a number of choices that would be economically destructive.

All these incentives push parents to be demanding of their children and to have high expectations of them. Research[52] confirms that parents communicate these expectations to their children, as their parents did before them, and the children respond. These incentives operate even on parents who might otherwise be inclined to be indulgent with their children and would prefer easy popularity with them today, rather than greater chances of economic security for the whole family later.

But all these calculations, it would appear, are subtly undermined by the growth of the welfare state. Suddenly, state retirement benefits mean parents have far less invested in the economic success of their offspring, however much they might want to see them succeed for the personal satisfaction it might bring to the children. The consequences of poor choices of mate or career are blunted by the state being willing to be an absentee parent writing cheques, especially at the lower end of the income scale.

In a fascinating confirmation of this observation, the empirical link between welfare availability and generosity on the one hand and the propensity of people at the bottom end of the income scale to marry is quite strong. Professor Doug Allen of Simon Fraser University wrote about this several years ago and noted that there was little surprise in the fact that higher welfare payments led to higher levels of dependence among lower-income women than among higher-income women, just as it led to lower participation in the workforce by lower-income women but did not affect better-off ones.

What did surprise him, however, was that "welfare seems to have a relatively large impact on decision regarding family status."[53] More precisely he finds that an increase in welfare entitlement of $100 to $200 per year leads to a 5 per cent increase in the probability of being a lone parent, a 2 per cent increase in the probability of a child being born out of wedlock, and a 1 per cent increase in the probability of divorce.[54]

Similarly, there is evidence that high welfare rates discourage young men from working[55] and marrying[56] although whether this is because they are less interested in marrying or because they are less eligible marriage partners, or because there are welfare benefit disincentives, or some combination of the above, is unclear. Especially among those with the fewest skills to offer employers and who therefore receive the lowest levels of income, then, high levels of welfare not only discourage adults from working, they discourage them from marrying, while acting as an incentive for women to have children on their own in addition to not working.[57] The effects on men and women and children and families are devastating.

Education costs are often borne by the state, and social insurance, public spending, and state employment all help to tide people over job loss, unemployment, and recession. Not so many years ago, these would have been costs borne chiefly by the family. What hitherto had been seen as decisions of huge consequences for grandparents, parents, and children (i.e., whether or not to marry or to have children or to work) have come to appear more as mere personal (and private) preferences. And the stigma attached to not working or to being dependent has been gradually worn away as abandonment of the work norm becomes more common and the state becomes more willing to make up income lost through divorce or failure to marry in the first place.

If this view of the interaction between family and the welfare state is correct and if the values our parents transmit to us are the most important ones forming our character, then you might expect the evidence to show that those children raised in the absence of the welfare state would not have their work ethic much changed by the sudden appearance of a welfare state in their society. Because their approach to work was already set, as it were, the existence of newly available benefits would not change their behaviour much. On the other hand, we might think that the succeeding generation would have a very different view, as welfare dependency becomes "normalized" and as the economic incentives on parents to make sure their children acquire their work ethic are muted.

Such a generational difference in welfare state reliance is just what we find. One pair of researchers noted, "While the main increase in tax rates, as well as in the coverage and generosity of the benefit systems [of the welfare state] took place between the late 1940s and the late 1970s, clear indications of negative effects on work did not emerge until the 1980s and 1990s, i.e., with a considerable time lag."[58] The rise of extremely well-developed welfare systems in northwestern Europe has been shown to coincide with a fall in attitudes valuing work as the route to success in life. Of the forty-two countries in the 1998 World Values Survey, "the seven countries ranking the lowest in terms of the percentage of respondents who regard 'hard work' as a quality especially important for children to learn at home are advanced European welfare states." The countries include Denmark, Sweden, Finland, Norway, Netherlands, Austria, and the former West Germany.[59] Were he living in northern Europe today, Max Weber, the nineteenth-century German sociologist, likely could never have written *The Protestant Ethic and the Spirit of Capitalism*, a work about the importance of the work ethic, self-discipline, and sacrificing current pleasure for more important future goods.

The incentives associated with easily available state benefits, then, not only make parents less able to communicate to their children the importance of work, and make children less receptive to that message, but those same incentives also lessen the power of family ties and weaken the family as the chief means of passing values and traditions across the generations.

Remember that the traits and behaviours that confer success in work and life are, generally speaking, ones that must be acquired. This causes tension between parents and children because parents try to inculcate in their children values that will stand the children in good stead in later life, but whose importance will not seem evident immediately. Children prefer present enjoyment, parents worry about their future achievement.

When children are bound to their parents by economic ties as well as ties of affection and respect, both sides have a direct and material interest in making the relationship work. But when children can turn to the state to supply many things previously available only through family ties and obligations, and when the state is specifically constrained from attaching expectations of good behaviour in exchange for its aid, parent-child relations are powerfully altered. Not so long ago, parents of even modest means could often, through the threat of economic sanctions, rein in even adult children behaving destructively. But especially at the low end of the income scale the amounts of help that could be offered or withheld could be relatively small and therefore the economic levers those parents enjoyed in shaping the behaviour of their children were relatively few.

Now, with the state willing to fork over amounts of support that might well replace or even exceed such modest help, the shoe is on the other foot. It is now the grown-up children who can threaten with impunity to withhold affection, contact with grandchildren, and the thousand other little ways in which generations share the joys and burdens of growing older together. Attempts to establish high standards of behaviour, at least in some segments of the population, are sacrificed. Parents quickly learn that their authority is a tenuous one, and children quickly see that parents, unless they are strong-willed and clear-eyed, can easily be cowed by children's threats to call the state to their aid. Even those instruments of the state, such as teachers, judges, and police, on whom parents used to be able to rely to buttress and support their authority, their standards, and their expectations, are now often complicit with children in devaluing the coin of parental influence.

Forget the Village; It Takes Parents to Raise a Child

We return, then, to Aristotle. Home is the place we are first expected to act habitually as if we care about others and are prepared to restrain our appetites in the name of a greater good, namely, family life. To listen to many advocates for professional child care or early childhood education, you might be led to conclude that the notion of family as the most desirable place to raise a child is a quaint hold-over from a bygone era, belied by the dysfunction of many actual families and the damage they have done to vulnerable children through abuse and neglect.

Surely putting children in the hands of the "professionals," those with child-care certificates and education degrees and Ph.D.s in psychology, is vastly to be preferred to leaving them chiefly in the hands of amateur parents whose only qualification is the physical ability to reproduce. But to become preoccupied with the failings of some individual families, however distressing and painful, is to miss the strength of family as an institution for child-rearing, to mistake the exception for the average, the unusual for the trend.

> Children of divorce face higher probabilities of virtually every social ill one can think of relative to children from intact marriages, even when such marriages are "bad." Having a dad at home is important. Divorce is creating a large cohort of children with low human capital. What will happen to the[se] children when they become adults?
>
> John Richard and Doug Allen, *It Takes Two*

The best way to see this strength is, again, to contrast it with the alternatives. Formal child care or early childhood education or even elementary and secondary schools are staffed by well-meaning professionals whose investment in the success of any one child is necessarily limited. Even the most gifted teacher or child-care worker can give only a small part of their attention to knowing, understanding, and dealing with the needs of each child. And knowing that each child will deal with many professionals with a wide array of special knowledge and skills, both within any class or year and across the many years that children will spend in educational institutions, the responsibility each professional can feel for each child will necessarily be quite small.

Contrast this with parents and the relationship they have with their children. There will be no new class of children after recess, no new intake in the autumn, no hope of sloughing off difficult children on a colleague. Your children are yours; you live with them and get to know them intimately as complex individuals. And because you share a home together for twenty years or so, as opposed to a classroom for a few hours each day for a year, you not only have the biggest store of knowledge about them, their needs, and personalities, you also have the biggest investment in civilizing them. A child with no self-control in your classroom is merely a trial. At home it is misery-making, both while they are your dependants and later when you, as aged parents, might need to be able to rely on their goodwill and commitment to you.[60]

In other words, the buck stops at home in a way it can never quite do anywhere else. Only parents have the intimacy with their children and the investment in the outcome of their upbringing that makes them the indispensable guardians of their children's welfare. Only parents hear about their children's hopes and fears every day, about the scraped knees, the cruel remarks from other children, the scholastic successes, the sporting failures, the Halloween treats, and the secret Christmas or birthday desires. And the average parent is also quite observant about how their child compares to others in how they speak, their physical coordination, ability to deal with school work. They see the way their children behave with their friends and acquaintances, with their brothers and sisters, with older children, and with adults. No other adult can have so comprehensive a view of a child as his or her parents.

Nor can any other adults see their self-esteem as so bound up with the success of a particular child as its parents. Teachers and daycare workers can boast about the successes of a few of their charges and be silent about the failures, while parents have a much more limited field and much more at stake over a longer period.

As one author noted, with teachers and school administrators, if there is a poor fit between a teacher and a child, the reaction will often be "Oh well, perhaps it will be better next year with a different teacher." But for the child, a year of forgone educational success may be disastrous. Parents cannot be so cavalier about their limited brood.

Finally, parents have the most interest of any adults in the later success of their children. Even though state and private pensions have undermined to some extent the reliance of aged parents on their children, the personal care and attention of children for their parents can no more be fully replaced by institutional care than the personal attention of parents can be replaced by daycare centres or schools. In both cases the personal attention only family can provide can be usefully supplemented by professionals, but they are hardly perfect substitutes, or even close equivalents. And even though pension provisions are now better than they have ever been before, and even though the rate of poverty among the elderly is therefore lower than in the population as a whole, many children still make major contributions to the mental and physical comfort and well-being of their parents. The future is a murky and surprising place, and the rational person would hope to have children around as insurance against all kinds of possibilities, such as outliving one's savings or unexpected reform of pension schemes that rely on the shifting generosity of taxpayers.

Family and Love Stage a Comeback

Across the ideological spectrum there is, happily, an increasing awareness of the unique and irreplaceable role played by the family in the life of children.[61] The

Brookings Institution's Isabel Sawhill was one example from the United States cited in a previous chapter. In a prominent Canadian example,[62] John Richards and Douglas Allen write, "Marriage is an efficient institution. Were there a more efficient means to raise children, marriage would not have lasted over the millennia as the primary form of organisation for procreation and social structure."[63] And as Sawhill's and Allen and Richards's data all show, the rise in child poverty in recent decades has been the direct outcome of the state making it easier to escape the obligations of marriage and insinuating itself as a highly imperfect substitute breadwinner and enforcer of child support orders.[64] It is the undeniably unsatisfactory performance of the state as substitute father (having released many real fathers from many of the traditional responsibilities that accompanied that role) that no doubt has caused many a potential mother either to forgo having children or to limit their exposure to social and economic disaster by having as few as possible, and certainly fewer than the number they tell pollsters they would like to have.

Love I have not mentioned. I wanted to spend some time on the institutional, practical, and very down-to-earth reasons that parents alone can, on the whole, be expected to make greater investments in their children than any other adults. These incentives in no way depend on love.

Yet love is also intimately tied to family. Not every family is characterized by love, but most are, and most parents say that making their marriage succeed and being good parents are the two most important goals they have in life.[65]

Suppose Canadians wanted more children and thus a more balanced population, and wanted to reward and not punish loving behaviour.[66] To achieve these goals we would need to think more about how to support and encourage families and less about how to make divorce easier. At our behest governments have taken the opposite tack over the past few decades and have, on balance, caused more harm than good for men, women, and especially children. And in a future in which children with education, good character, and sound values will be one of our most precious resources, the state has succeeded in making this happy outcome much less likely than when mums and dads were in charge together.[67]

How Marriage Changes Adults

Marriage and the family that results change the behaviour of husbands and wives compared to their unmarried counterparts. There are economic and social aspects to this difference that are well documented, but the place to start this discussion is with the undocumented and possibly undocumentable because the differences are rooted in feelings such as love and deeply private understandings.

Marriage matters because husbands and wives matter to each other in ways that cannot be exhaustively enumerated and that are demonstrably different from the way that unmarried cohabiting partners, for example, matter to each other. On the whole, married people tell researchers that they like and trust one another and are committed to each other.[68] And because getting married involves an enactment of that commitment, a visible public exchange of promises and mutual commitment, it helps to increase the likelihood that those promises and that commitment will be honoured. Marriage is therefore an institution in which love can and does flourish because love requires trust, but individuals are weak and sometimes find the constraints of a relationship onerous. The spirit is willing but the flesh is weak.

Since the greatest human achievements, however, take time to come to fruition, they require us to find ways to bind ourselves to long-term goals even when our short-term selfish interest draws us in other directions. Marriage is thus another institution suited to human nature, in that it allows our better self to bind our weaker self to a larger personal and social good: the founding and nurturing of our families. Family as an institution echoes the great themes that this book concerns itself with: the importance of char-

Married and single men who are not in school are differentiated by five labour market attributes. They [married men] have higher wages, are more likely to be in the labour force, less likely to be unemployed because they had quit their job, have lower unemployment rates, are more likely to be full-time and are less likely to be part-year workers. In each and every dimension the married men have stronger labour market attachment than the unmarried.... The wages for the married men are slightly higher. For example, married men with just 12 years of education between 20 and 24 years of age and 25 and 29 have 11 and 14 per cent higher wages than their respective single counter-parts. The differences in labour force attachment are indeed dramatic. Single men 20 to 24 with this amount of education are more than three times as likely to be out of the labour force as married men. If in the labor force, a single man of that age and educational attainment is 75 per cent more likely to be unemployed than a married man with similar traits. Similarly, the fraction of such men working full year full-time if married is almost 40 per cent greater, 70 per cent for the married, compared to 50 per cent for the single. A single man 20 to 24 with just 12 years of education is 50 per cent more likely than a comparable married man to be unemployed because he quit his last job. Age 25 to 29, he is more than twice as likely.

George Akerlof, *Men without Children*

acter and responsibility for self, and the difficulty of disciplining our immediate desires to allow slow-maturing goals of inestimably greater import to take root and bear fruit. Family builds character and expresses great intentions across time, especially insofar as it is an institution where parents invest in each other and in their children, pooling resources to allow the greatest development possible of all the family's members.

But is there evidence for this claim that married couples have different attitudes and behave differently toward each other and their children compared to cohabiting couples?

Happily, the evidence concurs with a view that our grandmothers would have regarded as perfectly self-evident. In other words, just like the value of work and the dangers of dependency, it is another instance where we had to abandon tradition for its value to become evident.

Living common-law is a statement of a different kind compared to the statement made by marriage. It is a statement of absence of commitment, that the relationship will last just as long as it is convenient to both the partners.

That is why, for example, much of the mythology that surrounds common-law relationships is not borne out in the facts. Common-law couples often think of the relationship as a kind of "test drive" to see if they are suited to marriage (a wonderful image if you are the potential car buyer, as one wag put it, but a terrible one if you think of yourself as the car ...). But the reality is that marriages that follow common-law unions are less successful (in the sense of being more divorce-prone) than marriages where the couple did not cohabit before marriage.[69] Cohabiting is the institutionalization of a non-married relationship, where each party is acutely aware of what is theirs and what belongs to the other, not of building and sharing goods the relationship alone makes possible. And one of the most common sources of violence to both women and their children is unmarried cohabiting boyfriends. In fact, so great is the difference that marriage makes that a child's biological father, living common-law with the child's mother, is more likely to abuse the child than a man who marries the child's mother and assumes the father's role, even though he is not the child's biological parent.[70]

While there has been much discussion in recent years, then, about how legislation and the courts have made cohabiting more and more like marriage, with most of the legal obligations that married people undertake and protections they enjoy, I would argue that what has happened is really the reverse: through legally effortless no-fault divorce and the end of the social and other stigma attaching to divorce, especially where children are present, we have made being married more and more like cohabiting.[71] Part of the point of marriage is that, facing a

binding commitment that it is hard to escape, one is choosier about one's partner. The qualities one values in choosing them will be different because trust,
mutual confidence, and deep commitment will be sounder foundations on which
to build. Women especially will find this to be true. After all, it is they who are taking the biggest risk if the couple has children, since the chances are great they
will be raising them alone and in poor economic circumstances if the marriage
does not succeed.[72]

Easy divorce, high divorce rates, various forms of state-funded assistance to
lone parents, higher levels of child support following divorce, and greater economic opportunities for women, however, are just some of the factors that have
encouraged people to see marriage as a level of commitment much more akin
to living together than to traditional marriage. The skill with which people pick
partners and the support that they used to enjoy in this from their wider family has declined.[73] By removing many of the consequences of poor choices (in
other words, by lowering the cost of choosing mates badly and for the wrong
reasons and entering the marriage relationship in the wrong frame of mind), we
have made such poor choices more common. The fact that married people in
Canada are so overwhelmingly committed to the health of their marriage and
doing a good job together as parents is strong evidence that marriage is no mere
piece of paper, nor solely a legal agreement. Instead, marriage arises out of a
deep human need to which every society has attached legal and social buttresses,
not to trap people in bad marriages, but rather to help support people through
the moments when the effort might not seem worth it, even though the long-
term emotional and economic benefits are usually significant.

We have already seen that families with two married parents present are the
most economically, socially, and emotionally successful and robust of places in
which to raise children, but part of the reason that is true is the changes in behaviour that marriage makes possible among the parents. For example, fathers
who are married to the mothers of their children work harder and longer, not
because they are unhappy and want to get out of the house (married people
consistently report themselves as happier than singles and common-law couples[74]), but because they think it is their responsibility to do so.[75] Thus, while
many feminists see the hand of patriarchy and sexism in the earnings differentials between men and women, they neglect to see the significance of the earnings differentials *between men*, and one of the most powerful explanations for
those differences is that men who have promised to look after their wives and
their children take that promise seriously and work hard to honour it.[76]

In Canada in 2007, for example, among men under 25, the share of married
men in the workforce was nearly 90 per cent, whereas among the unmarried it

was 65.6 per cent; the respective unemployment rates were 7.5 per cent and 12.8 per cent.[77]

Canadian survey data on the values of married parents versus singles and common-law couples confirm this difference. Among married couples the two values they hold most dear are to "maintain a good stable marriage" and to "be a good parent." In other words, these are other-oriented values.[78] Marriage expands who the "self" is, and married Canadians in very large majorities clearly take seriously their vows to love their partner as themselves and to count their partner's good as their own.

For unmarried Canadians, by contrast, the single most important value was the self-regarding one of "having a job that gives you personal fulfillment." That was one of the top two priorities for 54 per cent of unmarried Canadians. For married Canadians, by contrast, only 23 per cent made it one of their top two priorities.[79] In other words, much as work is a source of fulfilment for everyone, married people value a *personally fulfilling* job much less than they do maintaining their marriage and being good parents. Their position requires them to make sacrifices and compromises for the good of their family, compromises they are very happy to make; their fulfilment simply comes via another route. Similarly, making lots of money falls down the priority list as parents adjust their work commitments to be consistent with their overriding priorities of being committed to each other and to their children.

Thanks for Nothing

It is a good thing, by the way, that making lots of money falls down the priority list when you marry because your reward for forming a family unit, forgoing some income, sacrificing in order to promote the interests of your spouse and children, and expending the enormous effort to civilize those children so that they can be in their turn productive members of society, is that the taxman takes a bigger bite out of your income compared to a family or common-law couple where both work. Economist Jack Mintz sums the facts up nicely:

> Consider two Ontario families, each with two children—one with two working parents earning $35,000 each and the other with one working parent earning $70,000. Assume the only credits used are for basic personal and child exemptions: The two-earner family pays $10,364 in 2007 federal and Ontario tax while the one-earner family pays $14,165 in tax, or 37% more. With rent, mortgage payments, car lease obligations, food, clothing and other demands, the additional $315 monthly penalty is a burden on the single-earner family.[80]

Better, then, from the taxman's point of view, that both parents work. The price the state puts on being married just keeps on rising.

How to Have It All

As women have entered the labour force in larger numbers and worked more hours and weeks over the last forty years or so, women's attitudes toward the work-life balance has changed. It used to be that women were happier than men with the work-life balance, as they spent more time with their children and less at work. Now that women are in the workforce to an even greater extent than they were, however, they are less happy than men with their work-life balance, and their level of satisfaction on this point has been declining.[81]

The now-conventional explanation is that women are victims of sexism and discrimination that demands ever greater work effort from them while they get less and less support from men in return. But this explanation fits the facts far less well than another one: that women prefer to spend more time with their children than they do working, but that economic insecurity occasioned by the increasing unreliability or unavailability of marriage is forcing them to work more than they wish to or than they believe is good for their children. In other words, the issue is not that sexism gives women a double workload compared to men. Rather it is a growing lack of trust between men and women that means women are increasingly anxious that they dare not rely on marriage to provide the economic security they feel is the foundation that might allow them to spend the time they wish with their children.[82]

Easy divorce and other factors listed above, while undoubtedly liberating some women from bad marriages, have also made good marriages less dependable and made women less able to trust even good husbands. In fact, the ease with which marriages can be dissolved seems to create perverse incentives in which husbands and wives, sensing the impermanence of marriage, do not invest in the marriage or their spouse as much as they would if marriage were regarded as more permanent. Instead, the incentives are for each spouse to invest primarily in their market-earning capacity (i.e., their career): "a spouse who thinks the marriage may be in trouble has every incentive not to put money into common assets but instead to invest in his own or her own career."[83] Houses and stocks and pensions and children may all end up being left behind, but one's career is indisputably one's own, even if the income from it must be divided, at least for a time.

Underlying this line of thought concerning the desires of women for more children but the disincentives contained within a regime of easy divorce, of course, is the following heretical proposition: there might be a fruitful division of labour between men and women with regard to working versus child-rearing. Men might, on the whole, actually function best with a balance skewed toward work, while women might, on the whole, prefer a balance skewed to rearing their children. Marriage, in other words, when it is functioning as it should, unleashes the economically productive power of men to an unprecedented degree[84] and unleashes the fecundity and maternal instincts of women to a similar extent.

This is a proposition for which I will be pilloried, for it is *verboten* now to suggest that men and women might be suited *by their nature* to different social, economic, and reproductive roles, and it will doubtless not save me if I say that no one is proposing that women be forced into child-bearing roles or in any way prevented or discouraged from working. Rather, I am suggesting that women should be given *more* choices, and the one that seems to be most appealing to them based on their expressed preferences and observed behaviour is that they would like to work less, spend more time with their children, and have more children in total. It is a side benefit that such behaviour is in our interest as a society.

This argument in no way implies that women should not work if they wish to, or that they should earn less than men for the same amount of work of comparable quality; it only means that women themselves are signalling their deep dissatisfaction with having to work so much when they want to be able to have more children[85] and to spend more time with them when they do.

Indeed, as Harvard's James Q. Wilson has observed,[86] motherhood is probably more compatible with working outside the home than at any time in human history. Women need to spend far less time pregnant in order to achieve their ideal number of children because infant mortality has fallen to virtually negligible levels, so no "extra" children have to be born as an insurance policy against child death. Contraception and abortion give huge (albeit imperfect) control over fertility, making the timing of births more manageable. Combine this with the effects of modern technology and universal free public schooling, and mothers with even minimally competent management skills can quite successfully balance child-rearing and work outside the home if they wish, especially if they are married— for marriage, as already remarked, allows for a high degree of specialization within the family, far more than in other kinds of domestic relationships such as common-law or lone parenthood.

Breaking up Is Hard to Do

Just as being married changes people's behaviour, so too does getting unmarried, in the sense of divorce. A woman once could reasonably expect that if she married a man he would attend to the material needs of her and their children throughout their lives. Today women look at divorce rates and tell themselves that however much they might wish that to be true, they cannot count on it. They thus invest more than they really wish to in a career to gain a measure of income security beyond a husband, in the sense of working longer than they really prefer, and delaying having babies until it is physically difficult or even dangerous. Nobel laureate Gary Becker, who really started the modern economic study of marriage and the family, remarks,

> Fertility is reduced when divorce becomes more likely, because child care is more difficult after a marriage dissolves. There is evidence that couples who anticipate relatively high probabilities of divorce do have fewer children. The labor force participation of women is also affected when divorce rates increase, not only because divorced women participate more fully, but also because married women will participate more as protection against the financial adversity of a subsequent divorce.[87]

For men the experience is, of course, somewhat different. Once, a man knew that he was the main if not sole source of support for his family. His role and value to the family were clear and assured. And while no one is so naïve as to think there was no sex outside marriage, marriage was a far surer source of sexual satisfaction than any other. Now women are often largely economically self-sufficient, thus reducing the economic value of a husband, especially at the low end of the income scale, and the state is ready and willing to step in and play the role of breadwinner, however badly and inadequately it may do so. Sex is relatively easy to come by, and, if experience is anything to go by, if the marriage falls apart, access to the children may well be difficult and capricious and the economic burden crushing, especially if the father starts another family with a different woman.

The amazing thing today is not that the divorce rates are so high, but that anyone gets married at all.

What Do Women (and Men) Really Want?

If you actually ask women what they want (as we are so often encouraged to do), among other things they express a desire for stronger relationships, less time at work, more time with their children, and more children over-all.[88] This era of allegedly greater freedom for women to make their own choices has resulted in their getting less of what they say they want.[89] And the reason is clearly at least in part related to the decline of marriage, for many of the things women want are just impractical in the absence of marriage. Other forms of relationship simply do not perform the same role for women, and the generosity of the welfare state seems to deprive certain groups of women of all that as well as of the most promising route to self-reliance and independence.

As we have already seen, sometimes the best way to understand the most important functions of traditional institutions is to see what happens to people in their absence. If we want to see how marriage can affect the lives of women and mothers, we might start by looking at how they fare under different forms of relationship to spouses and the state.

> To the extent that increases in welfare payments encourage individuals, and women in particular, to choose lifestyles that do not provide the same institutional protection, they may actually worsen their economic position.... If a 20-year-old woman opts to live as a common-law spouse or as a single parent in order to capture higher welfare benefits, human capital investments in herself or her partner are likely to be too risky given the lack of legal protection and bargaining power over such investments when not married. Similarly, since welfare reduces the incentive to participate in the labour force, welfare recipients suffer further reductions in human capital relative to higher income groups. Hence, a poverty gap is created and exacerbated by increases in welfare payments.
>
> Doug Allen, *Welfare and the Family in Canada*

Single mothers who marry, for instance, are very likely to escape dependence on social welfare by doing so. The same is true for single women without children. Getting married means, other things being equal, becoming part of a self-reliant family unit; it means moving up. On the other hand, becoming a divorcée or a divorcée with children reduces the chances of getting off welfare, "sometimes to extraordinarily great degrees," to quote one set of researchers.[90] And the more generous the welfare rates, the more they act as an alternative to working and therefore to gaining the experience and skills that improve one's value in the marketplace, especially for single women and lone mothers. According to the same researchers, raising the welfare rates by $1,000 annually raises welfare dependency as much as a 1 percentage point rise in unemployment. It works in reverse as well. Welfare reform in the 1990s in Ontario that resulted in an effective decline in benefits of approximately $5,000 per annum was credited with a big decline in welfare dependency in the second half of that decade.

Marriage is key. Mothers who have never been married are much more likely to be on welfare and much less likely to be in the workforce than married mothers, even when you take account of age, education levels, and wages.[91] Worryingly, during precisely the period when we were ramping up the size and generosity of the welfare state in Canada, we were drawing more and more young mothers into dependence on welfare rather than into marriage, where their economic and job prospects are much better. In fact, between 1973 and 1991, the share of lone mothers who had never been married more than doubled from 22 per cent to 46 per cent. At the same time the percentage of lone mothers reliant on welfare as their primary source of income climbed to over 40 per cent, while a mere 6 per cent of married couples with children had welfare as their main income.[92]

The State Loves Me, It Loves Me Not, It Loves Me, It Loves Me Not ...

If the conventional wisdom of the last forty years is allowed to prevail, this state of affairs poses no problem because welfare creates no dependence, it is never abused, and no one is ever on it willingly. Certainly no one should ever suggest that being in a relationship with a man would be a superior alternative to being in a family relationship with the state, which is far more respectful of the autonomy and choices of individuals and never beats or abuses women or children. Any argument to the contrary is an unfeeling attack on the most vulnerable and therefore means the person making that argument is a social regressive who does not deserve an audience. Alas, however, it is those who defend the heavy reliance by young mothers on the welfare system who do the most to condemn them to social and economic isolation and vulnerability.

Marriage, from an institutional point of view, is designed to increase the bargaining power of the partner who is more vulnerable, especially where that vulnerability has been created by the marriage relationship.

Think about the wife who works as a server to pay for her husband to attend medical or law school. She sacrifices income and possibly professional satisfaction because as a couple they have decided that they can improve their family situation by getting him a highly valued professional qualification. But if, once qualified, he decides to up sticks and take up with someone else, all the value of the sacrifice the wife has made is captured by the departing husband, who takes his higher income with him, while she is left with the costs, particularly where she might have invested in building her own career if she and her husband had not decided to maximize their collective income by investing in his education. Ditto for women who forgo some or all of a professional life in order to stay at home and raise the children. In order to feel safe in doing so, the vulnerable spouse needs to feel that the marriage tie protects that investment and prevents her vulnerability from being exploited.

No-fault divorce eliminates precisely that protection. Where there is a fault-based approach, the party who wants to maintain the marriage has powerful leverage, more ways to protect her (because it is usually a her) investment in the relationship and the family at the expense of her career. When either party can simply apply to have the marriage cancelled because it has now become inconvenient, it becomes vastly riskier for spouses to make this kind of investment in each other or in their children because they must maintain their value in the marketplace instead. Or else, where the economic value a spouse brings to the household might be relatively low to begin with, they might simply prefer reliance on welfare where benefits are high enough and never marry at all, or they might live common-law to maximize benefits by avoiding clawbacks for married couples.[93]

Some might see a contradiction here. If our concern is with tight labour markets looming on the horizon, surely we should be finding ways to get more women into the workforce, not with encouraging stronger marriage so that women may feel freer to have more children.

Aside from the fact that I am arguing for more options for women, including making it easier to combine work and child-rearing, however, this criticism misses an important point: marriage is a partnership between men and women, and *both* parties are changed by it in ways that matter, including in the context of work.

As already noticed, married men work harder than unmarried men. Moreover, young unmarried men in Canada have got a poor record of working and looking for work, whereas the participation of young women has been rising steadily. Men have proven increasingly unattractive partners at the low end of the income scale[94] (where women have been drawn to the big-spender state), whereas higher up the income scale women have been drawn more to their careers as the means to guarantee their economic future. As a result, women are indeed working harder and in larger numbers, but having fewer babies, and expressing unhappiness at both. On the other hand, we are getting less work out of men.

If we could match the ambitions and expressed preferences of men and women for the right work-life balance, the right number of children, and the right legal protections for vulnerable marriage partners, we might well get the trifecta: we'd get more work out of Canadians, our standard of living would rise, and we'd have more children, to boot. And the bonus on that particular winning ticket might well be that we were able to love each other more as the desires of the human heart and the institutions of our society pulled together rather than being at cross-purposes.

Beyond Marriage: Family across the Generations

The rise of the overbearing state has affected more than just the way we raise our children, how many children we have, and whether we marry, live common-law, or become dependent on various kinds of transfers.

A further central family function usurped by the state was to look after the aged when they were too old to work; this is another fascinating area where the imperial ambitions of the state have wrought long-term changes no one expected and that make sustaining the state's current size almost impossible as our population ages. Government's attempts to take over the functions of the family carried within them the seeds of their own destruction.

One of the reasons that people in earlier generations had children was to provide them with security in their old age. Parents brought children into the world, reared them, equipped them to be productive, and then expected to be looked after by them when they (the parents) became too old to work. Many children equalled a comfortable retirement.

We got rid of this necessity because of an illusion that the baby boom created for us. Societies with growing populations can pay social security–type benefits to today's retirees out of today's tax revenues, on the grounds that the next generation's benefits will also be paid by *their* children's taxes, and so on indefinitely. This is known as pay-as-you-go, or PAYGO. PAYGO is essentially cash in, cash out.

PAYGO means the socialization of the risks of old age. Whereas in the past children contributed to the welfare of their individual parents, under compulsory state-funded PAYGO retirement schemes, every child is jointly responsible with all other members of their generation for some of the retirement income of every adult of their parents' generation. That state-enforced responsibility of the children's, however, has no counterpart for their elders. Members of their parents' generation can and do benefit from that security without doing their share, which was to pay the costs of having and rearing enough children of their own to take their place in the workforce.

As Canadians become increasingly sceptical that they can rely on tax-financed benefits to see them through their old age, their retirement behaviour will certainly change. They will work longer (as is already happening). The political resistance of the productive part of the population to paying taxes to support an older generation that broke the social contract by having too few children to support PAYGO will become intense. Given our poor productivity record, the only way the current PAYGO schemes can be supported is through crushing levels of taxation on the relatively shrinking productive population. And open borders and relatively easy emigration for our most valuable workers mean that even if what the British call the wrinklies have the votes, their depredations will be constrained by other realities. A goose driven to escape across the border lays you no golden eggs.

While PAYGO works brilliantly when the population is growing and limps along reasonably satisfactorily when the population is stable, however, it becomes a crushing burden on the rising generation when their parents choose not to have enough children to replace themselves in the workforce. Canada's baby bust threatens the sustainability of many social programs based on PAYGO principles. We have already had to shift the Canada Pension Plan from a wholly PAYGO approach to one where we are now investing a part of current premiums in order to build up a fund out of which future pensions can be partly paid. But many other programs, such as medicare, whose resources will be sorely taxed by aging, remain *pure* PAYGO programs today.

Similarly, recent research from the United States demonstrates[95] that as the tax burden to fund social benefits (such as pensions) rises, there is a fall in fertility. Nobel laureate Gary Becker has argued that social security taxes tend to reduce the amount of resources children give to their aged parents.[96] In other words, as the state seeks to crowd out the functions of the family, it literally crowds out the family itself. As Canada will need to boost, not cut further, the number of babies its people bring into the world, understanding that high rates of taxation reduce the size of the future population will put a real crimp in the trend to replace the family with the state.

Suppose that, under all these pressures, the state rolls back its ambitions, and Canadians in turn roll back their expectations of what the state can do for them. Family is almost certain to fill at least some of the gap. Philip Longman argues, "The absolute population of Europe and Japan may fall dramatically, but the remaining population will, by a process similar to survival of the fittest, be adapted to a new environment in which no one can rely on government to replace the family...."[97] And on current trends, Canada will not be far behind.

Nationalism and Welfarism in Quebec and the Consequences for Canada

The place to start is by recognizing that the "Quebec model," associated with the Quiet Revolution, is neither a model nor exclusive to Quebec. In fact it is the Quebec version of a generalized politicization of society taking place in Western societies over the last 40 years. Europe has led the way, and Quebec has only pushed a bit further than the Europeans its commitment to collectivism, corporatism, dirigisme and statism. [Author's translation]

JEAN-LUC MIGUÉ, *LA RÉVOLUTION TRANQUILLE, UN TOURNANT POUR LE PIRE*

There was nothing inevitable in Canada's response to the wave of workers that washed over us as the Boomers strode onto the scene. We could have stuck with our relatively laissez-faire approach, not interfered too much in labour markets, not made benefits a lot more generous, not ramped up debt and taxes and public-sector employment overmuch, not pulled so many people into dependence.

Other countries with similar demographic challenges, such as the United States and Australia, took this route, and while they experienced some unemployment, it was no worse than Canada's and on the whole much better. The economy in those countries was quite able to put most people to work. The United States also experimented with liberalized welfare, but rapidly found the experience unsatisfactory. Welfare reform came early to many U.S. states compared to our leading edge in Alberta and Ontario, and President Bill Clinton signed a far-reaching national welfare reform bill in the mid-nineties. The United States never grossed up public-sector employment to the extent we did, nor did the tax burden or the size of the state ever approach the levels we quickly reached.

Why did we break ranks and turn our backs on our own past and values, values that had nevertheless served us well? Because, in a word, we were frightened.

Quebec chose that moment in history to pursue a nationalist strategy that had the intended effect of building its constitutional and political negotiating power within Confederation. Unfortunately for both Quebec and Canada, it also had the largely unintended effect of undermining Quebec's own economy while creating a convenient scapegoat for its troubles in the shape of the rest of the country. Out of its largely self-inflicted economic wounds Quebec found additional fodder for repeated national crises and the battle for the hearts and minds of Quebeckers. The chief arms in that battle were transfers, welfare, massive public employment, and pseudo-work.

Moreover, the demonstration effect of Quebec's behaviour was powerful: other provinces followed in Quebec's footsteps, lobbying to get "their share" of federal largesse and expanding their provincial apparatus in response. In other words, the emergence of a big-government, social welfare state in Canada was not the manifestation of a more left-wing country to the north of the United States; doubtless the general state-friendly zeitgeist in the Western world played its part, but was more importantly an *ex post facto* rationalization. As Cy Gonick's remark, quoted earlier, to the effect that the United States by 1964 had discovered poverty whereas Canada had not shows, nationally we were still the traditional Canada mistrustful of high taxes, big spending, and dependence on the state.

But in Quebec the growth of the state was underway already on a massive scale: in part as catch-up to the rest of the country, in part as an expression of a desire by the French-speaking majority to bring more of Quebec society under its political control, and in part as an effort to find work for the burgeoning wave of young French-speaking workers. That started a process of growth of government not just within Quebec but across the country, as federal transfers were ramped up everywhere, even though their real justification was to combat the appeal of millenarian nationalism in Quebec. The other provinces simply sat back and let Quebec do the work of winkling billions out of Ottawa. They were then happy to spend the money, especially since its arrival coincided with the big rise in the workforce. They now had big money and a social problem to spend it on.

Be Careful What You Wish For:
The Consequences of the Nationalist Strategy

There can be little doubt that one of the side effects of the rise of Quebec nationalism was a loss of economic confidence and a slow leakage of capital, both financial and human, from the province. The policies of successive governments of Quebec were not disastrous—merely deeply damaging. Private-sector investment dried up; old natural resource industries declined but found few New Economy replacements. But because of the language barrier, moving somewhere else was often not an option for French-speakers, or at least seemed far more personally costly than for people in other parts of the country.[1] The economy did not die but simply became increasingly arthritic, while provinces to the west outstripped Quebec in economic and population growth.

Other jurisdictions faced with a similar relative decline might normally have sought to reverse policy course. Not Quebec, however, for it had to hand two far more comforting explanations of their failure to keep up. On the one hand, *c'était la faute aux Anglais*; if only Quebec had control of all the levers of economic and fiscal power, the performance gap with other North American economies would rapidly close. On the other hand, there was the idea that a lower standard of living was simply the price one paid for the moral superiority of a more caring community committed to both justice for its members and the preservation of French as the symbol of belonging to that community.

Whichever of these mutually contradictory explanations one chooses, thus did a policy-induced economic decline, coupled with a post-war baby boom and the growth of the welfare state it brought in its train, generate a powerful strategy for Quebec in its relations with the rest of Canada. The "neverendum" was born: the constantly repeated threat to leave brought a shower of benefits financed by the rest of the country to "compensate" for this chronic economic underperformance. Indeed, the abandonment by Ottawa of its traditional rather laissez-faire economic and social policy was not the result of a loss of faith in the economic efficacy of that policy, although that may have been the rationalization. Instead, Ottawa came, as we saw earlier, to recognize the political and constitutional efficacy of the social justice state, throwing economic caution to the winds in a headlong rush to defeat Quebec separatism by outbidding the Quebec government for the fickle allegiance of Quebeckers, no matter what the cost in social injustice and loss of national economic performance.

On reading this account of the history of the economic and social outcomes produced by fifty years of rivalry between Ottawa and Quebec City for the loyalty of Quebeckers, the bellows of outrage from the nationalist movement in Quebec will be deafening. Few articles of faith have proven so enduring in Quebec as the notion that the economic manifestation of nationalism, the so-called Quebec Inc., has proven a remarkable success worthy of emulation rather than sceptical criticism.

That has started to change, as the declaration of the so-called *Lucides*[2] and the mild economic liberalism of Mario Dumont and l'Action démocratique and even Jean Charest's tax cuts and hesitant welfare reform attest. But this questioning of the predominant role of the state remains so far a minority taste.

In assessing the success of the Quebec model of economic and social progress, we have to know what its chief elements are. I would argue that we are at a minimum, looking at a government-driven economic strategy premised on the notion that government planners are well placed to identify those industries and sectors in which Quebec enjoys some competitive advantage, and then ensuring that those sectors have the support they need from both the government and other economic agents within Quebec society. That, in turn, requires that business and labour be represented at the *table de concertation*[3] where large policy decisions are made and the economic energy of the entire society directed toward the appropriate ends.[4] And because such politically dominated economic decision-making has to be subject to some high degree of popular support, economic decisions are often justified as somehow contributing to the "solidarity" of Quebeckers. In exchange for the right to work and invest in the province, high levels of taxation are imposed on profits and wages,

> A simple chart of the economic growth of the Ontario and Quebec economies would show that both economies have largely evolved in parallel between the 1870s and the mid-1960s. It is only from the 1960s that the Quebec economy starts showing signs of growing at a lower rate than Ontario. It is therefore difficult to find evidence in these economic growth series that the shackles of the traditional society and of the Duplessis regime have been debilitating for Quebec or that the Quiet Revolution has catalyzed accelerated economic growth.
>
> Gilles Paquet, What if There Had Been No Quiet Revolution in Quebec ...

and the money so raised is used by the social justice state to make sure no one is left behind by economic progress. Similarly, rules are imposed about the language of work, so that contributing to the linguistic solidarity of a French-speaking Quebec is equally a condition of participating in Quebec Inc.

At least that is the idealized mythology put about by those in Quebec who have derived rich benefits from Quebec Inc. If we measure Quebec Inc. by its actual results rather than what its friends would like us to believe about it, I believe an altogether less flattering portrait emerges, a portrait foreshadowed in the review of the nationalist strategy laid out in an earlier chapter.

Far from being a model that has secured the economic success of Quebec, Quebec Inc. has created the conditions in which people and capital have fled the province, in which population renewal through both births and immigration has faltered, in which governments politicize economic decision-making for short-term electoral gain at the expense of long-term progress, and in which powerful and essentially parasitic interest groups organize to capture large benefits from the bloated Quebec state while spreading the costs over not just the entire society of Quebec but the entire country of Canada.

One of those costs is the creation of massive unemployment that can be masked only by equally massive welfare programs and pseudo-work in both the public and private sectors. Another is the destruction of the work ethic in large segments of the Quebec population and a vigorous attempt to substitute the state for many of the traditional support roles played by the family. Quebec Inc. has impoverished Quebeckers while ironically making the millenarian nationalist dream of a sustainable and prosperous French-speaking state in North America a distant prospect. By undermining individual commitment to work and family, promoting heavy dependence on government-funded transfers and services, and promoting the impression that the most aggressive interest groups can expect the biggest rewards from the state, Quebec Inc. has changed the character of Quebeckers for the worse.

This is a serious indictment. Can it be sustained? I believe that it can. In doing so, let us ask ourselves what sort of tests we might apply to see if Quebec Inc. has produced a secure and prosperous society with high levels of opportunity.

We can begin by setting Quebec's overall economic performance in context, remembering that part of what justifies the vast expansion of the state, and the state's role as "directing mind" of the Quebec economy, is the superior economic results that it should produce compared to other, relatively more laissez-faire jurisdictions in North America.

In 2004 only three North American jurisdictions had a poorer ability than Quebec to generate wealth for its citizens (i.e., GDP, per person): those economic powerhouses of Arkansas, West Virginia, and Mississippi, three of the very poorest U.S. states.[5] While Canada's economic performance, both in GDP growth and in productivity, has been poor relative to the United States over much of the last fifty years, Quebec's performance has lagged behind almost all other peer jurisdictions and helps in large part to explain why Canada's overall performance has not been better. In that same year, 2004, for example, Quebec's GDP per person stood at $35,117 or 13 per cent less than Canada as a whole (at $40,351) and 16 per cent less than Ontario at $41,703. For more than twenty years, Quebec has been unable to close a persistent real per person GDP gap compared to the rest of the country of about 11 percentage points. Productivity too has lagged: between 1987 and 2004, for instance, productivity per hour worked in Quebec has grown at an annual rate of 1.27 per cent, versus 1.44 per cent in Ontario.[6] And this is no mere continuation of a gap that has always existed between Quebec and Ontario. The gap emerged and widened over the decades after 1960.[7]

This was all comprehensively documented in Jean-Luc Migué's book *Étatisme et déclin du Québec: Bilan de la révolution tranquille*, which was a bestseller in Quebec in 1999. In an op-ed in *La Presse*, Migué summarized his findings:

> Since the end of the 19th century until the end of the 1950s, Quebec enjoyed strong economic growth, which paralleled that of Ontario. This increase in wealth has never been reproduced since. It is therefore true that the Quiet Revolution was a turning point in the economic and social evolution of Quebec, but it was a turning point for the worse. Whether one measures the decline by the relative decline of investments, by demographic change (rapid decline in the birth rate and recruitment of immigrants), by job growth, or by income per person, Quebec has lost ground relative to its North American partners.[8]

Productivity per person, which is the real measure of the strength of the economic base of any society, is consistently 17 to 20 per cent lower in Quebec than in Ontario, and Ontario is a laggard with regard to comparable competitor jurisdictions in North America. In fact, of sixteen peer jurisdictions in North America that include Quebec, Ontario, Michigan, Texas, and Georgia, Quebec comes significantly behind them *all* in its ability to put all its factors of production (i.e., capital, labour, and technology) to work at the highest levels of productivity. Ontario, against whom Quebec usually benchmarks itself, performs better, at thirteenth out of sixteen, but is hardly a paragon—a topic to which we shall return.[9]

Total wealth production in Quebec (overall GDP) has also languished over much of the past decades. Between 1981 and 2006, average annual growth in Quebec's real (i.e., inflation-adjusted) GDP was 2.3 per cent, compared to 3 per cent in the rest of Canada. The cumulative effect of such a gap is devastating. For Quebec, this represents a 77.6 per cent rise in real GDP over that quarter century, in contrast to 109.9 per cent in the rest of the country. Quebec's real GDP accounted for only 20.5 per cent of the Canadian total in 2006, down nearly 3 full percentage points from 1981 and well below the province's share of the national population.[10] Over roughly the same period (1981 to 2001), Ontario saw its economic weight rise from 39 per cent to 42 per cent of the national economy, which is four percentage points more than its demographic weight of 38 per cent.[11] Even if these proportions have been slightly knocked off course by the downturn and its disproportionate impact on Ontario,[12] they are based on long-term underlying realities that likely transcend these cyclical swings.

There are other valuable resources that societies are in competition with each other for. One of them is capital. The ability of the *modèle québécois* to attract private capital has been poor, and it has therefore been forced to pursue a policy of replacing private capital with public capital, with predictable consequences.

Private Investment: Come Flee with Us

In 1867 Montreal was the second-most important commercial city in the British Empire. By the 1960s, the flight of corporate head offices, to choose just one measure, was picking up pace, and now Montreal is a very poor second in Canada in head offices, having been overtaken not merely by Toronto but now by Calgary and Vancouver taken together.

Similarly, Quebec only gets 17 to 18 per cent of private investments in Canada, which is well below its share of both GDP (20.5 per cent) and population (24 per cent). For the sole period of 2000 to 2006, the difference between the share of private investment in the GDP of Quebec versus its share in the GDP of the rest of Canada was 2.75 percentage points, amounting to a $6.6-billion investment deficit in Quebec in 2006.[13]

Now you can compensate to some extent by *public* spending on business investment, and that is clearly what the Quebec model does. For example, according to Statistics Canada, over the period 1990 to 2005, Quebec's transfers to business varied anywhere between roughly 40 and 50 per cent of all the subsidies to business paid *by all the provinces combined* in any one year.[14] When you consider that the Quebec economy represents only a little over 20 per cent of the national economy, that puts the level of subsidization of Quebec business by the provincial government truly in a class of its own.

And these figures describe only what is done directly and explicitly through the provincial budget. There are many other ways in which Quebec uses public money to try to make up for the shortfall in private investment. The shortfall helps, for example, to explain why Quebec has been so keen to commandeer pension savings (through the Caisse de dépôt among others) as part of the Quebec model: the market is clearly signalling that the investment climate is not attractive in the province compared to other places, and so the logical solution for Quebec Inc. is to engineer pools of captive capital that invest for political, not economic, reasons. The Caisse is not precluded from investing in non-Quebec companies, but according to one researcher, there has always been a clear expectation that priority would be accorded to "Quebec" corporations.[15]

The Caisse has also been quite explicitly used as a kind of captive in-house financier of the debt of the province of Quebec, an action that would not be necessary were the debt instruments of the province offered to the market at a price that reflects the true risk associated with holding Quebec government debt. One historian notes, "From the outset, Quebec's interest in a provincial pension scheme had less to do with providing benefits to the elderly or 'maîtres chez nous' than with the need to fill provincial coffers."[16] Indeed, this role that the QPP and the Caisse would be called upon to play was explicitly recognized and underlined in the 1963 report to the Quebec legislature on the creation of the plan: "Such a reservoir of capital would fill a serious gap in the province's financial arsenal," it stated, "by providing a steady flow of money greater than that available on the open market, and supplying the financial means to carry out the economic plan the [Quebec government economic council] was preparing."[17] The significance of the Caisse in financing Quebec's public sector can hardly be overestimated. This is demonstrated in the proportion and absolute value of the Caisse's investments accounted for by bonds issued or guaranteed by the Quebec government and its agents, and other public-sector organizations in the province. These have ranged from a high of 75.7 per cent of the total value of the Caisse's investments, or $144.6 million in 1966, to 50.3 per cent, or just under $8 billion in 1985.[18]

In effect, by commandeering much of the pension savings of Quebeckers the government was able to reduce the upfront cost of its destructive economic policies, creating what one author called a kind of defensive central bank, buying up Quebec bonds whenever the government needed to borrow.[19] There can be little other explanation, for example, for the Caisse's behaviour in 1976–77. In 1976, one of the most volatile years in Quebec history, the Caisse purchased $395 million in provincial bonds, issued a $50-million loan to Hydro-Québec and bought about $30 million in bonds issued by the state-owned and loss-making steel company Sidbec.[20] In 1977, the stormy year immediately following the Parti Québécois's election victory, the Caisse increased its purchase of Quebec bonds to $560 million.

Normally if a government runs down the long-term growth of the economy, and hence the government's ability to repay its debt, one would expect the market to demand a premium for holding that government's paper. By having the Caisse buy the debt on essentially non-market terms, the Caisse has protected the credit rating of the province at the expense of future retirement earnings for Quebeckers. Indeed, while Canada's chief actuary holds that the Canada Pension Plan is solvent for the next seventy-five years, the Quebec chief actuary has sounded the alarm bells about the Quebec Pension Plan, which is solvent for only the next forty-five years.[21] And that was the position of the Caisse before the recent economic downturn. When the markets blew up, the Caisse's exposure (and hence the QPP's) was far more pronounced than the CPP's.[22] The

Quebec government spent months fending off opposition calls for full disclosure of the damage to the Caisse's assets. It finally had to accede to demands for an inquiry in mid-March 2009.[23]

Yet the Caisse has been in the investment game since its inception, whereas the CPP got into genuine investment of a share of premiums only after the Paul Martin reforms of 1996. In 1986, the Caisse, at $8.5 billion, was the "largest diversified investment portfolio in the country,"[24] although in a curious sense it was not "diversified" at all, but had its investments dangerously concentrated in an economy with a poor history of economic performance and was often making investments for political reasons rather than on the basis of sound long-term investment principles.

Unfortunately for Quebeckers, few serious businesses locate anywhere because of government subsidies of the kind offered by both the provincial government, the Caisse, or the Société générale de financement (SGF)—often matched by Ottawa, as we shall see; they seek out open markets, stable or falling taxes, stable or falling public debt, a well-trained and plentiful labour force, good-quality infrastructure, and a good cost-benefit balance between taxes paid and services received.[25]

Subsidies impoverish society because they bribe companies to abandon their independent judgment about where it makes best business sense to invest and make taxpayers pay for business risks that should be shouldered by investors. It gives rise to the problems of companies and others seeking benefits for themselves at the expense of taxpayers (i.e., rent-seeking or PUPPETRY) that I outlined in a previous chapter.

This explains—for the most part—the superficial paradox of the relatively high productivity of workers who are actually lucky enough to have a job in Quebec, while the province's productivity per person is poor. Because the Quebec model makes the cost of employing someone very high, employers must keep their workforces relatively small and invest to make those few workers productive. Any employment beyond that economically justified level can occur only through government subsidization of one kind or another (tax breaks, cheap electricity, below-market cost for access to provincially owned resources, markets protected by laws and non-tariff barriers, and straightforward cash subsidies). But this means that the fruits of the higher productivity of a few workers must be confiscated by the state and used to subsidize business investment and to compensate the most vulnerable in society, who are simply priced out of work.

Let no one be under the illusion, by the way, that cosmopolitan, multicultural, internationalist Montreal, home to a great share of the province's private sector, a concentrated urban market, and many great universities and other institutions of international renown, escapes the effects of these policies. According to one study of Canada's twelve largest cities, Montreal had the highest unemployment rate, the highest incidence of low-income households, and the highest proportion of residents receiving some government assistance. It had one of the highest shares of its population earning less than $25,000, and one of the lowest shares earning more than $50,000. All this despite having the highest share of people with a university education.[26]

The Taxman Cometh

How heavy is the burden on the productive in Quebec relative to the rest of the country? Let's look at the tax burden that the provinces put on their respective provincial economies (looking at provincial own-source and local revenues as a percentage of GDP).

A clear divide is revealed between the more economically successful and the less developed provinces. In 2008, Alberta had a provincial government fiscal burden of under 20 per cent of GDP. Most of the other provinces were grouped together in the 21 to 22 per cent of GDP range. This is quite representative of their traditional tax burden in recent years.

In most years, by contrast, the size of Quebec's provincial and local government as a percentage of GDP is much larger than in the other provinces, and it has remained largely stable over a long period, while the size of provincial government in most other provinces declined relative to their economy in the decade between 1994 and 2004.[27]

In 2008, while no other province had an own-source revenue burden that exceeded 22.3 per cent of GDP, Quebec's own-source taxation burden reached 27 per cent of GDP, five to six full points higher than the bulk of provinces and nine points higher than Alberta.[28] This should help put paid to the notion put about by the Quebec government that its recent income tax cuts redressed the tax situation for Quebeckers compared to taxpayers in other provinces. By looking at total tax burden as a share of the provincial economy, we can establish that the overall tax burden on Quebeckers remains significantly higher than that imposed by other provincial governments, regardless of how this or that particular tax rate has been adjusted.

Not only is the overall tax burden heavy, it comes in the form of

> In fact, Quebec has among the highest personal income tax burdens in the world.
> TD Bank Economics Special Report, April 2007

extremely damaging taxes. To take but one example, highly progressive income taxes are a poor policy in a society with a major productivity problem. Such taxes are in effect a tax on effort or work, and the more progressive the tax system, the bigger the tax burden on the most productive workers. That discourages them from working as much as they might. In 2008, Quebec's marginal tax rate on income earned from working was the highest in Canada at 49.9 per cent.[29] If you make the mistake in Quebec of working an extra hour, you can expect the state to reward you by confiscating one-half of your extra earnings. It is perhaps therefore not surprising that one of the main factors explaining the productivity differences between Quebec and other parts of Canada and the United States is the low number of hours worked per employee.[30]

Social Solidarity: Who, Whom?

So taxpayers bear a big burden. But the cost of Quebec Inc. is by no means limited to the cost of taxes. Much of the redistributionist effort of the social justice state in fact penalizes the most vulnerable and rewards the politically powerful. In this latter regard, it is instructive to look at a few policies of Quebec Inc. and the social justice state. There are many we could look at, such as the impact of heavily subsidized daycare,[31] which has been documented to benefit the middle class far more than the economically weak and vulnerable, or the artificially low levels of university tuition fees, that also disproportionately benefit the middle class (and coincidentally the politically volatile and noisy student population). For our purposes, however, I have chosen two other examples. On the one hand there are the very high rates of trade unionism in Quebec and on the other what has fairly consistently been the highest minimum wage in North America.

In an earlier chapter, I showed how trade unionism as it is practised in much of the Western industrial world is in reality a fairly transparent effort to achieve a monopoly by unions on the supply of labour. This allows unions to force up wages for their members at the expense not of employers, but of the unemployed and underemployed. People who would have been willing to take work at lower wages than union members expect are forbidden by the union contract from doing so. I also pointed out, however, that in the private sector in most of North America, the power of trade unions to push this monopoly are rather limited because of, for instance, the ability of consumers to pick non-union suppliers and by the fact that employers are entitled to bring in non-union labour to replace striking union employees who do not have a contract.

In Quebec, these constraints have to a large extent been abolished by law. In the construction industry, for example, employers may not hire non-union labour. More importantly, the provincial government has extended the effective reach of union monopoly by preventing employers from bringing in replacement workers during strikes. All this, by the way, is the perfectly predictable outcome of the bribery state created by the bidding war with Ottawa: unions in Quebec are one of the privileged corporatist "social partners" that belong at the negotiating table where Quebec Inc. parcels out the booty. Unions in Quebec have won legal privileges unmatched anywhere else in North America because that is the price of keeping them favourable to nationalism, and not because having a union stranglehold on the economy is in the economic interests of Quebeckers.

One of the rare times that nationalists dared to challenge union power was in the aftermath of the 1980 Quebec referendum. In the run-up to that vote, the Lévesque government had given clearly unsustainable pay increases to Quebec civil servants, thinking thereby to make them strong proponents of a sovereign Quebec. When the referendum failed and the wage bill arrived, the government blanched and rolled back the wage increases, knowing, presumably, that there would be no more referendums in the near future.

As the natural consequence of these favourable conditions that allow unions to win benefits at the expense of less privileged workers, more workers must seek to join unions or else risk being frozen out of the state-awarded benefits that flow to union members. If you had a choice between benefiting from privilege and paying the bill for that privilege enjoyed by others, you would probably make the same choice. Among the ten provinces and fifty states in North America, Quebec is therefore the jurisdiction with the highest rate of unionization: 40 per cent in 2004. The corresponding averages are 31.8 per cent for the rest of the Canadian provinces[32] and 13.8 per cent for the U.S. states.

Very unusually, Quebec's higher rate of unionization is not limited to the public sector, so that the large public sector in the province does not explain in itself the higher rates of trade unionism overall. In the private sector, Quebec's rate of unionization reached 26.7 per cent in 2004, the highest among the Canadian provinces by a long shot. Looking at the U.S. example, the contrast is even more striking: the most highly unionized state, New York, which also encourages trade unionism through some very permissive labour legislation, has a lower *overall* unionization rate—26.4 per cent, public sector included—than the private sector alone in Quebec.

Private employers, as we have seen, can on the whole tolerate the cost of artificially high union wages as long as they can make the job cuts and capital investments necessary to keep the workforce small and productivity high. Alternatively, the state can compensate for this legal prohibition on paying employees a market-justified wage by offering subsidies to keep employment levels higher than they would be otherwise, thus transforming a certain portion of this private-sector employment into pseudo-work. Since Quebec has made employing workers such an expensive proposition, even the levels of subsidy it is willing to pay (including indirect subsidies such as artificially low electricity prices or taxes deferred by large-scale government borrowing or artificially cheap public credit thanks to the Caisse's effective confiscation of a significant share of the future retirement income of Quebeckers) can only partly make up for the burden on employers. The result: high structural unemployment (that is, unemployment not caused by ups and downs in the economic cycle, but rather by the economy's permanent inability to put some people to work. Structural unemployment is almost without exception caused by poor policy rather than by the economy's inability to put people to work if left to its own devices).

And the need continually to buy the allegiance of the trade union movement means that it is not merely favoured companies that get to tap the taxpayer for money. The cronyism that infects the business community is also present in the relationship between the government and the trade unions. Indeed the members of any powerful group that can effectively demand a share of the booty that Quebec has to shower on its fickle but voracious *partenaires sociaux* will find their mouths stuffed with gold.

I could give a hundred examples of just what happens in Quebec (and elsewhere) when the dividing line between economic decision-making and petty politicking is crossed—we could look at the Caisse, the SGF, Hyundai, Paccar, Provigo, or Hydro-Québec, but I will limit myself to only one painfully pertinent example of the Quebec government, the private sector, and the trade union movement in bed together to fleece the taxpayer: La Gaspésia, an industrial complex in the Gaspé heavily supported by Quebec government investment. According to Alain Dubuc's account of this fiasco in *La Presse,*

> This escapade, which rested to a very large extent on public money (both direct and indirect), never gave any signs of having a profitable future.... Already such a context should have caused the partners in this project to be more demanding and rigorous in their analysis of the business case. Alas, it is the opposite that occurred, and the cost overruns ended up making an economic nonsense of the project, leading to the closure of the construction project only after $300 million had been ploughed in.
>
> This cost explosion, as the public inquiry is only now starting to reveal, can be explained by several factors, including the complex retooling of the mill and a weak management, but also by a literal reign of terror by the unions,

where the representatives of the Fédération du travail du Québec (the FTQ) kept out members of other trade unions, thus contributing to the worsening work climate on the job site and to the fall in productivity.[33]

In other words, scandals like La Gaspésia, and many others, are the inevitable outcome of the kind of cozy relationship between politicians, business people and trade union leaders that state domination of economic decisions produces. The money that is invested in enterprises like this contributes nothing to a *projet de société*. It is simply wasted, full stop.

Minimum Wage, Maximum Damage

A classic destroyer of jobs much beloved of trade unions and social-justice-state advocates is high minimum wages. For years, Quebec has vied for the title of jurisdiction with the highest minimum wage in North America, and in many of those years has in fact emerged as the undisputed title holder. Anyone with a lick of common economic sense knows, for reasons I laid out earlier, that when minimum wages are set higher than the value that the lowest-productivity workers in society can produce, those workers will not be employed. Trade unions love to remove that low-wage competition and to force upward this legally established floor under the whole wage structure. This truly is an example of a rising tide lifting all boats. Unfortunately, low-productivity workers don't have a boat in these circumstances, so the price is unemployment among the most vulnerable.

The folly of this policy is only obvious, however, if you forget to place the high minimum wages in the context of both the social justice state and the bidding war for the loyalty of Quebeckers. In the social justice state, many of the good things in life are not distributed by markets, but by the state. The state ensures that everyone gets a living regardless of their contribution to the economy, which in turn proves that the state provides social justice. As for the bidding war between Ottawa and Quebec City, Tom Courchene, one of Canada's leading social thinkers, saw the dynamic at work back in 1981:

> Quebec has had, until recently at least, the highest minimum wage on the continent, let alone in Canada. This does not make economic sense but it exists in large measure because Quebec does not have to bear the full financial and economic costs of such a policy decision. As unemployment rises, Ottawa comes to Quebec's aid with Unemployment Insurance (UI) transfers, increased equalization payments, and one half of welfare costs. But even that is not the

end of the story. Because of its high unemployment, Quebec can then lobby (successfully) for such things as quotas and tariffs on its beleaguered industries. The solution is, of course, to alter the incentives embodied in the transfer system so that one province cannot export, via Ottawa to the rest of Canada, the costs of its decisions on the economic front.[34]

Courchene is bang on in his analysis until he reaches the point where he explains how the rational economic agent would fix this obviously perverse set of incentives. What he did not then see was that *the destructive outcome he was describing was in the interests of both Ottawa and Quebec City in the bidding war for the loyalty of Quebeckers*. Both levels of government found openings here to create dependence on themselves: Quebec could argue (plausibly but incorrectly) that the high minimum wage guaranteed a higher standard of living for socially vulnerable Quebeckers, and the government would further benefit from the fact that those who fell on welfare because of their poor productivity would then become dependent on cheques with fleur-de-lys on them, and unions (social partners much solicited in the bidding war) would find their bargaining power on behalf of their members enhanced.

Ottawa could send maple leaf cheques to UI recipients, remind people at referendum and election time that the welfare benefits of the Quebec state were financed in part through large federal transfers, and could add their subsidies to business to those of the province in the always close-run race to raise those subsidies faster than the burden of taxation and regulation causes business profitability to decline.

What Price Winning?

This winning political strategy for both governments, however, was bought at a steep price. That price was not only the accelerating debilitation of the Quebec economy, but more importantly the moral corruption of an ever-growing circle of people, companies, and institutions that came to see that their success was better assured by a life of taking rather than making.

Take, for example, the work ethic in Quebec. As a result of the many employment-destroying policies imposed on Quebec by both Ottawa and Quebec City, Quebec has a participation rate (i.e., people in work or looking for work) in the workforce which is thirteenth among sixteen peer jurisdictions in North America, and three and a half percentage points below Ontario, a situation rendered all the more tragic when one realizes that Quebec has the highest proportion of working-aged people in its population of the entire group of sixteen peers.[35] When people do work, they work fewer hours than their counterparts elsewhere,[36] no doubt reflecting in part the punishing tax burden on extra income from work, as well as the state-financed alternatives to working.

Between 1981 and 2006, the total number of jobs rose by 34.9 per cent in Quebec, 49.5 per cent in the rest of Canada, and 43.8 per cent in the United States. During this period, Quebec generated 18.8 per cent of the jobs created in the country as a whole, again significantly less than its share of the population or of the economy. If, over the last twenty-five years, Quebec had created jobs at the same pace as the rest of Canada and the United States, there would have been 261,000 more jobs created there.[37]

In the world where workers, companies, and governments are trying to build the economy, results such as these would be regarded as evidence of failed policy. Not, however, if you are a government out to create dependence on your benefits on as wide a scale as possible. On the maple leaf cheque scoreboard, we have, for instance, EI. Year in and year out, never fewer than 30 per cent (and in some years as high as 37 per cent) of Canada's EI recipients come from Quebec, while the provincial population is now around 24 per cent of the nation's total.[38] The mathematically inescapable result is a much higher rate of dependence on EI than the Canadian average: 61.3 recipients per 1,000 inhabitants aged twenty to sixty-four in Quebec, compared to 47.8 per 1,000 in the rest of Canada in 1986. In 2006, the figures were 37.4 per 1,000 in Quebec and 22.3 per 1,000 in the rest of Canada.[39]

On the fleur-de-lys cheque scoreboard, the proportion of social welfare beneficiaries as a share of the Quebec population is consistently higher than in nearly all the other provinces. Newfoundland has been the only recent exception. In 2005, for instance, 6.8 per cent of the population of Quebec was in receipt of welfare benefits, while the Canadian average was 5.2 per cent and Ontario 5.4 per cent.[40]

In 1995 (a referendum year), fully 11 per cent of the provincial budget in Quebec was devoted to social welfare. In constant dollars, between 1980 and 1993, welfare spending increased by nearly 60 per cent, and the number of households on welfare increased in the same proportions, reaching 450,675 households in 1993. Lone-parent households on welfare increased at a slightly lower but still alarming 40 per cent, for a total of 89,366 such households in 1993.[41]

According to McGill's William Watson, writing in 1994,

> More than 450,000 Quebec households, accounting for 700,000 people, receive welfare. That is more than 10 per cent of the population. Another 450,000 are unemployed, the vast majority of whom receive unemployment insurance benefits. Counting the children of the unemployed, roughly one-fifth of Quebecers are on social assistance of one form or another.[42]

And while the minister responsible at the time, Manpower and Income Security Minister André Bourbeau, argued that these high levels were due to the recession then underway,[43] the evidence I have cited elsewhere in this book shows that this was in the heart of the period when rises in welfare dependency in recessions were not followed by declines in the subsequent upswing, making welfare dependency a one-way ratchet. Only serious welfare reform makes a difference.

Like other provinces, of course, Quebec did reform welfare over the course of the nineties, and welfare rates and the share of the population on welfare were brought down. On the other hand, even at lower overall levels, welfare dependency in Quebec remained higher than in the provinces to the west of the Ottawa River and in some cases higher than almost all the other provinces.

In the case of single people on welfare, for example, Quebec and Newfoundland actually fought the downward trend in welfare dependency over the nineties, with their rates rising sharply in 1993 (like most provinces), but then remaining high throughout 2000. Quebec finished the 1993–2000 period with the highest rate of welfare dependency in this category of all the provinces, at 21.4 per cent.[44] In the category of couples with children, Quebec spent most of the period with the second-highest level of dependency over the period, with Saskatchewan overtaking them only in the last year. In the couples without children category, Quebec again vied with Newfoundland for the top dependency rate among the provinces, ahead in the first half of the period, slightly behind for the rest. Only in the lone mothers with children category did Quebec trail the pack.

Thus, while the welfare reform period of the nineties saw welfare dependency decline across the board, Quebec remained one of the jurisdictions with the highest rates of welfare dependency overall and saw the disparity between itself and the more economically dynamic parts of the country open up. According to a StatsCan study of this period, Quebec had the lowest level of people leaving welfare, relatively high rates of people getting on welfare, and relatively little fall-off in welfare dependency during the growth years in the second half of the decade. The result: "the highest annual incidences of [social assistance] participation of all the provinces."[45]

Quebeckers also retire earlier from the workforce than other Canadians, withdrawing their labour and drawing pension entitlements, often at the taxpayer's expense. On average, the early retirement rate in Quebec is second highest in the country at nearly 60 per cent (i.e., 60 per cent of those eligible for early retirement took advantage of it). The national average is 42, per cent and Alberta is around 30. This helps to put the median retirement age in Quebec at 59.4 years of age, about a year and a half lower than the Canadian average and over two years lower than in Ontario.[46]

This retirement behaviour is itself surely influenced by the high degree of reliance on the public sector for work in Quebec. Public-sector workers generally have a very different retirement pattern than other workers, reflecting in part the very generous pension arrangements awarded by politicians to their unionized employees at the expense of taxpayers, who have to retire much later. In 2005, about 56 per cent of public-sector workers in the country took early retirement, whereas private-sector workers could manage only about half that rate (33 per cent) while 80 per cent of the self-employed soldiered on instead of retiring early. The average public servant retires two and a half years before his or her opposite number in the private sector.[47]

As we have seen, the long-term dependence created as a result dampens the desire and even the ability to work. In place of a work ethic that is focused on making grows the mentality of dependency and entitlement: a culture of taking.

Of Fighter Planes and Milk Quotas

Other interest groups lined up for their share of benefits and came to accept it as simply normal that income, privileges, barriers to competition, and other special advantages should be procured by aggressive bargaining with both the federal and provincial states, now founts of dependency-inducing spending and other privileges. I've talked about subsidies to business, trade unions, welfare recipients, etc. Over and above those, anyone whose political allegiance might be up for sale is entitled to be an aggressive *demandeur* of booty with a consequent coarsening of political life.

Just two quick examples: in 1986, the Mulroney government awarded the contract for the maintenance of the CF-18s, its new fighter planes, to a Montreal firm, despite the fact that a Winnipeg company, Bristol Aerospace, had won the tender by virtue of the superior quality of its bid. There then ensued a dialogue of the deaf in which Manitoba, supported by several other provinces, expressed outrage that an ostensibly meritocratic bidding process had been subverted, while the Mulroney government, deeply rooted in Quebec, saw only an opportunity to distribute some largesse in the Ottawa-Quebec bidding war.

From Ottawa's point of view, to call foul on this transaction was to fail to understand the stakes and "the way things are done." For Manitoba and its supporters, this was a classic example of the anger that is generated when government benefits are distributed for some other reason than merit or equality. They thought that they were involved in a merit-based process where the best bid would win, whereas they came to understand that they were involved in a sham whose real purpose was to provide a fig leaf of legitimacy for an essentially corrupt process. Many commentators date the birth of the Reform Party and the ultimate loss of support for the Mulroney government in the west from the CF-18 debacle, even though the government was obliged to beat at least a partial retreat. Even so, they never thought they had done anything wrong, and they almost certainly thought that the Reform Party that emerged afterwards was laughably naïve in its expectation that Ottawa could treat everyone in the country in the same way and on the basis of merit. Ottawa finds this view incomprehensible and its tenants simple-minded.

In the 1995 Quebec referendum, by way of a second example, Quebec dairy farmers came to epitomize the corrupt stance of bargaining for private advantage by holding both Ottawa and Quebec City hostage. The dairy farmers were concentrated in politically sensitive constituencies that swung back and forth between separatist and federalist politicians in Quebec and that were major referendum battlegrounds. In 1995, dairy farmers perfectly summarized the logic of how PUPPETRY and the bidding war have corrupted behaviour. Analysts found that Quebec dairy farmers voted in a majority for sovereignty in that year's referendum but those farmers saw no contradiction between this vote and the fact that they held milk quota for about 47 per cent of the Canadian marketplace[48] while the province represented only about a quarter of the Canadian population. These farmers were quite confident that they would continue to be guaranteed nearly half the Canadian market if ever Quebec left Confederation, and their politicians abetted them in this view.[49]

In a world where such a position makes sense, no one is committed to anything and no sacrifices can be demanded of anyone. Everyone expects to seek advantages through political bargaining, with that bargaining ideally taking place at the moment of greatest leverage (i.e., around elections and referendums), playing the two governments off against each other to maximum effect, no matter what the cost to the larger society.

Psssst, Buddy. Need a Job?

Beyond business subsidies, trade union appeasement, welfare entrapment, and special interest buy-offs, there is a further area in which Ottawa and Quebec City excelled in their bidding war: public-sector jobs. For individuals, perhaps the most satisfying form of dependence on one government or the other is getting a job in government, which carries at least the possibility of producing something for society and therefore earning one's paycheque. But for the two contending governments, such moral niceties were neither here nor there. The struggle between them unleashed a wave of essentially parasitic public employment that is almost comic in scale—most of it solely for the political benefit of being able to run up the score on the dependency count.

In Quebec, about 780,000 individuals officially work for the public sector—the provincial, federal, or municipal governments, as well as state-owned corporations.[50] One employed person out of five is a federal, provincial, or municipal employee, down from more than one in four over most of the eighties and nineties. That level is still considerably higher than Ontario, which has hovered around 17 per cent for most of the past decade (and that includes the disproportionate number of federal civil servants concentrated in Ottawa). Quebec's rate of public employment is not only higher than in the rest of Canada, it is also higher than in all G-7 countries with the sole exception of France.[51] And the growth in this employment exactly coincides with both the rise of Quebec nationalism and the move of Boomers into the workforce.

In 1960, the Quebec provincial public sector employed 36,000 people. A decade later, in 1971, almost 350,000 people were employed in its administration, in public enterprises, and in health and educational services—that is, an increase from 2 per cent to 15 per cent of the labour force, a stunning growth rate even if one accepts that Quebec had some catching up to do following the withdrawal of the Catholic Church from the provision of many kinds of social services. These figures are, in any case, a gross underestimate of the number of people paid by provincial tax money and state enterprises. The expenditures of the federal, provincial, and municipal sectors in Quebec grew from just over a third of the Quebec GNP in 1961 to nearly half in 1970.[52]

That is a lot of people getting cheques from both governments inside Quebec. It would, of course, exclude civil servants in Ottawa (but include those on the Hull side of the Ottawa River). But Ottawa most emphatically could and should be included in this survey of how the strategies of the two governments played out in battle for the loyalty of Quebeckers.

Bilingualism as Affirmative Action

Think, in this context, about the real meaning of a federal policy of bilingualism in the civil service at a time of rapid expansion of the public sector. Whatever its benefits in ensuring a government capable of serving its population in both official languages, and whatever its benefits in redressing any historical wrong occasioned by a traditional under-representation of French-speakers in the federal government, at a time of struggle over the fate of Canada, its real benefit was quite different: it was effectively a job reservation scheme for French-speakers.

To call it such will cause offence in certain quarters, but it is hard to know what else to call it. It is a fact that knowing English is of greater economic value to French-speakers than knowing French is to English-speakers, except in the very particular and artificial circumstances of Quebec with its language laws. All other things being equal, in the North American context there will be a higher degree of bilingualism among French-speakers than among English-speakers, and this means that the farther one moves geographically from centres of French-speaking population the more difficult it will be to recruit bilinguals to work in the public service.

The problem becomes more acute as one moves up the federal public sector hierarchy. Line employees in British Columbia or Newfoundland may easily get away with being unilingual English-speakers, but the higher one rises, the more the lack of bilingualism becomes an obstacle to further promotion. Bilingualism thus effectively excludes from competition for many federal government jobs the vast majority of Canadians who are unilingual English-speakers and contributes mightily to the alienation of a significant part of the population from its government in Ottawa. Solving one injustice (the historical under-representation of French-speakers) in Ottawa by perpetrating another equally unacceptable injustice is hardly sound policy.

But perhaps the two injustices are not equally unacceptable, and perhaps this bilingualism arrangement is not really about justice at all. Instead, perhaps it is about offering a federal response to deep-seated fears in Quebec about the continued survival of the French language. That would allow Ottawa to contest Quebec's attempt to monopolize the title of government most committed to the survival of French in North America. Handily, it would also guarantee a large share of public jobs for French-speakers whom Ottawa was desperate to draw into dependence on its payroll. And contrary to the protestations of the federal bilingualism police (of whom the Commissioner of Official Languages is only the most prominent), the policy will not have succeeded if it creates a large class of bilingual officials who are native English-speakers. That is because the purpose of the policy is not, at bottom, to create a public service open to all who can master both languages. On the contrary, the emergence of a large number of perfectly bilingual English-speakers who could out-compete native French-speakers for civil service jobs would be an unmitigated disaster if the real purpose is to give Ottawa more chips to play with in the high-stakes bidding war with Quebec for the loyalty of French-speakers.

Even before bilingualism became official policy, expanding the share of French-speakers in the federal public service was already a top priority after 1960. And it is hard for us to remember today the pace and scope of the explosion of the federal public service at the beginning of the Boomers' arrival on the scene. Between 1960 and 1968, for example, the federal public service added nearly 70,000 employees, an increase of over half. Between 1969 and 1976, the public service grew handsomely again, the total number of employees reaching 273,167. In 1977, the Public Service Commission of Canada found that there were 283,000 federal employees, another record, while Statistics Canada counted 330,000 federal employees in the "general government" category, and another 144,000 in public enterprises. By the time this expansion was over, French-speakers, who had been traditionally under-represented in Ottawa's ranks, were heavily over-represented. By 2005,[53] French-speakers (who represent 23 per cent of the national population) held 32 per cent of the federal civil service jobs, meaning that on a per capita basis they were over-represented by about one-third. In the national capital, where the top civil service jobs are heavily concentrated, French-speakers do even better: there they hold 42 per cent of the civil service jobs, or almost twice their share of the population as a whole.

The Grantrepreneurial Economy

Nor is bilingualism any more than a small part of the federal contribution to the building of a broadly based state of dependence in Quebec, driven by competition with Quebec City for the loyalty of Quebeckers, and aiming to make separation too economically daunting a prospect. I've spoken of EI and public-sector jobs, for example. But what about pseudo-work, subsidies to business, and regional development programs?

A great deal of the Quebec economy, for instance, was heavily dependent not only on formal civil service employment in Quebec and Ottawa. To pick one apt illustration, Air Canada and CN, two major federal Crown corporations, had their corporate head offices in Montreal, offering many high-quality, high-paying jobs that existed chiefly for political reasons. Even though now privatized, these companies are both required to keep their head offices in Montreal, regardless of whether that makes business sense. Both companies are now major North American operations (often with American CEOs) and widespread share ownership. The chances that they would freely choose Montreal as their corporate headquarters are slim.

Through regional development programs and business subsidies that go to industries concentrated in Quebec, such as aerospace, railcar, and transit, Ottawa has helped to create a larger share of pseudo-work in Quebec than would be justified by its share of the population. To illustrate this, Quebec received 48 per cent of the $6.6 billion doled out under Ottawa's flagship corporate welfare programs—the Defence Industry Productivity Program (1982–1996) and Technology Partnerships Canada (1996–2006).[54] In other words, the province got in *federal* transfers to business under these major programs about twice what its share of the national population or the national economy would justify, almost exactly the same proportion we saw in the case of *provincial* subsidies to business. The amounts I've mentioned are in addition to the $4.2 billion[55] distributed by the federal regional development agency in Quebec, CED-Q, between 1992 and 2005.

Remembering that business subsidies are by definition subsidizing private-sector activity, it makes no sense comparing, say, per capita transfers to business between Ontario and Quebec to get a sense of how heavily subsidized Quebec business is. The correct point of comparison would of course be the total subsidy flowing to Quebec *in proportion to its share of the total private sector in Canada*. This would make the level of disproportionate subsidy of Quebec business by federal taxpayers even more stark.

It is a bit tricky, of course, trying to nail down exactly the scale of the federal effort in Quebec because spending on Quebec is often buried inside national programs and is hard to winkle out. Neither Ottawa nor Quebec has any interest in transparency in the amount of explicit or implicit transfers to the province. The examples offered here are, therefore, no more than indicative of the scope of the effort.

Suppose, however, that we wanted to take a stab at it. First, we'd have to figure out what share of the Quebec economy is generated in the private sector. One way of calculating this would be to look at shares of employment between the public and the private sector, something on which we do possess reasonably good data. Between 1997 and 2007, the average public-sector employment in Quebec has represented 21.2 per cent of total employment in the province, implying that 78.8 per cent of the population works in the non-governmental sector, including for-profits, not-for-profits, and NGOs. Recalling now that Quebec's total economy represents 21 per cent of the national economy, slightly less than four-fifths of that would be the private sector in Quebec. In other words, the Quebec private sector represents about 16.5 per cent of the national economy based on employment.

That 16.5 per cent of the national economy already gets, as we know, about one-half of all provincial subsidies to business as defined by Statistics Canada. The federal largesse is no less impressive, however: that same 16.5 per cent of the national economy also gets nearly one-half of the federal Defence Industry Productivity Program and Technology Partnerships Canada, plus nearly a third of all federal regional development spending (which until the current economic downturn was not available at all in southern Ontario, which represents about 40 per cent of the national economy).

If, then, we add together (a) direct federal transfers to the province; (b) direct federal program spending and business and other subsidies; (c) direct transfers to persons through instruments such as EI, pensions, and income supplements; and (d) the share of the provincial population in both Quebec and Ottawa working for the federal government, the dependence that has been created on the federal taxpayer is truly awe-inspiring.

Governments Are Known by the Companies They Keep

Let's stop for just a moment to dig a little further into the pseudo-work that the federal and provincial efforts have created jointly within Quebec.

One way of measuring private-sector pseudo-work would be to calculate what share of private-sector employment is dependent on federal-provincial subsidies. To arrive at a back-of-the-envelope calculation of the scale of pseudo-work in the private sector, I took StatsCan's average weekly earnings for each year, multiplied it by 52 to get an annual figure, and then divided total federal-provincial business subsidies by this amount. This is a rough and ready measure of the number of people whose jobs would depend wholly on these subsidies if those people were paid the average wage. For the decade 1995 to 2004, the annual average was roughly 125,000 workers in the private sector in Quebec whose jobs could be thought of as entirely reliant on federal and provincial subsidies to business.[56] That is equivalent, on average over the same decade, to almost exactly 5 per cent of all non-governmental employment. The equivalent figure for Ontario is 1.23 per cent.

But of course this is not the way that subsidies to business are experienced by the workforce or the community. When the province or the feds or both give money to a company, it is not some small share of the company's workforce that considers it owes its entire job to the subsidy. Every single member of that workforce feels that their job has been "supported" by the government, and every single member of their families and everyone who supplies the company and local consumers feel the same. Certainly the politicians who are behind the transfer to business in the first place will take great pains to make them feel that way. When you consider how such a large absolute amount of transfers to business ripples across interlocking and interdependent groups—workers, families, local suppliers, and more—the political impact can only be huge.

How Do You Say "Tipping Point" in French?

So we might conclude from this vast statistical portrait that, if we add up the attention lavished on Quebec by both levels of government, Quebec society has long since passed any reasonable threshold past which the size of government becomes a brake on growth and a source of burgeoning social contention. I argued earlier that there appears to be a tipping point that is reached in an economy when the size of government gets too large. Stay below that level and one avoids the worst excesses of a bloated state and lost economic growth while retaining the civilizational benefits that Oliver Wendell Holmes associated with taxation. Go beyond that, however, and you unleash a destructive dynamic in which the energy and attention of society is progressively distracted from making and focuses ever more tightly on taking. And in earlier chapters of this book, I laid out the long-term effects of an overweening state on the moral and social health of society and on institutions such as work and the family.

The record I have laid out here suggests strongly that the allegedly distinctive society that both Ottawa and Quebec City claim exists in Quebec may be attributed at least as much to their bidding war for the loyalty of Quebeckers as to any fundamental cultural differences between Quebec and the rest of Canada. That bidding war has itself generated many of the differences that do exist between the behaviour of Quebeckers and people in other parts of Canada because those differences, such as higher levels of public services and employment, more tolerance for the corruption of character that results in unproductive social behaviours such as welfare dependency, and higher levels of taxation, are exactly the behaviours one would predict would be exhibited by a society that has shifted its focus from making to taking. The main difference between Quebec and the rest of Canada on this score is simply that Quebec got started earlier, moved farther into these dysfunctional behaviours in the first few decades of the Boomer generation, and has been correspondingly slower and more timid in trying to change them once the damage they cause had become too obvious and costly to ignore.

That would also help to explain the poor economic performance of Quebec relative to the rest of the country and the continent. In fact, the burden of my argument is that these phenomena have become linked in a downward spiral of social, economic, and moral decline.

As we have seen, economic decline, erosion of work ethic, increase in dependency are all of a piece. Moreover, the likelihood is that those parts of Canada that moved farthest down the track of state dependence would exhibit higher levels of these dysfunctions. This is clearly what the data presented here suggest: that Quebec is more deeply mired in these pathologies than other parts of the country, except for places like the Atlantic provinces. That region has also been ensnared in the growth of the taking state but was merely collateral damage, as it were, created by the primal struggle for dominance between Ottawa and Quebec City, as Ottawa expanded national programs for purely Quebec-centric purposes, causing by ricochet untold harm in other economically weaker parts of the country.[57]

The Quebec Family: An Endangered Species

I also predicted, however, that it wasn't only the work ethic and a sturdy independence from the state that would be more damaged in Quebec than elsewhere. I also suggested that the family would be more deeply damaged, with all that that implies for the future of work, fertility, and valuable personal and social traits like self-discipline and self-control. Again, that is what the data show.[58]

Common-law unions are much more prevalent in Quebec. The 2006 census showed that 44.4 per cent of all common-law families in Canada lived in Quebec, whereas the province represents less than a quarter of the population.[59] Montreal had the highest proportion of common-law and lone-parent families of the four major metropolitan areas (the other three being Vancouver, Toronto, and Ottawa-Hull) and, at 36 per cent, a rate much higher than the national average of 26 per cent. Montreal also had the lowest proportion of married couples of the four metropolitan areas.[60] And children living with married parents are also becoming the exception. In addition to high rates of lone parenthood, Pollard and Wu note that according to the 1996 Census, the rate of children living with cohabiting (rather than married) couples was twice as high in Quebec (31 per cent of all children under the age of six) than nationally (14 per cent).[61] And that tells us nothing about whether the cohabiting couple was composed of the children's biological parents.

In fact, the decline of marriage has been so severe in Quebec[62] that it has caused Canadian national marriage rates to diverge with those of the United States, while the rates in the rest of Canada are not that different from our southern neighbours.[63]

Two-thirds of unmarried women in Quebec were of the view that marriage was "not very important" or "not at all important," according to the GSS-95 data, whereas only 37 per cent of women in the rest of the country shared this view.

Even for those who can make their way through this emerging cultural resistance to marriage and actually wed, the prospects are dim. After the 1969 liberalization of divorce, the number of divorces in the province each year "rose from 2,947 in 1969 to 15,186 in 1976, falling back to 13,899 in 1980 only to climb again to 19,931 in 1981 (a gain of 38 per cent in one year), levelling off at 16,845 in 1984. Quebec is close to a situation whereby only half of the population marries, and of that half, between a quarter and a half divorces."[64]

One of the few comprehensive reviews of this data, which attempted to arrive at a cultural explanation of the differences in marriage rates between the rest of Canada on the one hand and Quebec on the other, arrived at the very unsatisfactory conclusion that they could not explain the difference based on any of the usual cultural or social factors. The authors' explanation was that the data showed that while Quebec women weren't keen on marriage, they ranked the importance of a long-term relationship to their happiness as higher (94 per cent) than their counterparts in the rest of the country (84 per cent). "Clearly," the authors conclude, "the rejection of marriage in Quebec does not reflect a rejection of a long-term relationship, only of the traditional nuptial route to union formation."[65]

> Within the last 20 years the declines in marriage rates and prevalence have been much more pronounced for Quebec than for the rest of Canada. The total first marriage rate for Quebec women (age 15–49) in 1994 was only 373 per thousand, compared with 608 per thousand for women in the rest of Canada. Comparable figures in 1985 were 515 and 682, respectively.
>
> While the crude marriage rate in the United States fell from 9.9 per thousand population in 1987 to 9.1 in 1994, Canada's plummeted from 7.1 to 5.4 during the same period (United Nations 1992, 1995).... The recent trend toward later and fewer marriages is not simply a continuation of a long-term process. The continuation of marriage as an institution is in crisis, particularly in Quebec.
>
> Michael Pollard and Zheng Wu, "Divergence of Marriage Patterns in Quebec and Elsewhere in Canada"

That would be one way of putting it. A different one would be that Quebeckers have created the conditions in which marriage, which implies constraints on one's personal preferences and choices, and the putting in common of many life projects, is simply an unnecessary and burdensome cost that confers little in the way of real benefits. If you can get the pleasure of the long-term relationship without burdening it with the inconveniences of marriage, why not? Especially if the state will ensure that your children are cared for, your income assured, your aged parents looked after, your retirement savings provided for, and so forth. The state provides so many of the things one traditionally looked to a husband or wife for, and the state is always there, whereas husbands and wives, as the divorce courts eloquently demonstrate, come and go.

In earlier chapters we saw evidence about the social and economic importance of family. Family is the place where many of the key attitudes and behaviours are inculcated that confer success on children. We also looked at the social pathologies that follow from family breakdown and the impossibility of governmental institutions replacing the socializing role to which families are uniquely suited. That evidence also suggested that high degrees of welfare dependency undermined the work ethic of children as well as parents and that this effect gathered speed and force across generations. The evidence equally strongly supported the proposition that an easing of restrictions on divorce, and especially the introduction of no-fault divorce, increased the incentive for the less-committed spouse to bail out and reduced the bargaining power of the spouse who wished to maintain the marriage. The outcome was a state-induced rise in the numbers of lone-parent families and therefore the number of children living in poverty.

Quebec has, as one might therefore expect, low levels of marriage, high levels of divorce, high levels of lone parenthood and child poverty, and low levels of fertility. These are social dysfunctions that the state has encouraged and rewarded to the great cost of families and especially children, as well as the economic future of the province.

We also saw how government taking over economic functions traditionally associated with the family, such as helping to ensure an adequate retirement income, were related to falling fertility. Quebec has clearly gone further in the direction of taking over many traditional functions of the family than in other parts of Canada, driven by a need to find new programs to create dependence by both governments.

The point has now been reached in Quebec where the family is in many instances regarded as an illegitimate interloper in matters that now concern chiefly the state. This is best illustrated by a story told by Gary Caldwell, a well-known commentator and social analyst who lives in the Eastern Townships. Caldwell wanted to care for his aged parents in his home, but the social worker sent by the Quebec government to inquire into the suitability of this arrangement was nonplussed by it. She insisted that there was no official category into which she could fit children looking after their aged parents at home, and if there was no official category it could not be countenanced by any responsible state official. A category was finally identified that satisfied her bureaucratic soul, but a better illustration of the imperialism of the Quebec state over the family could hardly be hoped for.

The chief difference between Quebec and the rest of the country, then, is not that our cultures are irreconcilably different and always have been, but that Quebec has merely moved well ahead of the rest of Canada in its dependence on the state.

But Are You Really Happy?

Perhaps all this information about the poor economic performance of Quebec; its welfare dependency; its excessive levels of public employment, union power, and heavy taxation; and the decline of marriage is beside the point. We are constantly invited by some thinkers and philosophers to give up our preoccupation with the "more is better" materialist approach of modern capitalism. Instead of Gross Domestic Product, Pierre Trudeau once mused, perhaps we should think in terms of Net Social Benefit. Others have wondered if human happiness might not be the better measure of human progress. What sort of measures might help to reveal to us that despite having a lower material standard of living, people in Quebec are nonetheless happier with their lot in life?

Despite having the most complex and well-developed welfare state in the country, which presumably would eliminate at least one kind of anxiety from life, Quebeckers report themselves to be the most anxious people in Canada. According to a recent study,[66] Quebeckers are more stressed out than other Canadians. A total of 22.7 per cent of Quebeckers aged fifteen and older indicated symptoms of high psychological stress, the highest level of any of the provinces. The highest proportion of respondents suffering from stress—31 per cent—was found among unmarried Quebeckers.

Such high levels of stress are doubtless related to another measure of the state of "subjective well-being" or happiness in Quebec: the suicide rate. Between 1975 and the present, Quebec's suicide rate has consistently eclipsed the rates in other provinces and, for some time, was the highest in the world. In fact, despite a concerted effort by the provincial government to reduce the province's incidence of suicide in recent years, Quebec still has the highest rate in the country and the fifth highest in the world.[67] The province was home to 1,136 suicides in 2006. In other words, nearly three Quebeckers per day kill themselves.[68] Between 1999 and 2001, the rate of suicide among Quebec males was 30.7 per 100,000 people. The rate among men in Ontario, Alberta, and British Columbia was 16.1 per 100,000.[69] Even after a major suicide prevention program by the provincial government, suicide is still the leading cause of death for Quebec men between the ages of twenty and forty. And yet before 1975, suicide in Quebec was less common than anywhere else.

Among the more interesting explanations of this unspeakably dreadful phenomenon was that given by none other than former Parti Québécois premier Bernard Landry: the Quiet Revolution and resulting disavowal of Quebec's founding values. He noted at a 2007 conference on suicide prevention, "The revolution [of the 1960s] changed so many things in such a short period. We made a break with Catholic morality and have been trying to build an ethical and moral code that is not linked to religion ... and we haven't yet found a good way to do that. This isn't what directly provokes a suicide, but it can create a context that makes life more difficult."[70]

Other kinds of choices might similarly reveal something about how Quebeckers feel about the quality of life, about how much satisfaction they are getting; in other words, these choices might be indirect indices of happiness.

For example, people have choices about where to live and whether to have children. A happy society, one might suppose, would be one that attracted new people to live there, whereas unhappy societies might be exporters of people looking for a better life. Likewise, people who are happy might well think that they would like to share that happiness with children, that they might pass along to a new generation the satisfactions that they have gained in life. Indeed, one might argue that a society's ability to reproduce itself, whether through births or immigration, is a key measure of happiness and of a society's success wherever family size and place of residence are free choices.

Looked at this way, how does Quebec measure up? Is it able to reproduce itself by making babies or attracting new residents from the outside?

Where Did Everyone Go?

On the fertility side, Quebec scores poorly. Cumulatively Quebec has had over recent decades one of the lowest birth rates in the industrialized world. The situation has been somewhat improved in recent years thanks to the efforts of the Quebec government to subsidize the production of babies, but this modest improvement has been purchased at a prohibitively high cost per additional birth.[71] If you think that the desire of its citizens to make more little citizens to populate its future is a measure of a society's happiness, this is a major problem. In fact, not only are Quebeckers reluctant to make new little Quebeckers unless the state pays them fairly generously to do so, even when nature starts the process, residents of Quebec are much more eager than in other parts of Canada to just say no to children. The province's high incidence of abortions led the CBC to call Quebec the "abortion capital of North America" in 2000.[72] And while the historical record is poor before the late eighties, what data we do possess show Quebeckers' predilection for abortion over parenthood deepening. In 1995, Quebec and Ontario shared a ratio of 31.5 abortions per thousand live births. A decade later, in 2004, Quebec's rate had risen by nearly a third to 41.3,[73] while Ontario's rate had steadily fallen by nearly a fifth to 26.5. The national average that year was 29.7.[74]

Low birth and high abortion rates are, one might think, somewhat offset by the language barrier. Unilingual French-speakers would likely have limited job prospects outside Quebec, making the French-speaking population somewhat less mobile than workers in other parts of the country. If, however, we looked at the total number of people *born* in Quebec and now living in other parts of the country, and not merely annual in- and out-migration, we would find that Quebec has suffered a stunning loss of (mostly but by no means exclusively English-speaking) people (and all the knowledge, education, and skills they represent) over the last forty years.

An analysis of census and other data suggest that as many as 250,000 English-speakers,[75] for example, left the province for other parts of Canada between 1971 and 1996. English-speakers were already leaving before then, and the exodus has undoubtedly continued since 1996, so the actual total is almost certainly higher. Nor is the exodus finished. It will be completed largely by the undertaker: the older you are, the more likely you will be unwilling or unable to absorb the costs of moving to a more welcoming place. The effect is particularly important for older English-speakers: a one-year increase in age increasing by two-thirds of one percentage point the probability of staying.[76] The young don't stay, increasing the weight in the English-speaking population of older Canadians. When, in due course, that generation dies off, it will essentially sound the death knell of a native-born English-language community that had been a vital part of Canada for two hundred years. There will still be English-speakers, of course, but fewer, and with few ties to the historic English-speaking community of Montreal and the province.

The number of native English-speakers in Quebec fell from 789,185 in 1971 (or 13 per cent of the population) to 557,040 (or 7.6 per cent) in 2001.[77] To that must be added the net out-migration of those of all mother tongues other than French or English, in other words among the traditional immigrant populations that had come to Montreal. The total net out-migration of non-French-speakers in the last forty years has been on the order of 425,000.[78] That net loss represented roughly 7 per cent of Quebec's population as it was in 1970, when nationalist policies really began to bite, when the PQ became a major electoral power, and when separatist-inspired terrorism (partly directed against English-speakers) reached its apogee in the kidnapping of British diplomat James Cross and the kidnapping and assassination of Quebec cabinet minister Pierre Laporte.

Such an absolute population and human capital loss (along with the children that population might have produced) was a big handicap for a provincial economy, but a boon for a nationalist movement trying to create economic opportunities for a large bulge of young French-speakers entering the workforce. There was also a side benefit. To the extent that the English-speaking emigrants were primarily unilingual and highly paid, the differential between the earnings of English-speakers and those of French-speakers would narrow.[79] That allowed the nationalist movement to claim a big victory for the allegedly endangered French-speakers ("We French-speakers are improving our performance relative to English-speakers") but did so by cutting off the top of the income distribution and depressing the average English-speakers' earnings rather than raising up French-speakers at the bottom:[80]

> As the outflow of more mobile (and likely higher-income) unilingual Anglophones increased, and as the inflow of highly-paid unilingual Anglophones diminished, their representation in the workforce not only declined, but lowered the average income of those who remained.[81]

Whether They Come Depends on What You Build

Of course there is another route to demographic renewal: immigration. Here Quebec's performance is also poor, again despite major government intervention. Quebec represents about a quarter of the population of Canada but routinely attracts only about 16 to 18 per cent of immigrants to the country, despite getting a disproportionate share of federal immigration funding, despite major recruiting efforts by the Quebec government of so-called *francophonisables*, and despite the now-official government policy of *interculturalisme* described earlier, whereby Quebec offers immigrants a "moral contract." In that contract, immigrants agree to do far more than to become Canadians. They become novitiates in the social justice community of Quebec, and their progress toward full rights to justice, paid for by the rest of the community, is conditional on their paying a price. That price is sufficient mastery of the sacred language of the community: French.

The fly in this ointment is that the moral contract is quickly understood by immigrants to ask them to pay a high cost (learning a new language is costly in many ways, and the economic value of French is falling all the time in a globalizing world where English is increasingly the lingua franca). In return they will be embraced by a community whose standard of living is low and declining relative to the rest of North America. It is not that you will not find people for whom the other opportunities to immigrate to North America may be limited, or who already enjoy some mastery of French, but they will be a small share of the pool of the most economically desirable immigrants. Most of them are willing to pay the high costs of immigration in order to secure a higher standard of living for themselves and their children, not in order to move into a community that apparently regards too much material success as a warning sign of a wavering member of the social justice and language community. If you have other options for immigration to North America, why bother with Quebec?

I am not the only one asking the question; clearly, many prospective immigrants are doing so as well. People heading for the exit is not the only reason that Quebec's share of the Canadian population has been declining fairly steeply in relative terms; Ontario, with less than 40 per cent of the country's population, attracts one-half of its immigrants, and British Columbia, with a population of only 4 million people, attracts as many immigrants as Quebec, with over seven and a half million. Migrants from other parts of Canada, a major source of growth for Ontario, British Columbia, and Alberta outside the current downturn, are also well below Quebec's share of the national population.

The question of "Why bother with Quebec?" is likely to become even more acute in the future as potential immigrants pick up on the same signals that have driven away so much of the English-speaking population. The public face of their languages is suppressed by Bill 101, and they are required by law to send their children to French-language schools, thus creating an obstacle to their children participating fully in the opportunities of a predominantly English-speaking North America. *Interculturalisme* is generating tensions between old-stock French-speakers and newcomers, unleashing a fractious debate over "reasonable accommodation."

The so-called reasonable accommodation debate has been triggered by a growing unease in Quebec caused by the belief that there is a burgeoning number of immigrants who are proving to be distressingly resistant to assimilation into the social justice and language community, thus allegedly yet again threatening the continued survival of a morally superior Quebec society and of the French language. This belief peacefully if incoherently co-exists with the facts laid out earlier, showing that French is now heavily favoured over English as the language of common communication adopted by immigrants.

Politicians are taking notice of the public's anxiety: the then leader of l'Action démocratique, Mario Dumont, made opposition to immigration a bit of a hobby horse and in March 2008 introduced a motion in the National Assembly to the effect that the government should "react to the setback suffered by French in Montreal ... and that it cancel the recent increase in the level of immigration and bring it back to the previous level."[82]

A poll a few weeks later showed that 51 per cent of Quebeckers agree with Dumont's position that Quebec should cut back on immigration. But interestingly, another poll around the same time revealed that while fewer than 10 per cent of Quebeckers would object to a black person becoming premier, nearly half of French-speakers would object to an English-speaker occupying that post.[83]

So just how attractive is Quebec society as measured by the growth of its population? Given the driving away of English-speakers and immigrants and the low fertility and high abortion rates, suffice it to say that over the thirty years between 1971 and 2001, Quebec's population grew by 1,209,715 or 16.7 per cent. The rest of Canada grew by 7,229,068 or 31.5 per cent, and Ontario's population grew by 3,706,941 or 32.4 per cent, in both cases roughly double the growth rate of Quebec.[84]

In a world where every society is in competition with others for scarce resources like people, Quebec's model has not proven attractive to people who have a choice as to where they live or whether they have children. The social justice state, the preoccupation with language, and the Quebec Inc. economic model, taken together, are the most likely explanation of this performance. If that is true, then the alleged distinct society marked out by these traits is literally squeezing the life out of Quebec.

8

Symmetry's Turning Point and a Tiny Window on the Future

Pushed along by the failures of socialism, the idea that a market economy provides the foundation for prosperity has gained widespread acceptance in recent years. Many countries have moved toward an environment more consistent with economic freedom and the smooth operation of a market economy. Trade barriers have been reduced, monetary systems have become more stable, marginal tax rates have been lowered, and various price controls—including exchange and interest rate controls—have been liberalized or eliminated. Yet in one critical dimension—the size of government—most nations have moved in the other direction. Over the past several decades, government expenditures as a share of GDP have been rising, resulting in more resource allocation through government.

ROBERT LAWSON, RANDALL HOLCOMBE, AND JAMES GWARTNEY,
THE SCOPE OF GOVERNMENT AND THE WEALTH OF NATIONS

In the 1960s television sitcom *The Beverly Hillbillies*, a running gag went like this: the Clampetts, a dirt-poor family from the Ozarks who had struck oil and moved into a Beverly Hills mansion, knew nothing about the conveniences of modern urban life.[1] In particular, they had never lived in a house with a doorbell. Whenever the doorbell rang, it set the mystified Clampetts scrambling in every direction in search of the ringing. They never were able to track it down, however, because for some inexplicable reason, after the bell had rung a couple of times and they were hot on the trail of its source, *someone always knocked at the door and distracted them.*

This was very comical for the audience, of course. They knew the ringing doorbell and the knocking were causally connected events. Only, the Clampetts failed to make the connection.

Watching governments in Canada over the last half century has come to feel more and more like watching this gag on *Beverly Hillbillies.* Unemployment up? Not enough government. Family dysfunction? Not enough government. Regional disparities? Not enough government. Child poverty? Not enough government. Poverty in general? Not enough government. They hear these bells ring and they reflexively search for a government program to respond. But in fact it is the government programs that are causing the bells to ring.

It is now clear, for example, that the unemployment that accompanied the move of the Boomers into the labour force in Canada was not due to the number of new workers at all. Rather the growth of government, first in Quebec, then in Ottawa, and finally in the other provinces, was the cause of our large-scale unemployment. Just one such unemployment-creating mechanism was the massive liberalization of UI in 1971, which hugely increased the disincentives to work.

One can go much further than just UI, however, and show there is strong evidence that government that looms too large relative to the economy is closely correlated with higher unemployment, as opposed to countries with smaller governments, which also tend to have lower unemployment.[2] The same can be said for the share of income enjoyed by the bottom 40 per cent of the population: the larger the size of government, the more their share of income declines. While the ideological justification for the expansion of the state has been to look after the weakest and most vulnerable, the evidence is that that justification is a sham: government that gets too large on the whole generates unemployment and worsens income inequalities.[3] A similar argument can be made for regional inequalities,[4] as well as for the causes of the decline of the family and the fall in fertility. While government professes to be the solution to these problems, problems that allegedly arise for mysterious reasons rooted in obscure things like "culture," the reality is that bad policy has caused many of these changes. Our "solution" of the last half century has, in fact, been the problem.

> Well, now, if government planning and welfare had the answer—and they've had almost 30 years of it—shouldn't we expect government to read the score to us once in a while? Shouldn't they be telling us about the decline each year in the number of people needing help? The reduction in the need for public housing? But the reverse is true. Each year the need grows greater; the program grows greater.
>
> Ronald Reagan, *A Time for Choosing*

Ironically, the evidence also shows that government can be part of the solution to social problems. My institute's work on transfers to Atlantic Canada, for example, shows that federal transfers and faster regional growth went hand in hand until the late sixties. After that, when transfers were pushed up to previously unimagined levels, the relationship turned negative. Too-high transfers undercut the growth as Atlantic Canada shifted from being a making to a taking society. The unemployment rates in Atlantic Canada had been steadily converging on the national rate until Bryce Mackasey and Co. liberalized UI in 1971. Immediately, the unemployment gap widened again, and the disparity was on the order of 2 to 4 percentage points for decades afterwards.[5] Government help is best given in homeopathic, not massive, doses.

This all suggests that we got causality wrong in our way of thinking about government and its role in the economy over the last fifty years. We came to believe that the reason we had unemployment and poverty over those decades was that government was too small and didn't do enough to absorb the wave of Boomers and women that entered the workforce. The solution, therefore, was to tax harder and spend faster. And if we hadn't done that, well, just imagine how dire things would have been has been the refrain. But instead, the evidence establishes quite strongly that if we hadn't force-fed government, the economy would have absorbed all these extra workers, as other industrialized democracies with smaller governments, such as the United States and Australia, were able to do quite successfully, and our productivity and standard of living would be higher.

In fact, it was the growth of government, motivated by the fear of Quebec nationalism and the possibility of unacceptable (i.e., nation-endangering) levels of unemployment without compensating social programs, that was a major factor driving our rising dependence, our lower productivity, and a growing pressure on the family. After all, it was vital that people in Quebec be aware that their well-being depended on the connection with Canada; who knew when the next referendum might come, and when the future of the county might be decided? Keeping Quebeckers sweet was far more important than ensuring they actually engaged in productive economic activity. And the rest of the country simply rode the cycle of rising transfers unleashing rent-seeking responses in the population, calling forth more government in response, although the extent of this imitation varied with local economic conditions, as the different evolutions of Atlantic Canada and Ontario, for example, clearly show.

Because we were frightened of what Quebec would do if ever we drew a line in the sand and said this far and no farther, no demand to be released from the exigencies of community membership could ever be definitively refused,[6] although there were always rearguard actions along the way, and regions unwilling to play the separatist card could be treated less accommodatingly. But when one member of the family can be refused nothing, it makes the refusal of anything to any other member of the family seem arbitrary and unfair. The result is that standards must eventually, slowly, but ineluctably, be jettisoned for all. Without the threat of separation, you can close steel plants in Cape Breton and fish plants in Newfoundland and pulp mills in Northern Ontario when they have outlived their economic usefulness. But if uneconomic steel plants and fish plants and pulp mills cannot be closed in Quebec, then the plants in Quebec and Cape Breton and Newfoundland and northern Ontario must all be accommodated until some fiscal crisis looms. And if people have their demand granted for welfare of various forms instead of working in Quebec, how can people in similar circumstances in other provinces be refused the same?

On the federal-provincial scene, the competitive dynamic I have described bound together Ottawa and Quebec City, to use René Lévesque's apt expression, like "two scorpions in a bottle."[7] But their dance of destruction did not leave everyone else as they had been. On the contrary. Every observer of the federal-provincial scene in the 1960s commented on the extent to which Quebec City took the lead in pressing Ottawa to send new transfers and to remove itself from jurisdictions that Quebec thought should be under its control. Even if many of the other provinces had no desire to see Ottawa get out of many of its traditional areas of responsibility, they were perfectly happy to take the money that Ottawa was spraying over the countryside. After all, this manna was falling at exactly the moment when masses of young people were entering the workforce and higher education. Schools and universities needed to be built, and there were anxieties about where all these young people would find work. Ottawa and Quebec City were blazing the trail, and public-sector employment was clearly the flavour of the month. Every province saw big increases in its budget and levels of employment, but clearly Quebec City and Ottawa were leading the parade.

The provinces also learned something about PUPPETRY (i.e., rent-seeking) behaviour when large sums are on the table. As we have seen, the size of the Canadian state rose quickly over the sixties and seventies. Both the rate of increase and the absolute size of the numbers meant that there was a lot of booty on the table, and Quebec was making no bones about wanting its share and more. In those circumstances, even the provinces that just wanted to be left alone and for Ottawa to take less of the national economy were drawn into asking constantly for more. If Quebec was getting hundreds of millions and even billions, why shouldn't Ontario or British Columbia or Nova Scotia get "their share"? In fact, if you were a provincial premier, failure to get "your share" in those circumstances would have been an invitation to your voters to retire you at the next provincial election. Quebec's success in getting federal booty generalized the bidding war across the country, and that, in its turn, drove the strategy that we employed to mop up the Boomers.

A key point for understanding what has happened and what will happen, then, is that the Baby Boomers became inextricably entangled with this grossing up of government. Just as our labour force was exploding, so too was the machinery of government, of dependency, and of pseudo-work in the public and private sectors. Many people with little attachment to a profession, a career, or even just a job burst onto the labour market and were quickly shunted into the expanding public sector. That gave a powerful impetus to the rent-seeking cycle at the same time as it undermined our individual and collective character.

So, while much of the change that Canada has undergone in the last fifty years has been made possible only by the wave of workers produced by the baby boom and the move of women into the workforce, that wave is now ebbing. That change will of necessity cause us to revisit things that many have come to regard as "settled" aspects of the New Canada somehow set free from its past. We will come soon to realize that the Canada and its values of the last fifty years or so will, or at least can, be supplanted by a Canada simultaneously new and old. The Canada that is already rising on the horizon will be much more drawn to the country's enduring traditional values than the passing ones that the special circumstances of the past few decades made possible. That is Canada's fearful symmetry.

The New Canada of recent decades will not go quietly, however. Some of the changes that are coming are inevitable and are simply dictated by the stark numbers of our future workforce and the distribution of the population among age groups and regions. In the rest of the book, I am going to sketch out what I think the very best outcomes are we can manage given the cards we have been dealt. But other outcomes are certainly possible. Here are two.

We are not the only society dealing with an aging population, although in the next few decades our population will age more quickly than in most other societies.

In considering the alternatives of how to deal with population aging we might, for instance, follow the trail blazed by the Japanese. Their response has chiefly been to run up the public debt to enormous proportions, with no end in sight.[8] The projections in early 2009 were for the annual budget deficit to rise to above 5 per cent of GDP and remain there for the foreseeable future.[9] Stimulus packages are already wreaking merry hell with those assumptions.

We've experienced the consequences of that strategy, and it wasn't pretty. One hoped that the one rule of fiscal probity that seemed well entrenched after our bitter experience with debts and deficits was "No budget deficits." If we had stuck to that rule, we would have closed off one of the easy but ultimately self-defeating responses to aging. Borrowing doesn't make the high cost of pensions and social programs and health care go away. It does, however, allow us to benefit from those services right away, while pushing the bills onto future taxpayers, with interest. It is an undisciplined and dishonourable solution. But it is one that can be popular because it looks like something for nothing, at least in the short run. And given politicians' propensity to find ways to excuse politically popular but anti-social behaviour, we will have to be on our guard against it, especially now that federal and provincial stimulus packages have let the budget deficits genie out of its bottle again. Politicians promise a return to balanced budgets when the economy recovers, but it is easier to promise cutting off the flow of tax dollars to powerful interest groups than it is actually to close the taps.

The other main alternative (which is quite compatible with pushing up public debt) is to hit the accelerator on the redistributionist state and simply raise the taxes to pay for it. Much of Western Europe has followed this course. As we have also learned from the experiences I have outlined in earlier chapters, however, the results are equally unpleasant. Job creation weakens. The public sector swells. Incentives to work are damaged. Fertility falls. Thousands march in the streets, as they have done in France, to protest efforts to rein in runaway spending, such as bringing rich public-sector pension plans a little closer to the benefits available to the taxpayers who foot the bill. And because the politicians still are unwilling to make current taxpayers pay the full cost of their popular policies, debt tends to rise anyway and economic decline causes politicians to return again and again to their voters with "reform plans" to shrink the state and improve competitiveness, with very mixed success.[10]

Neither of these solutions is causing the collapse and disappearance of the societies employing them. But neither are they thriving. We can and should do better, and demographic change will press us to do so. We can fight those changes or we can embrace them for the renewal of Canadian society they portend.

Why the Rest of the World Cannot Save Us

Whatever the benefits of immigration to Canada's economy and society, and to immigrants themselves, immigration cannot relieve Canada of the challenges of an aging population. The need to encourage work and saving by an older population and to deliver pensions and healthcare efficiently and sustainably will be as pressing in a future of high immigration as it would be without it.

WILLIAM ROBSON AND YVAN GUILLEMETTE, *NO ELIXIR FOR YOUTH*

Many Canadians' reaction to all this talk of labour shortages is to yawn and say, So what, can't we just let in a few more immigrants? And indeed immigration will be a part of the response, but only a small part. Immigration is projected to supply only a relatively small share of new workers for the Canadian economy. Four-fifths of the next generation of workers will come from the Canadian school system, not immigration.

Can't we just open the gates and increase that proportion coming from immigration? If only it were that simple.

There is a lot of confusion about just how much immigration Canada already accommodates. Many people assume that Canada has been achieving an oft-mooted net immigration target of 1 per cent of our population annually, but nothing could be further from the truth. The 1 per cent target has been a pious wish circulated in Ottawa for many years. In 2001, the (Liberal) minister responsible stated that the government "remained committed to increasing immigration levels to approximately 1 percent of the population over the long-term, but that Canada's ability to absorb and integrate increased numbers would dictate the pace."[1] In 2006, the (Conservative) minister of immigration stated, "Over the years there have been many reports and alleged promises of a one-percent immigration intake target for Canada. However, government statistics show that not once in the past 13 years has Canada's immigration intake met a target of one percent of the population."[2]

During the seventies and eighties, the net inflow of immigrants to Canada averaged about 75,000 per year, a relatively paltry number compared to recent years, where we have been hovering around 200,000.[3] To put that in perspective, since 2004 or so we have been allowing net immigration on the order of one-half of 1 per cent of the population (that is a gross intake of roughly three-quarters of 1 per cent minus a gross outflow of one-fifth of 1 per cent).[4] Federal projections are for a slight increase (to 0.54 per cent) by 2020 and for it to remain at that level afterwards.[5]

This level of immigration, however welcome it may be in helping to plug specific skill gaps in the economy, will leave the problem of our aging domestic population pretty much unaffected.[6] Only changes in behaviour by Canadians will be able to influence the consequences of our aging. We cannot outsource our problem to the younger populations of other countries.[7]

Even a substantial increase in the number of immigrants could not stop Canada's population aging. For example, if Canada was to admit four times as many immigrants per year, the population's median age would still increase, from the current 38.8 to 44.1 years in 2056. This would mean an average of about one million immigrants per year for the next 50 years. Regardless, the proportion of seniors would increase from the current 13.2% to 22.3% in 2056. These results are obtained from the medium-growth scenarios of Statistics Canada's most recent demographic projections and by adjusting the number of immigrants by a factor of four.

Statistics Canada, *The Daily*, October 26, 2006

It may be counterintuitive, but the reality is that immigration cannot substitute for domestic population growth. This seems to be the case for two main reasons. First, the age profile of immigrants is not all that different from that of the population as a whole.[8] Immigrants tend to arrive when they are around thirty years old, and then they age just like everybody else. And they may bring their aged parents, thus offsetting their own youthfulness in the age distribution of the population unless they have more children to compensate.

Achieving an annual gross immigration level of 1 per cent of the population rather than the current 0.75 per cent could, by some measures, *prevent* an additional 10 per cent *decline* in real GDP per capita due to aging.[9] In other words, immigration could ward off an even worse economic outcome than might otherwise befall us, but that too would take a number of years to achieve. There is just no getting around the fact that immigration is small relative to the population as a whole. Raising immigration levels can therefore mitigate only very partially the economic consequences of a broad social phenomenon like aging.

The second reason that immigration is a poor substitute for domestic population growth is that there has been a deterioration in the economic success of immigrants in recent years compared to the earlier post-war experience (although certain classes of immigrants are actually improving their performance), suggesting that the average new immigrant is making a smaller and smaller contribution to the country's prosperity.[10] The downward trend in earnings for both immigrant men and women relative to their Canadian-born counterparts is unmistakable, even after ten years in the country.[11] These gaps persist even when we control for education levels and are actually widest for the best educated.[12]

Canada has been less successful in recruiting immigrants suited to our economic needs in recent years, *and* we are rather poor at putting to work the skills and knowledge immigrants do bring with them. Immigration will likely be most important in allowing us to fill specific skill shortages (rather than to change the demographic profile of the country). To repeat: it can only be a contributor on the margins to resolving the issues created by an aging population (whatever other costs and benefits may attach to immigration). To put it baldly, only by allowing annual net immigration levels at roughly seven times our current levels and imposing draconian restrictions on the age of immigrants could we make a serious dent in our problem of population aging.[13]

In the context of thinking about the political, let alone the practical, consequences of such huge increases in immigration from current levels, consider the results of one Strategic Counsel survey in 2005. It found that three-quarters of those polled thought that Canada was already accepting too many immigrants.[14] It would be a brave politician indeed who wanted to defend the proposition that immigration levels needed to rise seven times in a country already accepting more immigrants, relative to its population, than any other.[15]

Immigration's Contribution

For the first time in Canadian history, more of our population increase is now due to immigration than to natural increase and, moreover, "Canada's population growth will stagnate and may even decline by 2026 if our immigration rates do not increase significantly."[16]

Before being alarmed by the National Research Council's conclusion, of course, we must be able to show both that (a) immigration such as we are able to attract will in fact make a significant economic contribution to the country, especially when we set the benefits against the real costs; and (b) higher levels of immigration in the future would result in better levels of economic success for both Canada and the new immigrants than we have been able to achieve in recent years.

Recent international research[17] has suggested that when all public expenditures and taxes are taken into account, the fiscal benefits of immigration are uncertain and depend crucially on the educational attainments of the immigrants. This point is contested by others, who claim to be able to demonstrate that in small, open economies such as Canada's, all income and age groups benefit from immigration, even if the newcomers are low-skilled and net beneficiaries of the pension system.[18] On balance, the consensus seems to be that immigration's contribution to GDP growth per capita is not very great either way. There can be little doubt, however, that low-skilled immigrants struggle to integrate successfully into the Canadian economy, and as we shall see, they are likely to form a growing share of those seeking to immigrate to Canada. Thus changes in the overall composition of immigrants may create different outcomes than in the past for both immigrants and for Canada. Indeed, it will likely require rising levels of spending by Canada (in education, language training, acculturation, integration, etc.) to get the same levels of economic benefit from immigration as in the past.

Canada's past history suggests that immigrants can and should make a major contribution to the country's and to their own well-being, and there is no doubt that certain classes of immigrants have been doing better. Again, this points to a need to think deeply about how to come up with an immigration policy that serves the needs of the country.

Who Is in Charge Here Anyway?

It's time to re-examine the process whereby immigrants are chosen. For example, economist David Foot[19] summarized the qualities that ideally would characterize the most desirable immigrants from an economic point of view: they would be of working age; likely to participate in the workforce; likely to be employed, hard workers, and highly productive. Thus these criteria should, as Foot sensibly recommends, form the basis of how immigrants are chosen. Along these lines, much has been made in recent years of the extent to which the Economic Class of immigrants has come to dominate overall immigration numbers, thus implying that people chosen for their ability to contribute to the Canadian economy are the most significant group of immigrants.[20] For example, in 2005 the composition of landings by immigration class was as follows:[21]

Economic	60%
Family	24%
Refugee	14%
Other	3%

And the trend in recent years has strongly favoured the Economic Class. However, this badly misrepresents the extent to which Economic Class immigrants in fact are chosen for their job skills and ability to be economically productive. Of the 133,746 Economic Class immigrants landed in 2004, 60,424 were skilled workers, entrepreneurs, self-employed, investors, provincial/territorial nominees, and live-in caregivers. The balance, or 73,322, was spouses and dependants of these principal applicants. In other words, fewer than half were admitted because of their capital or jobs skills. Now, it goes without saying that these principal applicants would not have come if they could not have brought their families, just as it is obvious that their spouses may well be equipped to make a welcome contribution to the economy. But the issue is rather that barely a quarter of the immigrants granted permanent residence in 2004 were bona fide economic immigrants, chosen for their objectively measured ability to make an immediate and significant contribution, not the 60 per cent suggested by the official statistics.

Even with Ottawa's 2008 reforms designed to reinforce the weight of genuine economic criteria in choosing immigrants the fact is that bureaucrats are no more successful at picking winners among immigrants than they are in other fields, such as government investments in business or "industries of the future." If we go back to Foot's list of criteria for economically successful immigrants, note that these are precisely the qualities that every employer seeks in every employee, immigrant or not. And employers are probably better than anyone else at assessing the chances that a potential employee will "pay off" in the sense of becoming a valued employee.

So if what we want are immigrants who succeed more in the economy, why do we allow bureaucrats instead of employers to pick our immigrants? It surely cannot be because bureaucrats enjoy some information advantage over employers as to what skills are most in demand—it is the employers who actually are the ones doing the demanding, and so each employer knows his or her requirements in greater detail and with greater precision than any bureaucrat can ever hope to do.

It used to be thought that the costs of matching employers and employees internationally were prohibitive, and it was more sensible to bring potential immigrants to a single Canadian window for processing. But technology has made all this redundant. Anybody who has been on monster.com knows that anybody anywhere in the world with access to a computer can find out more about the current state of the job market in Canada with a few keystrokes than any government office can ever tell him, and that information will be up to the minute. If we allowed employers to hire people from outside the country and bring them in to fill jobs immediately, with no queuing, it is also clear that a market would emerge in which entrepreneurs matched employers and employees for a fee. This cannot be morally objectionable since employment agencies and head-hunters already do a roaring trade within Canada. Why not let them do the same across the border? Basically, our policy should be that any potential immigrant who can get a formal job offer from a Canadian employer and pass the security and health checks should be granted immediate status. Such arrangements would, of course, have to be subject to after-the-fact spot audits to prevent fraud.

And as for recognizing immigrants' qualifications, the current obstacles are a scandal that should cause the people responsible to hang their heads in shame. Theirs is a transparent effort to protect not the interests of supposedly vulnerable and ignorant consumers (who are generally quite able to look after themselves) but rather the interests of those already exercising these professions in Canada. We should move aggressively to push aside these protectionist barriers as unworthy of a society that has grown through offering opportunity to people from all over the world. New arrivals should be given the chance, within a very short period of time, to challenge directly, through one or more exams and other appropriate tests, the professional standards of Canada and any of the provinces and get their professional qualifications recognized as equivalent. Mentoring and apprenticeship programs should be automatically provided for those trying to get qualifications recognized in large and complex fields such as medicine, where the period required to establish equivalency might be relatively long, thus allowing them to exercise their profession temporarily under the supervision of recognized Canadian practitioners.

Don't Call Us, We'll Call You: Immigrants

Yet just as Canada is coming to realize that it may need to be more thoughtful about its immigration program, Canada's relative attractiveness as a destination for immigrants is declining and the competition for the best immigrants is intensifying in every part of the world.[22] For example, Chinese students, who in the past might well have come to study in the West and then attempt to stay, are now returning in large numbers to China after completing their education.

Many developing countries, especially in Asia, that were once lands that the ambitious and talented sought to flee, are now places of huge opportunity. Nearly 70 per cent of executives of Indian origin living in the United States indicated in a recent survey that they were actively looking for opportunities to return home. In 1987, the then Communist Party general secretary, Zhao Ziyang, described China's exodus of talent as "storing brain power overseas."[23] They are now doing everything in their power to lure it back. There is no reason to think that once Canada has attracted high-talent immigrants that they will stay in Canada for life. In fact, over a quarter of immigrants to Canada don't stay now, and the chances are this proportion will increase.[24]

> The cost of an Indian graduate is roughly 12% of that of an American one. Indian graduates also work more: an average of 2,350 hours a year compared with 1,900 hours in America and 1,700 in Germany. The bottom line is that you can buy almost ten Indian brains for the price of one American one.
>
> *The Economist*, October 7, 2006

This should cause us to call into question the comfortable assumption too often made by Canadians and their governments that we can attract as many immigrants as we wish at whatever levels of education and skills we need.

Both China and India, for example, project severe shortages of the talented people they will need to make a modern industrial economy function, and they are almost certainly keeping at home many of those who might, in another era, have been emigrants. Consider the Indian IT sector. Because salaries are lower and Indian graduates work longer hours than North Americans or Europeans, you multiply by a factor of ten the brainpower that you buy per dollar when you outsource work in this sector to India, although wage inflation and other factors are eroding some of that advantage.[25]

The industry in India is already butting up against labour shortages of its own. One industry group predicts a shortfall of 500,000 IT professionals within two years. Reportedly, GE Capital, part of a large U.S.–based multinational, has signs posted throughout its Indian offices already: "Trespassers will be recruited."[26] Executives in India are more than twice as likely as their Canadian counterparts to report that their employees have been approached by a competitor with a view to recruitment.

Yet places such as India and China are the very countries that, in recent years, have been significant sources of immigration to this country. According to Kathleen Newland of the Migration Policy Institute in Washington, D.C., "Based on the experience of countries like Spain, Portugal, Greece and South Korea, emigration usually slows when income per person approaches a threshold level in relation to income in the richer countries where the migrants are heading."[27] That ratio may be as low as four or five to one, meaning that the most desirable immigrants that Canada might traditionally have wanted to recruit, those with high levels of skills and knowledge, are going to be increasingly hard to attract from traditional source-countries where the middle class is growing richer fast.

Moreover, as Demetri Papademetriou, head of the Migration Policy Institute, notes, the range of host countries eager to recruit the most economically valuable immigrants is much broader than it used to be. Long gone are the old days of the immediate post-war era when Canada was one of a tiny handful of countries with relatively open immigration and a high standard of living. With absolute population declines in some cases, rich but previously largely closed European countries, for example, are taking an aggressive approach to immigration promotion.[28]

On the other hand, Canada may see increases in immigration numbers from less traditional sources. Africa is an example, because the wage gap between, say, North America and Africa is now double what it was between North America and low-income Europe during the nineteenth century, a time of mass migration.[29] Like much of Latin America, Africa's population is very young, but the education and skills of its population are poor.

The result is likely to be that while Canada may continue to be able to attract large numbers of immigrants, their ability to contribute to the Canadian economy will, on average, be lower than what we have traditionally expected. Immigration will be more costly because we will have to spend more money to bring language and other skills up to a level where newcomers can integrate successfully. Immigration will be no silver bullet, but openness to the movement of people will be essential to our future.

Don't Forget International Trade in Goods

Essential, too, will be openness to the international movement of goods and services and capital. Canada's success in dealing with the challenges of population aging will almost certainly depend as well on our remaining open to trade, including so-called offshoring, or the transfer of jobs from Canada to other countries.

The reason, of course, that trade plays such an important role is that every economy has its characteristic mix of strengths and weaknesses. International trade maximizes the ability of each economy to improve its standard of living through specializing in those things in which it has the greatest advantage compared to others.

This is surely just as true with regard to demographic characteristics as any others. It is not that the world will be short of young workers. Indeed, the population will continue to grow significantly in the Third World as Canada's stabilizes; production processes requiring large numbers of young and relatively inexpensive workers will naturally tend to be transferred to those jurisdictions with a lot of young people. Canada, on the other hand, with its highly educated and increasingly experienced (because older) workforce, will have a great deal to offer other countries short on managerial, scientific, institutional, and other expertise. Access to the industrial production of growing economic giants such as the BRIC countries (a convenient shorthand for some of the most important emerging economies: Brazil, Russia, India, and China) helps to keep cost-of-living increases low for Canadians, including retired populations on fixed incomes, and allows us to keep interest rates low. Finally, openness to international capital markets means that Canadian investors can earn better returns on their investments while promoting diversification and risk reduction, thus improving the retirement prospects of Canadians.

> The same forces that drove European emigration before 1914 are even more powerful in Africa today.... For example, European-African wage gaps are double those for the New World and low-income Europe in the 1800s.... With the young adult share of the African population expected to rise by several percentage points by 2015 ... African emigration could reach the same pace as European emigration in the 1870s.
>
> Jeffrey Williamson, The Inaugural Noel Butlin Lecture

Thus it will be a policy imperative for an aging Canada to protect existing levels of international trade openness and to seek to expand them where possible, including through multilateral and bilateral trade agreements. Canada may therefore need to revisit some of its own policies, such as Ottawa's dogged determination to protect the supply-management system in agriculture, that have reduced this country's prestige and bargaining power in international trade negotiations.[30] This is a classic example of the kind of choices we will be faced with if we intend to use the demographic changes that are coming as a way to escape the dead hand of the last fifty years on our growth, standard of living, and most importantly on our character.

Note that while increased trade with foreign economies and immigration may be thought of as similar, in that both use workers of foreign origin to increase the supply of goods and services at home, they are not strictly interchangeable sources of labour.[31] Immigrants themselves consume goods and services in their new host country, and so immigration itself increases the demand for labour more than foreign trade does. By contrast, immigrants in Canada and other Western countries may be expected to be more productive than in their country of origin *and* there are some things they can produce only if they are present in Canada. Immigrants, in fact, play a disproportionate role in providing services such as home care for the sick and elderly and child care, which will be of increasing importance but cannot be provided remotely.

In any case, the conclusion is pretty clear: the rest of the world will not rescue us from the folly of the last fifty years, although they will certainly lend a hand. Most of the heavy lifting will have to come from us, in the form of removing the barriers to growth that we erected to satisfy rent-seekers, not retiring so early and having more babies.

The Two Nations in Canada's Future: Lord Durham Updated

Sustained economic growth—even if one narrowly defines it as sustained growth in income per person—is everywhere and always a process of continual transformation. The economic progress that rich nations have enjoyed since the Industrial Revolution would not have been possible had people not undergone wrenching changes. Economies that cease to transform themselves are destined to fall off the path of economic growth. The countries that most deserve the title of "developing" are not the poorest of the world, but the richest. To stay rich, countries like Canada must engage in a never-ending process of economic development and transformation.

PETER HOWITT, "INNOVATION, COMPETITION AND GROWTH"

My ancestors, Laurence and Honora Crowley, arrived in Canada in the 1840s from Ireland and immediately set about clearing what became the family homestead at a place that became Kincora (or Kinkora) in Ellice Township, near Stratford, Ontario. Like most Canadians of the time, they and their descendants lived and worked on the land. According to the Canada West census of a few years after their arrival, Honora was illiterate, and she was doubtless not alone in the family.

My grandfather, Lee, born in 1892, was the first Crowley to leave the family farm for a university education (according to family legend, his studies were largely financed by pool sharking, and knowing him as I did this seems to me a highly credible claim—alas, I was graced with his name but not his skills with a cue). He never returned. He was part of a vast movement of people in Canada that saw the overwhelming majority of the population living on the land in 1900, but only a tiny fraction a century later. This shift of people drove the growth of Canada as an industrial and economic power and saw our standard of living soar as Canada's growing population found better education and more sophisticated and diverse work in the cities. Far from regretting my grandfather's decision as the desperate act of a man forced by circumstance to leave a rural idyll, all his descendants bless his name as the man who opened before us the prospects of a cosmopolitan, varied, and rich existence in the city.

Let My People Go

No discussion of raising Canada's economic game to respond to our demographic challenges can neglect movement within Canada as one of the traditional motors of economic growth and improved individual standards of living.

While every part of the country has had its share of state-sponsored schemes for soaking up surplus workers, these schemes have been relatively less important in parts of the country with strong economies capable of pulling most people into real work. While it is unpopular to say so, we would certainly have been able to find more work for more people had workers in less favoured parts of the country been willing to move to where the jobs were. But one of the moral certainties of the decades since the late sixties was that no person should ever have to leave their home in pursuit of work and opportunity. Instead, it was the obligation of the state to deliver opportunity to people wherever they happened to live. If our governments could not do so, they had an obligation to deliver an income, unconnected to working, instead.

The result was the gumming up of the mechanism that had permitted most Canadians to improve their lot in life in earlier times as governments threw more and more sand in the works of this conveyor belt to prosperity. Movement between provinces went on a slow steady decline from a high in the 1970s to a deep low in the early part of this century. But in another sign of the big changes that are afoot, between 2004 and the recession of 2008-09, there was an unprecedented spike in that movement. People were being pulled out of parts of the country in economic decline or stagnation as never before. The population of Alberta rose by an almost unheard-of 3 per cent in one year alone (2006), although the downturn has temporarily cut the flow. Newfoundland and Labrador's population has been in decline for several years (although high oil prices stabilized it for a few years, and now some workers returning from Alberta may temporarily help too), and Quebec's

> Regional barriers to mobility have always been a serious problem for Canada. But in a knowledge-based economy, the problem is even more serious because technical change is rapid and unpredictable, and those who are unwilling or unable to move are at the mercy of fortune. Removing mobility barriers would result in a more adaptable workforce, which, in turn, would reduce the premium the economy pays for adaptability, thereby lowering overall wage and income inequality.
> Peter Howitt, "Innovation, Competition and Growth"

population, while still growing, is growing more slowly than the country as a whole. So StatsCan foresees in 2031 a Canada whose population is distributed vastly differently than it is today:[1]

> Five provinces/territories are likely to have a smaller population in 2031 than their estimated population in 2005: Newfoundland and Labrador, New Brunswick, Saskatchewan, Northwest Territories and Yukon.
>
> Ontario, Alberta, [and] British Columbia ... would see an increase in their share of the total population between now and 2031. Ontario's population would be between 14.8 and 17.5 million in 2031, more than 40% of Canada's population in every scenario, compared with less than 39% in 2005. Alberta's population, 3.3 million in 2005, would break the 4 million barrier in 2031, increasing the province's share of the national population, which was 10% in 2005. With a population in excess of 5 million or even 6 million ... in 2031, compared with 4.3 million in 2005, British Columbia would account for 14% or 16% of the Canadian population.
>
> With a population of 7.8 to 8.9 million in 2031, Quebec would see its share of the total population fall from 23.5% to 21.6% at best [and 20.9% at worst].[2]

There are all kinds of ways in which the movement of people matters. Consider, for example, that if we were able simply to get the same proportion of people working in the five easternmost provinces as the current national average, we would put another 156,000 workers into the workforce.[3] And one of the ways that we would do that traditionally would be to encourage people to move to higher-opportunity parts of the country.

When I say "encourage," I don't mean exhortation by government. I mean letting people read the unfiltered signals that the economy is sending about where their skills are most needed and are therefore most valuable. After years of governments making those signals hard to read, they are now shining through unmistakably.

As a result, in the years immediately before the downturn, the movement of people in Canada was on a tear, bidding fair to exceed the highs known in much earlier decades. But note that if you compare the graph showing the recent history of interprovincial movement (i.e., long-term decline in mobility from roughly 1962 to 2002, but a stunningly rapid rise since then) with the graph showing the differences in incomes between regions, you will find that they are almost identical. In other words, as income disparities have grown between regions, people have been drawn from low-income regions to higher-incomes ones. Put the other way around, when governments' efforts to redistribute income reduce the rewards to workers of moving, they don't move. When regionally concentrated labour shortages sharpen the income differences, movement takes off. To give a concrete example, when just a few years ago the average wage in Atlantic Canada was 90 per cent of the average wage in Alberta, Atlantic Canadians stayed put. When the average wage in the region fell to only 80 per cent of Alberta's, people couldn't move west fast enough. Such free movement of workers means higher growth for the Canadian economy as people find better fits between their job skills and available work.

> The Atlantic region and Quebec are the fastest aging regions and their economies are more severely affected by this trend than the rest of Canada. In these regions, the negative labour supply shock is exacerbated by early retirement behaviour and a greater proportion of inactive adult population. The negative impact [of population aging] on real GDP per-capita in the Atlantic region and Quebec ranges from 4.6% and 6.9% in 2026 to 28% and 22.8% in 2050, respectively.
>
> Maxime Fougère and Simon Harvey, "The Regional Impact of Population Aging in Canada"

The higher shares of the population working right across the country also showed that the expansion of available work was not just limited to fast-growing regions. As workers move from lower- to high-growth regions, that migration often opens up opportunities for work in the lower-growth regions for others who might not otherwise be working.

Today even economic downturns are different in their effects on workers. The unemployment rate in mid-March 2009 was 7.7 per cent. To put that in perspective, the unemployment rate from 1974 to 1999 was *always* higher (8.1 per cent in 1990 was the lowest during the period). Moreover, during a similar worldwide recession in the early 1980s, the Canadian unemployment rate was in double digits for four years (1982 to 1985), peaking in 1983 at 12.7 per cent. While obviously we cannot know exactly how the current malaise will play out, we haven't seen double-digit unemployment since 1994 (10.4 per cent).[4]

So in ordinary circumstances, Canada's dynamic national labour market works exactly as it should, spreading opportunity across the country and not just in high-growth regions, something that decades of regional economic development programs could not achieve. In fact, the redistributionist policy of the past few decades has been much more successful at closing the income disparity gap between regions than the production gap in Canada.[5] It is just so much easier to write people cheques for much of the difference between what they earned in

Chicoutimi or Sydney compared to what they might have earned in Calgary or Vancouver than it is to actually close the productivity gap that causes the income gap in the first place.

The return of income disparities shows just how wrong-headed this redistributionist emphasis has been, in the sense that recent evidence seems to suggest strongly that rising income disparities are an important signal to Canadians about where the opportunities are. Government income support programs have drowned out those signals. It is this that has confused Canadians about exactly where the best opportunities were to be found over the past few decades.

Two Nations Warring in the Bosom of a Single State

If it is the case that *rising* income disparities has been an important driver of movement of people around the country, this has important implications for the future because the impact of aging will not be uniform across the country.

On the contrary, because it is by far the largest recipient of immigrants and has relatively high productivity, Ontario will be spared some of the pain of population aging, as will high-productivity Alberta, at least for several decades. Like Alberta, Manitoba and Saskatchewan will enjoy high birth rates and therefore also fare reasonably well. By contrast, in Quebec and the east generally, with low immigration rates, high out-migration, low productivity, and trends to earlier retirement, the outcomes are likely to be much less rosy. In Quebec over the last twenty-five years, for example, the number of people over 65 has risen faster than in the rest of Canada, while those under 15 have declined faster.[6]

All this implies a further acceleration of the already marked divergence in the situation of the two parts of the country on either side of the Ottawa River. West of that boundary, higher immigration, higher productivity, and, in some cases, higher fertility will mute the problems caused by population aging. In the east, by contrast, unless we can shift the trends (e.g., in when and how people retire), rapid aging will tend to remove a large proportion of workers from the labour force, who will by and large not be replaced by either immigrants or native-born children. This will constrain economic growth while at the same time causing a rapid rise in demand for certain kinds of workers (such as health care workers) because of the different patterns of demand caused by an older population. The "*deux nations*" in Canada will no longer be English Canada and French Canada but a predominantly "making nation" (young, English-speaking, multicultural, western, and on the rise economically) on the one hand and a predominantly "taking nation" (old, predominantly French-speaking, eastern, and in relative decline) on the other.

Here is how this new two-nations policy has worked.

Areas that had the least need of federal cash and whose economies provided the extra cash for transfers to other provinces—such as Ontario and Alberta—were also the provinces that enjoyed the highest rates of population growth, the highest levels of immigration, (with occasional lapses) the lowest levels of provincial taxation and debt, and the lowest shares of provincial GDP devoted to government. They therefore became relatively less enmeshed in domestic versions of PUPPETRY (rent-seeking). They empowered interest groups less than more dependant parts of the country did. They put more of the young workers into genuine work and less into public-sector work, pseudo-work, and welfare dependency. They focused more on making and less on taking. As a result, those parts of the country continued to progress economically faster than the rest of the country. This progress was all relative, of course; they fell back relative to their U.S. counterparts, where the size of the state was much less again and grew more slowly, but they remained the economic bright spots of Canada throughout these decades. Temporary downturns in the auto industry and falls in oil prices are unlikely to change this long-term underlying reality.

On the other hand, provinces caught up in the big-government rent-seeking extravaganza have seen their economic and population lights dim.

Thus many of the major policy changes of the last half century, defended as contributing to greater equity and fairness in Confederation, produced or at least reinforced a major regional divergence in Canada. Those regions, such as Ontario and Alberta, that enjoyed the most successful and dynamic private economies, were least drawn into the shift from making to taking because the private-sector opportunities were greater, thus rewarding the maintenance of more traditional behaviours. Because these behaviours confer success, just as Canadians traditionally had believed, these regions enjoyed more economic success than those regions that found taking more profitable than making. Major population and economic shifts resulted, although these were driven more by higher fertility and higher levels of immigration than would usually have been the case. Interprovincial mobility of Canadians, traditional motor of the economy, was discouraged by the new redistributionist mentality that saw regional variations in levels of opportunity as a grievance calling for compensation rather than as positive signals of how to raise everyone's standard of living.

Those economies least caught up in dependency and rent-seeking grew strongly. That is the explanation for the phenomenon already noted, that Ontario, for example, with only 38 per cent of the population has enjoyed a prolonged period of high productivity during which it has produced as much as 42 per cent of GDP (even if that number has been temporarily depressed by the downturn),[7] whereas Quebec contains a little less than a quarter of the national population, but officially produces barely 20.5 per cent of the national wealth.[8] Even that figure is probably too high because it counts the disproportionately high ratio of pseudo-work in the Quebec economy as if it produces real value. This divergence in performance occurred even as the better-performing parts of the country were burdened with an ever-larger bill to pay for the redistribution that was undermining the performance of its recipients.

The main bright spot for the traditionally weaker regions such as the Maritimes in the coming decades is likely to be the more severe scarcity of workers in the eastern half of the country than elsewhere (because of aging), the knock-on effect of which is likely to be significantly reduced dependence on EI and other social benefits as rising wages pull more people into work. If the recently observed effects of rising wage disparities on inter-regional migration are any guide, this would have the effect of increasing job opportunities and wages in the east, drawing migrants from other parts of the country, and increasing the returns to education and training for workers already in the east.

Again, though, this positive outcome can occur only if these provinces are not relieved of responsibility for current destructive policies that prevent economic growth from manifesting itself more vigorously. As we have already seen in the case of Quebec, the result of counterproductive but politically popular provincial policies under the current regime of massive wealth redistribution is that the poorly performing provinces are further entrenched in their bad policies by a combination of rent-seeking behaviour (i.e., PUPPETRY) by governments and their voters and easy money from federal transfers.

It would thus be important for governments not to repeat the mistakes of the past by reacting to increased income disparities nationally by increasing transfer payments to traditionally less-developed parts of the country. Too often those transfers are uncoupled from work and productivity, which are going to be vital elements of a strategy to cope with population aging. Instead, we should rely on those proven adjustment mechanisms that reward work, mobility, and productivity.

This is just as true of Quebec as other parts of the country. The argument is usually made that unilingual French-speaking Quebec workers cannot be expected to move to English-speaking parts of the country for jobs. Since they cannot therefore participate in the increase in economic well-being that movement makes possible, equalization and other transfers are just the price of preventing the death of a French-speaking society through dispersion and assimilation, or the alternative: separation. All this might be more convincing if Quebec and Ottawa didn't spend so much time competing to keep French-speaking populations in Quebec from moving *within Quebec* to areas of greater opportunity.

The areas of greatest economic decline within the province have also often been the greatest battlefields in the struggle to keep Quebec within Canada. The bargaining power of many rural communities in the Eastern Townships, the Saguenay-Lac-St-Jean, the Gaspé, and elsewhere has been strong, resulting in the propping up of their declining natural resource industries to prevent painful economic renewal. It isn't just movement between provinces that has been squeezed, but also movement within provinces. Even though the data show that Quebec (like Ontario) has a relatively high rate of movement within the province (reflecting the fact that large provinces have more places to move to than smaller ones), the fact remains that large shares of the population remain in areas of low opportunity, driven in part by the state's willingness to subsidize such choices. In fact, the decline in migration by workers within Quebec has followed the same generally downward trend as interprovincial migration nationally over the last forty years.[9] The one major difference is that Quebec has not experienced the spectacular rise in mobility over the years preceding the downturn. Aging will produce rising demand for workers and therefore rising wages in economically dynamic parts of the province in the future, however— if the state doesn't seek to suppress those effects through redistribution. In any case, though, even if migration within Quebec picks up, the province's generally low levels of productivity mean that movement will not produce the same kind of rise in the province's standard of living as interprovincial mobility does nationally in Canada.

In Atlantic Canada, the years before the recent downturn saw an acceleration of out-migration to the west, although the flows have temporarily reversed because of falling natural resource prices. Migration from the countryside to the region's cities also sped up in the good years, and those two trends together dragged down unemployment and raised the productivity of those in work. But we have a lot of lost time to make up as we shed the policies of the past decades that rewarded people so handsomely for staying put where there were few opportunities and local industries were in decline.

Why We Will Hear More from Those Who Foot the Bill

The argument so far shows how the less well-developed regions of the country were harmed by past policies and also how their economies and politics are likely to be transformed by the aging of Boomers. What deserves more attention, though, is the other half of the regional equation: not the recipients of this "largesse," but those who paid the bill. In the face of such stark evidence about

the self-defeating nature of much inter-regional redistribution, why did Ontario in particular remain so silent over the years, only to become an increasingly
vocal critic of such redistribution since the mid-nineties?

While the increasing evidence of the failure of these inter-regional redistributive policies has become hard to ignore in the past few years, the true cause
of Ontario's change of heart does not come from looking at the bad effects of
regional policy on Quebec and the rest of the taking nation, primarily the country east of the Ottawa River. Ontario's increasing angst and anger is much more
due to how free trade and continental integration have changed the political
economy of Confederation than it is to the manifest failings of EI or the Atlantic Canada Opportunities Agency.

The move to free trade is having subtle but increasingly irresistible influence
on what we have called "regional policy" over the last forty years. Much of that
policy, at least in its current form, will have to go, largely as a consequence of the
competitive pressures arising from continental integration. Given the failure of
these programs, this is no bad thing.

To understand how continental free trade is going to drive changes in
today's regional policy, we have to understand how very different the context
was in which much of that policy was originally put in place. According to former Quebec and Ottawa cabinet minister Eric Kierans,

> When I was a member of the Lesage government in Quebec in the early 1960s,
> I attended a first ministers' meeting in Toronto. A proposal was on the table to
> create a new federal transfer program, the effect of which would have been to
> take millions of dollars out of the wealthy provinces and distribute it to the
> poorer ones. No province would foot a higher bill than Ontario, yet then-
> premier John Robarts looked on benignly and supported the proposal. My
> curiosity piqued, I cornered Robarts in the corridor and asked him why he
> looked with such equanimity on a proposal that would cost his province dear.
> Robarts' response spoke volumes about the political understandings which
> underpinned all the transfer programs that emerged from those febrile times.
> Ontario had no quarrel with these programs, he said, because the money came
> right back to Ontario in the form of the purchase of goods and services. The
> transfers were simply a way of ensuring that people in the regions had the
> money to buy Ontario's products.[10]

Whatever the economic merits of Ontario premier John Robarts's view, as
reported by Eric Kierans, as a picture of the political economy of Canada at that
time it had a certain logic. Canada had been created as an act of political will,

in defiance of natural economic ties. Those ties had led Canadians in every region to look chiefly south for the source of their prosperity. Politics, in the form of Sir John A. Macdonald's National Policy, had contrived to make that much more difficult, throwing up a tariff wall at the border and investing massively in the CPR (i.e., east-west infrastructure to tie the new national economy together).

But embracing continental free trade in 1988 was a conscious decision to repudiate the National Policy (which Sir John A. had always believed was a poor substitute for free trade, but American resistance meant that free trade was not an option open to him) and to revive the north-south links that had played second fiddle to the nation-building efforts of Canada's first century.

The consequences for regional policy are not far to seek. Free trade means that those transfer dollars are no longer shepherded back to Ontario, but may in fact be used to purchase goods and services from Ontario's competitors in Boston, New York, or Chicago. The old political understanding is breaking down.

And while transfers, such as equalization,[11] are often justified on the grounds that they protect the equality of Canadians in their access to provincial services, that is less and less convincing when we see how equalization has in fact been used, not to guarantee equal levels of services, but to guarantee, for instance, relative levels of provincial government employment and pay in the recipient provinces[12] that exceed those offered in Ontario and Alberta. That is the classic outcome of rent-seekers scrambling to capture the spoils that transfers have put on the table.

Putting equalization and much of the edifice of inter-regional transfers (such as the notorious regionally extended benefits under EI) out of their misery is only a matter of time. It isn't just that the transfers don't work and do create a vicious cycle of PUPPETRY. They have become an intolerable burden on the industrial heartland of the country; that burden, moreover, is about to grow, creating a competitive drag on the success of some of our most successful workers, regions, and industries just when we need them to be as robust and productive as possible.

The case for EI reform is pretty straightforward, and I have already explained why reform in that area is almost inevitable as political support for programs that pay people not to work and discourage mobility evaporates in an era of labour shortages. Equalization is a little harder for people to grasp, so without getting into the arcane details of how it works, let me try to summarize crudely the problem. Much of the "disparity" between the revenues enjoyed by various provincial governments was driven by natural resource revenues until the recent downturn. And we're not just talking about the revenues flowing to Alberta. British Columbia was receiving large sums in auctions for natural gas exploration rights, for example. And Saskatchewan and Newfoundland, two long-time equalization recipients, were riding the natural resource commodity wave to new heights.[13] Even though natural resource prices have come off that peak, however, there is little reason to think that they will not return in due course. With countries like China, Brazil, India, Russia, and others trying to drag millions of their citizens into relatively modern conditions, the demand for resources will return when the economic cycle turns anew. We have been through these cycles before, and every time, the rise in natural resource prices puts intolerable pressure on the equalization system. The current downturn only wins us some breathing space. The problem will not go away. In fact, because the equalization system now smoothes revenues over time, the big spikes in natural resource prices will continue to drive equalization entitlements up in the next few years, even though the actual revenues to resource-rich provinces have fallen significantly.

The reason that all this matters is that an unreformed equalization program must somehow make up the alleged disparities created be-

> "The Newfoundland and Saskatchewan economies have gone from stagnant to stellar," declared Statistics Canada in its May 2008 Economic Observer. "These two provinces have moved beyond old stereotypes and stepped into a new era of prosperity."
>
> Both provinces led the country last year in the growth of provincial exports, in the rate of housing starts, and in GDP growth—the only provinces along with Alberta whose per capita GDP was above the national average.
>
> In June, 2007 a report by the TD Bank Financial Group called Saskatchewan "Canada's commodity superstore," and said if the province was a country it would rank fifth in the world among OECD nations in terms of GDP per capita, trailing only Luxembourg, Norway, the U.S. and Ireland. (Alberta would come second if ranked on the same list.)
>
> As for Newfoundland and Labrador, over the past decade its per capita GDP has gone from $10,000 below the national average to $10,000 above: the fastest, 10-year turnaround of any province in Canadian history.
>
> Richard Foot, "Have-not no more," *Leader Post*

tween provinces with vast natural resource endowments and those not so blessed. I say "alleged" because the whole premise is, of course, nonsense. The idea that natural resources are an unfair "leg-up" that less-endowed provinces must be compensated for is the exact reverse of the truth. Most economists will tell you that vast natural resource wealth is a curse, not a blessing, because of the rent-seeking PUPPETRY they unleash. Resource-rich places such as Russia,

Nigeria, and much of the Middle East are bywords for corruption, autocracy, and poverty. Even Louisiana, with one of the best resource endowments in the United States, consistently figures at the bottom of economic development tables in that country, and corruption there is reputed to be endemic. It is the very exceptional jurisdiction, such as Norway or Alberta, that has derived more benefit than harm from such wealth.

On the other hand, if you think about many of the wealthiest societies in the world—Switzerland, Singapore, Taiwan, Hong Kong, Japan, Israel, and many more—they have virtually no natural resources. They have had to pursue in a disciplined manner making rather than taking as an economic strategy and have invested in the productive capacity of their people. People are and always will be the true source of all ability to produce wealth. Pointing fingers at Alberta or Saskatchewan or Newfoundland and Labrador because oil and other resources make them "unfairly wealthy" just proves that the people doing the pointing have no idea how real wealth is created in the long term.

Be that as it may, assuming that we did want to use equalization to temper the disparities being created by high natural resources prices, how much would it cost? Before the downturn, some experts saw those prices driving up the current cost of equalization from roughly $14 billion today to $30 billion in ten years.[14] Even though that timetable may be somewhat delayed, in a world where billions of people are entering a new era of industrialization and rising living standards the demand for natural resources will return, and sooner than many expect. Whenever it does occur, remember that the disparity in revenues between provinces is created in large part by vast natural resource revenues flowing to some provincial governments. Ottawa, however, and not the provinces, funds equalization out of *its* tax revenues, and it is constitutionally barred from taking a share of natural resource revenues such as royalties, which are reserved to the provinces. Equalization is financed solely out of federal tax revenues, chiefly the GST and personal and corporate income tax and *these come disproportionately from Ontario.*

The perverse outcome, then, is that Ontario will bear a disproportionate share of the cost of new higher equalization payments and will therefore find its industries struggling with a heavier than necessary tax burden while resource-rich provinces reduce debt and tax rates. Ontario will inevitably become more vocal about this as it is more heavily taxed to support provincial governments like Quebec's that offer more public services (e.g., $7-a-day daycare) and have higher levels of public employment, higher rates of welfare dependence, lower levels of workforce participation, and higher levels of early retirement. The mother of all federal-provincial battles looms, regardless of whether Ontario is an equalization recipient, for that is yet again more churning, with much of the money for Ontario's equalization payment coming from federal taxes on Ontarians.

Essentially, then, we will have a choice in the future between increased redistribution and accelerated economic decline, especially in recipient or taking regions, or increased productivity and an accelerated rise in our standard of living. If we choose the latter, we will almost certainly find that ratcheting back transfers, and especially equalization, to make taking regions accept more responsibility for their policy choices, will be essential. Too many countries and regions have succeeded in escaping underdevelopment through judicious policy (South Korea, Chile, Israel, the Asian Tigers, many former Eastern Bloc countries, and others come to mind) for us to accept that underperforming regions of Canada are simply the victim of forces beyond their control. What they cannot control is their appetite for transfers.

Getting More from Less

I have frequently referred to raising Canada's productivity as a key part of the solution to the puzzle of aging, but this is a word that is badly misunderstood.

Sadly, productivity is a word that political parties, their advisers, and pollsters have decreed shall be banished from our vocabulary. And indeed polling indicates that most Canadians are turned off by a big word that they think is code for chaining people to their desks and sewing machines and brandishing a cat-o'-nine-tails at them. In other words, it is conceived as *taking something from people.*

The truth, however, is that productivity is a beautiful word that means the art of getting more from less, and specifically getting more value out of each hour of our labour. Not working harder: more result for the same or even less effort. A single worker on the production line controlling an industrial robot that does the work of several line workers works less hard physically than any of the people he and his robot displace, requires less strength and stamina, and earns a higher wage. The bus driver who drives an articulated bus works no harder (and likely enjoys more pleasant working conditions than in the older buses) but moves more people around. The teacher who uses distance education teaches the same lesson but reaches more students.

In other words, productivity, properly conceived, is *getting something extra for people.* It is the cornerstone of our future prosperity and will become ever more important as an aging population means fewer Canadians will be working relative to the population as a whole.

One obvious response to a faltering labour supply is for the smaller number of workers that remains to produce more wealth. This is another of the natural adjustment mechanisms that labour shortages trigger: as the availability of workers tightens, wages will tend to rise, which in turn provides incentives for employers to cut back on their use of labour and to use machines and other labour-saving techniques wherever possible. However, Department of Finance projections I have seen that make some reasonable assumptions about productivity improvements over the next forty years give results that are disappointingly low for anyone who hopes to see the country grow its way out of the demographic and economic challenge presented by an aging population. Canada's productivity performance over the past few decades has been poor, and the projection is that we will not shift course significantly. In fact, the department's projections, to the extent that they see productivity growth following the path of the last ten years, may be optimistic; if our performance turns out to be closer to the average of the last thirty years rather than the last ten, the consequences for our standard of living would be grave.

Canada's aging economy faces being saddled with an ugly mixture of lower growth and higher inflation unless the country improves its "very disappointing" productivity record.... David Dodge said the labour force will start to noticeably shrink as early as 2009 as waves of Baby Boomers begin to retire, lowering the economy's "potential output," or the rate at which it can grow without generating inflation. Only by squeezing more output out of fewer workers and raising productivity growth could the country offset the trend.... Without an increase in productivity growth, inflationary pressure is bound to slow the growth of the Canadian economy as a whole. Ultimately, that could mean higher interest rates and borrowing costs for Canadians without all the benefits of stronger growth.

Jacqueline Thorpe, "Economy Risk Real: Dodge," *National Post*

We have already paid a terrible price in lost productivity over the last few decades.[15] While it is true that Canada's economic performance on many fronts in recent years, such as our improved fiscal performance, has been the envy of many other industrialized countries, the fly in the ointment is that our productivity performance is poor. It is not just bad; it has been getting worse. Our labour productivity since 2000 has deteriorated compared to both our own performance in the latter half of the 1990s and to American performance since 2000. In both cases, our performance since 2000 has been one-third of these two benchmarks. The productivity gap between Canada and the

United States has gone from 17 percentage points to 26.[16]

Canada's manufacturing productivity performance since 2000 has been even worse than the business sector performance. Output per hour advanced at only a 0.6 per cent average annual rate between 2000 and 2006, compared to 5.5 per cent per year in the United States. In other words, U.S. manufacturing labour productivity growth before the downturn was nearly *ten times as fast* as that of Canada!

The result, of course, has been a divergence in standard of living between Canada and the United States,[17] and a decline in our standing among OECD countries as measured by our productivity performance. Our output per hour worked, the third highest in the OECD in 1973, had fallen to sixteenth in 2006. Although our output has risen, we have been overtaken by many others who saw their relative standard of living advance more quickly. Thus while it may be true that America's productivity performance was somewhat overstated during the boom leading up to the current slowdown,[18] that brief historical moment can in no way explain the long-term nature of our own poor productivity performance.

Increased productivity would significantly lighten the economic burden of population aging. But the story of the past few decades should help us to understand why that is easy to say and extremely hard to achieve.

Why Creative Destruction Is Good for You

Why would better productivity be hard to achieve? Because that poor productivity performance has been the result of a fear of Quebec nationalism and a resultant use of the power of the state both directly and indirectly, to draw Boomers into dependence on the state. And we had so many workers and potential workers we could afford to be profligate with them.

One of the ways that this has been accomplished has been to use the state to prevent any kind of unpleasant economic change. Declining industries, such as the fishery or pulp and paper, declining regions, and workers with skills of declining value have all been assured by the state, especially in Quebec, but elsewhere too, that they would not have to suffer from any difficult adjustments. After all, what if this requirement of sacrifice should sour someone on the future of Canada and cause them to vote *oui* one day in a referendum on the future of the country?

Thus, for example, we have subsidized industries in declining regions and paid workers not to leave those regions, and we have found various ways to bail out declining industries to prevent them from having to go out of business. Every potential job loss has been seen as an economic calamity; every scheme to bail out declining industries has received powerful political support. Dalton McGuinty's pleas on behalf of the Ontario auto sector are only the most recent performance of a well-known but increasingly shopworn tune.

Yet this view of the economic world has actually retarded our economic progress and pulled down our productivity. That is because productivity is most improved by shifting people and capital out of declining industries and into growing ones, and out of declining companies and into ones that are on the way up.

Those responsible for national economies increasingly see the wisdom in Joseph Schumpeter's description of the operation of market economies as "creative destruction."[19] Some economists have argued that two-thirds of all economic growth is generated by innovation, which simply means new ways of doing things. We all like that "creative" part because it means new jobs and industries and we all like to feel progressive and at the forefront of change. But we tend to want to eliminate the "destruction" part that is its necessary precursor. In fact, genuine economic progress and growth invariably creates winners and losers, and unless we confront that squarely and make the case why this is a price worth paying, we will continue to get knocked off course as we seek a better standard of living for Canadians.

Fortunately, increased productivity creates new wealth, part of which can be used to compensate the

OUT WITH THE OLD, IN WITH THE NEW

Capitalism, then, is by nature a form or method of economic change and not only never is but never can be stationary. And this evolutionary character of the capitalist process is not merely due to the fact that economic life goes on in a social and natural environment which changes and by its change alters the data of economic action; this fact is important and these changes (wars, revolutions and so on) often condition industrial change, but they are not its prime movers. Nor is this evolutionary character due to a quasi-automatic increase in population and capital or to the vagaries of monetary systems, of which exactly the same thing holds true. The fundamental impulse that sets and keeps the capitalist engine in motion comes from the new consumers, goods, the new methods of production or transportation, the new markets, the new forms of industrial organization that capitalist enterprise creates.

... The opening up of new markets, foreign or domestic, and the organizational development from the craft shop and factory to such concerns as U.S. Steel illustrate the same process of industrial mutation—if I may use that biological term—that incessantly revolutionizes the economic structure from within, incessantly destroying the old one, incessantly creating a new one. This process of Creative Destruction is the essential fact about capitalism.

Joseph Schumpeter, *Capitalism, Socialism and Democracy*

losers, just as the emerging era of labour shortages should, if managed properly, reduce the impact of economic change. If we coordinate the massive withdrawal of retiring workers with the rationalization of sectors of the economy, we can produce major gains for the economy at relatively little cost. And even modest improvements in productivity growth can have major effects as they are compounded over the years.

Creative destruction is all around us. Look, for example, at employment growth. In 2005, about 250,000 jobs were created. But that was the net figure. In fact, nearly 3.5 million jobs were created, and well over 3 million disappeared.[20] Twenty-one per cent of all employees finished the year with a different employer than at the beginning of the year. This is no purely Canadian phenomenon: according to *The Economist*, in the last two decades of the twentieth century all the net job growth for U.S. workers came from firms that were five years old or less.[21] And speaking of new firms, in Canada about 60 per cent of them fail within their first five years.[22]

Of all the jobs that existed within companies in 1989, nearly 40 per cent of them were gone ten years later because firms shrank or went out of business. Conversely, however, 43 per cent of the positions that existed in 1999 had been created in the preceding decade by expanding firms or by new firms that entered the market. That was the process by which declining industries shed resources that were then shifted to expanding businesses.[23]

Manufacturing is not exempt from the benefits of creativity, but nor is it exempt from the destruction by which the growth in our prosperity creates losers as well as winners. While manufacturing is declining as a major employer, Canada is doing no worse than other industrialized economies in the manufacturing sector, and our weak dollar probably even softened the blow of the transition in the nineties. Some industries undeniably stand to lose from this shift in production; the overall impact will continue to be positive, however, as gains in technology-intensive manufacturing and in services continue to outweigh the employment losses by a wide margin.

Productivity growth comes principally from this kind of creative destruction. During the period 1989 to 1999 in Canada, two-thirds of productivity growth came from two sources: more productive firms expanding and gaining market share at the expense of less productive ones, and more productive firms entering the market and less productive firms leaving. Only one-third came from productivity improvements within firms.[24]

If only politicians and voters saw it this way. Markets tend to promote industries and entrepreneurs of the future; businesses bet on future productive capacity, whereas politics tends to favour established industries with large employment bases (because large numbers of happy workers and their families are also often happy voters) and therefore to prefer old industries to new ones. Ten good jobs tomorrow will not, in the political calculus, compensate for one job lost today, even though creative destruction's disruptions of recent years have been accompanied by a slight increase in average pay levels across the economy, widely held opinions to the contrary notwithstanding.[25]

Nor is it only the creative destruction of industries and firms that raises the standard of living of Canadians. It is also the movement out of communities with poor opportunities and into ones with greater possibilities. Researchers from the Centre for the Study of Living Standards found a way to measure the impact of interprovincial migration in Canada; they found that its contribution to both output and productivity growth increased in recent years, fuelled by heavy migration to high-productivity Alberta.[26] Thus migration and productivity increases are closely linked. Taken together they are an important part of the explanation of the emergence of a taking and a making state within Canada.

Some people see in this welcoming of creative destruction a heartless indifference to the human costs of economic change. Real people lose real jobs, and in an earlier chapter we saw the terrible cost that unemployment exacts on the unemployed, through depression, illness, family breakup, and more.

By contrast, the argument to this point establishes pretty clearly that the wrong response is to try to prevent economic change. It is not just wrong for the economy overall; it is wrong for the vast majority of those displaced by economic change. When we trap workers and capital in old industries whose day is done, we prevent those people and that money from producing the greatest benefit for Canadians and from producing the vibrant labour market that maximizes the chances of displaced workers finding new jobs. When we let creative destruction work, more wealth and more jobs are created than if we try to prevent it. And when change means more wealth than existed before, we can compensate those who lose from economic change and still leave society wealthier and more productive than it was before.

Unemployment insurance is a good example. When properly used to help displaced workers maintain their incomes temporarily as they move from one job to another, such insurance helps to promote economic growth. When workers use it as part of their annual income, as so often happens in Canada in declining seasonal industries, it has the opposite effect.

The person who had the balance right between the social benefits of creative destruction and the individual costs of job loss was U.S. president Bill Clinton. Clinton was a master at making displaced workers feel that he empathized with their plight when he assured them that he "felt their pain." However, he never promised there would be no pain, only that it would be shared. He repeatedly told his audiences that economic change was a reality that had to be accommodated, but that displaced workers would not be left behind. He happily backed measures like training programs for workers displaced by free trade, for example. And yet he was immensely popular in states that had been hard hit by creative destruction. The lesson to be learned is that most people do not expect economic change to be abolished; they want to be assured that their individual sacrifices will not be forgotten and they will be helped to move to a new job where they can again be self-supporting. Remember that Bill Clinton was both the president who felt people's pain and the president who abolished welfare as we had known it.

Tax Me, I'm Productive

Of course it is not just regions that are net payers or net recipients under the redistributionist state. It is also companies and individuals. And since it is the productivity of companies and individuals that together make up the productivity of places, the effects of the redistributionist state on these basic elements of the economy is key. We've dwelt on how the behaviour of individuals and firms is harmed by being on the receiving end of these "benefits." How about those who pay?

This requires us to think about how we finance these activities of the state, and the answer, of course, is taxes, remembering that if we finance these activities by borrowing, that is merely deferred taxes. Ultimately all the state's activities must be paid for by taking a share of the productive efforts of Canadians.

The problem in the context of the imperative to improve our productivity is that the tax burden required to finance redistribution must, by definition, fall on the economically most successful companies and individuals. The tax burden is not something that leaves unaffected those who bear it. It doesn't just leave them disgruntled. It changes their behaviour, just as the structure of welfare state benefits changes the behaviour of recipients and the structure of federal-provincial transfers changes the behaviour of provinces.

Consider individuals first. Our objective, namely to raise the productivity of every Canadian worker as the first line of defence against the cost of aging and population change, must mean putting everyone to work who is capable of working, and to do so at the highest possible levels of productivity.

But think about a progressive income tax. This is a tax that taxes you harder as your income rises, and your income is one of the best measures we have of your individual productivity. In other words, a progressive income tax is a tax on productivity, and the steeper the progressivity, the higher the tax. And any economist worth his salt will tell you that the more you tax something, the less of it you will get. If we want to increase productivity, a heavy tax burden on the most productive individuals, and a tax burden that rises in lockstep with their work effort, is the exact reverse of what we want and need.

There is lots of evidence to back up this proposition that high and progressive income taxes deter work effort. It is one of the reasons that explain, for example, the productivity gap with the United States, where the tax burden on individuals, while still progressive, is flatter than in Canada. That means that high-productivity people are less penalized in the United States compared to their opposite numbers in Canada. When taxes on effort are high, as they are here in Canada, for example, the inclination to take more leisure (i.e., time off) is increased, since the pay earned from extra work is taxed, whereas the benefit you get from time off is not. This helps to explain that extra month's work Americans put in compared to Canadians—they work 145 hours more in the course of a year than Canadians, or about four workweeks of thirty-five hours each.[27]

Confronting our need to raise productivity as well as to encourage older people to remain in the workforce after they become eligible for various kinds of retirement income will mean, therefore, that there will be strong limits on the steepness of income tax progressivity, as well as on tax rates per se.

Similarly, too-high tax burdens turn workers' and investors' attention from where they can derive the most benefit from investing their work or their money and focuses it instead on how to defeat the efforts of the taxman. Both tax evasion and tax avoidance become important national sports, and the game of PUPPETRY gets focused on the tax system, with each special interest looking for a credit or a deduction or an exemption that protects their little interest from the taxman's attention. Politicians are happy to grant such targeted benefits because of the magic formula of dispersed costs and concentrated benefits we reviewed in the earlier discussion of rent-seeking.

Unhappily, each one of those special measures can be paid for only by keeping the general burden higher than it needs to be overall, meaning that the politically powerful get tax breaks, and the politically less connected do not. And we now know that the politically powerful are the old industries with lots of employees, located in politically sensitive parts of the country, who will also generally be those companies with low productivity. These are the companies and industries you would expect to have the lowest tax burden. On the other hand, you would expect new emerging industries with high growth potential and high productivity to have higher tax burdens. If you doubt that this principle holds in the area of taxation, you might want to consider that in 2007, as a result of further special tax measures to shore up manufacturing, the gap in effective tax rates between the manufacturing industry and the most highly taxed industry (communications—surely an industry of the future if ever there was one) jumped to 18 percentage points from an already substantial gap of 7 percentage points the year before.[28]

Yet there is every reason to think that a low and uniform tax burden on business, making little or no distinction between industries or businesses, makes much more sense. That way managers and investors make business decisions based on the strength of the business case for, and not on the tax consequences of, one course of action versus another. If the tax consequences of all choices are pretty much the same, the tax system ceases to be a factor in business decision-making. And there is evidence that in the United States the range of difference in tax treatment meted out to firms and industries is much narrower than in Canada and that this likely helps to account for the higher productivity of U.S. firms.[29]

> A new OECD study, "Taxes and Economic Growth," examines national tax burdens and their impact on growth and incomes in member countries. It concludes that "corporate taxes are most harmful for growth, followed by personal income taxes, and then consumption taxes." The study adds that "investment is adversely affected by corporate taxation," and that the most profitable and rapidly growing companies tend to be the most sensitive to high business tax rates.
>
> "America the Uncompetitive," *Wall Street Journal*

The friends of the redistributionist state, however, think that business taxation is a kind of free ride. We can free individuals, especially low-income people, from the burden of personal taxation by simply taxing corporations more vigorously. Leaving aside the obvious problems of tax competition between countries (i.e., the possibility that other countries will attract footloose companies through aggressive corporate tax lowering), the flaw in this logic from a productivity point of view is not hard to see.

Corporations ultimately do not pay the great bulk of business taxes. They may write the cheques, but they then pass most of those costs along to others. Workers pay through lower wages, customers pay through higher prices, and investors pay through lower returns on their investment. Ultimately it is individuals who pay, whether the original bill is paid by companies or not.

But that does not mean that the behaviour of companies is not affected by the tax burden, precisely because companies' ability to attract the best workers, to sell competitively to their customers, and to attract investment capital will be affected by the tax regime under which they operate. Companies will gravitate to those jurisdictions with competitive tax regimes, and tax regimes that do not discriminate among industries and companies will attract those new entrants into the economy who are responsible for the lion's share of productivity growth. Tax policy can create virtuous as well as vicious circles.

The government of Canada has announced a long-term policy of getting federal corporation tax down to 15 per cent and is trying to get the provinces to move to a companion 10 per cent rate, making for a combined rate in Canada of 25 per cent—fairly competitive in today's international environment. With its 2009 budget, previously lagging Ontario finally joined the most economically dynamic parts of Canada in converging (albeit slowly) on this business taxation standard. In fact, there is a marked convergence of economic and taxation policy among the three western most provinces that will help to consolidate their status as high-productivity-growth poles within the country.[30]

The long and short of it, then, is that the tax burden we can impose on both businesses and individuals will be subject to strong constraints, especially when we recall that other countries will be confronting similar or even worse demographic challenges than our own and are already adjusting tax policy in consequence. Throughout the industrialized world, personal income taxes are being flattened (i.e., the degree of progressivity is being lowered), tax rates are falling on both individuals and corporations,[31] and the tax burden is being shifted in favour of consumption taxes (like the GST) that don't affect the incentives to work. America may be the main exception if President Obama's plans for big stimulus packages, universal health care, fixing social security entitlements and balanced budgets come to fruition. It is hard to see how those objectives can be met without a significant increase in taxes today or in the near future.

Add this competitive international taxation world together with the foreseeable costs to taxpayers of population aging as Pierre Fortin laid them out for us in an earlier chapter. If we want the benefits of a strongly rising productivity and standard of living in the face of population aging, if we want to keep our best and brightest individuals and companies in Canada rather than seeing them leak abroad, and if we want to be a destination for both investment and high-productivity individuals, the state in Canada will be under tremendous financial strain with little room to raise taxes. Either shrinking the state by abandoning ill-advised and counterproductive redistributionist policies, or a borrowing and taxing binge to sustain the fruits of decades of aggressive PUPPETRY, are the two main choices that will be available to us. The choice we will make between them will be conditioned by our character, our expectations of ourselves, and our sense of responsibility to generations that come later.

In the coming battle between makers and takers for the soul of Canada, Ontario will almost certainly be the key battleground. If the forces of taking can push that province over definitively into the takers' column, joining Quebec and most of the other smaller provinces, it is hard to see how the national battle can be won.

Some of the elements of the takers' case in Ontario are already quite clear. The province's manufacturing, on this account, is in severe decline, and only aggressive PUPPETRY by both Ottawa and Queen's Park can "save" the sector. Much of the argument is made by the powerful rent-seeking triumvirate of the province, the unions, and the Rapidly Shrinking Three carmakers and is made all the more attractive, as always, by the possibility that a good part of the cost of Ottawa's contribution will be passed on to taxpayers in other parts of the country.

But the consequences of succeeding in the campaign to bail out Ontario manufacturing without expectations that the companies and workers will raise their productivity game would be disastrous. We already know that the policy of the Ontario government of bribing large manufacturers like the car companies has been a signal failure, as Christina Blizzard documented even before the downturn gathered a full head of steam:

> The McGuinty government has given $400 million to the Big Three automakers—and those companies have cut 10,000 jobs in this province. GM was given $235 million to retain 900 jobs; Ford got $100 million to retain 4,000 jobs and Chrysler got $76.8 million to retain 5,200 jobs under the Liberals' 2004 automotive investment strategy. Meanwhile, GM slashed 5,500 jobs, Ford laid off 2,700 and Chrysler cut another 2,000. Under the strategy, GM had committed to keep 16,000 jobs in the province and now has 14,850.[32]

What the Ontario government doesn't seem to understand is that it is in the interests of the province, the companies, and their workers that this policy fail. To understand why, let's look at the example of the American manufacturing industry coming out of the last manufacturing recession in the early years of this decade.

The thing everyone remembers about that episode is that the United States came out of it with 3 million fewer workers in manufacturing, and the idea became widespread that this meant that U.S. manufacturing was dying.

We should all hope to look so good on our deathbed. Here are a few facts about U.S. manufacturing prior to the latest downturn, most of them underlined by a report for the Clintonite Progressive Policy Institute in Washington, D.C.:

American factory output nearly doubled in the last 15 years, (in constant 2000 dollars) from $0.9 trillion in 1992 to $1.5 trillion in 2005. More money goes into U.S. manufacturing from abroad than goes from the United States to other countries. From January 2005 to September 2006, for example, U.S. manufacturers invested $78 billion in foreign facilities; foreign firms put $100 billion into American manufacturing facilities. In real dollars, manufacturing made up 12.9 percent of the U.S. economy in 1992, and as of 2005, accounted for 13.8 percent. (Still down, though, from a 14.5 percent peak in 2000.) The U.S. share of world manufacturing was slightly down, but only slightly—from 21.4 percent in 1993 to 21.1 percent in 2005—as the shares of China, Korea, and some other developing countries rose sharply and those of the EU and Japan dropped. American manufacturing exports jumped in 2005 and boomed in 2006, rising by about $100 billion—easily a record in value terms and the highest percentage rate of growth in at least 20 years.[33]

The year 2006 was a record year for output, revenues, profits, profit rates, and return on investment in the manufacturing sector. According to Daniel Ikenson of the Cato Institute, "The [United States] remains the world's most prolific manufacturer—producing two and a half times more output than those vaunted Chinese factories in 2006," and America's exports to China more than tripled between 2000 and 2007.[34]

What we have to remember, however, is that the sector's successes were made possible only by the improved productivity that the loss of 3 million jobs made possible. If Washington and the states had stepped in and subsidized those manufacturers to keep those jobs in place, the industry could have looked forward to many years of declining profitability, shrinking markets, technological stagnation, and debilitating political battles to keep the subsidies flowing. Instead, they bit the bullet and reaped the rewards.

Most importantly, that loss of 3 million manufacturing jobs coincided with a generational low in unemployment. That doesn't mean that the transition wasn't miserable and painful for many of the people involved. What it does mean is that a vigorous job market with lots of employers ensures that those costs are minimized while putting people back to work as quickly as possible. And when you focus on lubricating the process of adaptation to new circumstances and allow productivity to rise, that means more tax revenues to support the social programs that help in the transition. Workers get the money and are helped to move on, as opposed to companies getting the money and shedding the workers anyway in response to competitive pressures.

The views of the Ontario government hang in the balance at the moment.

They have spent the past few years pillorying the federal government for being reluctant to prop up the car industry or to try to bribe them to keep workers they don't need. The downturn has loosened Ottawa's purse strings, meaning that both governments are now pursuing a PUPPETRY policy. However, Ontario has now moved, as already remarked, on bringing its previously uncompetitive tax regime in line. That is an anti-PUPPETRY policy aimed at improving the competitive conditions in which Ontario manufacturers work.

Resisting the siren song of PUPPETRY will almost certainly be the sounder long-term strategy, however. We've already seen that the old strategy of subsidizing companies to do what you want doesn't work in any case. More fundamentally, though, Canada in general and Ontario in particular are about to enter into a new economic era when the recession ends. Canada should, if we do not squander our hard-won advantages, enjoy a period of significant economic strength compared to the United States. That country is going to be wrestling with rising taxes and deficits, significant disruptive restructuring of its corporate sector, and a long hangover from its debt binge. Even if we have fallen off the wagon temporarily, Canada has either fixed many of the problems that the United States has yet to confront (balancing the budget, reducing debt, and fixing social security) or has avoided many of the excesses that brought on the current recession (such as an exaggerated asset price bubble and much-weakened financial institutions). Even with our own demographic challenges, Canada, and our manufacturing heartland in Ontario, should enjoy a strong competitive advantage for several years. But only if we don't waste it.

One final comment about creative destruction in the context of the current downturn. Some will seize on the greater impact current circumstances have had on Ontario and Alberta compared to, say, Quebec, to argue that this proves that the big-government model works better. After all, in the spring of 2009, for the first time in many years the unemployment rate in Ontario exceeded that of Quebec. Again, however, this is to confuse short-term fluctuations with long-term trends. Ontario has enjoyed decades of superior economic performance to that of Quebec by virtually every measure, and that is a more reliable guide than the unusual circumstances of the current recession.

Moreover, if the argument about the ill effects of governments preventing economic change from occurring is correct, certain things follow. One of them is that in a downturn those economies open to creative destruction might well find their performance temporarily fades relative to economies mired in PUPPETRY, where governments are more inclined to bail out faltering industries. But having avoided the adjustments during the downturn, the rent-seekers never reap the later gains, the foundations of which have been laid by creative destruction. It won't always be the case that flexible economies will be hammered by recession; it will depend on the factors causing the recession and the structure of the economy. A recession caused by declining natural resource industries, for example, might not affect too badly an economy based on manufacturing. It turns out that this recession is hitting manufacturing (and hence, Ontario) particularly savagely. But it is hitting every other manufacturing region in the world as well. And if Ontario stays the course and doesn't shift from a making to a taking society, there is every reason to think it will emerge from the downturn economically invigorated, while Quebec will return to its mediocre performance of recent decades.

What It Looks Like on the Ground

If all this discussion of raising productivity and intensifying competition within the economy appears hard to relate to anything concrete, here is a brief and incomplete list of measures that would achieve just the kind of outcomes we are looking for.[35] Unsurprisingly, every item on our to-do list is also encrusted with rent-seeking interests that have so far fought efforts at reform to a standstill or at least a snail's pace.

- removal of ownership restrictions on telecoms, banking, and airlines;
- privatization of many of the utilities that the U.K. experience has shown can reap such huge productivity gains by being taken out of the public sector (including airports, seaports, and other infrastructure currently in unsatisfactory halfway houses);
- removal of restrictions on bank mergers;
- getting politics out of business-financing decisions;
- ending regional agencies' tendency to subsidize low-productivity work under the guise of "maintaining jobs";
- genuine Open Skies, with the United States and across the Atlantic;
- completing international trade negotiations (the Doha Round) with generous liberalization for trade in services and agriculture;
- stopping the subsidization of low-performance provincial governments through excessive equalization and other transfers;
- shifting of much post-secondary education (PSE) support into student vouchers so that universities must compete for students, and the removal of all obstacles to the emergence of private universities to provide some genuine competition to the too-often-complacent existing oligopoly;
- more rigorous measuring of the success of our primary and secondary

education institutions to ensure that the workforce of the future gets the skills they need when they are in school;

- federal legislation to guarantee the economic rights of Canadians to live, work, exercise their profession, invest, buy, and sell wherever they wish in Canada.

Each item here represents a choice we must make between the status quo of relative decline compared to many other industrialized countries and the kind of improved productivity that alone will allow us to improve the standard of living for our shrinking workforce while guaranteeing a decent retirement for the aging Boomer generation.

Happily, the move into retirement of the baby boom bulge and the emergence of labour shortages can and should create circumstances in which it is politically much easier to make the case that workers and capital should be shifted to where they can make the greatest contribution to our standard of living. If we were to succeed in making such a political shift, the economic benefits could be substantial measured by improved productivity, and the result would be a much more manageable cost of population aging. The bad news is that for this to succeed will require both politicians and voters to break reflexive habits of the past fifty years, habits formed at a time when labour was plentiful and jobs scarce and Quebec was scaring the daylights out of the country. If we cannot break those habits, the gulf separating the two Canadas that are emerging will widen and deepen, and the politics of the next fifty years will be disfigured by repeated and increasingly bitter battles over redistribution between them.

Do Not Go Gentle into That Good Night: Work for All and All in Work

Though much is taken, much abides; and though
We are not now that strength which in old days
Moved earth and heaven; that which we are, we are;
One equal temper of heroic hearts,
Made weak by time and fate, but strong in will
To strive, to seek, to find, and not to yield.

ALFRED LORD TENNYSON, *ULYSSES*

Ever dream of what the investment advisers like to call Freedom 55, the ability to thumb your nose at your boss and head out to the golf course or into the garden when you hit your fifty-fifth birthday? Apparently a lot of Canadians have acted on that dream, because over the past few decades Canada has done a relatively poor job of convincing people to stay in the workforce after fifty-five. This is despite the evidence that we saw in earlier chapters about the desire people have to be productive active members of society. That desire, however, like most desires, can be and is shaped by incentives. And the incentives we have created for many over-55s have made work unattractive.

The reason Canadians' propensity in recent decades to retire early matters is that the economic pain of population aging is muted if workers stay in the workforce longer rather than retiring, because this means more workers per retiree in the population. Compared to the top five countries in the OECD on this measure, however, we have significantly fewer men over age fifty-five still in the workforce.[1] The difference for women is less marked but still important.

If we were able to match the labour force participation rates of *all* age groups with those projected for the top five OECD countries we would, by 2010, have improved the ratio of workers to retirees from about 3.25 workers to each retiree to roughly 4.6 workers per retiree. That represents a significant reduction in the cost of population aging because that means both more people working and fewer people depending on programs financed by those workers through their taxes.

By 2030, on current form the ratio in Canada is expected to be two workers per retiree. If we again met the participation rates of the top five OECD countries, the ratio would be just over three to one. Still painful, but a big improvement over what it would be otherwise. Moreover, it is not as if Canadians are unwilling to change their traditional retirement behaviour—according to the OECD, in this country, "between 1994 and 2004, the participation rate of older men and women aged 50–64 has increased by around 5 and 13 percentage points respectively—well above the average increase across OECD countries."[2] That means that while the proportion of over-55s working is lower than in many other industrialized countries, the rate of increase of Canadian over-55s at work is closing the gap already. Maybe those famous self-adjusting mechanisms really do work after all.

This increase has been driven by a number of factors, such as growing demand for workers, declines in asset values (i.e., the equity market's decline following the tech bubble, which caused some workers near retirement to delay retiring), and so-called cohort effects, particularly for women.[3] Just as importantly, however, the expectations of workers themselves are changing, as people realize that idyllic pictures of early and prolonged retirement without work are in fact not that attractive. According to one survey, for instance, nearly half of Canadians of working age already expect to work beyond the age of sixty-five, and not just for economic reasons: "Nearly all of those who expect to work beyond age 65 cite one or more lifestyle reasons, including remaining mentally active, enjoyment of their jobs and the interaction with their co-workers."[4] In other words, future retirees are coming more and more to realize that work (although not necessarily any particular job, a distinction many people seem to have difficulty grasping) is closely related to happiness.

Just as is the case with regional development policy and inter-regional transfers and EI, labour shortages are going to make the transition to a more sensible retirement behaviour easier. We saw how labour shortages, for example, are sending stronger signals to workers to move to places where their job skills are in bigger demand while at the same time making dependence on EI, say, less attractive.

In the case of retirement behaviour, trying to do anything with the retirement regime in Canada has seemed, just like social security in the United States, the third rail of Canadian politics, the one that kills you if you touch it. But that was all premised on two assumptions. The first was that our main problem was unemployment, and therefore that people retiring was a good thing, as they were no longer in the labour market and they had an income they could count on. The second was that the only way to change people's retirement behaviour was to reduce their retirement income. Just as with EI reform, this was a politically touchy issue because the policy could so easily be portrayed by the demagogically inclined as an attack on the poor and vulnerable.

But think back to what we learned about when workers move. Basically, they don't move when the costs of moving are high and the benefits low relative to those costs. Revealingly, when the number of Canadians moving between provinces took off in about 2002, it was not because we suddenly squeezed EI benefits, for example. Instead, it was because the reward from working (i.e., wages) suddenly rose while the benefits available from not working stayed fairly steady. People respond to incentives.

Retirees and potential retirees, it appears, are no different. They quite carefully calculate the balance between the costs of working (including lost leisure time) and the benefits (such as higher income). If the difference isn't very great, they prefer not to work and to enjoy more leisure time. Therefore *the key is the disparity in income* between working and not working for those people able to work, which, given modern medical technology among other things, is a very large share of most people over fifty-five.

If, then, labour shortages are indeed going to improve the rewards of working, as the evidence suggests they will, the key will be to keep retirement benefits relatively steady and allow the rewards to working to grow over time.

The benefits of such a policy are hard to overstate. For example, we know that people who work are happier and healthier than those who do not, including those over fifty-five. With life expectancy rising for men and women, and the expectations that more of the years after fifty-five will be spent in good health, there is every reason to think that more people working later in life would not only produce good results for the economy, but result in better quality of life for older people themselves. And of course our public finances would benefit from older people spending more time contributing their work and taxes and less time drawing retirement benefits and paying much lower taxes.

The impact of encouraging people to work longer would be bigger than almost any other single policy one could imagine. If our retirement behaviour were to remain as it is, by about 2030 there would be roughly 17 million people in the labour force in Canada. If we were able to match the workforce participation seen in the top five OECD countries, the number would be almost 20 million. That is a difference worth having, especially if it is achieved by making people feel that they prefer working to being retired.

As we know, changing our retirement behaviour is far more effective at changing our future prospects than increased immigration. If we raised the current CPP retirement age of sixty-five by three months a year starting in 2008 and continued with that incremental shift until 2024, our retirement age would then be seventy (i.e., it would be back to what it was before we ramped up the size of the dependency state in the sixties and seventies[5]). Our old-age dependency ratio would go from about three workers per retiree (the current projection) to about five by 2025. On the other hand, as we know, even rather extreme increases in immigration levels barely shift the trend at all.

Redefining retirement is hardly an original idea, but every time it has been mooted, politicians have drawn back because it required them to reduce benefits to a politically powerful group. Old folks have become rent-seekers just like everyone else, and they are especially concentrated (for all the reasons we have already seen) in Quebec and the other declining parts of the country.

In place of the traditional assumption that people should work as long as they are able to, politicians kept moving the bar down, as they competed with each other to release older people from their traditional moral and practical obligation to work. Old-age pension cheques from Ottawa were frequently mentioned by observers as an important part of the federal dependency arsenal during referendum campaigns.[6] And there was little political push-back. With every part of the country wrestling for decades with high unemployment, we were busy trying to move the retirement age as young as we could. Employers in particular were happy to be released from their obligations to expensive older workers when there was a huge supply of cheaper youngsters.

Now consider how circumstances are going to be different. Employers facing retirements for which there are few younger replacements available are going to resist those retirements by existing workers by improving incentives for them to stay. Rather than buyout packages, people will be offered "buy-in" packages. Water-cooler conversations will revolve around what various people have been offered to stay instead of what they have been offered to go.

With productivity rising, labour markets tightening, and wages being brought up in their wake, older workers will find their relative cost to employers declining. Older people will be increasingly aware of the physical and mental health benefits of working, just as they will be aware that too early a retirement creates the risk of their running through their retirement savings before death, leaving them at the mercy of the public pension system just when those retirees are oldest and therefore most vulnerable. If, as seems likely, long-term returns to equities will decline relative to the unrepresentative post-war period, private and public pension plans are liable to be less rich. And everyone, including older people, will be aware of the economic opportunities we are forgoing as we age, just as they will be looking increasingly enviously across the border as our standards of living continue to diverge in favour of America.

All these factors make it possible to think that we can successfully encourage people to adjust their retirement behaviour. Rather than approaching it as making people feel they are having something taken away, we will need to approach it as increasing the choices people have for handling their gradual withdrawal from the labour force.

Governments and employers are already taking measures. In 2007, for example, the federal government announced that, in order to encourage older workers to stay in the labour market, phased retirement will be permitted. Also, the age limit for converting a registered retirement savings plan (RRSP) has been increased.[7] There remains a very great deal more to be done, however, to make working compatible with income security for our aging population. There are clawbacks under both the OAS and Guaranteed Income Supplements that discourage work; to get CPP benefits you must show that you have "substantially ceased working"; the CPP penalizes those who delay getting benefits until age seventy, and those penalties are more severe after seventy; there are clawbacks on the tax credit for those sixty-five and older; and there are provisions in the Income Tax Act that prevent people from simultaneously drawing benefits from a defined benefit pension plan and accruing benefits in that same plan.[8] And speaking of defined benefit (DB) pension plans, employers are even starting to look at bringing them back (DB plans have been falling out of favour for fifteen years or so). DB plans promise a specified level of pension benefit in exchange for regular contributions, rather than defined-contribution (DC) plans, which invest your pension contributions but offer no guaranteed benefit level. DC plans suit employers because they shift the risk to employees that market returns over the life of the plan won't be adequate to ensure a comfortable retirement. But increasingly employers are recognizing the attractiveness of DB plans as a recruitment tool:[9] "they can serve as a powerful tool for attracting and retaining staff."

In Quebec it won't be easy to shift retirement behaviour given the large share of the population already retiring early, but things will be more promising than at any time in recent years. The QPP is in much worse shape than the CPP: before the rout in the financial markets, its reserve fund was slated to disappear in forty-four years, and since then the markets' decline has severely worsened the QPP's position, not least because the plan had huge exposure to what turned out to be some very risky investments, such as asset-backed commercial paper. The CPP's reserves, while reduced in the short term, are still expected to keep on rising in the long term,[10] although that assumption may be unwarrantedly optimistic. QPP premiums were already going to have to rise to something like 12.6 per cent of pay, much higher than the already painful 9.9 per cent for the CPP, making it more expensive to employ people in Quebec and driving employment to other more competitive parts of the country. And because the province's population is aging more quickly than the population in more economically dynamic parts of Canada, the number of beneficiaries, already quite high, is expected almost to double by 2030.[11] Yet Quebec's labour force will fall in absolute terms over the next forty years.

The pressure on Quebec to improve its economic performance by enticing older workers to work longer will be intense—if we don't let them off the hook by compensating them for bad policy as we have so often done throughout the Boomer era. One such scheme was put forward recently, making the case that Ottawa should in effect prop up the QPP by lending it part of the accumulating surplus in the CPP.[12] That is the exact reverse of the policy we need to be pursuing, because it only prolongs Quebec's self-inflicted suffering while sending yet again the message to rent-seekers that the messes created by their worst excesses will always be cleaned up by someone else, thus encouraging yet more bad and irresponsible behaviour later.

Moreover, bailing out the QPP would be deeply unfair. In addition to the creation of a vast pool of government-controlled investment capital it created, one of the reasons that Quebec found it worthwhile to opt out of the CPP when it was created in the sixties was the larger proportion of young people in the province's population compared to the Canadian average. In 1966, a mere 4.6 per cent of the population was over sixty-five. The corresponding share of over-65s in the rest of the country was 9.3 per cent, or more than twice as high.[13]

In a pay-as-you-go system, a largely youthful population means that you can either set premiums lower or accumulate a bigger investment pool. Quebec took the latter option since, as we've already seen, the main justification for the QPP in the first place was to create such a pool. By mirroring the premium rate set for the CPP, Quebec's younger population generated a lot of money for the Quebec government to invest.

Because Quebec took advantage of its different demography at the outset, it is unclear why the rest of the country should bail the province out when the perfectly foreseeable demographic tide has turned against it.

Encouraging older Canadians to work longer is, of course, only one strategy for us to use to reduce the costs of aging while spreading more widely the benefits of working. There are populations in Canada that have consistently poor participation rates, such as young men, Aboriginals generally, some rural populations, and people trapped by the welfare wall in various forms (including those on the seasonal work/EI cycle). According to StatsCan, in 2001 only about two-thirds of recent immigrants were employed, 16 percentage points lower than the rate of nearly 82 per cent among Canadian born.[14] I mentioned earlier that if we were able to reach OECD best-practices levels of employment for those over fifty-five, we would have nearly 20 million workers in 2030, as opposed to the projected 17 million or so. If we were able to achieve best-practices levels across the board for all groups, that would add yet another million workers.

The next fifty years will be an age of labour force inclusiveness such as the social engineers of the employment equity movement could never have imagined.

Family's Comeback and Fertility's Return

Marriage is the most basic form of social cooperation. It is the institution in which children are born and reared. When spousal cooperation breaks down, the substitutes for it are intrusive, ineffective, and expensive.

JENNIFER ROBACK MORSE, "CHEERLEADING FOR DIVORCE"

Family is the greatest social welfare institution we have....

DAVID FRUM, *COMEBACK*

So far we have spent a lot of time thinking about the current generation, their retirement behaviour, the recruitment of new Canadians through immigration, encouraging people to move to where the best opportunities are, and improving the productivity of everyone in the workforce. But encouraging Canadians to work longer will carry us only so far because even if we get another ten or fifteen years' work out of many Boomers, they will still retire someday and they will die. Yet unless something changes the demographic slump we face will last for fifty years. That means that beyond longer working lives, higher productivity, and more intelligent immigration policy, we should spend some time thinking about Canadians and their willingness to have children.

We would not be facing these challenges if Canadians had been having enough children to replace themselves. There was no need for them to keep making babies at 1950s-style rates, which were well above the rate at which the population replaces itself. But we have now fallen well below that replacement rate (generally regarded as an average of 2.1 children per woman of child-bearing age). And while an increase now in the number of babies Canadians bring into the world would not help us with our short-term scarcity of workers, that scarcity is projected to last for half a century. Much more than immigration, the decision to have children today is the one that determines much of what the labour supply will be like twenty years from now, just as the decision how and in what circumstances those children will be raised will determine to a large extent their ability to participate to the fullest extent in work.

The key fact, then, is that Canadians do not have nearly enough babies to re-place the current population (a national birth rate of just over 1.5 per woman of child-bearing age ([higher in the Prairies at roughly 1.9 and lower in New-foundland at 1.3]), versus a replacement rate of 2.1).

The Great Demographic Outlier

It is worthwhile exploring for a moment what these trends might mean for Canada. One of the best ways to do so is to contrast what the future currently has in store for us compared to our southern neighbours. I draw this compari-son not because we should want to ape the Americans, but because the differ-ences illustrate the great extent to which Canada's population future is neither fixed nor controlled by immutable and inscrutable forces. The differences be-tween Canada and America are the result of adding up all the individual choices of millions of Canadians and Americans. If the aggregate of Canadians' deci-sions is a bleak future in which Canada loses influence in the world and in which Canadians' standard of living stagnates, we have it in our power to try to influ-ence those decisions, to make Canadians want to choose another path for them-selves and their families.

The rate at which Canadians choose to have babies, to create the next gen-eration of the bearers and exponents of our society's values, is in marked con-trast to that of Americans. They are having enough children to replace themselves (a birth rate of almost 2.1), supplemented by the largest absolute number of immigrants of any Western country (to the extent that immigration to the United States can be correctly estimated, given the high rate of illegal im-migration likely not captured by any official statistic).

In this regard, it is interesting to reflect on the observation *The Economist* newspaper made several years ago about the different experiences of the United States and Europe with regard to population aging:

> At present, West European countries are following what seems to be a normal demographic path: as they became richer after the 1950s, so their fertility rates fell sharply. The average number of children borne by each woman during her lifetime fell from well above the "replacement rate" of 2.1—the rate at which the population remains stable—to less than 1.4 now. The United States followed that pattern too, until the 1980s. But then something astonishing happened: the American fertility rate reversed its decline, and even rose quite sharply, back almost to the replacement rate.[1]

According to Hania Zlotnik of the UN Population Division, "America is the world's great demographic outlier."[2] More on this in a moment.

You can see some of the consequences of these different trends captured in the age pyramid for Canada in 2030 compared to that for the United States in the same year. The age pyramid of a country simply represents the distribution of the population among different age groups. A normal distribution would be broad at the base where the children are represented, and then taper off as it rises through the different age groups, reflecting the attrition of death and net migration. Comparing the "shapes" of the population of Canada and the United States twenty-five years from now is sobering. Our pyramid is shaped like a vase: narrow at the bottom, because we have too few children, wide at the shoulders, where the 40- to 70-year-olds are concentrated. The American pyramid, by contrast, is almost cylindrical. There are as many children under 5 as there are 35- to 40-year olds. By 2020, the proportion of children in the U.S. population will be higher than China's.[3]

While demographic projections as far out as 2050 have to be subject to some qualification, the current projection for the Canadian population in that year is 43 million, whereas the American population in that year could be as high as 500 million to 550 million, with our median age being 42 versus America's 36 (and Europe's 52.7).[4] Not only will the age and ethnic profiles of the two countries diverge fairly markedly over that period, but Canada's total demographic and economic weight relative to its major trading partner and ally will likely also decline. This divergence will take place just as the centre of population in the United States is shifting increasingly south and west, meaning a smaller share of the U.S. population will have direct experience of Canada. And if current trends are borne out too, we will live very differently on our respective sides of the border. Canadians are congregating more and more in a handful of cities. Americans are increasingly moving to the outer suburbs, the exurbs, and even the countryside.[5] Some of the fastest-growing states in the United States now include places such as Nevada, Utah, Idaho, and Colorado.

The consequences of these shifts are worth pondering. They are, of course, in addition to the already significant differences in incomes and productivity growth, differences that have widened over the last quarter century. Projected into the future, these trends imply a sharp divergence in the standard of living of our two nations. *The Economist* remarked, referring to the trends facing America domestically and internationally, "These trends suggest that anyone who assumes the United States is now at the zenith of its economic and political power is making a big mistake." Half a billion Americans, with the highest productivity in the world; a relatively young, flexible, and highly educated workforce; and a willingness to spend a significant share of GDP on defence would be a superpower perhaps even more influential and formidable in 2050 than today—and possibly even less inclined to pay attention to Canada's interests.

If the World Needs More Canada, You Know What to Do

Canada won't just be changing relative to the United States as a result of its population growing older. In fact, Canada will undergo a relative aging more marked than any major industrialized country, save Japan.

Population renewal is not merely an economic issue. In fact, economics has nothing to tell us about how many children people *should* have, since the economy is supposed to serve people, and not the other way around. To have or not have children is just a choice that people can make, and all economists can do is to make clear (a) what the trade-offs are in our standard of living from making one choice or the other and (b) how our society's incentive structure (including public policy) may be influencing people's choices to have babies or not.

Beyond economics, an aging population has social and other consequences that societies ignore at their peril. In his recent book, *America Alone*, Mark Steyn makes an intriguing case that societies with young populations are powerful in foreign policy and economic terms, as well as militarily. They have the means to act on their values.

Aging societies such as Sweden and Japan and Italy may be able to organize their population decline gracefully and even keep their standard of living relatively stable, at least for the time being. But there can be little doubt that they are effectively deciding that over time the world needs less Sweden and Japan, that they shall matter less. In its 2002 cover story on demographics in Europe and America, *The Economist* spent considerable time discussing the various ways in which demographic divergence between the two was going to result in a divergence of interests and sympathies and hence of incentives to work together. Having more or fewer babies can be a momentous decision in more ways than is commonly understood.

A self-confident Canada that believes life here is good, that our institutions are robust, and that we want to be a force for good in the world must at least be ready to ask itself two questions. First, whether those aspirations are compatible with relative population decline. Second, whether our self-image as a great country with much to offer the world can be reconciled with Canadians' unwillingness to replace themselves, to bring enough children into the world to ensure that Canada continues to grow, to thrive, and to be a beacon of tolerance and civility to the world. Immigration, as we have already seen, cannot begin to make up for this unwillingness of Canadians to replace themselves through having babies.

If the answer to these questions is no, then we have some soul-searching to do. What is it about Canadians and the culture and society we have created for ourselves that makes us unwilling to contribute a rising generation commensurate with the one that will soon enough pass from the scene?

Government as Contraceptive

In seeking answers to these questions, we must, of course, ask ourselves what governments may be doing that discourages Canadians from having children they might otherwise have and how we can reverse those policies. Governments do not make children; they do, however, help to create conditions in which it is more or less attractive for Canadian families to have them. While it is not the government's business to tell people how many children to have, neither is it the government's business to make having children more economically onerous than it needs to be or than is compatible with our individual desires regarding family size. Yet, the case can be made that a series of policies discussed in the earlier chapter on the family all conspired to make marriage and children a much less likely outcome for many Canadians—despite the fact that government cannot substitute for the social, economic, and personal benefits that family produces for adults and children as well as society as a whole.

But while policy wonks will often make it seem as though government holds all the keys to unlock the fertility puzzle, and that the solution to fertility decline is more government—more state-financed daycare, more subsidies to children, better tax treatment for parents, more legislated parental leave—I believe that the weight of evidence leads to a different conclusion. That different conclusion is that overweening government has undermined families over the past fifty years. That growth in government has been driven in part by the zeitgeist, by contraception, and by other changes universal to Western society. But it has also been an unintended consequence of the struggles to keep Quebec within Canada, to absorb the Boomer generation, and to accommodate the rise of women in the workforce.

Many societies have tried to encourage higher birth rates (Quebec prominent among them) by a series of policy measures, such as grants and tax advantages for parents, subsidized daycare, generous parental-leave policy, etc. In no industrialized country have these policies been very successful, except perhaps in slowing the decline in the birth rate, as in the case of, say, Sweden, which has one of the higher birth rates in Europe (but at 1.7 or so, while slightly above Canada, is still below replacement rate and the cost of such policies per extra child produced is exceptionally high).[6]

By contrast, the United States and the United Kingdom, neither of which has pursued a big government policy of promoting larger families, have enjoyed a demographic renaissance, and France, which has not gone as far down the activist pro-fertility road as some Scandinavian countries, also has nearly a replacement-level fertility rate.[7] And Quebec, after all the effort I have described, still has a fertility rate well below that of Alberta, Saskatchewan, and Manitoba, and only marginally above that of Ontario,[8] whereas none of these provinces have the full range of extensive and expensive "pro-birth" policies of Quebec. What might explain these differences?

Earlier I sketched out what I think the answer is, and it is only partly related to the tax burden on families or the level of provision of state-funded daycare. Instead, it has much to do with: the breakdown of trust between men and women; a decline in our ability to love and trust each other enough; the undermining of marriage, the institution in which such love and trust best flourish; marriage laws' elevation of the desires of adults over the well-being of children; governments' desire to push women to work more in the wage economy than women themselves say they wish to do; and, finally, those same governments' willingness to act as a very poor-quality substitute parent in the case of the breakdown of marriages with children.

What's Love Got to Do with It?

One way of putting it, then, is that the decline in fertility of Canadians is partly a matter of incentives, but at least as much and probably more a matter of character. We are less inclined to make sacrifices for others, more bound up with our own desires, more determined that government will look after our needs for security and support than earlier generations, who relied on hard work and the family to protect their future.

If the shift in our character has, in fact, been chiefly the product of the expansion of the state and the decline in the need to work to support oneself, then the vision of the future of the Canadian economy and society that underpins this book means yet another sea change is in the offing.

Driven by the need to put everyone to work, and at the highest levels of productivity, together with the need to restore Canadians' ability to have the number of children they say they desire to have but are not currently having, we will have to change the institutional supports around the family just as we will have to change the way the workplace is organized.

On the family front, I have already observed that the most economically productive workers are married men, and that as marriage has declined, the relationship of young men to the workforce and to education has deteriorated as well. This is especially true for young men whose education, skills, and abilities might have made them only marginally employable in the Canada of the last fifty years. The state has to some considerable extent crowded them out as suitable marriage partners: social welfare programs of various descriptions were serious alternatives to work, high minimum wages and other legal requirements on employers made low-productivity workers hard to hire, and in an era of abundant labour supply, employers always chose the better qualified candidates.

All these conditions are about to change in Canada. Population aging is going to press the state to reduce its size (as it is already doing in countries like Sweden). Social programs are going to be further revamped (after the first mini-wave of reform in the mid-nineties) to push people into work rather than present barriers to work. Wages are going to rise. Marginal tax rates on labour income are going to fall. Employers will be under tremendous pressure to find ways to supplement the poor productivity of under-skilled workers by giving them more intelligent tools to work with. We will become acutely aware of the problems caused by poorly brought-up children who enter the workforce without having acquired the skills that make them valuable employees, let alone desirable mates and parents. And we will have to surrender to the powerful evidence that daycare, schools, and other institutions cannot ever hope to replace the character endowment that intact families, on average, bequeath to their children and, through them, to society as a whole.

The increased proportion of people in real work, the shrinking of the rent-seeking state, the increased need of individuals to rely on themselves and their families, will all thus produce a change in our character, a change toward something recognizable by the people who founded Canada.

But there will be more to be done in the area of the family. We will not be able to wait for the changes in character that will come in due course, and we will need to give those changes some institutional support. There is no need to roll back the progress that women have made economically and socially, and indeed there is no reason to wish to do so. What we need to do is to reflect on the way that we have shifted the balance of costs and benefits related to marriage over the past fifty years, to see if we can find a new equilibrium. That new equilibrium would recognize the importance of marriage for both adults and children, the socially and economically desirable behaviour that it unleashes in both parents, and the need to help women strike the better balance they seek between working and having children.

Because these matters all touch vital areas of personal freedom, however, there are limits to how much the state can or should do to redress the balance. Saying that there are limits on what can be done, however, is not to say there is no room to work.

Entire books have been written on the interplay between the modern welfare state and marriage and the family. Let me just mention three things that I think would be enormously helpful in reinstating the centrality of marriage and family to Canadians' lives.

Make Young Men More Attractive Marriage Partners by Increasing Their Economic Value

The highly desirable rise of women in the workforce has been accompanied by a decline in the participation rate of certain groups of young men in both work and education. As the economic value of women rises in the workplace and the state offers no-strings-attached support for lone mothers, the economic value of marriage and family is undermined, most powerfully for people on low incomes. One of the consequences appears to be a class of eternally adolescent young men who are hardly attached to work, education, or family. One author writes, "For whatever reason, adolescence appears to be the young man's default state, proving what anthropologists have discovered in cultures everywhere: it is marriage and children that turn boys into men."[9]

Pressure on young men to get into the workforce will grow as labour scarcity improves the incentives to work, which will also improve the incentives to complete an education. It may be important, however, to find ways to make it easier to combine working and studying, and to lessen the emphasis on university education in favour of technical and trades occupations that may prove more attractive to young men alienated from traditional post-secondary education.

Ironically, one of the effects of labour shortages that we were already seeing in Alberta is that the pay one can get even for relatively unskilled work is so great that it draws young people out of education and into work. We shouldn't be too quick to condemn this development. Not everyone is suited to a prolonged period of education, and a more fluid mix of education and work may help especially some young men to do more of both. Moreover, there is evidence that part of the decline of marriageability for certain classes of young men has been the deteriorating low-wage and low-skill labour market, as the earnings premium payable to workers with higher levels of education has risen and more low-productivity, low-value work has been exported.[10] The evidence gleaned from the severe labour shortages already seen in some provinces in

Canada prior to the downturn holds out the hope that the economic rewards to working at all levels of education and skills will improve. Social welfare reform, discussed below, may complement that development.

Most importantly, getting the character-changing benefits of work—the discipline, the responsibility, the rewards for productive behaviour—at an early stage may change a lot of things. For young men it may make them less self-indulgent, more committed to work, and more aware of the benefits of marriage, including two incomes, shared household responsibilities, and complementary skills. For young women, it may make the pool of economically and socially attractive potential partners wider. If there are strong reasons that we as a society want to encourage work, marriage, and family, then it makes no sense to create the conditions in which women see little value in a significant number of men as potential partners. Giving such men little alternative to either real work or real education at the earliest possible moment in their young adult lives will give them something substantial to offer women and an awareness of the real benefits of longer-term stable relationships.

It would probably help if parents were less indulgent toward their children of either sex. Growing up and taking responsibility for yourself is hard at the best of times. If the process of maturation is obstructed by parents who pay the bills, rarely challenge destructive choices, and indulge bad behaviour (such as letting children live at home long past the age when they can and should be self-supporting), it only delays the point at which children will get on with their own lives and damages their character to boot. The parents of the Boomer generation were dragged into adulthood by their experiences of the Depression and the war. While we do not wish to re-create the fifties that resulted, neither should we lose sight of the tremendous social, economic, and cultural vitality that was thereby unleashed. To say that we want to rediscover the latter is not a wish to return to the former.

Make Marriages with Children Harder to Get out Of

Take together all that we have learned about the importance of marriage and family to children, including the extent to which intact families are the place where children learn first and best the character traits that confer success in our society and economy. Look at the other side of the coin, namely, the documented evidence of chronic poverty, poor cognitive and emotional development, school-dropout rates, behavioural problems, and other dysfunctions for children associated with lone parenthood.[11] Can there be any doubt that in our rush to accommodate the desires of adults, we have bought their freedom to escape marriage at the expense of the most vulnerable members of our society, our children?

I laid out earlier as well the consequences of no-fault divorce for the bargaining power of the parent that has the greatest interest in keeping the marriage together. Divorce reform has, therefore, created the conditions in which the spouse who is least committed to the marriage is the one who holds the keys to the marriage's dissolution, regardless of the financial consequences (i.e., division of assets, child and spousal support) that may flow from that decision.

No one wants to return to the days when bad marriages were an inescapable trap. On the other hand, there were sound reasons why we as a society made it difficult to escape marriage, and chief among these was that children, who had little means with which to protect their interests, were on balance damaged by it. Similarly, it was widely recognized that the sexual division of labour, in which women stayed at home and looked after the children, meant an economic sacrifice by women that could not be undone by dissolving the marriage, and so men needed to be bound to honour their economic commitments to the family even if their pleasure in doing so had been replaced by less appealing emotions.

Conditions are now different. Women do not need men economically to the same extent. On the other hand, if I am right that the undependability of marriage is one of the chief reasons that women delay marriage and child-bearing so as to establish a career that is indisputably theirs (and therefore not endangered by marriage breakdown) and end up having fewer children than they might otherwise prefer to have, we have not got that balance between adult freedom, marriage, and children right. Many of the other policy ideas I have laid out here would help, but there is no substitute for women—who must make the decision to bear the children, and who in the great majority of cases must raise the children alone in the case of marriage breakdown—feeling that they have strong and reliable institutions to support them in that choice.

How can this be reconciled with the freedom of adults to make the life and relationships that they wish? By remembering that our choices have consequences, and that mature individuals and mature societies hold individuals to account for the consequences of their choices, especially where those choices affect others. Above all else, that must mean that adults who are mature enough and responsible enough to make a child together should be in no doubt that that brings with it expectations that those parents will accept responsibility to raise the child together.

Thus if we decide, as I believe we will, that we are not satisfied with our declining propensity to have babies, that we want to renew our population and make Canada matter more in the world, we will doubtless want to consider marriage reform. Couples marrying, for instance, might have a choice of two kinds of marriage. Where no children are contemplated, they might choose a form of marriage such as we have today, in which each party is free on their own initiative to dissolve the relationship.

Where the plan is to have children, however, a deeper form of marriage commitment might be contemplated in which both parties agree that the marriage would be indissoluble by unilateral action by either of the spouses until their youngest child reaches the age of, say, sixteen. The power relationship within such a marriage would shift tremendously. Now the parent with the least or no interest in seeing the relationship dissolved would, in essence, have a right of veto, giving them powerful bargaining leverage and a greater sense of confidence that economic sacrifice made early in the relationship would not be repaid with betrayal and abandonment later on. The only exception would be where one of the parties could demonstrate fault on the part of the other spouse, fault grievous enough to justify allowing them to escape their commitment, such as mental or physical cruelty.

In the same vein, we might, as a matter of law, automatically convert the first kind of marriage into the second where children are produced.

We could not, of course, force people who did not wish to marry to do so, nor would it be desirable if we could. Not every social problem can be resolved by the compulsion of the law. On the other hand, one of the ways in which our character has become corrupted has been the extent to which we are very reticent to use non-legal means to encourage appropriate behaviour. Legal institutions such as marriage can complement but not replace love and trust, and as I have already said, part of the problem is that we do not love each other well enough.

One of the ways in which we do not love each other well enough is that we have low expectations of one another—parents of children, spouses of one another, unmarried couples of each other, friends and relations of such couples. In the face of the evidence about the benefits of marriage, especially where children are present, but even in the absence of children, we should be prepared to speak out more forcefully about the right way to behave to one another, to stigmatize irresponsible parental behaviour in divorce, to encourage our children to marry, to expect that partners who say they are committed to us enact that commitment and give it force beyond the desires of the moment. Such social pressures are not improper but are rather a manifestation of the care that we owe to one another. No one is obliged to act on the basis of social disapproval of their actions, but no one is entitled to have their actions exempt from criticism where they affect the well-being of others. Being free also means being accountable.

Think More Seriously about the Behaviour We Want to Reward

Earlier I talked about Isabel Sawhill of the Brookings Institution, who spoke about the importance in social policy of being clear about the behaviour governments wish to encourage, and then making sure that government policy ensures those people who "play by the rules" are always made better off by doing so. This is vital, because marriage and family are hard work, and even though their benefits for society and the vast majority of families are considerable, we have worked diligently over the years to reduce the rewards for such desirable behaviour.

The key is that the higher the economic value of women's time away from the home, the greater the incentives for women to work outside the home, and the more the benefits to both men and women of marriage decline. We are thus faced with the difficulty of finding ways to increase the value to both partners of being married without decreasing the value to women of working. Or, as a Goldman Sachs report[12] noted recently,

> In countries where it is relatively easy for women to work and have children, female employment and fertility both tend to be higher. Economies where the problem of population aging is most acute—such as Japan and Italy—also tend to be those where female employment is lowest.

Here are three examples of things that we should do to make things better. The first is to reform social welfare in all its guises. The second is to reform taxes. The third is to reform the workplace.

Social welfare currently makes little distinction between those whose behaviour we want to reward and those whose behaviour we want to discourage. The only thing that really matters is lack of income, although clearly different classes of welfare recipients (single without children, married without children, and married or single with children) have differing levels of access to welfare benefits.[13]

As the experience of the eighties and nineties taught us, welfare rates matter enormously. The movement of large numbers of people off welfare and into work in the nineties was accompanied by a serious decline in the value of benefits, and we have already seen the evidence that high levels of benefits increase, to a remarkable extent, the danger of young people being trapped on benefits, and in the case of women, the chance that they will have children alone and have little chance of marriage later on.

So part of making marriage more attractive is to decrease the attractiveness of the alternatives. In welfare reform terms, that takes us back to my earlier argument that escape from poverty for those who will not do so under the impulse of their own values can come only from outside pressure to change their behaviour. Some of that can and must be accomplished through improved incentives, but there are still limits to our ability to improve "positive incentives." Increasing the flow of benefits to low-income people or attacking income inequality by levelling incomes down will not merely fail, it will actively undermine the most promising route out of poverty.

So what is needed is not more money, but rather an improved ability for social welfare to discriminate between those using government support to tide them over an exceptional and temporary life crisis, on the one hand, and those whose values and consequent behaviour condemn them to poverty and long-term dependency on the other. And we then need to put in place policies that make it progressively more difficult for the latter to remain on benefits in the long term.

But the state is ill equipped to undertake these social welfare roles. The state is quite good at issuing cheques based on abstract and objective criteria, such as low income, unemployment, or old age. It is very poor at discriminating between people whose values and behaviour will lead them to escape poverty and those who are liable to remain trapped by it.

Moreover, in the liberal-democratic state, it is not at all obvious that we want the state dictating behaviour or that the courts will even let it do so. I am more and more convinced that our rights-based culture will consistently undermine attempts to impose behavioural conditions on receipt of social welfare benefits, on the grounds that such discrimination is, well, discriminatory, no matter how rational and beneficial it may be. There is nothing wrong with discrimination, as long as it is based on rational and justified criteria. There are in fact differences between people, and policy that is incapable of giving to each person what they need is likely to create great damage. But the modern state cannot achieve this kind of targeted and rational discrimination.

It is precisely for this reason, in my view, that we have seen in both the United States and the United Kingdom a growing use of the private sector, including the not-for-profit and so-called faith-based charities, for the delivery of social services. The main attraction is not that this necessarily saves money—real welfare reform doesn't save money, and that's not the objective—but rather that such private agencies may be more demanding of their clientele and expect more in the way of improvements in behaviour. An officer in the Salvation Army, for instance, is likely to be more personally committed to the success of those he is responsible for, as well as less accommodating of bad behaviour, than a government welfare administrator.

In addition, the existence of many such private agencies allows a wide variety of strategies to be employed in the effort to move people off benefits and into self-sufficiency. Because the needs and capacities of people trapped on welfare vary enormously, so too do the programs that might help inculcate in them the values that they need to succeed. I predict, then, that Canada will begin to experiment much more extensively with contracted-out provision of welfare services, with payment to agencies being based, not on how many people are passively maintained on income support, but rather how many people are successfully moved off benefits and into employment over some sustained period of time.

Thus an increased reliance on private delivery of welfare services might make it easier to have higher expectations of how welfare recipients will behave, including marrying when there are children present and moving into work whenever and wherever possible.

A related strategy would use the new federal Working Income Tax Benefit (WITB) and its provincial equivalents to reward work more strongly on the lower rungs of the income ladder. WITB-style programs aim to do exactly what Isabel Sawhill suggested: to ensure that people who play by the rules (in this case who work rather than remaining on social benefits of one kind or another) find their income enhanced rather than reduced by doing so.

The American experience, by the way, shows unambiguously that this approach is far more effective in getting low-income, low-skilled people into work than raising the minimum wage, which is disruptive of low-wage job markets, forces businesses to pay for social policy with no regard to business conditions nor the cost imposed, and is poorly targeted if the objective is to reduce poverty. Nada Eissa, who is the chief analyst for the U.S. government of the effect of their equivalent of the WITB (called the Earned Income Tax Credit or EITC), says that, compared to the alternatives, such as higher minimum wages, the EITC unambiguously increases labour-force participation and reduces poverty.[14]

Just as we have in recent years worked to open up the income differential in favour of work (as opposed to dependence), we should examine ways in which we can further increase the difference in the benefits that flow from work to married parents as opposed to single people or lone parents with children. In our efforts to reduce child poverty, we have increased the flow of social spending on low-income parents with children, for example through the Canada Child Tax Benefit, but we have not sought to differentiate between the marital status of parents. And yet the evidence we have looked at here shows strongly that the decline of the family, in part spurred by the growth of the welfare state, has been a principal motor of the growth of child poverty. If family is indeed the greatest social welfare institution we have, we have got to have the courage to support it and use it.

Social welfare reform is thus one tool. Another is tax policy. Jack Mintz has documented how tax policy discriminates against a family with a single-earner parent,[15] compared to one with two earners, even though the family unit might have the same overall income. Mintz puts the tax penalty for this structure at over $300 a month for an Ontario family with a single earner earning $70,000 as opposed to another family with the same income but split between two earners. Remember that one of the reasons for the declining attractiveness of marriage to women is their increased earning power in the marketplace. The effect of such a tax policy is to increase an already punishing economic penalty for staying home with the kids, because the income forgone by the stay-at-home parent is so significant. If on top of that forgone income, the tax burden borne by the parent who works is higher than cases where the income is split, not only are we not rewarding the behaviour we want, but we are actually penalizing it. Reversing this relationship between marriage, parenthood, and the tax system must be a top priority.

The key, I think, is to increase choices for parents by reducing the costs of their choices but without taking from them the responsibility for those choices. That's why the federal government's universal child benefit is such a good model.

When the government makes decisions about how to spend money, it does so in accordance with its priorities. The Liberal government of Paul Martin wanted to encourage women to work while it built a political support base through yet another new extension of state-sponsored employment, this time in a new quasi-state-monopoly on daycare. The experience in Quebec has been that such a system, as we have already seen with so many other such programs, is sold as favouring the poor, but it is in fact an inflexible one-size-fits-all solution to the child-care problem that benefits chiefly the middle class, who also finance it with their tax dollars.[16] Such an approach also implicitly suggests that parents who stay at home with their children are performing a less valuable service than those parents who go out to work and use professional state-sponsored child care. The child benefit, by contrast, gives choices to parents about their priorities, makes no distinctions between the value of choices parents make, and returns the money to the hands of the parents and makes them responsible rather than allowing the state to use the money to build political support among well-organized rent-seekers. If more money is to be put by governments into supporting parents' child-care choices, it should take this form.

Finally, if we want to encourage marriage and children *and* continue to enjoy the benefits of women's full participation in the labour force over their working lives, we will have to think about the rules concerning how the workplace is organized.

Over the past few decades, trade unions and their way of thinking about labour relations and the workplace have come to dominate our thinking. But as any economist will tell you, it is a labour shortage and not a trade union that is the worker's best friend, because it gives the individual worker real bargaining power. Women and others will have unprecedented power to shape the terms and conditions of their employment, making the marriage of work and parenting more feasible than ever before.

In the brave new world that is looming, it is not just trade unions that will find their raison d'être vanishing. It is also the assumption that without a benevolent state to protect their interests through inflexible workplace legislation and regulation, employees would be at the mercy of rapacious exploitative employers. If it really is true that a labour shortage is a worker's best friend, then we are entering a worker-friendly era the likes of which has rarely been experienced in Canada.

The new direction labour relations will take was presaged by the tremendous labour shortages, especially in the information technology (IT) sector, that occurred in the lead-up to the tech bubble several years ago. IT companies were famous for the imaginative ways in which they tried to woo employees by offering them perks that matched the desires of their prospective employees.

Given that the recruitment pool was young and "cool," workplaces were quickly transformed accordingly. Out went corporate suits, 9-to-5 work schedules, carefully coiffed hair, and industrial cafeterias; in came blue jeans, flextime, bed head, video games, and espresso machines.

There is, however, an alternative strategy for workers to use to change the balance of power in the workplace in their favour, and that is labour legislation won through political rather than economic power. Thus the years of the baby boom bulge of workers were also an era characterized by a significant growth in regulation of the workplace. The problem is that such regulation, which is often relatively rigid and inflexible, becomes an obstacle to workers and employers negotiating mutually satisfactory workplace arrangements.

When one considers that the flexibility of workplace arrangements may also be a key factor in attracting older, previously excluded, and marginal workers into the workforce, as well as in making parenting and work more compatible, reform of the law governing employment and the workplace will almost certainly have to be part of the response to the labour shortages on the horizon.

Interestingly, this is exactly the conclusion reached by the 2006 Federal Labour Standards Review.[17] Among other things, the report recommends allowing employers and employees to agree to opt out of many one-size-fits-all labour standards and notes that "workers need more control over their time at work and after work in order to fulfill their responsibilities as family and community members, and employers need more flexible working time arrangements in order to compete in a highly volatile global marketplace." It also recommends that there be more room for workers and employers to strike a new balance between security and flexibility, so that employers get more flexibility to adopt new technologies while workers get better access to retraining and other resources to keep their skills up to standard.[18]

Workplace flexibility is also related to the issue of raising our productivity. Annual hours worked per employed person in Canada, as already noted, were about 145 hours lower than in the United States between 1997 and 2004.[19] This represents one month less per year spent on the job for every Canadian worker relative to the average American worker. In addition to our more progressive tax system, a lot of the gap is due to more stringent and inflexible labour standards in Canada that act as stronger work disincentives, as well as higher levels of trade unionism where unions are substituting their own judgment for what workers would actually choose for themselves in workplace conditions and practices. Giving Canadians more control over their working conditions could help to shrink this gap.

What this means, among other things, is that rather than relying on governments to force inflexible rules on employers and employees that then meet the needs of neither party, the assumption underlying workplace rules in the future will be of the competence of workers to represent themselves and their interests directly. With jobs plentiful and workers scarce, lumbering employers with all kinds of restriction will no longer be seen as in the interests of employees, who will find their interests better served by a wide variety of employers competing for their services.

Quebec's Power Within Canada: High Tide and After

After a century of political tutoring, the francophone population of Quebec understands intuitively that its surest power lies in the negotiating process itself, the menace of separation combined with the demand for special status, to increasingly enlarge the political autonomy of the Quebec government, and reduce that of Ottawa. Quebec has no interest in finding an angle of repose in this eternal struggle.

REED SCOWEN, *TIME TO SAY GOODBYE: BUILDING A BETTER CANADA WITHOUT QUEBEC*

Changing Canada in the next few decades will be a game of inches, not yards. Demographic change, and particularly the end of the economic premium that the Boomers represented in the seventies and eighties, has already unleashed a series of incremental changes that have pushed Canada slowly in a new direction. Looking back, we can see that the battle to defeat the deficit, the reform of the CPP, modest changes to social welfare and the tax system, and a modest decline in the overall size of government, have all been responses to population change as well as other factors. Tiny incremental shifts in the character of Canadians, especially as reflected in their political attitudes, are already observable. Fiscal rectitude, welfare reform, high shares of the population in the workforce are all notable trends that are different from the recent past.

The next frontier—reining in the state, shifting a higher proportion of the population into productive work, more significant reform of our whole philosophy of social welfare, flattening the tax structure and lowering rates, greater reliance on the family as an institution promoting social well-being as well as economic efficiency, changing the retirement behaviour of Canadians—all this lies in the future, although many of these changes are already observable in embryonic form. These changes will likely evolve gradually, driven among other things by the cumulative incremental pressures of a much bigger wave of population change. These pressures will likely incrementally change our political and individual character even further.

But there will be forces pushing the other way. The most powerful force pushing us in the direction of an expanded and redistributionist state was not the Boomer generation, but rather the arrival of a millenarian separatist movement in Quebec and the bidding war for the loyalty of the young French-speaking Boomers. The rent-seeking dynamic this brought into play has been most powerful in Quebec,[1] but has also captured economically more vulnerable regions such as Atlantic Canada. The result has been a growing division of the country into regions that live predominantly by making (Ontario, Alberta, British Columbia, and increasingly Saskatchewan) and those that expend more energy on taking (Quebec, the Maritimes, and Manitoba, with newly rich Newfoundland's future behaviour largely unknown).

Quebec's Bargaining Power Leaking Away

But the place that really matters is Quebec. The other parts of the country that have become enmeshed in character-corrupting rent-seeking (or PUPPETRY) on a large scale were never powerful enough to have caused the growth of the state that made such rent-seeking attractive in the first place. These other places were merely collateral damage. Without Quebec and the profound changes unleashed there by the Quiet Revolution and the Boomer generation, I am convinced that Canada would not have trod the path of massive state expansion we did. But while Quebec still matters, the reality is that it will matter less in the future, in large part because of the changes that it has itself unleashed.

The growth of the state in Quebec and the bidding war between governments has undermined economic growth; raised welfare dependence of all kinds; vastly expanded pseudo-work; given trade unions, companies, and other rent-seekers disproportionate economic power; undermined the family; driven away a major part of the population; and made the province inhospitable ground for immigrants. As a result, Quebec's political, economic, and demographic weight are all slipping noticeably, and these trends will only intensify unless the governments of Canada and Quebec change course with respect to the province. And if they don't change course and Quebec continues its relative decline, its ability to sustain the bidding war and win rewards for aggressive PUPPETRY will slip away by subtle degrees. Quebec's bargaining power may not disappear, but it will be an anorexic relic of its former glory.

As we have already seen, by 2031 StatsCan projects that Quebec will be a bare fifth of the Canadian population, implying a big drop in its relative weight in the House of Commons from 75 out of 308 members today to roughly 75 out of 375 members. British Columbia, Alberta, and Ontario together, by contrast, will represent roughly 250 members; winning three-quarters of those seats would give a political party an overall majority in the House of Commons without a single Quebec seat, or indeed a seat in any other province.

Immigrants, who have little invested in the French-English quarrels of the past and certainly feel no guilt over historical wrongs that might have been done to French Canadians, will represent an even bigger share of the population in this newly dominant coalition of provinces that will quite likely also include Saskatchewan and possibly even Newfoundland.

The old coalition of underdeveloped provinces (known by the hateful expression of "have-nots," itself a product of the new redistributionist state) that once could pretty reliably count on seven members and sometimes eight (when poor policy occasionally dragged British Columbia into the recipient column for equalization) is foundering. Ontario may have joined the ranks of equalization recipients for the moment, but it is hard to imagine that state of affairs continuing much beyond the end of the current downturn. On current form, then, Quebec will soon find only four other provinces at its back in the federal-provincial rent-seeking sweepstakes, those powerhouses of the Maritimes and Manitoba. Even that group could be further reduced. Manitoba could escape reliance on equalization and become a "have" province simply by selling its electricity at prevailing market prices[2] instead of at a steep discount. And Premier Sean Graham of New Brunswick is taking aggressive steps to move his province out of dependence on transfers and into self-reliance, including an imaginative tax plan that would make the province an attractive destination for business investment and productive workers.[3]

The newly enlarged grouping of provinces that are net payers into the vast churning cauldron of interprovincial transfers are going to be increasingly reluctant to see the fruits of their labours sucked away by other jurisdictions who will be ever more obviously the authors of their own misfortunes.

This new power coalition (Making Canada) will not only represent political numbers. It will also represent economic weight—perhaps 70 per cent or more of the national economy and of the national tax base. Compared to Quebec and the rest of Taking Canada, it will have a younger population, higher fertility, higher immigration, a higher share of its population working and at higher levels of productivity than the disparities in these fields that already exist with Taking Canada. And unlike past years, when the plea that there wasn't enough work to go around got a sympathetic hearing, everyone in these economically dynamic parts of the country will be acutely aware that there are jobs available for anyone who wants to work. That will make continued support for Quebec's extensive welfare state provisions, high rates of early retirement, and high levels of dependence an even tougher sell—to the extent that they are propped up by transfers from elsewhere.

The changing political economy of Confederation will also undermine Quebec's power. The story told by Eric Kierans illustrated the old mentality that saw Canada as a closed economic system dominated by the central Canadian industrial economy. Ontario and Quebec, jurisdictions of fairly equal size, were the political coalition and the complementary economies that powered that arrangement. Now the manufacturing economy of southern Ontario is deeply integrated into the North American industrial heartland[4] and can buy its supplies freely in the world market, just as Quebec increasingly looks to New York and New England as significant economic partners. Crucially, though, Ontario will be unable to be competitive within that North American economic heartland if it is weighed down by an unproductive and growing tax burden to finance transfers to underperforming parts of Canada when Michigan and Ohio and Pennsylvania bear no comparable redistributionist burden.

In 2031, Ontario's population will be roughly twice the size of Quebec and will be far less dependent on it economically. Within Canada, the vast expansion of the Alberta energy industry and the growth in western Canada more generally are creating significant new customers for Ontario's manufacturers. New economic coalitions are being forged domestically and internationally. Quebec will find itself increasingly bypassed, and the domestic political support for the redistributionist agenda that has kept the province afloat will be planed away by incremental change, one shaving at a time.

The Precursors

This shift in political attitudes to a less accommodating stance toward Quebec is not located solely in the future. Its precursors are there for all who want to see. The independence-minded nationalists in Quebec have now had two referendums with fudged questions and been unable to get a victory; now they suffer from the boy-who-cried-wolf syndrome. Fatigue with Quebec's demands, made under threat of taking the country to pieces, has hardened the hearts of many in the rest of the country, opening the door to many changes in the last decade or so that would have been previously unthinkable.

Take two examples. In the 1995 federal budget, Paul Martin completely revamped the way that Ottawa shared costs with the provinces over social welfare. The old Canada Assistance Plan (CAP) had committed Ottawa to picking up 50 per cent of the tab for most social welfare spending by the provinces. As part of the strategy to defeat the deficit, Martin did away with the old system and instituted the "infamous" cap on CAP, substituting a fixed lump sum payment for the open-ended invitation to provincial welfare spending at federal taxpayer expense.[5]

Quebec was outraged, and given the intertwining of Quebec nationalism and the social justice state, one might have thought that this would have become a *cause célèbre* in that province, proof of Ottawa's Anglo-Saxon hardheartedness and inability to understand Quebec's compassionate *projet de société*. And while the usual suspects railed against these reforms in Quebec, the political fallout there was fairly minimal, and the rest of the country did not shy from backing reform despite the potential for alienating Quebec. The fact that the cuts in transfers to the provinces that helped to bring Ottawa into budgetary surplus have been more than restored subsequently does nothing to undermine the general point that when Ottawa acts in good faith with a plausible case that it is doing so in the national interest, it can get the job done. While the BQ and PQ may call down curses on the heads of federalists everywhere, their ability to turn that to good nationalist account is clearly on the wane, and the reflexive waving of the white flag by the rest of the country is over.

Far more daring and dangerous, however, was the Clarity Act. Its history ran like this.

In the autumn of 1996, Reform Party MP Stephen Harper introduced a private member's bill (Bill C-314), which established the conditions that would apply to a referendum regarding the separation of Quebec from Canada. In this he spoke for a Canada traumatized by two referendum campaigns in which Ottawa essentially let Quebec set the terms of the question and the debate. Jean Chrétien, to his great credit, ignored those who, fearing the reaction of *indépendentistes*, counselled appeasement. Instead, Chrétien followed Harper's lead.

His government submitted three questions to the Supreme Court for clarification on the legality of a unilateral declaration of independence and the federal government's constitutional ability to respond.

In August 1998, the justices ruled that Quebec did not have a right to secede unilaterally, either under Canadian or international law, no matter how great a majority they might obtain in a referendum. To be lawful, secession would have to respect the Canadian Constitution, which would mean a constitutional amendment, thereby in effect giving Ottawa and the other provinces a right of veto.

In response to the Supreme Court's decision, Chrétien's government brought in the Clarity Act at the end of 1999, defining the conditions under which the federal government would accept to negotiate secession. Chrétien faced down the outrage of nationalists successfully, in large part because the nationalists got no support from the population of Quebec. Again, an Ottawa with the courage to act and a reasoned case to be made not only overrode the vitriolic attacks of the PQ and BQ, it did so with the support of Quebeckers as well as Canadians in other parts of the country.

Quebec's Awakening

While the incremental changes that will pull more people into work, reduce the take and the size of the state, result in more babies, and make people more reliant on family will almost certainly be less marked in Quebec than elsewhere, that does not mean they will pass unnoticed or unfelt. I have already pointed out the forerunners: plans by the Quebec government to put welfare recipients to work (under the supervision of the trade unions, *bien sûr*), Jean Charest's efforts to reduce Quebec's tax rates, the welfare reforms of the mid-nineties that reduced overall numbers dependent on benefits. Even the emergence of an articulate and thoughtful market-oriented public policy think-tank (the Montreal Economic Institute under the leadership of Michel Kelly-Gagnon) in Quebec, the growth of a new historiographical appreciation of the ideological diversity of traditional Quebec society[6] (including a more nuanced interpretation of the Quiet Revolution[7]), and prominent Quebec journalists like Alain Dubuc writing books praising the importance of wealth creation[8] are all signs of the times. Nor should we neglect the large following enjoyed in the Quebec City region by conservative TV talk-show host and Independent MP André Arthur; after all there is nothing he enjoys more than sending up what he calls the "*gouverne-maman*," or what might loosely be translated as "the mommy state." Even trade unionists are doing their *mea culpas*. When he retired as head of the CSN trade union central, Gérald Larose gave a front-page interview with *Le Devoir* in which he expressed reservations about the centralization and bureaucratization that have characterized Quebec society's evolution since the Quiet Revolution.[9]

There is every reason to expect that political debate within Quebec will be pulled along by the same forces as in the rest of the country as it struggles to meet the challenge of population aging, and it is behindhand because the rest of the country has so often relieved it of the necessity of responding to its true circumstances.

No doubt millenarian nationalists will continue to tax reformers with the accusation of being Anglo-Saxon Trojan horses, but the political success of Mario Dumont, even though it proved short-lived, still establishes the general proposition that Quebeckers are seeking a non-millenarian nationalist alternative to both the Liberals and the PQ, and that alternative will not only be non-separatist but relatively economically literate, seeking a smaller state as the way to rescue Quebec from its long-term decline. The ADQ is not the only vehicle that might deliver this alternative. For example, at their 2007 convention, the Quebec Young Liberals (from whose ranks Dumont originally emerged as a political force) favoured policies such as interprovincial free trade, tripling university tuition fees accompanied by an income-contingent student loan scheme, more English courses for children in elementary school, more democracy in labour unions, etc. Premier Charest was unable to give them much comfort that he would follow through on these ideas, but clearly there are stirrings of new ideas deep in Quebec society.[10]

Dumont and the Young Liberals and the political forces they represent are speaking out for a new political and economic class in Quebec, the young French-speaking Quebeckers who have never known a time when the entire economy was not open to them, who believe that globalization and openness to the world are the *sine qua non* of living their lives and their identity to the fullest. Daniel Dufort is one of the emerging leaders of this new generation of Quebeckers, and he speaks for many of them when he wrote recently:

> In all the new incarnations of the "*projet national*" you find this fear of assimilation and this urge to blame the Other (the federal government—who else?) for what in reality is the nationalists' own inability to manage soundly the Quebec state. We've had enough of this kind of talk, which is both defeatist and turned toward the past, not the future.... Our ancestors arrived here in the face of many obstacles; they survived bitter winters and built a life here through hard work requiring courage and endurance. They were no eternal pessimists, but rather people who didn't flinch from difficulties. They were not the kind of people who would have had much sympathy for victimology.[11] [author's translation]

People like Daniel Dufort, as well as Lucien Bouchard and the other *Lucides* who have argued for a more sensible and disciplined approach to public finances, productivity, and demographic change, will eventually be seen as visionaries who actually had the right prescription for Quebec. In fact, my guess is that the emerging French-speaking entrepreneurial class, the one that decades of language policy in Quebec helped to make room for, will now begin, ironically, to agitate for the end of the policies that put the levers of the economy in their hands within Fortress Quebec, because they want to succeed in international markets, not in a tiny protected one.

These voices of change are even reaching the inner recesses of the Parti Québécois. Jean-Herman Guay, a Quebec political scientist, shocked the leadership of the party when he addressed them in 2003 in these terms:

The programme of the Parti Québécois has largely been accomplished. Sovereignty has not been achieved, but that project helped to unleash major changes in the economic structure of society. Not every goal has been accomplished. Quebec has no seat at the UN, and not all legislative powers are in the province's hands.... But what made the Parti Québécois a powerful social movement is in part spent. The grapes of wrath have disappeared. Linguistic insecurity is no longer to be found in the workplace or in commerce, and our feeling of inferiority now is to be found chiefly in the history books.[12] [author's translation]

More recently, numerous PQ luminaries have expressed their displeasure with the Quebec model and the long-term decline it has brought in its wake. Along with former premier Lucien Bouchard, Joseph Facal, for example, was a signatory of the manifesto of the Lucides. Another former PQ premier, Pierre-Marc-Johnson, has said he agrees with much in that document. According to media reports, when he resigned from the National Assembly in June, 2009, prominent PQ front-bencher François Legault clearly was singing from the Lucide songbook: "almost 50 years after the Quiet Revolution 'Quebec is going into a quiet decline ... too often with resignation and indifference.' He warned of public 'apathy' toward Quebec's slow deterioration in prosperity and education relative to the rest of North America." He is said to be considering a run at the leadership of the PQ to promote these themes.[13]

Nationalism has always been a part of Quebec's makeup, and that will not change. Nor should it. Every people worthy of the name fights for respect for their past and room to develop by their lights in the future. But millenarian nationalism, a new breed of nationalism that only truly became credible after the Quiet Revolution, has, by an ironic twist of fate, become the motor of social and economic changes that have undermined the vitality of Quebec society, right down to its very ability to reproduce itself. After a half century of this insidious dynamic, Quebec cannot change overnight, any more than the rest of Canada. It will take a long time of incremental changes, that game of inches, not yards. But there is reason for guarded optimism, because of the changes that have already been unleashed in Quebec by earlier stirrings of the major changes that are bearing down upon us.

One of the imponderables about the future is who will hold the upper hand politically in Quebec when the battle over how to respond to these once-in-a-generation changes begins to rage internally. Whoever it may be, however, it is clear that the rest of Canada can influence the outcome hugely by its decisions about whether to continue to relieve that province of the economic consequences of poor policy. And the decision that will be made about that—or rather the series of decisions, for this will be a long process—will be determined not just by the relative bargaining power of Quebec and other parts of the country, but also by the kind of people we are, by the kind of character that will be formed in us by our experiences, by whether we want to confront our difficulties with courage and fortitude, as Jean Chrétien and Stephen Harper did with the Clarity Act. The alternative is to continue with the forlorn strategy of trying to buy the loyalty of Quebec, and then generalizing that policy to the rest of the country by the powerful twin logics of rent-seeking and federalism.

Common Ground

While Quebec's bargaining power is declining, however, it clearly will not fall to zero. Even at roughly 20 per cent of the national population and economy and with powerful constitutional tools in the hands of the province, Quebec will continue to matter significantly in all kinds of ways, even without the threat to break up the country. And it is in the nature of democracy to want to try to accommodate legitimate political and economic differences and grievances. A Quebec that was a good-faith partner in Confederation would and should expect no less, and the rest of the country should respond.

Fortunately, there is a good deal of common ground that the changes I have been describing open up. Quebec's interest lies in bringing as much policy under the control of its French-speaking majority as possible, particularly in the area of social policy. This is precisely the area of policy that the federal government became active in over the last half century in the bidding war to keep Quebec in the country. As the rest of the book's argument underlines, one main result has been to allow some provinces, and most importantly Quebec, to pursue destructive policies in effect supported and subsidized by the national tax base. Had they had to absorb and pay for all the costs of their choices, their high cost would have been apparent at an earlier stage and they likely would have had to change course earlier. The correct solution then is to end, to the greatest extent possible, access to the national tax base for provinces. This has the double benefit of making them confront the full cost of their poor policies and, equally important, to reap the full benefit of sound policy. Under the current equalization system it is the reverse: if a province, through sound policy, promotes genuine economic growth, the federal government deducts somewhere between 70 and 90 per cent of the new revenue from that province's equalization payment, effectively transferring the benefits to Ottawa, one of the best-financed governments in the country.

The solution is for Ottawa to get out of as much of these provincial social policy areas as possible, such as health care, education, and social welfare, leaving intact federal responsibilities for old age pensions, EI, and so forth. The justification for being in these provincial areas in the first place is slowly disappearing, as the Boomers pass from the scene and Quebec's ability to threaten the future of the country recedes as well. Instead of pulling people into dependence, we will need to push them into work. This also has the advantage of bringing us a little closer to the scheme of division of responsibilities that our founders created and that served us so well for generations. There was more wisdom in the scheme they designed in 1867 than we have been willing to credit them with.

There are many ways in which one could design such a scheme of easing Ottawa out of the inter-regional transfer and redistribution game, and this book is not the place to deal with the technical design of such a scheme. However, one idea that has received a great deal of currency in recent years is that of transferring to the provinces the sales tax field and allowing them to collect the GST and set the rate within their borders in exchange for an end to Ottawa's transfers in many areas of social policy. Such a transfer would appeal to Quebec, which has always wanted more autonomy from Ottawa in taxation matters. If they wished to finance a higher degree of social provision than in other provinces, they could always set their GST rate higher than elsewhere in the country, and if their voters approved, who could object? They would then be facing the full costs and benefits of their choices and should be free to set the level of social programs they want and are willing to pay for.

In addition, in order to sweeten the pot for provinces that might find the withdrawal of programs like equalization too daunting, Ottawa might offer them a supplementary deal: a debt-for-equalization swap. Ottawa would take over some part of the provincial debt and thereby clean up government balance sheets in provinces with weaker economies, reducing interest payments, and giving them much more room to finance their own activities out of their own revenues (including the newly transferred GST). Such a swap would not create the danger of provinces simply running up new debt if Ottawa made it clear that this was a one-time arrangement and that poor policy choices in future would not be compensated by renewed transfers. Interestingly, this idea of cleaning up provincial finances as a way to allow them to assume fully their constitutional responsibilities has a respectable Canadian pedigree: it was a now-forgotten recommendation of the Rowell-Sirois Commission. According to Sean Speer, Alex Skelton, the commission's able secretary, originally proposed just such debt relief to the commissioners, who were shocked by it but quickly came round to recommending it.

It became clear that the idea had merit for two primary reasons. First, debt-servicing charges were, by 1937, consuming over one-fifth of provincial revenues. Without some relief, the high cost of servicing debt threatened to undermine the commission's other provisions to place the provinces on a stable financial footing.... Skelton's proposal was, in this sense, consistent with classical federalism, and the commission's commitment to provincial autonomy. Second, the federal government was in a superior position to negotiate better repayment terms.... For these reasons—both Keynesian and provincialist—the commissioners endorsed Skelton's plan. The commission could now justifiably argue that, under its fiscal plan, the financial position of every provincial government, with no exception, would be improved.[14]

We might need a ten-year transition period from the old system to the new, but at the end of the transition we would have created a situation where one of the major friction points between Ottawa and Quebec—Ottawa's interference in social policy—would have been largely eliminated, and the incentives for every part of the country to put in place better policies that promote investment, growth, and productivity would have been vastly improved. Falling unemployment around the country would help to ease the transition politically. The existing constitutional provision regarding equalization certainly leaves huge latitude to Ottawa in how it works and what level of spending is required;[15] those obligations could certainly be honoured by some vestigial program at a much lower level of spending, a return to equalization's roots.

This is no scheme to emasculate Ottawa. On the contrary. One of the ironies of the last fifty years or so is that Ottawa has, in its headlong rush to compete with Quebec's social justice state, actually neglected the key powers that underpin central power in every federation in the world. The reason that federalism is such an attractive system is that it allows ethnically and culturally diverse countries to marry local autonomy with national economic efficiency and security. In particular, one of the key justifications for a central government is the creation of a barrier-free national economic space, and so authority over trade and commerce is an almost universal feature of central governments. Ottawa, however, has been extremely reluctant to use its completely legitimate power to tear down barriers to Canadians' right to live, work, invest, establish businesses, and buy and sell in every part of the country. Provinces, with Quebec at the head of the queue, have been eager to rush into this policy vacuum with barriers to the free movement of goods, services, people, and capital. Prodded by Ottawa, the provinces have made half-hearted attempts to develop an agreement on internal trade, but the results have been painfully slow to emerge and largely toothless in their effects.

As already noticed earlier in this book, Alberta and British Columbia, the provinces that have had the greatest experience to date with the labour short-ages that will soon cover the country, have moved ahead of the other provinces and struck their own more robust free trade regime, and the new economic cir-cumstances into which we shall shortly be plunged will cause the other provinces to be more open to free trade within Canada. But internal trade lib-eralization is a role that the logic and the practice of federalism around the world grants to central governments. In exchange for a historic fiscal settlement with Quebec and the other provinces over social policy, Ottawa should demand noth-ing less than the provinces' acquiescence in the federal government exercising the powers the Constitution already grants it to be the instrument of economic freedom and growth throughout the nation.

What if, in addition, Ottawa were to reinvigorate its use of the national de-fence power (the other key power of central governments in federations) to create an armed forces with a significant civil presence? The Canadian Forces could be much more important than they already are. National procurement policies, disaster relief, and Northern sovereignty protection are just three do-mestic roles in which they are widely recognized and act as a unifying force. By adding to that a more intensive research and development component in na-tional defence spending, playing a major training function in the economy and forming a symbol of national pride through its projection of Canadian values and interests abroad while protecting them at home, Ottawa would have done a very great deal to bolster the presence, the prestige, and the effectiveness of our national government.

Quebec would certainly oppose the new roles for Ottawa, and especially in the creation and management of the national economic space. But the other half of the bargain—a recognition that Ottawa's forays into a great deal of social pol-icy have run against the grain of the original Confederation pact and created more harm than good, and the creation of autonomous social policy and fiscal room for Quebec—would be a prize worth having for them. It is a deal they would likely make, especially when we realize that the areas where Ottawa could be newly active are entirely under the federal government's jurisdiction and do not require the agreement of the provinces, however much they might pretend otherwise. Quebec nationalists like to complain that they never signed the 1982 constitutional reforms. Quebec was a major negotiator and signatory of the orig-inal 1867 Confederation bargain, however. A promise of a return to something much closer to the 1867 division of power—Ottawa largely giving up its social policy pretensions and Quebec and the other provinces giving up their preten-sions to jurisdiction over the national economic space—is an agreement we al-ready struck once. We broke it, but not so badly that it can't be fixed.

14

The New Traditionalists

My point, remember, is not just that statecraft should be soulcraft. My point is that statecraft is soulcraft. It is by its very nature. Statecraft need not be conscious of itself as soulcraft; it need not affect the citizens' inner lives skillfully, or creatively, or decently. But the one thing it cannot be, over time, is irrelevant to those inner lives.

GEORGE WILL, *STATECRAFT AS SOULCRAFT*

What do governments have to do with the character of the people who live under them?

While some think that the character of individuals is simply given, that it is beyond the reach of governments and policy, anyone who has seen the effects of decades of Eastern European communism on individual behaviour, or the damage done to individual behaviour by lawless, corrupt, and arbitrary regimes such as Zimbabwe's or Nigeria's or Pakistan's will know that there is an unbroken continuum between individual behaviour and the institutions under which one lives. Under some regimes, it is quite impossible to live honestly and honourably. In others, good behaviour is simply discouraged or not rewarded. And in still others, formal and informal institutions serve to support and reward honesty, thrift, self-reliance, and independence of mind. That is why some writers have even spoken of "statecraft as soulcraft."

Here in Canada for the last half century or so, the once-traditional values of personal responsibility and autonomy, of a strong individual work ethic, of an aversion to the corrosive effects of dependence on character and of the desirability of the centrality of family to civilized life appeared to be on the wane. But if they appeared to be out of step with the times, that was only because the times were themselves exceptional. Our values and our character adjusted both to the rise of Quebec nationalism and to the bulge of workers by lowering our expectations of the contribution people could make to society. Traditional values appeared hard and uncaring and even dangerous in a world where having expectations of Quebec might push that province out and where real work was scarce, and the most socially vulnerable were the ones who would fare the worst in the battle for jobs.

Over the years since 1960, not working and being paid for it, or being in pseudo-work like Opportunities for Youth or most regional development programs or much of the east coast inshore fishery or teaching sociology, became socially acceptable as we struggled to get the bulge of workers through their working lives. But now those extraordinary circumstances have run their course. We now face the necessity of getting everyone to work who is capable of it. Yet, we are still lumbered with a cultural hangover that values work too little and sees virtue in relying on the efforts of others to pay one's bills.

But the disappearance of the surplus of workers that gave rise to this revolution in Canadians' attitude to work and dependence will almost certainly bring in its train the disappearance of the attitudes themselves. Many jobs will go unfilled in the Canada of the future. The inability to find workers will constrain economic growth, fuel inflation, and likely push up interest rates. The tax burden on the shrinking number of workers who must finance public services for a growing army of retirees will fuel social conflict. Every jurisdiction will tighten access to social welfare benefits to prevent them being an alternative to working.

We are on the cusp of a tremendous renaissance for Canada if we want to seize the moment. This looks set to be a time of huge and accelerating population shifts away from the regions most damaged by the policies of the last fifty years. The imperative of raising our economic game to respond to the costs of population aging likely will cause us to make every effort to put everyone to work who is capable of working, pulling hundreds of thousands of people out of dependency and pseudo-work and premature retirement. Real productive work could become the virtually universal norm. We could tear down barriers to Canadians living, working and trading anywhere they wish inside their county. We might see public services reinvented to eliminate wastefully high levels of employment that are unnecessary when modern management and technology are intelligently applied to the provision of services to the public. Immigration could change too—numbers would rise but the quality of immigrants would decline as we enter a period in which many more countries are actively recruiting the highest value immigrants. Family could become more important as the limits of the state's ability to replace family and all it represents become clear. All this creates an opening to push Canada in a direction easily recognizable by the country's founders, back toward the kinds of policies that underpinned our great success as a nation in our first century.

Quebec too could change. Having won the battle to make the province's economy operate in French, there is now an entrepreneurial class in Quebec operating successfully around the world. For this new generation, inefficient high-cost government is not seen as a benefit whose costs can be passed to people in other parts of the country but rather as an obstacle to competiveness. They will increasingly demand that workers be released from the public sector, from pseudo-work, and from welfare dependency.

In any case, Quebec will matter much less than it has done to the rest of the country. There is clearly a fatigue with Quebec's traditional demands and the repeated recourse to referendums that put the country at risk. There will be decreasing appetite for accommodation, and a hardening of the tone, a change of tactic foreshadowed by the Clarity Act in which the federal government unilaterally set constraints on Quebec's use of referendums as a weapon with which to bludgeon the rest of the country.

And Quebec will matter less simply because fifty years of pursuing self-destructive policies has shifted the population balance of the country, so that politically Quebec's weight, while far from negligible, is diminishing all the time.

A shift in political power is underway to regions that embrace values closer to the traditional values of our founders than the rest of the country, in part because they have themselves been more net payers than net beneficiaries of the dependency schemes of the last forty years. Consequently, their self-reliant character has survived more intact than in other parts of the country. They have grumbled under the burden of the yoke but lacked the political clout or the political will to take on the dependency syndrome. After all, this was a time when the bulge of workers and lack of employment made objections appear to be a hard-hearted abandonment of the most vulnerable in a world where there were no jobs. It was equally a time when the expansion of government had been sold to the country as a necessary response to the existential threat of Quebec separatism.

No more. Until the current downturn, Alberta's population had been growing so spectacularly because the shortage of workers had become so extreme. That insatiable appetite for labour will return, and soon. The geopolitical importance of the oil sands is such that the pressure to develop them is likely to be quite insulated from the momentary ups and downs of the international price of oil,[1] and no matter how enthusiastic we become in our pursuit of Kyoto and Son of Kyoto, oil will continue to power much of our economy for a very long time to come. By 2020, industry sources say that three-quarters of Canada's oil production will be from the oil sands, and all the future potential for production growth is there, rather than in conventional sources. The forecast for world energy demand between now and 2030 shows global growth requiring more of every kind of energy, including oil, placing the oil sands at the heart of the world's energy future.[2] And while Americans may wring their hands about "dirty oil," the reality is that the oil sands' environmental performance is improving significantly, and many of the sources of supply to the United States, such as Venezuela and Mexico, are also rich in hydrocarbons that require significant upgrading. In any case, oil is extremely fungible—if one market won't take your oil, there are many others that will. The ability of the world oil market to match supply and demand around the world is one of its most striking characteristics.[3]

Not only, therefore, are the provinces most receptive to traditional values going to be the ones that attract the most workers, but they will also attract the most immigrants. And it is there where the most babies will be born. Alberta not only has the highest rate of in-migration from elsewhere in the country, but it also has (along with Manitoba and Saskatchewan) the highest birth rate among the provinces, approaching replacement levels. Young Newfoundlanders and New Brunswickers and Manitobans move there and have their children, who will grow up Albertan.

And it is not just Alberta. The growth in places like Ontario and British Columbia is in the cities, but not just the metropolises of Vancouver and Toronto. The exurbs, places such as Burlington, Oshawa, Abbotsford, Chilliwack, are burgeoning as are the second-tier cities, such as Kelowna, Kamloops, Calgary, Edmonton, Saskatoon, London, Ottawa, Kitchener-Waterloo, Barrie. These will be the key political battlegrounds in the coming decades and they will be ripe for politicians that extol the traditional virtues.

Nor are the experiences driving the renaissance of traditional Canadian values restricted to the traditionally prosperous areas of the country. Consider Saskatchewan. There farmland values were kept artificially low due to decades of ownership restrictions that prevented non-residents from owning farmland. This opened up to all Canadians in 2003, and it could soon be opened up to an even broader audience in the near future.

Combine that opening of farmland to outside investors with the rapid long-term growth in India and China, which is changing diets (more demand for meat equals more demand for grain); subsidies to biofuels (such as ethanol) that have created a voracious new customer for prairie grain; rising farmland prices as Albertans realize you can sometimes buy five quarter sections in Saskatchewan for the price of one in Alberta; the Canadian Wheat Board's monopolies on barley and wheat sales that cannot long survive; the discovery of important diamond deposits; and the oil sands that extend into Saskatchewan, while the province is already benefiting from the commodity boom in uranium and potash and, increasingly, many agricultural commodities. All this presages a market-led boom. Already fairly traditional in its social values (not for nothing was Tommy Douglas's CCF government often referred to as "square socialism"), Saskatchewan will almost certainly become more like Alberta in the years ahead. Already it has reversed its long-running loss of population and will, on current form, soon join British Columbia, Alberta, and Ontario as the provinces whose weight in Confederation is rising rather than falling. It is even proving remarkably recession proof. According to the Canada West Foundation, Saskatchewan will be the only province in Canada to post real economic growth in 2009.[4]

In just a few short years, then, it could be the values of social-democratic welfarism that will seem a quaint echo of a receding past. Politically, any party that can capture the high ground of Canada's traditional values for the next generation will likely become the dominant party because it will speak directly to the anxieties of Canadians. These citizens will be increasingly aware that their standard of living is being squeezed because many jobs will go undone, new investments will be forgone, and profits will go unmade because not enough people are available to work.

This does not mean necessarily that this shift toward traditional Canadian values will result in Conservative governments. In fact, the traditional values that guided Canada in its first century were, for many years, the values of the Liberal Party of Canada. It is only in the years after 1960 that the party truly embraced a state-centred vision on a large scale for Canadians. Given their historical ability to remain free of ideological commitments and embrace whatever cause will win them electoral success, Liberals will be able to read the demographic entrails as well as anyone.

Happily, these new circumstances will also allow the party (or parties) that harnesses them to escape the charge of being flint-hearted. Voters will relax their instinctive assumption that there are no jobs and replace it with the new reality that there are not enough workers and jobs are going begging. Paying people not to work or paying them to do pseudo-work will then be transmuted from a social necessity decent people understand and support to a costly extravagance that causes political resentment and friction. Because work will *be* widely available and will *be seen to be* widely available, further welfare reform and elimination of pseudo-work will not be seen as an "attack on the poor" or "blaming the victim" but as a way to confer on them the individual and social benefits of working. Welfare in its various guises will not be eliminated but will shift from an *alternative* to working to an incentive *to* work. This can already be seen in the provincial welfare reforms that began in the 1990s. The introduction, in the

2007 federal budget, of the Working Income Tax Benefit, or WITB, is a more recent example; it will eventually guarantee that people at the bottom end of the income scale will be made reliably better off by working than by staying on benefits.

Similarly, the new natural governing party will be the party of social inclusion, because there are important parts of the population who have been previously unable to participate fully in the workforce. Aboriginals, some racial minorities, and some women are still not able to work as much as they may want to or up to their level of skill and ability. Decades of welfare for aboriginals and public-sector pseudo-work for all these groups has done too little to change their status. A labour shortage combined with a government's determination to open the benefits of work to all who are capable of it will make the new traditionalists the voice of real inclusion.

Immigrants too will be high on the traditionalists' priorities, as it will be imperative to make it easier to enter Canada, but the immigrants who will come will need more support to integrate successfully into the Canadian economy than has been the case in the past.

A country with too few workers is also a country compelled to be open to trade, for offshoring is merely Canadians using the labour force in other countries to produce the products, services, and profits (to fund their retirement) they need. Provinces begging for workers will gladly tear down the barriers to trade within Canada that have now become a constraint on their growth rather than a welcome protection for beleaguered workers threatened by a sea of unemployed. The TILMA (the Trade Investment and Labour Mobility Agreement) between British Columbia and Alberta that moves aggressively to tear down barriers to trade between two of our most economically dynamic provinces is only a precursor of a more liberal trade regime within the country as a whole.[5] Free trade will be a touchstone of the new traditionalism.

Identifying and removing the obstacles to Canadians having as many children as they would like will become a social and economic imperative and will place the resurgent traditional values at the heart of a renewal of family life. And we will re-evaluate relations between the sexes in our quest to encourage Canadians to have more babies, for our poor level of fertility is before all else a reflection of a profound malaise in relations between men and women. Basically, tax and other incentives to have children, while far from irrelevant, have at best a rather marginal effect on fertility; we need to learn to love and trust each other better and be more committed to each other and to put the needs of our most vulnerable, our children, ahead of the desires of adults. This will require us to revisit our experience with unilateral no-fault divorce, especially where children are involved. We will better align the incentives for parents who want to have more children and be close to them but cannot afford to neglect their careers when that is the one asset they take away intact from marriage breakdown.

The fiscal demands of aging plus the need to reduce the size of the state in order to improve our economic performance will lead to a rolling back of the state's ambitions to supplant much of the family's role, both because it is a poor parent and because it is too expensive in an era of population aging and labour shortages.

Also falling out from this renewed preoccupation with the family will be a re-examination of the old one-size-fits-all approach to labour legislation, workplace rules, and a host of other programs that will increasingly be shaped by labour shortages rather than the labour bubble of the post-war years. Working will be a more Protean idea, and workers will have more choices and more power in the workplace than perhaps they have ever known. Parenthetically, that will make antediluvian trade unions even more irrelevant than they are today.

Finally, all these new circumstances put within reach an historic new deal that might cement Quebec's attachment to Confederation for a generation: a withdrawal of Ottawa from much of its role as redistributor of wealth between parts of the country, ceasing to be an enabler of taking behaviour and giving up a major source of revenue to the provinces to give them both the power and also the ultimate responsibility for their social policy choices. In return, Ottawa can reinvigorate its presence and authority in the lives of Canadians by rejuvenating its proper role as protector of Canadians' economic freedom and prosperity, as well as of their national freedom and security from external threat. That this is essentially a return to 1867 and therefore our founding values makes this package even more attractive.

Put all this together: the demographic reversal, massive increase of movement of Canadians, labour shortages, the destinations of immigrants, the accelerating decline of regions caught in the past, the new political and economic power of growing and economically dynamic provinces such as Alberta, British Columbia, and Ontario (and, increasingly, Saskatchewan), the increasing irrelevance of Quebec's preoccupations to the rest of the country, the distribution of births across the country, a new congruence between traditional social values and the needs of the Canadian economy. That low rumble you hear is the traditionalist juggernaut gathering force across the land. When it reaches its full strength, it will leave nothing as it was.

notes

Chapter 1
Introduction: Symmetry's Halves

1. See Office of the Chief Actuary (OCA), Actuarial Report (21st) on the Canada Pension Plan as at 31 December 2003 (Ottawa: Office of the Superintendent of Financial Institutions).

2. With this important difference: before the Boomers, the dependency ratio was tilted toward under-15s. In the next forty years it will be tilted in favour of over-65s.

3. Richard Foot, "Despite recession, looming labour shortage big threat," *Telegraph-Journal* (Saint John), (May 2, 2009), E4.

4. Jean-Marc Burniaux, Romain Duval and Florence Jaumotte, "Coping with Aging: A Dynamic Approach to Quantify the Impact of Alternative Policy Options on Future Labour Supply in OECD Countries," *OECD Economics Department* Working Paper No. 371 (2004): 1-91; and "Canada faces severe worker shortage; A time bomb has been created by demographics," *Times-Colonist* (Victoria), (May 6, 2008), B2.

5. David Foot, *Boom, Bust and Echo: How to Profit from the Coming Demographic Shift* (Toronto: Macfarlane, Walter & Ross, 1996), pp. 18-20.

6. Doug Owram, *Born at the Right Time: A History of the Baby Boom Generation* (Toronto: University of Toronto Press, 1996), pp. xiii, 4, 31.

7. Nicole Morgan, *Implosion: An Analysis of the Growth of the Federal Public Service in Canada, 1945–1985* (Montreal: Institute for Research on Public Policy, 1986), p. 45.

8. Among economists, the view that government policy was responsible for the duration and severity of the Great Depression has become part of the general orthodoxy ever since Milton Friedman wrote his path-breaking book, *A Monetary History of the United States, 1867–1960.* For other examples of this line of thinking, see Milton Friedman and Anna Schwartz, *The Great Contraction, 1929–33* (Princeton, N.J.: Princeton University Press, 1965); W. Eliot Brownlee, *Dynamics of Ascent: A History of the American Economy* (New York: Alfred A. Knopf, 1979); and Ben Bernanke, *Essays on the Great Depression* (Princeton, N.J.: Princeton University Press, 2005).

9. Moses Abramovitz, a Stanford University economist, has explained the process. Migration, he wrote, "inhibited the rise of non-farm wages and so sustained the rates of return to investment in the face of large expansions of capital stock [in the 1950s and 1960s]. By permitting large productivity gains ... without provoking an unduly rapid rise in wages, it encouraged the expansion of industry and enlarged the scope for capital investment. The level of investment was raised and the investment boom prolonged instead of being cut short by falling profits." Quoted in Fred McMahon, "Welfare reform helps keep economy

working," *National Post* (September 9, 1999), D5.

10. With respect to the share of the economy devoted to the public sector, a great deal of data is offered later in on with respect to the Canada-US comparison. The Australian case is also important, however. Australia's public expenditures as a percentage of GDP were much lower than Canada's in 1960 (by about 7.5 percentage points of GDP). By 1996, the gap had widened to over 11 percentage points. Australia's public spending also remained much lower than the OECD average over the period, and tracked US trends quite closely. See Vito Tanzi and Ludger Schuknecht, *Public Spending in the 20th Century: A Global Perspective,* (New York: Cambridge University Press, 2000), p. 13. Further, Australia's average unemployment rate from 1973 to 1990 was 6.1 per cent. See David Meredith and Barrie Dyster, *Australia in the Global Economy: Continuity and Change,* (New York: Cambridge University Press, 1999), p. 244. The US's average unemployment rate for the same period was 6.9 per cent. See US Bureau of Labor Statistics, *Employment status of the civilian population, 1940 to date*: http://www.bls.gov/cps/cpsaat1.pdf. Canada's average unemployment rate for this period was 8.9 per cent. See Statistics Canada, Labour Force Historical Review 2007 (Table Cd1T46an), (Ottawa, Statistics Canada, 2008).

11. According to Andrew Coyne, "One event in particular stands out here: the 1971 reforms to unemployment insurance, brainchild of employment and immigration minister Bryce Mackasey. No single measure is more redolent of the era: benefits were increased from 40 per cent of earnings to two-thirds; as little as eight weeks of work was required to be eligible for benefits, which could be paid out for as much as 51 weeks. The program, until then self-financing, was topped up with a great dollop of subsidy out of general revenue, to pay for extended benefits in regions of high unemployment. The Mackasey reforms are credited with adding as much as two percentage points to the base rate of non-cyclical unemployment. Needless to say, they also substantially raised the cost of the program. From less than $700-million in 1970, UI benefits paid out soared to nearly $1.9-billion in 1972; to $3.8-billion in 1977; to more than $10-billion in 1985. Governments have been slowly pruning the UI program of the Mackasey excesses ever since, but the system of regionally extended benefits remains to this day." Andrew Coyne, "Social Spending, Taxes, and the Debt: Trudeau's Just Society," in Andrew Cohen and J.L. Granatstein (eds.), *Trudeau's Shadow: The Life and Legacy of Pierre Elliott Trudeau* (Toronto: Vintage Canada, 1999), pp. 233–34.

12. John Richards, "Reducing Poverty: What Has Worked, and What Should Come Next," *C.D. Howe Institute Commentary* No. 255 (Toronto: C.D. Howe Institute, October 2007): 1–32.

13. Kenneth J. Boessenkool, *Back to Work: Learning from the Alberta Welfare Reform Experience* (Toronto: C.D. Howe Institute, April 1997): 1–38.

14. Editorial, "Bankrupt Canada?" *Wall Street Journal* (eastern edition), (January 12, 1995), p. 14.

15. As one researcher points out, "New departments are created: Forests in 1960, Industry in 1963, and Consumer Affairs in 1966. The powers of other departments were considerably expanded: the Solicitor General ceased to be an appendage of Justice, and Manpower and Immigration were merged. Others ballooned under new responsibilities. For example, between 1962 and 1969, Agriculture went from 6,125 to 10,091 employees, National Health and Welfare from 3,053 to 6,114, External Affairs from 1,574 to 2,178 and Mines from 2,514 to 4,628." See Nicole Morgan, *Implosion: An Analysis of the Growth of the Federal Public Service in Canada, 1945–1985* (Montreal: Institute for Research on Public Policy, 1986), p. 54.

16. Brian Lee Crowley and Bobby O'Keefe, "The Flypaper Effect: Does Equalization Really Contribute to Better Public Services, or Does It Just 'Stick to' Politicians and Civil Servants?" *AIMS Commentary*, No. 2 (June 2006): 1–11.

17. See Barbara Boyle Torrey and Nicholas Eberstadt, "The Northern American Fertility Divide," *Policy Review*, No. 132 (August and September 2005): 39–55.

18. Documented, for example, in Charles Murray's indictment of the Great Society, *Losing Ground: American Social Policy, 1950–1980* (New York: Basic Books, Inc. Publishers, 1984).

19. Robert Lawson and Michel Kelly-Gagnon, "The Scope of Government and the Wealth of Quebecers," *MEI Economic Note* (February 2001), p. 1.

20. Daniel Drache, "The Canada-U.S. Income Gap," *CSLS Research Reports* (June 2000): 1–6.

21. David K. Foot, "Population Aging," in J. Leonard, C. Ragan, and F. St-Hilaire (eds.), *A Canadian Priorities Agenda: Policy Choices to Improve Economic and Social Well-Being* (Montreal: Institute for Research on Public Policy, 2007), p. 193.

22. Net federal debt in 1961–62, just as the Boomers were entering the labour market, was $14.8 billion. By 1996–97, it peaked at $609.8 billion, after more than twenty-five years of government deficit financing. For the data, see the third chart for net federal debt figures from 1961–62 to 2007–08, http://www.fin.gc.ca/frt-trf/2008/frt08_3-eng.asp.

23. Ross Finnie, Ian Irvine, and Roger Sceviour, *Social Assistance Use In Canada: National and Provincial Trends in Incidence, Entry and Exit*, Analytical Studies Research Paper, no. 245. Catalogue no. F0019M1E (Ottawa: Statistics Canada, May 2005), p. 5.: "The number of [social assistance] dependent individuals fell quite remarkably [over the nineties], from a peak of 3.1 million to under 2 million by the year 2000, and the value of benefits received by SA recipients fell from $14.3b in 1994 to $10.4b in 2001 (current dollars)."

24. Andy Radia, "Canada's birth-rate crisis," *Winnipeg Free Press* (March 2, 2009), A11.

25. Statistics Canada, *Labour Force Historical Review 2007* (Table Cd1T46an), (Ottawa: Statistics Canada, 2008), (Cat. No. 71F0004XCB); and Glen Norcliffe, "Regional Unemployment in Canada in the 1981–1984 Recession," *Canadian Geographer*, Vol. 31, No. 2 (1987): 150–59.

26. See a transcript of his remarks at http://pm.gc.ca/eng/media.asp?category=2&id=2469.

27. See Quentin Casey, "Concern mounts over lack of next-generation fishermen," *Telegraph Journal* (October 12, 2007), p. A1, and recent announcement of a loan program by the Nova Scotia government to encourage young people to enter the fishery, in which the average age is fifty: http://www.dailybusinessbuzz.ca/?p=7938&utm_source=ConstantContact.com&utm_medium=email&utm_campaign=DailyBuzz_20090408.

28. Brian Burton, "Oilsands pace puts heat on pipeline builders," *National Post* (March 10, 2006), EJ11.

29. Bruce Bartlett, "Large crowd turns out to hear pitch by Alta. company," *Telegraph-Journal*, February 6, 2009, C4. The company claimed that because of "an aging workforce and natural attrition it needs to hire more than 500 people per year."

30. "Unemployment hits highest rate in seven years," *Daily Business Buzz* (April 11, 2009), http://www.dailybusinessbuzz.ca/?p=8298.

31. Dr. J. McNiven with Michael Foster, *The Developing Workforce Problem: Confronting Canadian Labour Shortages in the Coming Decades* (Halifax: Atlantic Institute for Market Studies, 2009).

32. Canadian Restaurant and Foodservices Association, *Help Wanted: The Labour Shortage Crisis and Canada's Foodservice Industry*, (Toronto: CRFA, June 2006): 1-9.

33. Personal communication between the author and the Canadian Trucking Alliance.

34. According to a 2006 PricewaterhouseCoopers survey, nearly two-thirds of Canadian private companies said that the shortage of skilled workers was already slowing the growth of their companies. PricewaterhouseCoopers, "Insights into staff retention for private companies," *Business Insights*, (January 2007): 1-4.

35. In Ontario, where the economy has been battered recently, nearly 57 per cent of business leaders polled that same year, a strong majority, reported that their growth was hampered

by labour shortages. Eric Beauchesne, "Skill shortage mounts; Canadian firms face labour 'tsunami,' Beatty says," *Windsor Star*, (October 11, 2007), C1.

36. CFIB survey: Matthew Armstrong, "Help Wanted: Long-term vacancies grow for Canada's entrepreneurs," *CFIB Research*, (March 2007): 1-9.

37. See, for example, the June 13, 2007, speech in St. John's, Newfoundland, by then-governor of the Bank of Canada, David Dodge. According to the account in the *National Post*, "Canada's aging economy faces being saddled with an ugly mixture of lower growth and higher inflation unless the country improves its 'very disappointing' productivity record.... David Dodge said the labour force will start to noticeably shrink as early as 2009 as waves of Baby Boomers begin to retire, lowering the economy's 'potential output,' or the rate at which it can grow without generating inflation. Only by squeezing more output out of fewer workers and raising productivity growth could the country offset the trend.... [W]ithout an increase in productivity growth, inflationary pressure is bound to slow the growth of the Canadian economy as a whole. Ultimately, that could mean higher interest rates and borrowing costs for Canadians without all the benefits of stronger growth." Jacqueline Thorpe, "Economy risk real: Dodge, shrinking workforce must improve its productivity," *National Post* (June 14, 2007), A1.

38. For the classical economic perspective, see Moira Herbst, "Labor Shortages: Myth or Reality," *Business Week* (August 21, 2007); and Martin Wilkin, "Labour shortage is a myth: Companies can do more with less," *National Post* (July 5, 2006), WK. 7.

39. See Geoffrey Scotton, "The market works. The sky is not falling," *Calgary Herald* (August 30, 2006), A3.

40. Tom Blackwell, "MD uses lottery to cull patients," *National Post* (August 6, 2008), A1.

41. The first round of enrolment reductions occurred in 1993–94. In the academic year beginning in September 1994, the number of first-time admissions to medical-degree programs was reduced to only 1,610. Altogether, admission to medical school in Canada has been reduced by 15 per cent, from a peak of 1,894 students in the 1980–81 academic year to 1,610 students in 1993–94. See Eva Ryten, "Physician-Workforce and Educational Planning in Canada: Has the Pendulum Swung too Far?" *Canadian Medical Journal Association*, Vol. 152, No. 9 (May 1995), p. 1395.

42. Brian Lee Crowley, "Employment Insurance causes unemployment," *Chronicle Herald* (Halifax), (September 10, 2003):
http//www.aims.ca/aimslibrary.asp?cmPageID=192&ft=4&id=102.

43. Roger Sauvé, *Labour Crunch to 2021: National and Provincial Labour Force Projections* (Summertown, Ont.: People Patterns Consulting, March 2007), amended with updated Finance projections.

44. There were countless examples of this line of argument in the mainstream media and international political arena in early 2009. From French president Nicholas Sarkozy to Nobel Prize–winning economist Joseph Stiglitz, various commentators have called for the overhaul of liberal capitalism. See, for instance, Jeff Madrick, "Beyond Rubinomics (Cover story)," *Nation* (January 12, 2009), pp. 14–18; Rheal Seguin, "At gathering of leaders, Sarkozy to push for 'new form of capitalism,'" *Globe and Mail* (October 18, 2009), p. A16; and Anthony Faiola, "The end of American capitalism?" *Washington Post* (October 12, 2008), p. A1. In Canada, the perceived death of capitalism has been deplored by some, and celebrated by others. See, for instance, "American capitalism, R.I.P.," *National Post* (April 1, 2009), p. A10; and Mahmood Elahi, "Satanic optimism of capitalism haunts us," *Ottawa Citizen* (March 30, 2009), p. A9.

45. See Jon Meacham and Evan Thomas, "We Are All Socialists Now (Cover story)," *Newsweek*, Vol. 153, No. 7 (February 16, 2009): 22–24.

46. The objectionable case of the American insurance giant AIG has come to symbolize the worst excesses of this "entitlement mentality" among some on Wall Street. For more details, see "AIG pelted with virtual tomatoes," *Calgary Herald* (March 24, 2009), p. D1; and James Travers, "Public at tipping point on bailouts," *Toronto Star* (March 21, 2009), p. A10.

47. On this point see the work of Columbia University economist Xavier Sala-i-Martin on falling global economic inequality: http://www.columbia.edu/~xs23/papers/pdfs/World_Income_Distribution_QJE.pdf; UCLA's Deepak Lal's *The Poverty of 'Development Economics,'* 3rd edition (London: Institute of Economic Affairs, 2000); and Columbia University's Jagdish Bhagwati's *In Defense of Globalization* (Washington: Oxford University Press, 2004).

48. Gary Becker and Kevin Murphy, "Do not let the 'cure' destroy capitalism," *Financial Times* (March 20, 2009), p. 9.

49. In his Nobel Prize acceptance speech, economist F.A. Hayek laid out one of those fundamental reasons: the necessary ignorance of governments about the complex facts on the ground in a modern economy. "The Pretence of Knowledge," *Les Prix Nobel en 1974* (Stockholm, 1974).

50. "Briefing: China and the West, A Time for Muscle-Flexing," *The Economist* (March 21, 2009), p. 27.

51. See, for instance, Richard Gwyn, "Unchecked, unregulated greed breeds corruption," *Toronto Star* (March 20, 2009), p. A23; and Thomas L. Friedman, "Greed, stupidity, dishonesty, and the market collapse," *Times Colonist* (Victoria, B.C.) (December 1, 2008), p. A10.

52. John B. Taylor, *Getting Off Track: How Government Actions and Interventions Caused, Prolonged and Worsened the Financial Crisis* (Stanford: Hoover Institution Press, 2009), p. 14. The book is largely an expanded version of a lecture Taylor gave in Ottawa in honour of his friend and sometimes colleague in the international world of central banking, David Dodge, the former governor of the Bank of Canada.

53. On this, see Alex Castellanos, "The Tyranny of Good Intentions," National Review Online (September 25, 2008), http://article.nationalreview.com/?q=MWU2ODgzNzg2MmIyN2Y3ZWFjY2ZlODVmMTgzYjMwMjY=; and Thomas Sowell, "Subprime Pols," National Review Online (August 8, 2007), http://article.nationalreview.com/?q=YjgwYzI4Njg3OWMxOGUzYmY0ZDMwYzYwNzkzYjc1NDI=.

54. William Easterly, "Leaders Go Left, But Economists Get Back to Basics: In Trying Times, Even Protectionists Go Free Market," *Forbes* (January 29, 2009). http://www.forbes.com/2009/01/29/davos-economic-basics-opinions-contributors_0130_william_easterly.html?partner=email.

55. Contrary to the popular view that economists rarely agree on anything, Harvard economist Greg Mankiw recently listed fourteen propositions on which economists surveyed agreed in proportions of 80 per cent and higher. Here are three relevant propositions for this discussion, with the percentage of economists agreeing with the statement shown in brackets: tariffs and import quotas usually reduce general economic welfare (93 per cent); the United States should not restrict employers from outsourcing work to foreign countries (90 per cent); a large federal budget deficit has an adverse effect on the economy (83 per cent). http://gregmankiw.blogspot.com/2009/02/news-flash-economists-agree.html.

56. Network of Global Agenda Councils, "Discussion Highlights on Economic Growth and Development at the Summit on the Global Agenda," Dubai, United Arab Emirates November 7–9, 2008, http://www.weforum.org/pdf/GAC/Reports/EconomicDevelopment-Growth/EconomicGrowthandDevelopment.pdf.

57. Taylor, *Getting Off Track*, p. 34.

Chapter 2
Our Forgotten Political Tradition Vindicated

1. See Kenneth J. Boessenkool, *Back to Work: Learning from the Alberta Welfare Reform Experience* (Toronto: C.D. Howe Institute, April 1997), p. 3. "During the 1980s and early 1990s, the number of Canadians on provincial welfare increased nearly every year. In bad times, welfare enrolments shot skyward. In good times, they fell slightly in some jurisdictions and rose in others, but across Canada after each recession, welfare caseloads stayed well above the level that preceded the downturn."

2. William Watson, John Richards, and David Brown, *The Case for Change: Reinventing the Welfare State* (Toronto: C.D. Howe Institute, 1994), p. 3.

3. See William Watson's book *Globalization and the Meaning of Canadian Life* (Toronto: University of Toronto Press, 1998), and in particular the chapter entitled "The American Lead." It concludes: "The examples just cited put paid to the notion that the United States, in its practice as opposed to its preaching, had always been more dedicated to laissez-faire than Canada. In fact, on many important occasions in our history, we have copied their interventions whole cloth." See also David J. Bercuson's and Barry Cooper's research, which casts light on Ottawa's "administrative binge" in the 1970s. Bercuson and Cooper, *Derailed: The Betrayal of the National Dream* (Toronto: Key Porter Books, 1994).

4. Cited in Janet Ajzenstat et al. (eds.), *Canada's Founding Debates* (Toronto: Stoddart Publishing, 1999), p. 18.

5. Cited in Ajzenstat et al. (eds.), *Canada's Founding Debates*, p. 170.

6. Jean-Charles Falardeau, *Étienne Parent, 1802–1874* (Montréal: Les Éditions La Presse Ltée, 1975), pp. 145–70. Specific texts cited, in order: pp. 157, 157–58, and 161.

7. Original: *Vous comprenez, sans doute, que par l'oisiveté je n'entends pas seulement l'entière cessation de tout travail, mais aussi cette paresse de l'esprit qui vous empêche de developer dans le travail toutes les resource de votre intelligence, à votre avantage, comme à celui de votre pays et de l'humanité entière.*

8. Original: *Quelqu'un a dit que l'homme était un animal d'habitude: et c'est une grande vérité, si, comme on fait de certaines verities, on ne la pousse pas trop loin. Oui, messieurs, de bonne heure habituez-vous à un travail continuel et régulier, et je vous prédis ... que vous vous complairez dans votre travail, que vous l'aimerez pour lui-même, abstraction faite des avantages individuals que vous en attendriez; que l'oisiveté ou l'inaction, au-delà du repos indispensable qu'il faut à l'homme, deviendra pour vous une source d'ennui insupportable.*

9. Original: *Ainsi messieurs, faisons donc en sorte, par nos lois, par nos institutions, par nos moeurs, par nos idées, que tout le monde travaille chez nous.*

10. Quoted in Chris Leithner, "What on Earth Has Happened to Canada?" *Le Quebecois Libre*, No. 131 (October 25, 2003). http://www.quebecoislibre.org/031025-6.htm. Laurier's stature as a spokesman for a classical liberal small-government philosophy with deep roots in Quebec cannot be overstated. According to Jacques Rouillard, Laurier "was representative of the values that inspired his party. Drawing inspiration from British liberalism, he believed in free and representative government, in fundamental freedoms, in the respect of the equality of individuals before the law, in private property, in progress, in prosperity and in happiness—all eminently liberal values. He exercised enormous influence over liberals in Quebec and over the policies of the Quebec provincial governments of Marchand, Parent, Gouin, and Taschereau, all of whom followed the trail blazed by Laurier. They supported democratic institutions, aspired to progress based on economic development, ardently pursued American investment, and defended the autonomy of the State from the Church." [author's translation] Jacques Rouillard, "La Revolution Tranquille, Rupture ou Tournant?" *Journal of Canadian Studies*, Vol. 32, No. 4 (Winter, 1998): 23–51.

11. Doug Owram, *The Government Generation: Canadian Intellectuals and the State, 1900–1945* (Toronto: University of Toronto Press, 1986), p. 35.

12. Quoted in Bill Waiser, *Saskatchewan: A New History* (Calgary: Fifth House, 2005), p. 66.

13. Unemployment was simply not seen as the business of the state. According to social historian James Struthers, "No one kept unemployment statistics; there was no efficient state employment service; no public welfare department existed at the federal or provincial level and there were only four at the municipal level. In all of Canada before 1930 there were less than 400 trained social workers." See Struthers, *Canadian Unemployment Policy in the 1930s* (Peterborough: Windy Pine Papers Number 1, 1984), p. 3. As for Dennis Guest, "Applying for relief, as it was commonly referred to, was a demeaning and stigmatizing experience because it was widely regarded as clear evidence of personal incompetence and failure." Guest, *The Emergence of Social Security in Canada* (Vancouver, UBC Press, 1980), p. 1.

14. Stephen Leacock, "The Proper Limitations of State Interference," in *Empire Club of Canada Speeches 1924* (Toronto: Empire Club of Canada, 1924), pp. 109–24.

15. According to a recent analysis, Canada's government spending equalled 39.3 per cent of GDP in 2007. See Kim Holmes, Edward Feulner, and Mary Anastasia O'Grady, *2008 Index of Economic Freedom* (Washington: Heritage Foundation and *Wall Street Journal*, 2008), pp. 129–30.

16. Jack Mintz, *Most Favored Nation: Building a Framework for Smart Economic Policy* (Toronto: C.D. Howe Institute, 2001), p. 61.

17. Quoted in Guest, *The Emergence of Social Security in Canada*, p. 56.

18. See Watson, *Globalization and the Meaning of Canadian Life*, p. 109.

19. According to James Struthers, "Even more than Bennett, King was philosophically averse to expanding the role of the government." See Struthers, *No Fault of Their Own: Unemployment and the Canadian Welfare State, 1914–1941* (Toronto: University of Toronto Press, 1983), p. 140.

20. Quoted by Michel Kelly-Gagnon, "Our Free Market Past," *FCPP Perspective* (Winnipeg: Frontier Centre for Public Policy, August 1, 2005).

21. December 23, 1937, to be exact—a few days before Christmas, no less.

22. More formally known as the Royal Commission on Dominion-Provincial Relations.

23. Struthers, *No Fault of Their Own*, p. 205.

24. See, for example, Ramsay Cook, *The Politics of John W. Dafoe and the Free Press* (Toronto: University of Toronto Press, 1963), p. 232.

25. Watson, *Globalization and the Meaning of Canadian Life*, p. 109.

26. Robert Bothwell, Ian Drummond, and John English, *Canada Since 1945: Power, Politics and Provincialism* (Toronto: University of Toronto Press, 1981), p. 69.

27. Quoted in P.E. Bryden, *Planners and Politicians: Liberal Politics and Social Policy 1957–1968* (Montreal and Kingston: McGill-Queen's University Press, 1997), p. 22.

28. Bryden, *Planners and Politicians*, p. 31.

29. Michael Behiels, *Prelude to the Quiet Revolution: Liberalism Versus Neo-Nationalism, 1945–1960* (Kingston and Montreal: McGill-Queen's University Press, 1985), pp. 99–100. Nor was Duplessis in any way exceptional among Quebec politicians in his deep skepticism about the activist state. According to one historian, "Throughout the first four decades of the twentieth century, the government of Quebec occupied a unique position among provincial governments in Canada. Provincial government intervention in the regional economy lagged behind all of the other provinces; the Quebec government practised the strongest of laissez-faire strategies." Robert Armstrong, *Structure and Change: An Economic History of Quebec* (Toronto: Gage Publishing Limited, 1984), p. 276.

30. Angus L. MacDonald, *The Speeches of Angus L. MacDonald* (Longman's Green and Co., Toronto, 1960), pp. 75–76.
31. Walter Stewart, *The Life and Political Times of Tommy Douglas* (Toronto: McArthur and Company, 2003), p. 70.
32. Stewart, *The Life and Political Times of Tommy Douglas*, p. 70.
33. "On the political left it has become commonplace for the last century and a half to charge that modern, industrial people are alienated, rootless, angst ridden, superficial, materialistic, and that it is precisely participation in markets that has made them so. Gradually the right and the middle have come to accept the charge. Some sociologists, both progressive and conservative, embrace it, lamenting the decline of organic solidarity." See Deirdre McCloskey, "Bourgeois Virtues?" *Cato Policy Report*, Vol. XXVIII, No. 3 (May/June 2006); and McCloskey, *The Bourgeois Virtues: Ethics for an Age of Commerce* (Chicago: University of Chicago Press, 2006).
34. As historian John English has argued, in the early 1960s "Canada's liberals looked southward again for the breath of new life.... In one of those fundamental shifts in American history between reform and retreat that Arthur Schlesinger, Jr., Kennedy's friend and biographer, has argued are the salient feature of American history, the liberal hour had once again struck, and the sound reverberated in Ottawa as loudly as in Washington." See English, *The Worldly Years: The Life of Lester Pearson, 1949–1972* (Toronto: Alfred A. Knopf, 1992), p. 238.
35. William C. Berman, *America's Right Turn: From Nixon to Clinton*, (Baltimore: JHU Press, 1998), p. 18.
36. Canadian historiography is replete with research on this reformist impulse and its intellectual origins in the southern half of the continent. See, for example, Martin Robin, *Radical Politics and Canadian Labour, 1880–1930* (Kingston: Industrial Relations Centre, Queen's University, 1968); and Barry Ferguson, *Remaking Liberalism: The Intellectual Legacy of Adam Shortt, O.D. Skelton, and W.A. Mackintosh, 1890–1925* (Montreal and Kingston: McGill-Queen's University Press, 1993).
37. Cited in Bothwell, Drummond, and English, *Canada Since 1945*, p. 278.
38. See Michael Bliss, *Right Honourable Men: The Descent of Canadian Politics from Macdonald to Chrétien* (Toronto: HarperCollins Publishers, 2004), p. 192.
39. Lance W. Roberts (ed.), *Recent Social Trends in Canada, 1960-2000*, (Montreal and Kingston: McGill-Queen's University Press, 2005), pp. 35-37.
40. For more on the Lockean influence on Canada, see Janet Ajzenstat, *The Canadian Founding* (Montreal and Kingston: McGill-Queen's University Press, 2007); and Ajzenstat, *Once and Future Canadian Democracy: An Essay in Political Thought* (Montreal and Kingston: McGill-Queen's University Press, 2003).
41. Economist John Richards argues that Canada is somewhere in the middle of the road when compared to European countries. See Richards, "Now That the Coat Fits the Cloth: Spending Wisely in a Trimmed-Down Age," *C.D. Howe Institute Commentary*, No. 143 (June 2000): 1–60.
42. Nixon made this declaration before imposing price and wage controls on the American economy. Canada followed Nixon's lead with its own Anti-Inflation Program four years later in 1975. See Daniel Yergin and Joseph Stanislaw, *The Commanding Heights: The Battle for the World Economy* (New York: Simon & Schuster, 2002), pp. 42–43.
43. "Canada's was the loudest baby boom in the industrialized world. In fact, only three other western countries—the United States, Australia, and New Zealand—had baby booms," David Foot, *Boom, Bust and Echo: How to Profit from the Coming Demographic Shift* (Toronto: Macfarlane, Walter & Ross, 1996), p. 19.

44. The qualifier "in most circumstances" is necessary because occasionally circumstances arise where private sector pay escapes normal market constraints. The current controversies over executive pay and financial industry bonuses are examples. But they are also the exceptions that prove the rule. The vast majority of pay levels in the private sector are not subject to such controversy, and executive pay and bonuses are controversial precisely because they clearly do not meet the usual standards of market-determined pay based on productivity. While such forms of pay are clearly in need of reform, they are by their nature exceptions and therefore cannot be used to demonstrate a systemic weakness in the way the vast majority of market-based pay is determined. These exceptions generate such anger and resentment precisely because they appear to establish a double-standard—an uncontroversial one for the great majority of workers, and a highly contentious one for those in positions of great power.

45. For a term of relatively recent origin, "rent-seeking" has been widely adopted by many thinkers and analysts because the concept behind it helps to illuminate so many political activities and motivations even if the term is rather inelegant and obscure for non-economists. The term "rent-seeking" was coined by A.O. Krieger in his article "The Political Economy of the Rent-Seeking Society" published in the *American Economic Review,* Vol. 64 (1974): 291–303. Gordon Tullock, one of the founders (with Nobel Laureate James Buchanan) of public choice economics, claims that he originated the concept in "The Welfare Costs of Tariffs, Monopolies and Theft," *Western Economic Journal,* Vol. 5 (1967): 224–32, but it would be fair to say that the implied concept is easily recognizable in the work of some of the giants of early economic thought such as Adam Smith and Frédéric Bastiat.

46. Jonathan Rauch, *Demosclerosis: The Silent Killer of American Government* (New York: Times Books/Random House, 1994), pp. 30–31.

47. Bastiat's *The State* is available at http://www.panarchy.org/bastiat/state.1848.html.

48. As Watson notes, "Despite the Mulroney revolution, despite downsizing, despite the attack on the welfare state, despite the terrible neoconservative 1980s, our three levels of government currently combine to spend virtually 50 percent of GDP, which is not just a peacetime but an all-time high. In 1992, they spent a grand total of 51.2 percent of GDP.... The pre-1990s high, recorded in 1944, when our public sector was busy liberating Europe, was 50.0 percent." See Watson, *Globalization and the Meaning of Canadian Life,* p. 42.

49. Robert Lawson and Michel Kelly-Gagnon, "The Scope of Government and the Wealth of Quebecers," *MEI Economic Note* (February 2001), pp. 1–2.

50. See Jonathan Rauch, *Demosclerosis: The Silent Killer of American Government* (New York: Times Books/Random House, 1994).

51. Vito Tanzi and Ludger Schuknecht, *Public Spending in the Twentieth Century: A Global Perspective* (Cambridge: Cambridge University Press, 2000). In their survey of Western governments' spending in the twentieth century they found that "by around 1960, when public spending was, on average, below 30 per cent of GDP, most industrialized countries had reached adequate levels of social welfare. Public spending on essential services in health and education or in infrastructure and basic social security systems had provided most basic public services.... However; we could not find much evidence that the large growth of government spending over the post-1960 years contributed much to the further achievement of identifiable social and economic objectives" (p. 133). Moreover, they found that public spending changed its character after 1960, away from basic public services and in the direction of greater redistribution, with the result that "the earlier link between the growth in government spending and improvements in our social and economic objectives seems to have been broken" (p. 131). Finally, according to Filip Palda, "Fiscal Churning and Political Efficiency," *Kyklos,* Vol. 50 (1997): 189–206, "Most of the growth in

government spending and taxation since 1960 brought little or no measurable increase in the welfare of citizens, and ... citizens may even be worse off for such increases."

52. Palda, "Fiscal Churning and Political Efficiency," p. 190: "I define a transfer as churned when the person who receives it would have been just as well off, or better off, with a tax cut of the same size as that of the transfer. The familiar example of churned transfers is that of the middle class which is taxed, then given back a significant portion of those taxes in the forms of social security benefits or unemployment insurance. This sort of transfer is inefficient in the sense that it needlessly destroys resources. Money is taxed out of a citizen's pocket, filtered through a government bureaucracy, and funneled back into that same citizen's pocket. The tax and subsidy misdirect the individual's economic efforts and so create a deadweight loss." In 1990, Palda estimated, somewhere between 15.2 per cent and 49.2 per cent of government spending might be appropriately described as churning in Canada.

53. As two economists have recently shown, "In 1996, average governmental expenditures as a percent of GDP jumped to 45.0%, a historic high, led by Sweden with 64.2%. In 2002 average governmental absorption of GDP had come down somewhat to 43.5%. Interestingly, Sweden's governmental takings from GDP, which reached an all time high in 1993 of 67.5%, had come down to 52.6% in 2002." See Angel Alvarado and Hugo J. Faria, "Government Size, Quality and Growth," *CESMA Working Paper* (April 2007), pp. 2–3.

54. Fortin concludes, "The result would be a marked deterioration of public finances.... Tax revenues would drop by $21 billion; provincial spending on health care would increase by $17 billion; federal payments to seniors would rise by $12 billion; children's benefits, education spending, and childcare allowances could decrease by $10 billion. On net, if it were applied today, the age structure of 2020's population would make a $40-billion hole in government budgets for 2008.... After 2020 the problem will not disappear; it will in fact get bigger, as baby boomers continue to retire in large numbers and fewer young adults enter the labour force." See Fortin, "The Baby Boomers' Tab: Already $40 Billion in 2020," in Rudyard Griffiths (ed.), *Canada in 2020: Twenty Leading Voices Imagine Canada's Future* (Toronto: Key Porter Books, 2008), p. 44.

Chapter 3
Quebec and Ottawa: The Bidding War Unleashed

1. As Doug Allen rightly points out, "Until the 1960s, the timing, extent and progression of Canadian welfare legislation lagged the US experience." Douglas A. Allen, "Welfare and the Family: The Canadian Experience," *Journal of Labour Economics*, Vol. 11, No. 1 (January 1993): S203.

2. This is not to say that the *mission civilisatrice* was not also carried on internationally. It is so deeply ingrained in the cultural narrative of French Catholic Quebec that, as Radio-Canada reported, in the first half of the twentieth century, Quebec was a major source of Catholic missionaries carrying on the Church's work abroad. In the 1950s, for example, there was one French-Canadian missionary per 1,120 Quebec Catholics, the fourth-highest number per capita in the world: http://archives.radio-canada.ca/societe/religion_spiritualite/clips/6270/.

3. See, for example, Léon Dion, *The Unfinished Revolution* (Montreal and London: McGill-Queen's University Press, 1976), p. 16.

4. For a good overview of the new historiography of the Quiet Revolution and its antecedents, see Jacques Rouillard, "La Révolution Tranquille, Rupture ou Tournant?" *Journal of Canadian Studies*, Vol. 32, No. 4 (Winter, 1998): 23–51.

5. Claire Joly, "Le mythe de la Grande Noirceur et du Québec sous-développé" http://www.leblogueduql.org/2005/10/le_mythe_de_la_.html.

6. Many of the points in the rest of this paragraph are drawn from Lucia Ferretti's review of Michel Gauvreau's book *Les origines catholiques de la Révolution tranquille*. See Lucia Ferretti, "*Histoire—Une Révolution tranquille très croyante*," *Le Devoir* (April 12, 2008), p. F9.

7. Brigitte Saint-Pierre, "*Fernand Dumont—Un grand penseur de notre époque*," *Le Devoir* (May 3, 2008), p. G8.

8. See Jacques Rouillard's survey of work over nearly a century of business elites in Canada and Quebec in "La Révolution Tranquille, Rupture ou Tournant?" pp. 23–51.

9. Of course, other newspapers existed, such as *La Presse, Le Canada*, and *La Patrie*, and took an editorial line that was far more oriented toward individual liberty and economic development, although they were also stout defenders of the rights of French Canadians. See Ralph Heintzman, *The Struggle for Life: The French Daily Press and the Problems of Economic Growth in the Age of Laurier, 1896–1929* (Ph.D. thesis, York University, 1977).

10. "Ultramontanism in Canada, as in Europe where it began during the French Revolution, was the theory of those who rejected any compromise by Catholicism with modern thought, and demanded the supremacy of religious over civil society. Its central tenet was an attachment to the person of the pope and belief in the doctrine of his infallibility." See the definition in the online version of the *Canadian Encyclopedia*, http://www.thecanadianencyclopedia.com/index.cfm?PgNm=TCE&Params=A1ARTA0008196.

11. Léon Dion, *The Unfinished Revolution* (Montreal and London: McGill-Queen's University Press, 1976), p. 67. Ironically this comment only showed Dion's ignorance of his own society's intellectual history. For example, as Fernande Roy shows, it was precisely to this "American creed" that a significant proportion of the political and business elite adhered in the century and a half before the Quiet Revolution. "This liberal creed was widespread in the Quebec society of the time, well beyond the business community. In the 19th century, it was claimed, men were the product of their own efforts. This myth is propagated through success stories published in big city newspapers." [author's translation] See Roy, *L'Histoire des idéologies au Québec aux XIXe et XXe siècles* (Montreal: Editions Boréal, 1993), as well as her *Progrès, harmonie, liberté: Le libéralisme des milieux d'affaires francophones de Montréal au tournant du siècle* (Montreal: Editions Boréal, 1988).

12. Daniel Béland and André Lecours, "Sub-state Nationalism and the Welfare State: Quebec and Canadian Federalism," *Nations and Nationalism*, Vol. 12, No. 1 (2006): 93.

13. Millenarians are so-called here by analogy with Christians who believe the Second Coming of Christ will usher in a thousand-year period of paradise on earth, while before this decisive world-transmogrifying event, justice on earth is impossible

14. The term "*projet de société*" is not unique to the nationalist movement in Quebec (the environmental movement, for example, also has its version of such a *projet*); it might be translated as a "collective plan for social transformation." For the purposes of this book, however, I use *projet de société* to refer solely to the social justice project that is at the heart of the nationalist appeal in Quebec.

15. Béland and Lecours, "Sub-state Nationalism and the Welfare State," p. 79.

16. Béland and Lecours, "Sub-state Nationalism and the Welfare State," p. 80.

17. As one researcher explains, "Quebec was receiving, by the end of 1966, 23 additional personal income tax points and 1 corporate income tax point over and above the other provinces." See Odette Madore, *The Transfer of Tax Points to Provinces Under the Canada Health and Social Transfer*, Backgrounder BP-450E (Ottawa: Library of Parliament, October 1997): 1–17.

18. For more on the fiscal imbalance argument, see Brian Lee Crowley and Bruce Winchester, *The Mystery of the Missing Fiscal Imbalance* (AIMS: Halifax, February 2005).

19. Michael Bliss, *Right Honourable Men: The Descent of Canadian Politics from Macdonald to*

Chretien (Toronto: HarperCollins Publishers, 2004), p. 232.

20. "Quebec governments claimed the right to 'opt-out' of federal programmes while obtaining financial compensation through a transfer of tax points. They were successful in many instances (hospital insurance, social assistance and vocational training), but in others (for example, unemployment insurance) the federal government resisted. What is noteworthy here is that the Quebec government typically used this money to set up social programmes similar to the previously federally-administered ones ..., *which highlights that symbolism was crucial.* For Quebec politicians, the development of autonomous provincial social programmes was a statement about the province's distinctiveness and its desire to take control of policy areas related to identity building" [emphasis added]. Béland and Lecours, "Sub-state Nationalism and the Welfare State," p. 81.

21. "By the later 1990s, specific social policies were said to exemplify the distinctiveness of a Quebec society deemed more progressive, egalitarian and compassionate than the rest of Canada.... Quebec's nationalist politicians and interest groups made up of labour unions and other left-leaning organisations that are tightly embedded in the Quebec state maintain the existence of two societies with different values." Béland and Lecours, "Sub-state Nationalism and the Welfare State," p. 93.

22. These examples are drawn from William Johnson, "The latest target: Anglophones," *Globe and Mail* (January 31, 2008), A17. See also Johnson's May 2008 talk delivered at a conference of Civitas, entitled "Quebec and Multiculturalism."

23. Rheal Seguin, "Quebec pledges nearly $1-billion to boost work force," *Globe and Mail* (March 19, 2008), A11.

24. See, for example, Calvin Veltman, "De bonnes nouvelles," *La Presse* (February 11, 2008), A17; Michel Paillé, "Un progrès continu," *La Presse* (February 29, 2008), A17; and François Vaillancourt, Dominique Lemay, and Luc Vaillancourt, *Laggards No More: The Changed Socioeconomic Status of Francophones in Quebec* (Toronto: C.D. Howe Institute, August 2007).

25. Yves Boisvert, "L'autre secret sur le français," *La Presse* (January 25, 2008), A5. \

26. Matthew Fraser, *Quebec Inc.: French-Canadian Entrepreneurs and the New Business Elite* (Toronto: Key Porter Books, 1987), p. 93.

27. Pierre Arbour, *Quebec Inc. and the Temptation of State Capitalism,* (Montreal and Toronto: Robert Davies Publishing, 1993), p. 107.

28. For an insider's look at the failure of Quebec's public investments, see Pierre Arbour, *Quebec Inc. and the Temptation of State Capitalism* (Montreal and Toronto: Robert Davies Publishing, 1993).

29. Kenneth McRoberts, *Quebec: Social Change and Political Crisis* (Toronto: McClelland & Stewart, 1980), p. 131.

30. Albert Breton, "The Economics of Nationalism," *Journal of Political Economy,* Vol. 72, No. 4 (August 1964), pp. 384–85.

31. Charles Taylor, "Nationalism and the Political Intelligentsia: A Case Study," in Taylor, *Reconciling the Solitudes: Essays on Canadian Federalism and Nationalism* (Montreal and Kingston: McGill-Queen's University Press, 1993), pp. 18–19. Taylor's essay was also printed in *Queen's Quarterly,* Vol. 72 (Spring 1965): 150–68.

32. The emphasis here is on *political* institutions because to the extent that this account assumes that French-speakers did not control a number of important economic institutions, it is simply incorrect. The chambers of commerce, the co-op movement, the Mouvement Desjardins (i.e., the credit union movement), and the various institutions that ultimately became La Banque Nationale are all examples.

33. Michael D. Behiels, "Quebec: Social Transformation and Ideological Renewal, 1940–1976,"

in Michael D. Behiels (ed.), *Quebec Since 1945: Selected Readings* (Toronto: Copp Clark Pitman Limited, 1987), pp. 21–45 at p. 39, "the most pervasive and influential ideological force behind the Quiet Revolution proved to be neo-nationalism because the various sectors of the new middle class quickly perceived that if the modernization of Quebec society was accomplished by the state under the aegis of nationalist goals and aspirations, it was imperative to gain firm control over the levers of power. Only then would the new middle class, or at least one segment of it, emerge as the dominant social class, displacing the traditional Francophone petty bourgeoisie, the church, and, it might be hoped, the Anglo-Canadian and American bourgeoisies who controlled the economy. Neo-nationalism was a perfect ideology to appeal to the masses for the political support essential in a system of parliamentary democracy. Moreover, the emergence of a powerful new class (and the internal struggle between its various elements) was camouflaged by the rhetoric of collective rights and aspirations."

34. Behiels, "Quebec: Social Transformation and Ideological Renewal, 1940–1976," p. 24. See also McRoberts, p. 32.
35. Taylor, "Nationalism and the Political Intelligentsia," pp. 12–13.
36. Marc Renaud, "Quebec's New Middle Class in Search of Social Hegemony: Causes and Political Consequences," in Michael D. Behiels (ed.), *Quebec since 1945: Selected Readings* (Toronto: Copp Clark Pitman Limited, 1987), pp. 72–73.
37. Daniel Shapiro and Morton Stelcner, "Language and Earnings in Quebec: Trends over Twenty Years, 1970–1990," *Canadian Public Policy*, Vol. 23, No. 2 (June 1997): p. 117. "This policy makes obligatory the use of French as a working language and organizations with 50 or more employees are granted 'Francisation' certificates indicating that they have complied with the law."
38. According to a private communication with William Johnson of the *Globe and Mail*, "Pauline Marois proposed early in 2008 that people who are not competent in French should be ineligible to vote or run for public office. She also proposes that Bill 101 be rewritten so as to impose the obligation of francisation on all commercial enterprises, including the 175,000 with 1 to 50 employees. At present, only 5,640 businesses with 50 or more employees are subject to that constraint."
39. Arbour, *Quebec Inc. and the Temptation of State Capitalism*, p. 174.
40. Chris Kostov, "Canada-Quebec Immigration Agreements (1971-1991) and their Impact on Federalism," *American Review of Canadian Studies*, Vol. 38, Iss. 1 (Spring 2008): 91-103.
41. "Quebec after more francophones," *Montreal Gazette* (September 26, 1999), A4.
42. William Johnson, "A New Harmony?" *Globe and Mail* (May 23, 2008), A19.
43. Just to be clear: the suspicion of personal bilingualism is suspicion of the bilingualism *of others*, not of their own. Many nationalist leaders speak impeccable English—there was much comment at the time about the fact that the first PQ cabinet under René Lévesque was more bilingual than the Liberal cabinet of Robert Bourassa that it replaced. Some will object that I am overstating the opposition to bilingualism and that the objection is to institutional, not personal, bilingualism, except for a minority of extremists. But this objection misses two vital points. First, strong nationalist positions are the ones that pretty consistently win in Quebec politics; Liberal federalists often end up adopting nationalist positions far stronger than they would choose themselves in order to placate millenarian nationalists. Access to English-language schools and the language of signs are two good examples. Second, who wills the end wills the means, and the desirable end of personal bilingualism can happen for most people only with the institutional support of the schools. If it is true that only a minority of extremists sees personal bilingualism as a problem, why does the teaching of English in French-language schools remain such a fraught

topic, especially given clear demands by many French-speaking parents for improved English instruction? PQ leader Pauline Marois has recently found herself embroiled in just such a controversy where she has been vigorously attacked by nationalists for supporting greater access to English-language instruction in French-language schools (the bilingual nationalist intellectual Victor Lévy-Beaulieu, for instance, accused her of "treason"), forcing her to pen newspaper articles with titles like "No to a bilingual Quebec" (*La Tribune*, February 13, 2008, p. 15). Nationalist leaders of all political allegiances who ensure personal bilingualism for themselves and their children but deny it to the population at large through inadequate English-language instruction are, to put it as generously as possible, intellectually incoherent.

44. Donald Benham, "French issue won't go away for Pawley," *Financial Post* (March 29, 1986), 10.

45. Debbie Horrocks, "Ottawa sides with Quebec to limit English education rights; Harper government supports Bill 104 restrictions before the Supreme Court," *Montreal Gazette* (December 11, 2008), A23.

46. Claude Morin, *Quebec versus Ottawa: The Struggle for Self-Government, 1960–1972* (Toronto: University of Toronto Press, 1976), p. 13.

47. Morin, p. 50: "Confronting this position [Quebec's interest in extending its income support programs in 1971], Ottawa stated its determination to keep the upper hand in income security programs, adducing the large sums it allocated to them as proof of its indispensable role in redistributing the wealth of the country among the citizens, and as confirmation of its law-making prerogative. In addition, Ottawa skilfully stressed the reforms projected in its programs as implicit evidence of its innovative spirit and especially to highlight its deep desire to make policies in line with the objectives of the Quebec government. The proof: Ottawa's inspiration came largely from Quebec studies."

48. See William Johnson, Jeffrey Simpson, and Richard Cleroux, "Quebec angry but still undecided about federal sales tax reduction," *Globe and Mail* (April 12, 1978), A1.

49. "Bulldozer Federalism," *Globe and Mail* (May 2, 1978), A6.

50. Jeffrey Simpson, "Ottawa defies PQ with scheme for tax credits," *Globe and Mail* (May 16, 1978), A1.

51. Wendie Kerr, "Parizeau suggests a cooling of rhetoric," *Globe and Mail* (September 29, 1978), B1.

52. If this sounds rather similar to the anti-American rationale that fuels much self-destructive Canadian nationalist economic policy, it should. There is another book to be written about how Canadian economic nationalists in this period drew inspiration from Quebec's example, basing their appeal on the moral superiority of Canadian society and the importance of sovereignty over prosperity.

53. The federal government has been quick to point out at referendum time just how large the net transfer into Quebec is that federalism makes possible. Keith Banting, in his 1987 book, *The Welfare State and Canadian Federalism*, cites the example of federal minister Monique Bégin campaigning in the 1980 referendum: "In the case of income security programs, the big difference between special status and sovereignty would be financial, as the inter-regional transfers would stop, a point that was used to good political effect by federal spokesmen, especially Monique Bégin, minister of National Health and Welfare, during the debate leading up to the Quebec referendum. She argued strenuously that Quebec would lose some $680 million in implicit transfers, net of taxes, and that a sovereign Quebec would have to cut benefits, raise taxes, or increase its deficit. Ignoring the uncertainties surrounding the possible response, Bégin simply plunged on to imply that the result would be the elimination of benefits, especially means-tested benefits, such as the Guaran-

teed Income Supplement." See Banting, *The Welfare State and Canadian Federalism* (Kingston: McGill-Queen's University Press, 1987), p. 167.

Chapter 4
Work and the Meaning of the Content of Our Character

1. The package deal extends to "unpaid work" as well. Volunteerism has an important place in a discussion of work and its benefits; it is certainly not my intention to suggest that volunteer work is without value or that it does not represent a powerful way in which people may legitimately participate in community life. Remember, however, that volunteer work is, in an important sense, a privilege that must be earned. Such unpaid work only becomes possible when we, whether as individuals or as members of a family group, earn (or have earned) enough to pay for our material needs. Time left over from that indispensable activity is available for volunteering, among other things. For this reason, a discussion of the role of volunteerism can only be a derivative or subsidiary discussion to that about paid work.

2. Pontifical Council for Justice and Peace, *Compendium of the Social Doctrine of the Church* (Washington, D.C.: USCCB Publishing, March 2005), pp. 115–16.

3. Pontifical Council for Justice and Peace, *Compendium of the Social Doctrine of the Church*, p. 118.

4. Hannah Arendt, *The Human Condition* (Chicago: University of Chicago Press, 1958), p. 9.

5. See anonymous review of Murray, "Community without Politics," *Harvard Law Review*, Vol. 102, No. 4 (February 1989): 913–19.

6. Charles Murray, *Losing Ground: American Social Policy, 1950–1980* (New York: Basic Books, Inc. Publishers, 1984), p. 122.

7. Murray, *Losing Ground*, p. 127.

8. Arthur C. Brooks, "I Love My Work," *The American Magazine*, Vol. 1, Iss. 6 (September/October 2007), p. 23.

9. Brooks, "I Love My Work," p. 23.

10. See http://www.ipsos-na.com/news/pressrelease.cfm?id=3896.

11. This data was derived from a poll of 1,200 Canadians by the Royal Bank of Canada, reported by the CBC on January 30, 2008. See http://www.cbc.ca/news/yourview/2008/01/82of canadianswouldratherw.html.

12. For some recent examples, see Rafael Di Tella and Robert MacCulloch, "Some Uses of Happiness Data in Economics," *Journal of Economic Perspectives*, Vol. 20, No. 1 (Winter 2006): 25–46; and Roderick Hill, "Happiness in Canada Since World War II," *Social Indicators Research*, Vol. 65 (2004): 109–23.

13. See Richard Easterlin, "Will Raising the Incomes of All Increase the Happiness of All?" *Journal of Economic Behavior and Organization*, Vol. 27, No. 1 (June 1995): 35–48; and Easterlin, "Income and Happiness: Towards a Unified Theory," *Economic Journal*, 111: 473 (July 2001): 465–84.

14. As economist John Helliwell remarks, "For employees, neighbours and citizens to be engaged in doing things together, for the benefit of each other, is itself a potent source of happiness." Helliwell, "What makes people happy?" *Vancouver Sun* (October 30, 2007), B3.

15. See, for example, "The Price of Being Well," *The Economist*, Vol. 388, Iss. 8595 (August 30, 2008): p. 60: "Job insecurity, and the resulting stress, have a proven link with mental health."

16. See T.A. Blakey, S.C.D. Collings, and J. Atkinson, "Unemployment and Suicide: Evidence for a Causal Association?," *Journal of Epidemiology and Community Health*, Vol. 57 (2003): 598.

17. In one Australian study, the researchers found "welfare recipients often feel worthless, hopeless, and dissatisfied with life." See Peter Butterworth, A. Kate Fairweather, Kaarin J. Anstey, and Timothy D. Windsor, "Hopelessness, Demoralization and Suicidal Behaviour:

The Backdrop to Welfare Reform in Australia," *Australian and New Zealand Journal of Psychiatry*, Vol. 40, Iss. 8 (August 2006): 653.

18. David Dooley, Ralph Catalano, and Georjeanna Wilson, "Depression and Unemployment: Panel Findings from the Epidemiologic Catchment Area Study," *American Journal of Community Psychology*, Vol. 22, No. 6 (1994): 752.

19. Suzanne King, "Unemployment and Mental Health in French Canada," *Journal of Counselling and Development*, Vol. 67, No. 6 (February 1989): 358.

20. See Robert Jin, "The Impact of Unemployment on Health: A Review of the Evidence," *Canadian Medical Association Journal*, Vol. 153, No. 5 (September 1995): 529.

21. According to the 2002 General Social Survey (GSS) from the National Opinion Research Center at the University of Chicago, among adults who worked ten hours a week or more in 2002, 89 per cent said they were very satisfied or somewhat satisfied with their jobs. Only 11 per cent said they were not too satisfied or not at all satisfied. Cited in Brooks, "I Love My Work," p. 23. As for Canada, an international survey of over 60,000 workers in fifteen countries showed Canadian workers among the most satisfied with their jobs in the world. The survey, carried out by international recruiting firm Towers Perrin-ISR, said, "Canada was among the top-three-rated countries as far as workers' accounts of their companies' employee engagement, career development, communication, and stress, balance and workload." See Derek Abama, "Canadian workers happy with jobs, says research group," *Telegraph-Journal* (Saint John, NB) (September 8, 2007), p. E1.

22. From an interview Buffett gave to *Fortune* magazine: http://money.cnn.com/2006/06/25/magazines/fortune/charity2.fortune/index.htm.

23. Isabel Sawhill, a senior fellow at the Brookings Institution, in testimony before a congressional subcommittee, examining the roots of poverty in the United States. See Sawhill, "Solutions to Poverty," Testimony before the Ways and Means Committee, Income Security and Family Support Subcommittee, U.S. House of Representatives, (April 26, 2007).

24. Assar Lindbeck, "Hazardous Welfare-State Dynamics," *American Economic Review*, Vol. 85, No. 2 (May 1995): 11.

25. See Sawhill, "Solutions to Poverty."

26. John Richards, "Reducing Poverty: What Has Worked, and What Should Come Next," *C.D. Howe Institute Commentary* No. 255 (Toronto: C.D. Howe Institute, October 2007), p. 2.

27. Welfare reform in the United States and Canada in the 1990s produced, by all measures, astonishing results. By encouraging work and discouraging *dependency*, welfare dependants were encouraged to leave the welfare rolls and re-enter the labour force. The United States experienced a sharp decline in the number of welfare recipients from a high of 14.2 million in 1994, representing 5.5 per cent of the population, to 5.8 million in 2000, representing 2.1 per cent of the population. Of this group, one study noted that between 61 and 87 per cent were able to find employment. Meanwhile, in Canada, the number of welfare recipients fell from a high of 3.1 million in 1994, representing 10.7 per cent of the population to 2.1 million in 2000, representing 6.8 per cent of the population. Most Canadian research shows that, on average, 65 to 75 per cent of these former recipients successfully found work. For more information on welfare reform in the two countries, see Judith Havemann, "Most find jobs after leaving welfare," *Washington Post* (May 27, 1999), p. A1; Pamela Loprest, *Families Who Left Welfare: Who Are They and How Are They Doing?* (Washington, Urban Institute, 1999); Mark Heinzel, "Economists watch Canada welfare reform," *Wall Street Journal* (July 31, 2000), p. A2; Fred McMahon, "Welfare reform keeps the economy working," *National Post* (September 4, 1999), p. D5; and David Elton et al., *Where Are They Now? Assessing the Impact of Welfare Reform on Former Recipients, 1993–1996* (Calgary: Canada West Foundation, 1997).

Chapter 5
Perverting the Course of (Social) Justice: Pseudo-work,
Corporate Welfare, and Trade Unionism

1. Brian Lee Crowley and Bobby O'Keefe, "The Flypaper Effect: Does Equalization Really Contribute to Better Public Services, or Does It Just 'Stick to' Politicians and Civil Servants?" *AIMS Commentary*, No. 2 (June 2006): 1–11.

2. According to two sources—Joseph B. Rose, Gary N. Chaison, and Enrique de la Garza, "A Comparative Analysis of Public Sector Restructuring in the US, Canada, Mexico and the Caribbean," *Journal of Labor Research*, Vol. 21, No. 4 (Fall 2000): 601–25; and P.B. Beaumont, "Public Sector Industrial Relations in Europe," in Dale Berman, Morley Gunderson, and Douglas Hyatt (eds.), *Public Sector Employment in a Time of Transition* (Madison, Wisc.: Industrial Relations Research Centre, 1996), pp. 283–307—employment figures reveal that about 27 per cent of the Canadian workforce was employed in government and the broader public sector (e.g., health and education). As a share of total employment, public-sector employment in Canada is about 30 per cent higher than the U.S. and the OECD average.

3. W. Craig Riddell, "Unionization in Canada and the United States: A Tale of Two Countries," in David Card and Richard B. Freeman (eds.) *Small Differences That Matter: Labour Markets and Income Maintenance in Canada and the United States* (Chicago: University of Chicago Press, 1993), p. 123.

4. See Jason Clemens, Niels Veldhuis, and Amela Karabegovic, *Explaining Canada's High Unionization Rates* (Vancouver: Fraser Institute, August 2005). According to their report, the comparable unionization rate in the United States is only 40.8 per cent.

5. Andrew Coyne, "Social Spending, Taxes, and the Debt: Trudeau's Just Society," in Andrew Cohen and J.L. Granatstein (eds.), *Trudeau's Shadow: The Life and Legacy of Pierre Elliott Trudeau*, (Toronto: Vintage Canada Edition, 1999), p. 231.

6. University of Toronto professor Morley Gunderson has done extensive research in this field. See, for example, Gunderson, "Two Faces of Union Voice in the Public Sector," *Journal of Labor Research*, Vol. 26, No. 3 (Summer 2005): 393–414; Gunderson, "The Public-Private Sector Compensation Controversy," in Gene Swimmer and Mark Thompson (eds.), *Conflict or Compromise: The Future of Public Sector Industrial Relations* (Montreal: Institute for Research on Public Policy, 1984), pp. 1–44; and Gunderson, "Earnings Differentials Between the Public and Private Sectors," *Canadian Journal of Economics*, Vol. 12, No. 2 (May 1979): 228–42. More recent research by the CFIB pegs the public-sector pay premium at 15 per cent and at 23 per cent when you take account of non-cash fringe benefits. See Derek Picard, "A Comparison of Public-Sector and Private-Sector Wages," *CFIB Research* (October 2003): 1–19.

7. Maxim Boycko, et al., "A Theory of Privatisation," *Economic Journal*, Vol. 106, No. 435 (March 1996): 309.

8. Statistics Canada, *Table 183-0002—Public sector employment, wages and salaries, monthly*, CANSIM (database), Using E-STAT (distributor).

9. Much of the information for this survey of Crown corporations was drawn from W.T. Stanbury, "Government as Leviathan," in Thomas E. Kierans and W.T. Stanbury (eds.), *Papers on Privatization* (Montreal: IRPP, 1985): 243–74.

10. A.R. Vining and R. Botterell, "An Overview of the Origins, Growth, Size, and Functions of Provincial Crown Corporations," in J. R. S. Pritchard (ed.) *Crown Corporations: The Calculus of Instrument Choice*, (Toronto: Butterworths, 1983): 303-368.

11. See Bertrand Marotte, "CN profit jumps 41% in first quarter," *Globe and Mail* (April 25, 2000), p. B10; Oliver Bertin, "CN posts record results in '99," *Globe and Mail* (January 27,

2000), p. B5; Oliver Bertin, "CN chops 3,000 more jobs, railway has now cut half its staff since 1992; union chief condemns its 'greed,'" *Globe and Mail* (October 21, 1998), p. A1; and Harry Bruce, *The Pig That Flew: The Battle to Privatize Canadian National* (Vancouver: Douglas & McIntyre, 1997).

12. Thomas Walkom, *Rae Days: The Rise and Follies of the NDP* (Toronto: Key Porter Books, 1994), pp. 245–58.

13. See Sean Silcoff, "Delivering a new Canada Post; Is Privatization the answer for an antiquated system using decades-old machinery?" *National Post* (September 17, 2007), p. FP1.

14. Former American presidential economic adviser William Niskanen was the first to examine the growth of public bureaucracies from this perspective. See Niskanen, *Bureaucracy and Representative Government* (Chicago: Adline-Atherton, 1979) and Gordon Tullock's review of Niskanen's book in *Public Choice*, Vol. 12, Iss. 1 (Spring 1972): 119–24.

15. See Robert Bish, "Organization and Opportunities: Local Government Services Production in Greater Saint John," *AIMS Urban Futures Series*, Paper #4 (November 2004): 1–40.

16. Lipset makes this argument in several separate studies. See, for instance, Lipset, *The Paradox of American Unionism: Why Americans Like Unions More Than Canadians Do, but Join Much Less* (Ithaca, NY: ILR Press, 2004); and *Continental Divide: The Values and Institutions of the United States and Canada* (New York: Routledge, 1990).

17. W. Craig Riddell, "Unionization in Canada and the United States: A Tale of Two Countries," in David Card and Richard B. Freeman (eds.), *Small Differences That Matter: Labour Markets and Income Maintenance in Canada and the United States* (Chicago: University of Chicago Press, 1993), p. 138.

18. Some analysts argue that even this wage premium does not make it through to the unionized workers individually but is instead captured by the unions themselves in the form of the dues and initiation fees they collect from their members. See, for example, Thomas Palley and Robert LaJeunesse, "Social Attitudes, Labor Law, and Union Organizing: Toward a New Economics of Union Density," *Journal of Economic Behavior & Organization*, Vol. 62 (2007): 252; and John Raisian, "Union Dues and Wage Premiums," *Journal of Labor Research*, Vol. IV, No. 1 (Winter 1983): 6.

19 Donald McFetridge, *The Economics of Privatization* (Toronto: C.D. Howe Institute, 1997), pp. 31–32.

20. David Seymour, "Telecommunications Privatization, Services, and Provincial Well-being: A Comparison of Company Performance at SaskTel and MTS," *FCPP Policy Series*, No. 34 (October 27): pp. 4–5. Sir Roger Douglas, *Short Term Pain for Long Term Gain* (Halifax: AIMS, 1995); and Johan Hjertqvist, *Swedish Health Care in Transition: Markets and Competition Here to Stay* (Halifax: AIMS, 2001).

21. Hence Milton Friedman's careful distinction between public and private monopoly: "If society were so static that the conditions which give rise to a technical monopoly (one resulting from market outcomes) were sure to remain, I would have little confidence in this solution. In a rapidly changing society, however, the conditions making for technical monopoly frequently change and I suspect that both public regulation and public monopoly are less likely to be responsive to such changes in conditions, to be less readily capable of elimination, than private monopoly." See Milton Friedman, *Capitalism and Freedom* (Chicago: University of Chicago Press, 1964), p. 28.

22. University of Toronto economist Morley Gunderson argues, "The lower resistance to unionization on the part of public sector managers reflects the fact that the survival of public sector organizations is not jeopardized by unions flexing their muscles. This is in contrast to private sector firms—and increasingly so under global competition. In the public sector there is no 'residual claimant' who profits by resisting union; there is no great

cost to following the 'path of least resistance.'" See Gunderson, "Two Faces of Union Voice in the Public Sector," *Journal of Labor Research*, Vol. 26, No. 3 (Summer 2005): 398.

23. Crowley and O'Keefe, "The Flypaper Effect," 1–11.

24. In March 2008, the federal public service grew to 403,796, one of its highest levels in over a decade. See Statistics Canada, *Table 183-0002—Public sector employment, wages and salaries, monthly*.

25. The current economic circumstances have done nothing to curb the steady growth in public-sector employment. The recession, as one journalist has pointed out, "is attacking parts of Canada's economy with disproportionate force." In other words, the public sector has been largely inoculated from the economic downturn. In fact, Ottawa has seen an increase in its employment rate as more people are hired to administer employment insurance and other government programs. See James Bagnall, "1,300 Canadians lose jobs in March; but there's good news," *Ottawa Citizen* (April 10, 2009), p. A1; and Lee Greenberg, "Ottawa to buck negative trend, report says; stable public-sector employment shields capital from downturn," *Ottawa Citizen* (April 1, 2009), p. D1.

26. See Lucie Charron, "Canada's Pension Predicament: The Widening Gap between Public and Private Sector Retirement Trends and Pension Plans," *CFIB Research* (January 2007): 1–13.

27. Fred McMahon, *Retreat from Growth: Atlantic Canada and the Negative-Sum Economy* (Halifax: Atlantic Institute for Market Studies, 2000), pp. 101–2.

Chapter 6
Family and the Audacity of Love

1. Contemporary feminist and Marxist writers have characterized marriage as an inherently oppressive institution, akin to a prison or concentration camp. Social activists like Sheila Cronan have argued that "freedom for women cannot be won without the abolition of marriage," while others see marriage and capitalism as part of a "capitalist patriarchy" that invariably suppresses the feminist movement. See Betty Friedan, *The Feminist Mystique* (New York: W.W. Norton & Company, Inc, 1963), p. 337; E. Cudd, *Analyzing Oppression* (New York: Oxford University Press, 2006), p. 128; Sheila Cronan, "Marriage," in Anne Koedt, Ellen Levine, and Anita Rapone (eds.), *Radical Feminism* (New York: Quadrangle Books, 1973), p. 219; and Donna J. Harraway, "Gender for a Marxist Dictionary: The Sexual Politics of a Word," in Richard Parker and Peter Aggleton (eds.), *Culture, Society, and Sexuality* (Philadelphia: Routledge, 1995), p. 88.

2. At a recent colloquium in Mexico City, a Dutch representative of the United Nations Population Fund told participants that high rates of divorce and out-of-wedlock births represent the triumph of "human rights" over "patriarchy." See "World Congress of Families Reacts to UNFPA Leader Who Says Family Breakdown Is a 'Triumph' for 'Human Rights,'" *Mental Health Weekly Digest* (March 9, 2009), p. 298.

3. In many cases, households with only one parent in them may be described as "single-parent" or "lone-parent" households, with the former term more common in North America and the latter in Britain. Technically, however, "lone parent" is more correct than "single parent." Single parents are not married (i.e., "single" refers normally to marital status), but many parents who are alone may also be married—it is just that the spouse doesn't live with them. Others are not married plain and simple. The term "lone parent" puts the accent (correctly in my view) on the fact that they are the sole adult in the household, rather than on their marital status. I also understand that widowed lone parents often do not wish to be referred to as "single parents." For consistency's sake, I will adopt the British terminology, except where the context puts the focus on marital status, rather than on the composition of the household.

4. The editorial noted, citing the well-respected National Longitudinal Study of Children and Youth, "Children growing up in single-parent families are more likely to repeat grades, to possess poorer language skills, and to be less healthy than children living in two-parent families. These children are also less likely to get along well with friends and parents than children living in two-parent families." Problems of hyperactivity, aggression, or conduct disorders and other behaviour problems are also higher in single-parent families. See "No Replacing Traditional Families," *Globe and Mail* (September 13, 2007), p. A18.

5. Centre for Social Justice, *The State of the Nation Report: Fractured Families* (London: Centre for Social Justice, December 2006), p. 24.

6. Cohabitation data from the 1960s and 1970s are hard to come by because the British government did not ask questions about cohabitation in its household surveys until 1979. In the period from 1979 to 1998, the proportion of marriage-age women in cohabiting relationships tripled from 11 per cent to 29 per cent. One British scholar who has pieced together several data sources concludes that Britain's "cohabitation prevalence increased substantially in the 1970s and 1980s." See Michael Murphy, "The Evolution of Cohabitation in Britain, 1960–1995," *Population Studies*, Vol. 54, No. 1 (March 2000): 43–56.

7. Centre for Social Justice, *The State of the Nation Report*, p. 24.

8. Centre for Social Justice, *The State of the Nation Report*, p. 29.

9. Centre for Social Justice, *The State of the Nation Report*, pp. 46 and 49–51.

10. For a comprehensive study of the health effects of different family structures in Britain, see Anne M. McMunn, James Y. Nazroo, Michael G. Marmot, Richard Boreham, and Robert Goodman, "Children's Emotional and Behavioural Well-Being and the Family Environment: Findings from the Health Survey for England," *Social Sciences and Medicine*, Vol. 53, No. 4 (August 2001): 423–40.

11. Jill Kirby, *Broken Hearts: Family Decline and the Consequences for Society* (London: Centre for Policy Studies, 2002), pp. 18–20.

12. Centre for Social Justice, *The State of the Nation Report*, p. 71.

13. Centre for Social Justice, *The State of the Nation Report*, p. 55.

14. Jon Swaine, "Three million families living in jobless households," *Daily Telegraph* (August 28, 2008), p. 4.

15. Nasima Begum, "Characteristics of Short-Term and Long-Term Unemployment," *Labour Market Trends* (April 2004), p. 143. See also Iain Duncan Smith, *Breakthrough Britain: Vol. 2, Economic Dependency and Worklessness* (London: Centre for Social Justice, July 2007), p. 16.

16. Centre for Social Justice, *The State of the Nation Report*, pp. 56–57.

17. Smith, *Breakthrough Britain*, p. 3.

18. See Hymowitz, "Marriage and Caste in America: Separate and Unequal Families in a Post-Marital Age," *City Journal* (Winter 2006). In this article, Hymowitz argues that "the marriage gap" is becoming the chief source of inequality in the twenty-first century. She concludes, "Marriage may not be a panacea. But it is a *sine qua non*." She has developed this argument further in a book; see Hymowitz, *Marriage and Caste in America: Separate and Unequal Families in a Post-Martial Age* (Chicago, Ivan R. Dee, 2007).

19. David Popenoe and Barbara Dafoe Whitehead, *The State of Our Unions: The Social Health of Marriage in America, 2007* (Rutgers State University of New Jersey: The National Marriage Project, 2007), p. 19.

20. Patrick F. Fagan and Robert Rector, "The Effects of Divorce on America," *Heritage Backgrounder*, No. 1373, (June 5, 2000), pp. 3–4.

21. David Popenoe, *Cohabitation, Marriage and Child Wellbeing: A Cross-National Perspective* (Rutgers State University of New Jersey: The National Marriage Project, June 2008), pp. 16–17.

22. See Deborah Dawson, "Family Structure and Children's Health and Well-Being: Data from the 1988 National Health Interview Survey on Child Health," *Journal of Marriage and the Family*, Vol. 53, No. 3 (August 1991): 573–84.

23. Robert G. Wood, Brian Goseling, and Sarah Avellar, *The Effects of Marriage on Health: A Synthesis of Recent Research Evidence* (Washington, D.C.: Department of Health and Human Services, June 19, 2007), pp. 27–42.

24. Patrick Fagan, "The Real Root Causes of Violent Crime: The Breakdown of Marriage, Family and Community," *Heritage Backgrounder*, No. 1026 (March 17, 1995): 1.

25. James Q. Wilson, *The Marriage Problem: How Our Culture Has Weakened Families* (New York: HarperCollins, 2002), p. 169.

26. Patrick F. Fagan and Robert Rector, "The Effects of Divorce on America," *Heritage Backgrounder*, No. 1373 (June 5, 2000): 2–4.

27. These data are from http://family.jrank.org/pages/1578/Single-Parent-Families-Economics-Single-Parent-Family-Life.html.

28. Marjorie Starrels et al., "The Feminization of Poverty in the United States: Gender, Race, Ethnicity, and Family Factors," *Journal of Family Issues*, Vol. 15, No. 4 (December 1994): 590–607.

29. Mary Parke, "Are Married Parents Really Better for Children? What Research Says about the Effects of Family Structure on Child Well-Being," *Center for Law and Social Policy Brief* (May 2003), p. 3.

30. Even left-leaning public policy institutes are grappling with the consequences of family breakdown. In a 2001 study, the Pembina Institute concluded, "When a couple divorces, the ensuing family breakdown has an enormous impact on the social cohesion of the extended family, the community and the nation. The costs, both financial and otherwise (guilt, stress, anxiety), associated with family breakdown are substantial." See Amy Taylor and Mark Anielski, *The Alberta GPI Accounts: Family Breakdown Report #13* (Drayton Valley, AB: Pembina Institute, 2001), p. 4.

31. See, for instance, Jack Mintz, "Income Splitting Would Help Families," *National Post* (May 27, 2008), p. A12.

32. David Blankenhorn, a liberal, non-religious Democrat, has written extensively about marriage as a vital social institution. See Blankenhorn, *The Future of Marriage* (New York: Encounter Books, 2007).

33. Roger Scruton, *A Dictionary of Political Thought*, 3rd edition (London: Macmillan Publishing, 2007).

34. One comprehensive study concluded, "A substantial body of evidence suggests that family structure matters and that children do better, on average, when they are raised by the household of their own married mother and father." See Maggie Gallagher and Joshua Baker, "Do Moms and Dads Matter? Evidence from the Social Sciences on Family Structure and the Best Interests of the Child," *Margins*, Vol. 4 (2004): 180.

35. See David Murray, "Marriage and Economic Liberty," *Religion and Liberty*, Vol. 5, No. 6 (November/December 1995): 5–7.

36. It is worth underlining that Murray does not claim that all mates and parents manifest these qualities—only the good ones.

37. For more on this distinction and its consequences, see "The Absence of Fathers," *Globe and Mail* (July 31, 2007), p. A12.

38. According to two American researchers, "In short, married men are substantially more likely than their single counterparts to receive high performance ratings: high performance ratings, in turn, appear to increase promotion probabilities so that married men are also more likely to be promoted." See Sanders Korenman and David Neumark, "Does

Marriage Really Make Men More Productive?" *Journal of Human Resources*, Vol. 26, No. 2 (Spring 1991): 302.

39. The other, of course, is contraception, but that is not my concern here, because contraception is a means to avoid unwanted pregnancy, to control fertility. My concern is rather different. First, people are having fewer children than they say they want, which is not a problem of the effect of contraceptives, because contraceptives give control over fertility, not loss of control. Similarly, there seems to be an (unintended) correlation between certain kinds of public policy (e.g., social security to guarantee old age income) and fertility. We may thus be unintentionally discouraging people from having children that they wish to have. I am not the least bit interested in forcing people to have children they do not want. I am deeply interested, however, in removing the obstacles that may have been created to prevent people having children they *do* want.

40. *Falknier v. Ontario* (2002). For more information on the ruling and its impact on welfare policy, see Chris Schafer, "Welfare Reforms Jeopardized?" *Fraser Forum* (June 2002): 3.

41. See Murray, "Marriage and Economic Liberty," p. 7.

42. The vital importance of childhood experiences in shaping adult personality is widely known, and it has been estimated that about one-half of a child's full cognitive development is reached by the age of three or four. See Gabor Maté and Gordon Neufeld, *Hold On to Your Kids: Why Parents Need to Matter More Than Peers* (Toronto: Vintage Canada, 2005); John F. Conway, *The Canadian Family in Crisis*, 4th edition, (Toronto: James Lorimer & Company, 2001), p. 48; and Sylvia Brody and Sidney Axelrad, *Mothers, Fathers and Children: Explorations in the Formation of Character in the First Seven Years* (New York: International University Press, 1978).

43. While he was still leader of the Liberal Party of Canada, Stéphane Dion gave a good example of this view. When informed that Tory leader Stephen Harper had made comments that might have been interpreted as casting doubts on Dion's status as a "family man," Dion responded first with a comment to the effect that family is a private matter and therefore no one else's business: "Well, we'll speak about me. I'm a Liberal ... and we believe in this beautiful word we don't have in French, which is privacy, which is more than private life. It's the distinction between public and private life," he said, before finally allowing, "But I'm a family man. I love my mother, I love my wife. I love my daughter and my brothers, even my brothers." Siri Agrell, "Harper not the only family man in this campaign," *Globe and Mail* (September 7, 2008), p. A4.

44. See Angela L. Duckworth and Martin E.P. Seligman, "Self-Discipline Outdoes IQ in Predicting Academic Performances of Adolescents," *Psychological Science*, Vol. 16, Iss. 12 (December 2005): 939–44.

45. Wade Horn, a former U.S. assistant secretary for children and families explains, "Much of what is described as 'good character' or 'virtue' reflects the ability to delay or inhibit impulse gratification. When children tell the truth, even though they know that it will result in negative consequences, they are inhibiting the impulse to lie to avoid unpleasantness. When they show charity to others, they are inhibiting the impulse to behave selfishly. A civil society is dependent upon virtuous citizens who have developed this capacity to delay or inhibit impulse gratification—that is, persons who can control their behavior voluntarily." And as Horn shows, it is parents who play the formative role in instilling these values in children. See Wade F. Horn, "There Is No Substitute for Parents," *USA Today (Magazine)*, Vol. 127, Iss. 2642 (November 1, 1998): p. 34.

46. As Horn points out, there is no substitute for "traditional families [married couples] in socializing children." See Horn, "There Is No Substitute for Parents," p. 34. For Canadian research, see Lisa Strohschein, Noralou Roos, and Marni Brownell, "Family Structure

Histories and High School Completion: Evidence from a Population-based Registry," *Canadian Journal of Sociology*, Vol. 34, No. 1 (2009): 83–103; Don Kerr, "Family Transformations and the Well-being of Children: Recent Evidence from Canadian Longitudinal Data," *Journal of Comparative Family Studies*, Vol. 35, Iss. 1 (Winter 2004): 73–90; and Don Kerr and Roderic Beaujot, "Family Relations, Low Income, and Child Outcomes: A Comparison of Canadian Children in Intact-, Step-, and Lone-parent Families," *International Journal of Comparative Sociology*, Vol. 43 (April 2002): 134–52.

47. Lorne Gunter, "Court says no to sensible parenting; blatant state interference in father-daughter dispute sets dangerous precedent," *Edmonton Journal*, (June 22, 2008), p. A14.

48. See Carle C. Zimmerman, *Family and Civilization* (Wilmington: ISI Books, 2008).

49. Casey B. Mulligan, *Work Ethic and Family Background* (Washington, D.C.: Employment Policy Institute, April 1997): 1–32.

50. Mulligan, *Work Ethic and Family Background*, p. 27.

51. This area of empirical analysis was first advanced famously by University of Chicago economist Gary Becker. See Becker, "Family Economics and Macro Behaviour," *American Economic Review*, Vol. 78, No. 1 (March 1988): 1–13. It has become part of mainstream economic thought and is researched by contemporary family economists such as Doug Allen, Robert Barro, and others. See Allen, "An Inquiry in the State's Role in Marriage," *Journal of Economic Behavior and Organization*, Vol. 13 (1990): 171–91; and Becker and Barro, "A Reformulation of the Economic Theory of Fertility," *Quarterly Journal of Economics*, Vol. 102, No. 4 (February 1988): 1–25.

52. See, for instance, Jere R. Behrman, Robert Pollack, and Paul Taubman, *From Parent to Child: Intrahousehold Allocations and Intergenerational Relations in the United States* (Chicago: University of Chicago Press, 1995).

53. Douglas A. Allen, "Welfare and the Family: The Canadian Experience," *Journal of Labour Economics*, Vol. 11, No. 1 (January 1993): 202.

54. Allen, "Welfare and the Family: The Canadian Experience," p. 217.

55. Two researchers have concluded, "More generous social assistance benefits reduce the rate of employment probability of less-educated men without dependent children. The employment rate for this group of men drops by 3 to 5 percentage points in response to the higher benefits." See Thomas Lemieux and Kevin Milligan, "Incentive Effects of Social Assistance: A Regression Discontinuity Approach," *Journal of Econometrics*, Vol. 142 (2008): 807–28.

56. One pair of researchers points out, "The anti-marriage effects of welfare are simple and profound." See Robert E. Rector and Patrick F. Fagan, "How Welfare Harms Kids," *Heritage Foundation Backgrounder*, No. 1084 (June 5, 1996). See also Wade F. Horn, "Wedding Bells Blues: Marriage and Welfare Reform," *Brookings Institution Note* (Summer 2001).

57. As Rector and Fagan put it, "The mother has a contract with the government: She will continue to receive her 'paycheck' as long as she does not marry an employed man." See Rector and Fagan, "How Welfare Harms Kids."

58. Assar Lindbeck and Sten Nyberg, "Raising Children to Work Hard: Altruism, Work Norms, and Social Insurance," *Quarterly Journal of Economics*, Vol. 121 (November 2006): 1473.

59. See Ronald Inglehart, Miguel Basañez, and Alejandro Moreno, *Human Values and Beliefs: A Cross-Cultural Source Book* (Ann Arbor: University of Michigan Press, 1998).

60. In one study, a well-known psychologist and a physician and best-selling author chronicle the long-term consequences of peers replacing parents in the lives of children. Children, the two authors write, "seem less likely to take their cues from adults, less inclined to please those in charge, less afraid of getting into trouble." Only parents, they argue, ultimately have the capacity—and vested interest—to change their child's behaviour. See Maté and Neufeld, *Hold On to Your Kids*.

61. None of this argument about the centrality of family to the rearing of children should be taken as challenging the extension of the right to marry to homosexual couples. Precisely because family plays such a central role in human life, and precisely because loving human relationships are difficult to sustain but confer social as well as personal rewards and benefits, I can see little reason to deny to homosexuals the benefit of social institutions designed to shore up those relationships.

62. John Richards and Douglas Allen (eds.), *It Takes Two: The Family in Law and Finance* (Toronto: C.D. Howe Institute, 1999).

63. Richards and Allen, "Introduction," in Richards and Allen (eds.), *It Takes Two*, p. viii.

64. "The introduction of 'no-fault' divorce inadvertently went a long way toward promoting the unsustainable doctrine that marriage should be no more than a private contract between two equal partners, and has contributed to negative consequences that few anticipated. Perhaps the most dramatic effect has been the great increase in the number of children growing up poor and with only one parent." See Richards and Allen, "Introduction," in Richards and Allen (eds.), *It Takes Two*, p. ix.

65. According to one Canadian study, a significant majority of married people ranked "maintaining a good, stable marriage" (79 per cent) and "being a good parent" (68 per cent) as either the most or second-most important priorities in their lives. See Focus on the Family Canada, *Canadian Attitudes on the Family*, A National Survey Conducted by the Strategic Counsel (Ottawa: Focus on the Family Canada, 2002), p. 9.

66. A 1997 study suggests Canadian families, like families in several other countries, would like to have more children. A Gallup poll of sixteen countries on four continents found that people would be happy to have more children if their societies validated bigger families. In Iceland, Guatemala, and Taiwan, the average ideal family size was as high as three, while the mean number in Canada, France, Mexico, Singapore, and the United States ranged from 2.4 to 2.6. One in three Canadians said the ideal family size was three or more children. Significantly, there were no appreciable differences between men and women. Cited in Ian Dowbiggin, "Where Have All the Babies Gone? The 'Birth Dearth' and What to Do about It," A Presentation at the IMFC Family Policy Conference (Ottawa: Institute for Marriage and Family Values Canada, September 26, 2006), p. 4.

67. Richards and Allen, "Introduction," in Richards and Allen (eds.), *It Takes Two*, p. xi.

68. See, for example, Reginald Bibby, The Future Families Project: A Survey of Canadian Hopes and Dreams, (Ottawa: Vanier Institute of the Family, 2004); CBS News, Love and Marriage: A CBS News Poll, February 2001: http://www.cbsnews.com/stories/2001/02/25/opinion/main274410.shtml.

69. See Jennifer Roback Morse, "Why Not Take Her for a Test Drive?" http://www.jennifer-roback-morse.com/articles/cohabitation_fast_facts.pdf; and Padma Rao Sahib and Xinhua Gu, "To Tie the Knot or Not: Cohabitation, Marriage, and Individuals' Attitudes to Risk," *Demographic Research*, Vol. 6 (May 2002): 355–82.

70. Several studies have documented the pervasive link between cohabitation and child abuse. See, for instance, Robert Whelan, *Broken Homes and Battered Children: A Study of the Relationship between Child Abuse and Family Type* (London: Family Education Trust, 1993); and Robert E. Rector, Patrick F. Fagan, and Kirk A. Robinson, "Marriage: Still the Safest Place for Women and Children," *Heritage Foundation Backgrounder*, no. 1732 (March 9, 2004).

71. "The emphasis on marriage as a less than permanent phenomenon—one from which each spouse must emerge independent and self-sufficient if it ends in divorce—encourages both partners to invest in themselves and their careers rather than in the other spouse or the marriage itself. Marriage, therefore, comes to look more like cohabitation. A rational wife, for example, frequently makes sure she stays working full time because she may well end up

divorced. She therefore does not have as much time to devote to herself or to joint enterprises such as housework and children." Margaret F. Brinig, "The Effects of Divorce on Wives," in Richards and Allen (eds.), *It Takes Two*, p. 47.

72. A study by the Vanier Institute concludes, "Many people have come to believe that marriage is merely a matter of lifestyle choice and has few overall consequences or advantages over cohabitation. The two are equivalent. *The research literature does not support this view at this point. Rather, studies indicate that marriage, particularly a good and equitable one, carries many benefits for the spouses. It is above all highly beneficial to children, whether it is equitable or not between the parents* [italics added for emphasis]." See Anne-Marie Ambert, *Cohabitation and Marriage: How Are They Related?* (Ottawa: Vanier Institute, September 2005), p. 22.

73. This phenomenon is well documented in Pamela Paul's acclaimed book, *The Starter Marriage and the Future of Matrimony*. She writes, "Perhaps we now see marriage as the romance equivalent of the first job, that horrible, 'character-building' experience that left you feeling confused and undervalued yet in retrospect taught crucial lessons for your 'real' career ahead." See Paul, *The Starter Marriage and the Future of Matrimony* (New York: Random House, 2003), p. xx.

74. Married men are particularly happy. According to one comprehensive survey of young men, aged twenty-five to thirty-four, married men painted a positive picture of marriage—94 per cent said they were happier married than single, and 73 per cent said their sex life was better. See Popenoe and Whitehead, *The State of Our Unions*.

75. "Married men not only earn more per hour but also work more hours and weeks than unmarried men with similar job market characteristics. Marriage generally encourages savings and asset accumulation and reduces poverty." Robert I. Lerman, *Marriage and the Economic Well-Being of Families with Children: A Review of the Literature* (Washington, D.C.: Urban Institute, July 2002), p. 29.

76. George A. Akerlof, "Men without Children," *Economic Journal*, Vol. 108, No. 447 (March 1998): 294–96.

77. Morley Gunderson, U of T economist, private communication with the author.

78. Focus on the Family Canada, *Canadian Attitudes on the Family*, p. 9.

79. Focus on the Family Canada, *Canadian Attitudes on the Family*, p. 9.

80. Mintz, "Income Splitting Would Help Families," p. A12.

81. See Focus on the Family Canada, *Canadian Attitudes on the Family*, p. 12; and James M. White, "Work-Family Stage and Satisfaction with Work-Family Balance," *Journal of Comparative Family Studies*, Vol. 30, No. 2 (Spring 1999): 163–76. White shows that "mothers who work over twenty hours a week are less satisfied with the balance between work and family than fathers and mothers who work less than twenty hours or are at home full time."

82. Focus on the Family Canada, *Canadian Attitudes on the Family*, pp. 15–17.

83. Brinig, "The Effects of Divorce on Wives," in Richards and Allen (eds.), *It Takes Two*, p. 46.

84. See, for example, Wilson, *The Marriage Problem*, pp. 17–18: "Healthier men with a wife and children to support can and do work harder."

85. Focus on the Family Canada, *Canadian Attitudes on the Family*, p. 18: "Among the total sample, the average (mean) *ideal* number of children reported *per respondent* is 2.6." Current fertility rates are, of course, well below this level.

86. Wilson, *The Marriage Problem*, pp. 158–59.

87. Gary Becker, "Human Capital, Effort and the Sexual Division of Labor," *Journal of Labor Economics*, Vol. 3, No. 1 (January 1985): S34.

88. A Pew Research survey found that over 60 per cent of working mothers would prefer to work part-time. See Paul Taylor, Cary Funk, and April Clark, *From 1997 to 2007: Fewer*

Mothers Prefer Full-Time Work (Washington: Pew Research Center, 2007), p. 1. Similarly, a 2002 study of professional women found that more than a fourth of those who had children indicated they wanted more kids than they were ultimately able to have because of their careers. See Sylvia Ann Hewlett, *Creating a Life: Professional Woman and the Quest for Children* (New York: Talk Miramax Books, 2002), p. 2.

89. Two researchers conclude this "raises questions about whether modern social constructs have made women worse off, or alternatively about the interpretability of subjective well-being data.... Our findings raise provocative questions about the contribution of the women's movement to women's welfare." See Betty Stevenson and Justin Wolfers, *The Paradox of Declining Female Happiness* (Philadelphia: Wharton School, University of Pennsylvania, September 2007).

90. Ross Finnie, Ian Irvine, and Roger Sceviour, *Welfare Dynamics in Canada: The Role of Individual Attributes and Economic-Policy Variables*, Analytical Studies Research Paper Series, no. 231. Catalogue no. 11F0019-M1E (Ottawa: Statistics Canada, October 2004), p. 15.

91. In fact, in 2004, two Canadian researchers found that nearly half of Canadian single mothers received welfare payments in the eight years between 1992 and 2000. Their social assistance participation rate was much higher than single childless adults or married couples with children, even accounting for various socio-economic factors. See Roger Sceviour and Ross Finnie, "Social Assistance Use: Trends in Incidence, Entry and Exit Rates," *Canadian Economic Observer* (August 2004), p. 7.

92. Martin D. Dooley, "The Evolution of Welfare Participation among Canadian Lone Mothers, 1973–1991," *Canadian Journal of Economics*, Vol. 32, No. 3 (May 1999): 589–612. Another study found that female lone parents are the most likely households to be chronically in poverty, with only one-third above the poverty line. Marriage, the researchers found, was the most effective way to lift single women out of poverty. See Ross Finnie and Arthur Sweetman, "Poverty Dynamics: Empirical Evidence for Canada," *Canadian Journal of Economics*, Vol. 36, No. 2 (2003): 291–325.

93. Allen, "Welfare and the Family: The Canadian Experience," pp. 220–21.

94. Zheng Wu, "Recent Trends in Marriage Patterns in Canada," *Policy Options*, Vol. 19, No. 7 (Montreal: IRPP, September 1998): 3–6. He points out, "[Eighty-four] percent of men aged 15 and over were in the labour force in 1951. This percentage dropped to 76 percent in 1991 according to Canadian census data. A higher percentage of men, therefore, cannot 'afford' to marry."

95. John D. Mueller, *Family-Friendly Fiscal Policy to Weather 'Demographic Winter'* (Washington, D.C.: Ethics and Public Policy Center, May 2007).

96. Becker first made this case in his groundbreaking book, *A Treatise on the Family*. See Becker, *A Treatise on the Family* (Cambridge: Harvard University Press, 1981). See also Becker, "On the Economics of the Family: Reply to a Skeptic," *American Economic Review*, Vol. 79, No. 3 (June 1989): 514–18.

97. Phillip Longman, "The Return of Patriarchy," *Foreign Policy*, Iss. 153 (March/April 2006): 65.

Chapter 7
Nationalism and Welfarism in Quebec and the Consequences for Canada

1. In fact, according to William Johnson's submission to Bernard Lord during his cross-country consultations on official languages policy, it appears that an English-speaker is fifteen times more likely to move out of Quebec than a French-speaker. Johnson's data are based on work done by well-known demographer Réjean Lachapelle. Lord's follow-up report was released in February 2008. See Lord, *Government of Canada Consultations on Linguistic Duality and Official Languages* (Ottawa: Canada Heritage, February 2008).

2. Former Quebec premier Lucien Bouchard and a number of other luminaries from Quebec published a manifesto *Pour un Québec lucide* in 2005. In it they decried some of the same trends I am describing here and invoked the coming demographic changes as a call to action to change the course of Quebec's society and politics. They were, of course, virulently attacked by the nationalist and trade union movements for heresy. The manifesto is available at http://www.pourunquebeclucide.com/cgiole/cs.waframe.singlepageindex. See also Alain Dubuc's book on wealth creation, *Éloge de la Richesse* (Quebec City: Voix parallèles, 2006).

3. This very term is itself quite telling. It is more than a mere "negotiating table" and has no close equivalent in English. Its name implies not just negotiation among the parties at the table, but the bringing together of their efforts under some central authority to produce an agreed program of action.

4. As others have done before him, Michel Kelly-Gagnon traces the roots of this allegedly social democratic model of economic management back to the corporatism fashionable under. for example, Mussolini's fascist regime in Italy in the 1930s, as well as to those inspired by that model, such as Catholic social theorists in Quebec. "They thought they could control society by having an all-powerful government sit down with interest groups and business and union leaders to decide how to manage economic development. The economic summits so popular in Quebec are a direct descendant of this view." Michel Kelly-Gagnon, "Quebec Inc. must embrace globalization: Incestuous, government-supported model is outdated," *Montreal Gazette* (April 17, 2009), p. A17.

5. See Norma Kozhaya, "Quebec's Relative Poverty," *MEI Economic Note* (May 2006).

6. Much of this data is from Kozhaya's analysis of Quebec's economic position relative to the rest of North America. See citation 6.

7. Gilles Paquet, *What if There Had Been No Quiet Revolution in Quebec ...* (Ottawa: University of Ottawa Press, March 1997), p. 2.

8. Jean-Luc Migué, "Étatisme et déclin du Québec," *La Presse* (March 9, 1999), p. B3. [author's translation]

9. These data are drawn from *Measuring Ontario's Prosperity: Developing and Economic Indicator System*, Institute for Competitiveness & Prosperity Working Paper No. 2, (August 2002).

10. See Marcel Boyer, "Quebec's Disappointing Economic Performance in the Last 25 Years," *MEI Economic Note* (May, 2007).

11. See Chapter 2 in Government of Canada, *The Economy of Quebec and Its Regions: Analysis of Trends* (Ottawa: Department of Industry, January 2003).

12. Because Ontario has been particularly hard hit by the recession, its share of the national economy has temporarily declined to roughly 40.5 per cent, but even that remains well above its share of the national population. See Paul Vieira, "Ontario in decline; can Dalton McGuinty see the light and reverse the decay with his forthcoming budget?" *Financial Post* (March 21, 2009), p. FP1; and Jamie Sturgeon, "Jobs drought hits Ontario and Alberta; construction slump takes toll on former powers," *Financial Post* (March 13, 2009), p. FP6.

13. See Boyer, "Quebec's Disappointing Economic Performance in the Last 25 Years."

14. Based on author's analysis of Statistics Canada, *Table 384-0004—Government sector revenue and expenditure, provincial economic accounts, annual (dollars)*, CANSIM (database), Using E-STAT (distributor).

15. Stephen Brooks, "The State as Financier: A Comparison of the Caisse de dépôt et placement du Québec and Alberta Heritage Savings Trust Fund," *Canadian Public Policy*, Vol. 13, No. 3 (September 1987): 318–29.

16 P.E. Bryden, *Planners and Politicians: Liberal Politics and Social Policy 1957–1968* (Montreal and Kingston: McGill-Queen's University Press, 1997), p. 90.

17. Bryden, *Planners and Politicians*, p. 186.
18. Brooks, "The State as Financier," p. 321.
19. Matthew Fraser, *Quebec Inc.: French-Canadian Entrepreneurs and the New Business Elite* (Toronto: Key Porter Books, 1987), p. 81.
20. Sidbec swiftly absorbed several private firms after it was created in 1960. By 1979, its accumulated losses were $45.7 million due to "heavy losses" on steel production. See John Bradbury, "State Corporations and Resource Based Development in Quebec, Canada: 1960–1980," *Economic Geography*, Vol. 82, No. 1 (January 1982): 45–61.
21. See Régie des rentes du Québec, *Actuarial Report of the Quebec Pension Plan as at 31 December 2006* (Quebec City: Régie des rentes du Québec, December 2007); and Shannon Klie, "QPP Faces Crisis, CPP's Healthy Reserve Should Be Used to Cover Quebec's Shortfall: Report," *Canadian HR Reporter* (February 25, 2008), p. 1.
22. According to Lysiane Gagnon, "In 2008, the Caisse lost $40-billion—25 per cent of its value. A loss wouldn't have come as a surprise, considering the global financial crisis. The problem is, the Caisse's performance is by far the worst in Canada. The average loss of other Canadian pension funds was 18 per cent—14.4 per cent in the case of the fund that manages the Canada Pension Plan. The difference is due to two factors: The Caisse bought more asset-backed commercial paper than all the other Canadian pension funds combined, and it bears the cost of owning a great deal of real estate outside Canada, in places such as New York and London." Lysiane Gagnon, "Quebec's Caisse of the blues," *Globe and Mail* (March 9, 2009), p. A13.
23. Rheal Seguin, "Quebec yields to demands for probe of Caisse losses," *Globe and Mail* (March 13, 2009), p. A6.
24. Fraser, Quebec Inc., p. 80.
25. See Fred McMahon, *Road to Growth: How Lagging Economies Become Prosperous* (Halifax: AIMS, 2000).
26. Kazi Stastna, "We're nicely educated but poor: Montrealers tops in getting payments from government," *Montreal Gazette* (February 10, 2004), p. A1.
27. Quebec's government tax take (provincial and local taxes combined) persistently represented about 27 per cent of its provincial GDP between 1994 and 2004. The other provinces, by contrast, all significantly reduced their government-to-GDP ratios during this period. See Brian Lee Crowley and Bruce Winchester, *The Mystery of the Missing Fiscal Imbalance* (AIMS: Halifax, February, 2005), p. 4.
28. Author's calculations based on Statistics Canada, *Financial Management System* (Ottawa: Minister of Industry, 2008); and Statistics Canada, *Provincial Economic Accounts* (Ottawa: Minister of Industry, 2008). The Quebec numbers have been adjusted to take account of the federal tax abatement.
29. See Duanjie Chen and Jack Mintz, "Limited Horizons: The 2008 Report on the Federal and Provincial Budgetary Tax Policies," *C.D. Howe Institute Commentary*, No. 270 (July 2008), p. 7.
30. Quebec workers work fewer hours than workers in any other province with the exception of Nunavut. See TD Financial Group, "Converting Quebec's Strength into Prosperity," *TD Economics Special Report* (April 10, 2007), p. 29.
31. See John Richards and Matthew Brzozowski, *Let's Walk before We Run: Advice on Childcare* (Toronto: C.D. Howe Institute, August 2006), pp. 1–21; and Michael Baker, Jonathon Gruber, and Kevin Milligan, "What Can We Learn from Quebec's Universal Childcare Program?" *C.D. Howe Institute E-Brief* (February 1, 2006): 1–5.
32. See Jason Clemens, Niels Veldhuis, and Amela Karabegovic, "Explaining Canada's High Unionization Rates," *Fraser Institute Alert* (August 2005); and Norma Kozhaya, "The Consequences of a Strong Union Presence in Quebec," *MEI Economic Note* (September 2005).

33. Cette aventure, qui reposait en grande partie, directement et indirectement, sur des fonds publics, aurait eu une rentabilité incertaine.... Déjà, ce contexte difficile aurait dû mener les partenaires à la plus grande rigueur. Mais c'est le contraire qui s'est passé, et les dépassements de coûts ont finalement rendu le projet insensé et mené à la fermeture du chantier après qu'on y ait englouti 300 millions. Cette explosion des coûts, comme commence à le révéler la commission d'enquête, s'explique par la complexité de la reconversion de l'usine, par une gérance déficiente, mais aussi par un véritable régime de terreur syndical, où les représentants de la FTQ ont exclu les travailleurs des autres centrales et contribué au pourrissement du climat sur le chantier et à la baisse de productivité. [author's translation]

34. Thomas J. Courchene, "A Market Perspective on Regional Disparities," *Canadian Public Policy*, Vol. 7, No. 4 (Autumn, 1981): 509.

35. These data are drawn from *Measuring Ontario's Prosperity: Developing and Economic Indicator System*, Institute for Competitiveness & Prosperity Working Paper No. 2 (August 2002).

36. TD Financial Group, "Converting Quebec's Strength into Prosperity," p. i.

37. See Marcel Boyer, "Quebec's Disappointing Economic Performance in the Last 25 Years."

38. Based on author's analysis of Statistics Canada, *Table 276-0001-Employment Insurance Program, income beneficiaries by province, type of income benefit and sex, computed annual average (persons)*, CANSIM (database), Using E-STAT (distributor).

39. Marcel Boyer, "Quebec's Disappointing Economic Performance in the Last 25 Years."

40. Norma Kozhaya, "Quebec's Relative Poverty."

41. Bernard Fortin, Guy Lacroix, and Jean-Francois Thibault, "The Interaction of UI and Welfare, and the Dynamics of Welfare Participation of Single Parents," *Canadian Public Policy*, Vol. 25 (November 1999): 115–16.

42. William G. Watson, John Richards, and David M. Brown, *The Case for Change: Reinventing the Welfare State* (Toronto: C.D. Howe Institute, 1994), p. 3.

43. Philip Authier, "Quebec expects number of welfare households to fall; should be fewer cases because the economy is starting to pick up, minister says," *Montreal Gazette* (June 8, 1993), p. A6.

44. Ross Finnie, Ian Irvine, and Roger Sceviour, *Social Assistance Use in Canada: National and Provincial Trends in Incidence, Entry and Exit*, Analytical Studies Research Paper, no. 245. Catalogue no. F0019M1E (Ottawa: Statistics Canada, May 2005), p. 15.

45. Finnie, Irvine, and Sceviour, *Social Assistance Use In Canada*, p. 16.

46. P. Kieran, "Early Retirement Trends," *Perspectives on Labour and Income*, Vol. 2, No. 9, Catalogue no. 75-001-X1E (September 2001).

47. Lucie Charron, "Canada's Pension Predicament: The Widening Gap between Public and Private Sector Retirement Trends and Pension Plans," *CFIB Research* (January 2007).

48. See Grace Skogstad, "Canadian Federalism, Internationalization and Quebec Agriculture: Dis-Engagement, Re-Integration?" *Canadian Public Policy*, Vol. 24, No. 1 (March 1998): 27–48. She explains, "Since its full implementation in 1975, national dairy policy has directly benefited Quebec dairy producers who hold 47 percent of national industrial milk quota."

49. See, for example, the speech in the House of Commons by Mr. Jean-Paul Marchand (Québec-Est, BQ), Wednesday May 19, 1995, where he said, "This system is beneficial to all dairy farmers and will be maintained after Quebec achieves sovereignty. Quebec must achieve sovereignty, and it is in the farmers' interests to acknowledge that this will be good for the country as a whole because Quebec will want to repatriate the powers it needs in other sectors. However, dairy farmers in Quebec will be allowed to maintain this pooling system, which is beneficial to them and to their counterparts in other provinces. Upon achieving sovereignty, Quebec will be able to uphold the agreements in this sector and those that will be negotiated in other sectors."

50. Statistics Canada, *Table 183-0002—Public sector employment, wages and salaries, annual (persons)*, CANSIM (database), Using E-STAT (distributor).

51. Pierre Lemieux, "The (civil) servants rule," *Montreal Gazette* (March 11, 2002), p. D4.

52. Marc Renaud, "Quebec's New Middle Class in Search of Social Hegemony: Causes and Political Consequences," in Michael D. Behiels (ed.), *Quebec Since 1945: Selected Readings* (Toronto: Copp Clark Pitman Limited, 1987), pp. 48–49.

53. Marie-Eve Hudon, *Official Languages in the Public Service: From 1973 to the Present* (Ottawa: Library of Parliament, August 2006), p. 20.

54. See Statistics Canada, Table 384-0020—*Government subsidies and capital transfers, provincial economic accounts, annual*, CANSIM (database), Using E-STAT (distributor); Canadian Taxpayers Federation, *On the Dole: Businesses, Lobbyists and Industry Canada's Subsidy Programs* (Ottawa: CTF, January 2007), pp. 6–8; and Canadian Taxpayers Federation, *Peeling Back the Onion: A Taxpayers' Audit of Technology Partnerships Canada* (Ottawa: CTF, February 2002), p. 16.

55. Roughly a third of the nearly $13 billion in regional development money handed out by the four main regional development agencies that cover western Canada, northern Ontario, Quebec, and Atlantic Canada. Author's analysis based on the Government of Canada, *Public Accounts of Canada, Volume II: Details of Expenses and Revenues* (Ottawa: Public Works and Government Services Canada, 1988–2007); and Canadian Taxpayers Federation, *La Belle Province: Same Ugly Story, A 12-Year Quantitative Analysis of Canada Economic Development for the Regions of Quebec* (Ottawa: CTF, June 2002).

56. Thus if you add together all the federal, provincial, and municipal workers in Quebec, and then add to that number the number of full-time equivalent positions in the private sector that government transfers to business support, that means that in 2004 (a representative year and the last one for which we have total figures), 927,060 Quebeckers owed their job directly to the state, or over one-quarter of the 3,680,500 Quebeckers who had a job. In Ontario, the equivalent was only 18.7 per cent of total employment. Author's calculations based on Statistics Canada, *Table 183-0002—Public sector employment, wages and salaries, annual (persons)*; Statistics Canada, *Table 282-0012—Labour force survey estimates (LFS), employment by class of worker, North American Industry Classification System (NAICS) and sex, annual (persons)*; and Statistics Canada, *Table 384-0004—Government sector revenue and expenditure, provincial economic accounts, annual (dollars)*.

57. See, for example, Fred McMahon, *Retreat from Growth: Atlantic Canada and the Negative Sum Economy* (Halifax, AIMS, 2000).

58. Michael S. Pollard and Zheng Wu, "Divergence of Marriage Patterns in Quebec and Elsewhere in Canada," *Population and Development Review*, Vol. 24, No. 2 (June 1998): 329.

59. According to the census, 611,855 of Canada's nearly 1.4 million common-law relationships can be found in Quebec.

60. Focus on the Family Canada, *Canadian Attitudes on the Family, A National Survey Conducted by the Strategic Counsel* (Ottawa: Focus on the Family Canada, 2002), p. 33.

61. Pollard and Wu, "Divergence of Marriage Patterns in Quebec and Elsewhere in Canada," p. 348.

62. The total first-marriage rate for Quebec women (age 15–49) in 1994 was only 373 per thousand, compared with 608 per thousand for women in the rest of Canada. Comparable figures in 1985 were 515 and 682, respectively.

63. Pollard and Wu, "Divergence of Marriage Patterns in Quebec and Elsewhere in Canada," pp. 329–30.

64. "The number of marriages per thousand population [in Quebec] reveals a continuing decline since the middle of the seventies. Yet, the rate of total nuptiality of the never-married,

that is, the cumulative marriage rate of all age-groups under fifty, reveals an even more precipitous decline. In the case of men it passed from 906 per thousand in 1971, to 571 in 1981, to 493 in 1984; whereas in the case of women the rate for the same dates are 863, 579 and 514 respectively. This means, quite simply, that if present trends continue to prevail, one in two Quebecers will not marry." See Gary Caldwell and Daniel Fournier, "The Quebec Question: A Matter of Population," *Canadian Journal of Sociology*, Vol. 12, No. 1/2 (Spring 1987): 29.

65. Caldwell and Fournier, "The Quebec Question: A Matter of Population," p. 30.

66. "Quebecers most stressed-out Canadians; researchers urge study to probe root causes of high-anxiety levels of province's residents," *Edmonton Journal* (October 14, 2008), p. D6.

67. Janet Bagnall, "Quebec's saddest social challenge," *Ottawa Citizen* (February 28, 2008), p. A12.

68. "Society's great unspoken ill: The view from Montreal," *National Post* (June 6, 2006), p. A14.

69. Canadian Press, "Quebec men more likely to commit suicide," *Sudbury Star* (May 5, 2004), p. A7.

70. Kazin Stastna, "High suicide rate linked to Quiet Revolution," *Montreal Gazette* (February 6, 2007), p. A8.

71. See Kevin Milligan, "Quebec's Baby Bonus: Can Public Policy Raise Fertility?" *C.D. Howe Institute Backgrounder* (Toronto: C.D. Howe Institute, January 27, 2002), p. 1. "In 1988, Quebec introduced the Allowance for Newborn Children, a pro-natalist child benefit that paid up to $8,000 to a family after the birth of a child. Was the program successful? It achieved its goal of increasing family size, but only at a high cost per additional birth. Each child who would not have been born in the absence of the incentive cost the public purse more than $15,000. The main policy lesson from this episode is that, even if the response to an incentive policy is strong, the effective cost per desired result may be very high."

72. See http://www.cbc.ca/news/story/2000/03/10/abortion000310.html.

73. Having peaked at 43.2 in 2000.

74. Statistics Canada, *Induced Abortion Statistics, 2004*. Catalogue no. 82-223-XIE (Ottawa: Statistics Canada, July 2007), pp. 14–20.

75. This is a net figure. The gross outflow was roughly 400,000, but there was a much smaller inflow partially offsetting it. See Garth Stevenson, *Community Besieged: The Anglophone Minority and the Politics of Quebec* (Montreal and Kingston: McGill-Queen's University Press, 2003), p. 283.

76. Gilles Grenier, "Earnings by Language Group in Quebec in 1980 and Emigration from Quebec between 1976 and 1981," *Canadian Journal of Economics*, Vol. 20, No. 4 (November 1987): 781.

77. Louise Marmen and Jean-Pierre Corbeil, *New Canadian Perspectives: Languages in Canada, 1996 Census* (Ottawa: Public Works and Government Services Canada, 1999), p. 58.

78. Marmen and Corbeil, *New Canadian Perspectives*, p. 13.

79. Earnings disparities between English-speakers and French-speakers in Quebec have been a subject of concern since the publication in the mid-1960s of the results of studies done for the Royal Commission on Bilingualism and Biculturalism. Those results, based on the 1961 census, showed a very large earnings gap in favour of anglophones in the Montreal metropolitan area. In Montreal anglophone males earned 51 per cent more on average than francophone males. In 1970, the earnings differential decreased to 32 per cent, and, in 1977, to 15 per cent. See Grenier, "Earnings by Language Group in Quebec in 1980 and Emigration from Quebec between 1976 and 1981," p. 774.

80. Daniel M. Shapiro and Morton Stelcner, "Language and Earnings in Quebec: Trends over Twenty Years, 1970–1990," *Canadian Public Policy*, Vol. 23, No. 2 (June 1997): 100.

81. Shapiro and Stelcner, "Language and Earnings in Quebec," p. 126.

82. All this fuss is taking place at the same time as the evidence shows that on balance immigrants are integrating more and more into the French-speaking community in Quebec. According to Simon Langlois, for example, "Les nouveaux arrivants consomment de plus en plus de produits culturels en langue française au Québec. Ce changement est documenté par l'Office et il indique que les efforts de francisation de l'espace public et de l'espace du travail auraient un effet sur l'intégration des nouveaux arrivants, dont par ailleurs la langue maternelle est plus fréquemment le français, il faut l'ajouter. L'examen des indicateurs culturels complète bien dans le Bilan la lecture des transferts de langue au sein du foyer." Simon Langlois, "Un portrait juste," La Presse (March 6, 2008), p. A27.

83. See Pascal Faucher, "Chauvins, les Québécois," *La Presse* (June 30, 2005), p. A2.

84. Author's calculation based on Statistics Canada, *Table 051-0001—Estimates of population, by age group and sex for July 1, Canada, provinces and territories, annual (persons unless otherwise noted)*, CANSIM (database), Using E-STAT (distributor).

Chapter 8
Symmetry's Turning Point and a Tiny Window on the Future

1. While I think the preponderance of evidence points to the Clampetts having come originally from the Missouri Ozarks, the truth is that the show's producers kept it deliberately vague exactly where the family hailed from. Good cases can be made for West Virginia, Tennessee, Arkansas, Kentucky and several other states as well.

2. See Roger D. Congleton's book review of Vito Tanzi and Ludger Schuknecht, *Public Spending in the 20th Century: A Global Perspective in Public Choice* No. 108, No. 1–2 (July 2001): 197–200.

3. See Vito Tanzi, "The Economic Role of the State in the Twenty-First Century," *Cato Journal*, Vol. 25, No. 3 (Fall 2005): 617–39; and David L. Lindauer, *The Size and Growth of Government Spending: A Background Paper for the 1998 World Development Report* (Washington D.C.: World Bank, September 1998).

4. See, for example, Fred McMahon, *Retreat from Growth: Atlantic Canada and the Negative Sum Economy* (Halifax: AIMS, 2000).

5. See, for example, McMahon, *Retreat from Growth;* and *Looking the Gift Horse in the Mouth: The Impact of Federal Spending on Atlantic Canada* (Halifax: AIMS, 1996).

6. "But even these optimists will admit that the threat of separation is being used by all Quebec governments to extract concessions from the rest of the country. When we are conditioned to believe that a complete meltdown of our country is the only alternative to giving Quebec more federal tax revenues—or a special status in the Constitution—then we are truly hostages and no request may be refused." Reed Scowen, former member of the Quebec legislature, *Time to Say Goodbye: Building a Better Canada without Quebec,* rev. ed. (Toronto: McClelland and Stewart, 2007), p. 4.

7. "Quebec on the fast track to self-rule: Parizeau," Globe and Mail, (December 1, 1990), A1.

8. In fact, Japan has accumulated the largest government debt in the industrialized world. Its massive public debt exceeds 150 per cent of its GDP. For more on Japan's "debt explosion," see David Flath, *The Japanese Economy*, 2nd ed. (London: Oxford University Press, 2005); and Toshiki Tomita, "The Need for Redefining Japan's Government Debt Management Policy," *NRI Papers*, No. 42 (Tokyo: Normura Research Institute, February 2002): 1–16.

9. See: http://www.economist.com/Countries/Japan/profile.cfm?folder=Profile-Economic%20Data. Japan's deficit spending is no recent phenomenon either. In 1997, Milton Ezrati presciently observed, "... the government budget deficit will swell as the authorities struggle to meet public pension obligations that, by all accounts, are even less well funded than Social Security in the United States. At present, contributions to the Japanese equivalent

of Social Security and Medicare net the government surplus revenues equal to about 3.5 percent of GDP. While these contributions partially offset deficits elsewhere in the budget, they will disappear when the huge influx of pensioners takes its toll. The Ministry of Health and Welfare calculates that public pension obligations will swell the government budget deficit to 5 percent of GDP indefinitely. Public finances in Japan are already in deficit." Milton Ezrati, "Japan's Aging Economics," *Foreign Affairs* (May/June 1997), p. 98.

10 One well-documented account of the corrosive effect of Western Europe's dramatic growth in government and the continent's related demographic decline is Mark Steyn's book, *America Alone: The End of the World as We Know It* (Washington D.C.: Regnery Publishing, 2006).

Chapter 9
Why the Rest of the World Cannot Save Us

1. Roger Sauvé, *Labour Crunch to 2021: National and Provincial Labour Force Projections* (Summertown, Ont.: People Patterns Consulting, March 2007), p. 4.
2. Citizenship and Immigration Canada, *2006 Annual Report to Parliament on Immigration*, http://www.cic.gc.ca/english/DEPARTMENT/media/backgrounders/2006/2006-10-31.asp.
3. Statistics Canada. Table 051-0011 - *International migrants, by age group and sex, Canada, provinces, and territories, annual (persons)*, CANSIM (database), Using E-STAT (distributor).
4. "Immigration and emigration rates remained constant at 0.75% and 0.20% of the Canadian population respectively." See Mario Lapointe et al., *Looking Ahead: A 10-Year Outlook for the Canadian Labour Market, 2006-2015*, Catalogue no. SP-615-06E (Ottawa: Human Resources and Social Development Canada, October 2006).
5. Robert Banerjee and William Robson, *Faster and Younger? Not so much: Immigration's Impact on Canadian Workforce Growth and Age Structure*, (Toronto: C.D. Howe Institute, 2008), pp. 2-3.
6. William B.P. Robson and Yvan Guillemette, *No Elixir for Youth: Immigration Cannot Keep Canada Young* (Toronto: C.D. Howe Institute, September 2006), pp. 1–21; p. 2: "Whatever the benefits of immigration to Canada's economy and society, and to immigrants themselves, immigration cannot relieve Canada of the challenges of an aging population. The need to encourage work and saving by an older population and to deliver pensions and healthcare efficiently and sustainably will be as pressing in a future of high immigration as it would be without it."
7. Statistics Canada, *The Daily* (October 26, 2006), available at http://www.statcan.ca/Daily/English/061026/d061026b.htm.
8. See M.V. George, F. Nault, and A. Romaniuc, "Effects of Fertility and International Migration on Changing Age Composition in Canada," *Statistical Journal of the United Nations ECE* Vol. 8, No. 1 (1991): 13–24; p. 2: "Immigration effects are almost evenly spread over all age groups and so have much less influence on age structure [than initial age structure, fertility and mortality, in that order]."
9. Policy Research Initiative, *Population Aging and Life Course Flexibility: The Pivotal Role of Increased Choice in the Retirement Decision*, (Ottawa: Government of Canada, March 2004), p. 10.
10. Garnett Picot and Feng Hou, *The Rise in Low-Income Rates among Immigrants in Canada* (Catalogue no. 11F0019MIE), (Ottawa: Statistics Canada, June 2003).
11. Garnett Picot, "The Deteriorating Economic Welfare of Canadian Immigrants," *Canadian Journal of Urban Research*, Vol. 13, No. 1 (Winter 2003): 25-45.
12. Canadian Council on Learning, *Lessons in Learning: More Education, Less Employment: Immigrants and the Labor Market*, (Ottawa: CCL, October 2008), pp. 3-4.

13. See Robson and Guillemette, *No Elixir for Youth*, p. 11. "Only extreme and unpalatable policies, such as rapidly increasing immigration from less than 1 per cent of the population to well over 3 per cent for decades, could come close to stabilizing the [old-age dependency] ratio."

14. Sauvé, *Labour Crunch to 2021*, p. 14.

15. "Measured on a per capita basis, Canada is the world leader [in immigration], welcoming in recent times an average of 7 migrants per 1,000 population each year. This tops 6.2 migrants per 1,000 population for Australia and is well above 4.4 immigrants per 1,000 population in the United States." See Rudyard Griffiths, *Who We Are: A Citizen's Manifesto* (Vancouver/Toronto: Douglas & McIntyre, 2009), pp. 79–80.

16. National Research Council Canada, *Looking Forward: S&T for the 21st Century; Global Context—Changing Demographics* (Ottawa: Minister of Industry, August 2005), p. 3.

17. See, for example, James P. Smith and Barry Edmonston (eds.), *The New Americans: Economic, Demographic and Fiscal Effects of Immigration* (Washington D.C.: National Academy Press, 1997).

18. See Assaf Razin, "Notes on Demographic Changes and the Welfare State," in Jane Sneddon Little and Robert K. Triest (eds.), *Seismic Shifts: The Economic Impact of Demographic Change* (Boston: Federal Reserve, 2002), pp. 289–96.

19. David K. Foot, "Population Aging," in J. Leonard, C. Ragan, and F. St-Hilaire (eds.), *A Canadian Priorities Agenda: Policy Choices to Improve Economic and Social Well-Being* (Montreal: Institute for Research on Public Policy, 2007), p. 13.

20. I am intentionally excluding here those people admitted as temporary workers, precisely because they are not permanent immigrants, the class of people with whom we are concerned here. There is no denying, however, that such temporary workers are here in relatively large numbers. According to Sandra Elgersma, *Temporary Foreign Workers* (Ottawa: Library of Parliament, 2007), p. 4. "In 2006, 112,658 temporary foreign workers arrived in Canada. Although the number of temporary foreign workers has grown substantially in all provinces with significant numbers of foreign workers, this increase has been most pronounced in Alberta." Journalist Nicholas Keung reports that Canada admitted 165,198 such temporary workers in 2007, of which half were in technical and skilled trades, lower-skilled clerical and labour jobs, including farm workers and nannies. The downturn, however, is putting many of these temporary jobs at risk. See "Imported workers face uncertainty; a growing number of temporary foreign labourers now jobless, vulnerable in recession," *Toronto Star* (December 17, 2008), A16. The precariousness of such workers underlines why they are not part of this discussion, even though their presence in Canada is largely at the behest of employers: their admission is by definition temporary (even though some of them may go on to gain admission as permanent immigrants). My concern here is with the rules around those whom we admit permanently.

21. The numbers that follow are drawn from *Immigration, Labour Market Outcomes and Economic Impacts*, a presentation by Professor Arthur Sweetman of Queen's University to the annual Department of Finance retreat, May 28, 2007.

22. See, for example, *The Economist* survey called "The Battle for Brainpower," Vol. 381, Iss. 8498 (October 7, 2006), p. 3.

23. David Zweig and Chung Siu Fung, *Redefining the Brain Drain: China's Diaspora Options*, Working Paper No.1, (Hong Kong: Center on China's Transnational Relations, 2005), p. 4.

24. Drawn from Sweetman, *Immigration, Labour Market Outcomes and Economic Impacts*.

25. See "The Battle for Brainpower," *The Economist*, p. 3.

26. "The Battle for Brainpower," *The Economist*, p. 9.

27. Quoted in "Migration: A Turning Tide?" *The Economist*, Vol. 387, Iss. 8586 (June 28, 2008), p. 32.

28. Private conversation with the author.

29. See Jane Sneddon Little and Robert K. Triest, "Seismic Shifts: The Economic Impact of Demographic Change: An Overview," in Jane Sneddon Little and Robert K. Triest (eds.), *Seismic Shifts: The Economic Impact of Demographic Change* (Boston: Federal Reserve, 2002), p. 20.

30. See Allan Gotlieb and Milos Barutciski, "Wanted: leadership on trade," *National Post* (February 7, 2009), A19; and Paul Vieira, "Doha collapse to cost farmers $10M daily; Canada's position on supply management no help," *National Post* (July 31, 2008), FP3.

31. This argument is drawn from Sneddon Little and Triest's introductory paper in Sneddon Little and Triest (eds.), *Seismic Shifts*, pp. 12–13.

Chapter 10
The Two Nations in Canada's Future: Lord Durham Updated

1. See Statistics Canada, *Population Projections for Canada, Provinces and Territories 2005–2031*, Catalogue no. 91-520-xie (Ottawa: Minister of Industry, 2006).

2. Statistics Canada, *Population Projections for Canada, Provinces and Territories 2005-2031*, pp. 50–60.

3. Drawn from Brian Lee Crowley and Bobby O'Keefe, "The Flypaper Effect: Does Equalization Really Contribute to Better Public Services, or Does It Just 'Stick to' Politicians and Civil Servants?" *AIMS Commentary*, No. 2 (June 2006): 1–11.

4. Statistics Canada, *Labour Force Historical Review 2007, Table Cd1T46an* (Ottawa: Statistics Canada, 2008); and Glen Norcliffe, "Regional Unemployment in Canada in the 1981–1984 Recession," *Canadian Geographer*, Vol. 31, No. 2 (1987): 150–59.

5. Jim Milway and Roger Martin, *Enhancing the Productivity of Small and Medium Enterprises Through Greater Adoption of Information and Communication Technology* (Toronto: Institute for Competitiveness and Prosperity, May 2007).

6. Norma Kozhaya, "The Retirement Age in Quebec: A Worrying Situation," *MEI Economic Note* (June 2007).

7. The current number understates the gap in Ontario's favour because the difficulties facing the manufacturing sector in Ontario have temporarily slowed that province's growth relative to the national average in recent years. Several observers, including noted economist Jack Mintz, are confident that Ontario is still on a solid "growth path in the future" and that the temporary decline will ultimately reverse itself. See, for example, Jack Mintz, "Tough, but right choices made: Blended tax important step for growth," *National Post* (March 27, 2009), A4.

8. Marcel Boyer, "Quebec's Disappointing Economic Performance in the Last 25 Years," *MEI Economic Note* (May 2007).

9. See Statistics Canada, *Table 051-0035—Components of population growth, census divisions and census metropolitan areas, 2001 Census boundaries, annual (persons)* CANSIM (database); and Statistics Canada, *Table 051-0031—Components of population growth, census divisions and census metropolitan areas, 1981 census boundaries, annual (persons)* CANSIM (database).

10. Former federal Cabinet minister, Eric Kierans, private communications to author in 1992.

11. Equalization is a transfer from the federal government to poorer provinces to ensure that they can provide reasonably comparable (to wealthier provinces) services at reasonably comparable levels of taxation. The current level of transfers is over $14 billion in 2009–10.

12. Crowley and O'Keefe, "The Flypaper Effect," pp. 1–11.

13. Richard Foot, "Have-not no more: Canwest News Service Special Report," *Leader Post* (Regina) (July 19, 2008), p. B8.

14. Foot, "Have-not no more," p. B8.

15. Much of the following discussion is inspired by Andrew Sharpe's "Lessons for Canada from International Productivity Experience," *International Productivity Monitor*, No. 14 (Spring 2007): 1–18.

16. According to StatsCan, "In 2003, in the goods sector (agriculture and manufacturing), the level of labour productivity in Canada was about 72% of that in the United States; in the services sector, it was about 74%; in the engineering sector (transportation, communications, energy and construction) it was about 95%." See Statistics Canada, *The Daily* (July 21, 2008) available at http://www.statcan.ca/Daily/English/080721/d080721.pdf.

17. See Jim Milway and Roger Martin, *Commercialization and the Canadian Business Environment: A Systems Perspective*, Comments on Public Policy Support for Innovation and Commercialization in Canada (Toronto: Institute for Competitiveness and Prosperity, July 2005).

18. Eric Lascelles, "The 'new normal'; When the recession ends, what will the economy look like? Likely an era of reduced GDP growth for North America," *National Post* (April 11, 2009), p. FP 15.

19. For a recent Canadian example, see Peter Howitt, "Innovation, Competition and Growth: A Schumpeterian Perspective on Canada's Economy," *C.D. Howe Institute Commentary*, No. 246 (April 2007): 1–19.

20. Government of Canada, *Economic Adjustment in Canada*, (Ottawa: Department of Finance, February 2006).

21. "Innovation Survey," *The Economist*, Vol. 385, Iss. 8550 (October 13, 2007), p. 18.

22. Chris Parsley and David Halabisky, *Profile of Growth Firms: A Summary of Industry Canada Research*, (Ottawa: Minister of Industry, March 2008), p. 8.

23. John R. Baldwin and W. Mark Brown, *Four Decades of Creative Destruction: Renewing Canada's Manufacturing Base from 1961-1999* (Catalogue no. 11-624-MIE), (Ottawa: Statistics Canada, October 2004).

24. These figures derive from a private presentation by July 2005 presentation to the Department of Finance by John Baldwin, entitled "Innovation in a Small Open Economy." Baldwin's analysis is based on a previous book, Baldwin and Peter Hanel, *Innovation and Knowledge Creation in an Open Economy: Canadian Industry and International Implications*, (New York: Cambridge University Press, 2003).

25. On the issue of the impact of creative destruction on wages (i.e. does creative destruction result in people being pushed into low wage "McJobs"), a study by two Statistics Canada economists found that "the Canadian economy has not witnessed a deterioration in the relative importance of well-paid jobs since 1997. Likewise, there has not been a widespread increase in the relative importance of low-paid jobs since then." In fact, they find that wage increases in the service sector and new skilled manufacturing jobs ($25 per hour or more) have actually increased significantly over the period studied (1997 to 2004). See Rene Morissette and Anick Johnson, "Are Good Jobs Disappearing in Canada?" *Economic Policy Review*, Vol. 11, Iss. 1 (August 2005), pp. 26-28.

26. Andrew Sharpe, Jean-Francois Arsenault, and Daniel Ershov, *The Impact of Interprovincial Migration on Aggregate Output and Labour Productivity in Canada, 1987–2006* (Ottawa: Centre for the Study of Living Standards, November 2007).

27. Alberto Isgut, Lance Bialas, and James Milway, *Explaining Canada-U.S. Differences in Annual Hours Worked* (Toronto: Institute for Competitiveness and Prosperity, November 2006), p. 2.

28. See Duanjie Chen and Jack Mintz, "Limited Horizons: The 2008 Report on the Federal and Provincial Budgetary Tax Policies," *C.D. Howe Institute Commentary*, No. 270 (July 2008), p. 8.

29. Chen and Mintz, "Limited Horizons," p. 7.

30. For more analysis of provincial tax policy and its impact on productivity rates, see Jason Clemens and Niels Veldhuis, *Productivity, Prosperity and Business Taxes: An Occasional Paper for the Centre for Budgetary Studies* (Vancouver: Fraser Institute, January 2006), pp. 23–29.

31. For a comprehensive look at tax reform in OECD countries, see OECD, "Fundamental Reform of Personal Income Tax," *OECD Tax Policy Series*, No. 13, ISBN 9264025774 (May 31, 2006): 1–144; and OECD, "Fundamental Reform of Corporate Income Tax," *OECD Tax Policy Series*, no. 16, ISBN 9264038116 (November 2007): 1–174.

32. Christina Blizzard, *Toronto Sun*, May 14, 2008. See Andrew Coyne's blog at http://www2.macleans.ca/2008/05/14/mcguintonomics/.

33. Edward Gresser, "Healthy Factories, Anxious Workers—Or, Why Lou Dobbs Is Wrong," *Policy Report* (February 2007): 1–12.

34. Daniel Ikenson, "Thriving in a Global Economy: The Truth about U.S. Manufacturing and Trade," *Trade Policy Analysis*, No. 35 (August 28, 2007): 1.

35. See Sharpe, "Lessons for Canada from International Productivity Experience," pp. 1–18.

Chapter 11
Do Not Go Gentle into That Good Night: Work for All and All in Work

1. This discussion is based on Watson Wyatt Worldwide, *A Report on the World Economic Forum Pension Readiness Initiative* (Davos, Switzerland: World Economic Forum, January 2004).

2. OECD, *Aging and Employment Policies: Canada*, (Paris: OECD Publishing, 2005), p. 9.

3. See Steven James, Tim Sargent, Russell Barnett, and Claude Lavoie, *The Canadian Labour Force Participation Rate Revisited: Cohort and Wealth Effects Take Hold* (Ottawa: Department of Finance, January 2007).

4. Sun Life Financial media release, "Sun Life Financial study finds nearly half of Canadians will be working past 65" (January 28, 2009). http://www.sunlife.ca/canada/v/index.jsp?vgnextoid=1aaf570ea6d1f110VgnVCM100000a bd2d09fRCRD&vgnLocale=en_CA&chnpath=%2FsunlifeCA.

5. See Andrew Coyne, "Social Spending, Taxes and Debt: Trudeau's Just Society," in Andrew Cohen and J.L. Granatstein (eds.), *Trudeau's Shadow: The Life and Legacy of Pierre Elliott Trudeau* (Toronto: Vintage Canada, 1999), p. 234.

6. The importance of federal income security programs in general and old-age pension cheques in particular in the referendum campaigns is well documented in Keith Banting, *The Welfare State and Canadian Federalism* (Montreal and Kingston: McGill-Queen's University Press, 1987), pp. 167 and 177; and Daniel Béland and André Lecours, "Sub-state Nationalism and the Welfare State: Quebec and Canadian Federalism," *Nations and Nationalism*, Vol. 12, No. 1 (2006): 82.

7. Aaron Pereira et al., *Moving in the Right Direction?: Labour Mobility, Labour Shortage and Canada's Human Potential* (Vancouver: Action Canada, June 2007), p. 32.

8. Morley Gunderson, *Impact of Labour Market Institutions and Regulation* (Halifax: AIMS, forthcoming).

9. Then Bank of Canada governor David Dodge: http://www.bank-banque-canada.ca/en/speeches/2007/sp07-10.html.

10. Joseph Dawe, "Quebec pensions face crisis report; paper proposes lending some of the reserves of other Canadians' CPP to prop up ailing QPP," *Toronto Star* (January 17, 2008), B1.

11. Norma Kozhaya, "The Retirement Age in Quebec: A Worrying Situation," *MEI Economic Note* (June 2007).

12. Dawe, "Quebec pensions face crisis report," p. B1.

13. Author's calculations from Statistics Canada, "Census of Population (Provinces, Census Divisions, Metropolitans)," *1966 Census* (Ottawa: Minister of Industry, 1967).
14. Statistics Canada, "The Changing Profile of Canada's Labour Force," *2001 Census: Analysis Series* (Ottawa: Minister of Industry, February 2003), p. 12.

Chapter 12
Family's Comeback and Fertility's Return

1. "A Tale of Two Bellies; Demography in America and Europe," *The Economist*, Vol. 364, Iss. 8287 (August 22, 2002): 11.
2. "A Tale of Two Bellies," *The Economist*, p. 11.
3. Special Report, "Half a Billion Americans?—Demography and the West," *The Economist*, Vol. 364, Iss. 8287 (August 22, 2002): 22.
4. Special Report, "Half a Billion Americans?" *The Economist*, p. 22.
5. Even this may help explain divergence in birth rates. As Mark Steyn writes in the April 9, 2007, issue of the *Western Standard*, p. 53, "That in turn helps explain the healthy fertility rate: America is one of the cheapest places in the developed world in which to find a four-bedroom house with a yard. Who wants to raise three kids in a city apartment?"
6. According to David Foot, "Pro-fertility policies of many forms in many jurisdictions to date have had a minimal permanent impact on fertility rates. In general, they seem to be only able to ameliorate future decreases. In practice, the long-run inevitability of demographic transition is entrenched." See Foot, "Population Aging," in J. Leonard, C. Ragan, and F. St-Hilaire (eds.), *A Canadian Priorities Agenda: Policy Choices to Improve Economic and Social Well-Being* (Montreal: Institute for Research on Public Policy, 2007), pp. 192–93. See also Kevin Milligan, "Subsidizing the Stork: New Evidence on Tax Incentives and Fertility," *Review of Economics and Statistics*, Vol. 87, No. 3 (August 2005): 539–555.
7. See "A slow-burning fuse: A special report on ageing populations" *The Economist* (June 27, 2009), p. 5. Also, Sharon Lerner, "The Motherhood Experiment," *New York Times* (March 4, 2007), p. 20.
8. Statistics Canada, *Health Statistics Division, Births*, Catalogue no. 84F0210X (Ottawa: Minster of Industry, 2006), p. 21.
9. Kay S. Hymowitz, "Child-Man in the Promised Land: Today's Single Young Men Hang out in a Hormonal Limbo between Adolescence and Adulthood," *City Journal* (Winter 2008).
10. Daniel T. Lichter, Diane K. McLaughlin, and David C. Ribar, "Welfare and the Rise in Female-Headed Families," *American Journal of Sociology*, Vol. 103, No. 1 (July 1997): 112–43; p. 114: "The deteriorating low-wage, low-skill labor market has reduced women's incentives to marry and has undercut the economic foundations of existing markets."
11. See, for instance, Lichter, McLaughlin, and Ribar, "Welfare and the Rise in Female-Headed Families," pp. 112–13.
12. Kevin Daly, *Gender Inequality, Growth and Global Aging*, Global Economics Paper No 154 (New York: Goldman Sachs, April 3, 2007).
13. For more on Canada's welfare rates, see Ross Finnie, Ian Irvine, and Roger Sceviour, *Welfare Dynamics in Canada: The Role of Individual Attributes and Economic-Policy Variables* Analytical Studies Research Paper Series, no. 231. Catalogue no. 11F0019-M1E, (Ottawa: Statistics Canada, October 2004); and Finnie, Irvine, and Sceviour, *Social Assistance Use in Canada: National and Provincial Trends in Incidence, Entry and Exit*, Analytical Studies Research Paper, no. 245. Catalogue no. F0019M1E (Ottawa: Statistics Canada, May 2005).
14. Drawn from a presentation by Eissa to the Department of Finance, entitled "Tax-Based Transfers: Lessons from the Earned Income Tax Credit" (March 7, 2007).
15. Jack Mintz, "Income Splitting Would Help Families," *National Post* (May 27, 2008), p. A12.

16. See Michael Baker, Jonathon Gruber, and Kevin Milligan, "What Can We Learn from Quebec's Universal Childcare Program?" *C.D. Howe Institute E-Brief* (February 1, 2006): 1–5.

17. Government of Canada, *Fairness at Work: Federal Labour Standards for the 21st Century* (Human Resources and Skills Development Canada: Ottawa, 2006).

18. Extracts from the report:
    - Workers need more control over their time at work and after work in order to fulfill their responsibilities as family and community members, and employers need more flexible working time arrangements in order to compete in a highly volatile global marketplace. At present Part III does not adequately accommodate the interests of either workers or employers....
    - One size does not fit all....
    - Employers should be able to seek approval for adjustments to certain statutory standards directly from their workers....
    - Some of the problems of adjusting the competing interests of workers and employers concerning the regulation of time can be resolved only outside the context of labour standards and the employment relationship because they involve broad aspects of social and economic policy.
    - New unpaid leaves should be established that will enable workers to deal with family responsibilities, medical issues, bereavement, education or court attendance.
    - Labour standards should be part of a "flexicurity" initiative, which simultaneously provides more flexibility for employers to adapt to changing technologies and competitive conditions, while ensuring that workers are made more secure by being provided with retraining and other resources needed to adjust to new labour market requirements.

19. Alberto Isgut, Lance Bialas, and James Milway, *Explaining Canada-U.S. Differences in Annual Hours Worked* (Toronto: Institute for Competitiveness and Prosperity, November 2006).

Chapter 13
Quebec's Power Within Canada: High Tide and After

1. For a good summary of the dynamics of PUPPETRY at work in Quebec, see Jean-Luc Migué, *Étatisme et déclin du Québec: Bilan de la révolution tranquille* (Montreal: Montreal Economic Institute, 1999).

2. For more on the opportunity cost of Manitoba's subsidization of provincial electricity, see Pierre Fortin, "The Baby Boomers' Tab: Already $40 Billion in 2020," in Rudyard Griffiths (ed.), *Canada in 2020: Twenty Leading Voices Imagine Canada's Future* (Toronto: Key Porter Books, 2008), p. 46.

3. Marty Klinkenberg, "Liberals' Tax Plan Getting Noticed," *Telegraph Journal* (Saint John) (March 28, 2009), p. A1; and "Against the Current," *Globe and Mail* (March 19, 2009), p. A12.

4. See Thomas Courchene (with Colin Telmer), *From Heartland to North American Region States: An Interpretative Essay on the Fiscal, Social and Federal Evolution of Ontario* (University of Toronto: Centre for Public Management), 1998.

5. "Martinized," *The Province* (Vancouver) (February 23, 1994), A28.

6. Fernande Roy, *L'Histoire des ideologies au Québec aux XIXe et XXe siècles* (Montréal: Editions Boréal, 1993).

7. Reviewed in Jacques Rouillard, "La Révolution Tranquille, Rupture ou Tournant?," *Journal of Canadian Studies*, Vol, 32, No. 4 (Winter, 1998): 23–51.

8. Alain Dubuc, *Éloge De La Richesse* (Quebec City: Voix parallèles, 2006).

9. François Normand, "Larose est prêt à revoir le 'modèle québécois': 'Il faut décentraliser et débureaucratiser l'État,'" *Le Devoir* (May 13, 1999), p. A1.

10. For an account of the general tenor of the PLQ's youth wing's deliberations and Premier

Charest's response, see Gilbert Lavoie, "Congrès des jeunes libéraux: Charest calme le jeu," *Le Soleil* (August 4, 2008), p. 4.

11. Daniel Dufort, "Le soliloque national," *Métropolitain*, Vol. I, No. 4 (June 12, 2008): 8.

12. Text available at http://www.vigile.net/spip.php?page=archives&u=/archives/ds-souv/index-pq-congres.html as of September 8, 2008.

13. "Quebec's quiet decline continues apace," *Montreal Gazette*, (July 4, 2009), B6.

14. Sean Speer, *Technocrats and Provincialists: The Rowell-Sirois Commission's Conception of Federalism, 1937–1940* (unpublished Ph.D. paper, 2007).

15. See, for example, Brian Lee Crowley, "Equalization can be reformed: The Constitution is no excuse," *Chronicle Herald* (Saint John), (April 21, 2004).

Chapter 14
The New Traditionalists

1. See, for instance, Claudia Cattaneo's 2007 *National Post* column on U.S. oil analyst Henry Groppe's views of the oil sands. She quotes Groppe as saying "Canada, Alberta, because of the oilsands, is the only producing source for which we forecast continually increasing production as far into the future as we can see. Whatever problems arise—whether they be political, physical or resource-related—are going to be resolved ultimately, because it's essential to grow that oilsands supply for the world." See Cattaneo, "Oilman bullish on Canada; 'Essential to grow oilsands,'" *National Post* (June 26, 2007), p. FP2. And even in late March 2008, in the middle of the downturn and the precipitous fall in natural resource prices, *The Economist* newspaper was reporting, "Canada's tar sands remain an attractive investment because they provide long-lived reserves in a stable country—a rarity in the oil business these days." "Oil Mergers. Well Matched," *The Economist* (March 28, 2009), p. 75.

2. Energy Information Administration, *International Energy Outlook*, 2008, (Washington, D.C., 2008).

3. Eugene Gholz and Daryl G. Press, *Energy Alarmism: The Myths That Make Americans Worry about Oil*, (Washington, D.C., Cato Institute Policy Analysis no. 589, April 5, 2007). See also the account of Sino-Japanese rivalry to snap up oil reserves around the world in "Energy in Japan. Raising the Stakes," *The Economist* (April 11, 2009), p. 65.

4. Jacques Marcil and Owen Jung, *Against the Grain: Saskatchewan Economic Profile and Forecast* (Calgary: Canada West Foundation, 2009).

5. Neil Scott, "Western provinces talk of partnership," *Leader Post* (Regina), (March 14, 2009), A9; "A TILMA for all," *Globe and Mail* (January 15, 2009), A16; and Ben Shingler, "Labour tops agenda; Meeting Premier Graham and his Quebec counterpart to discuss economic, social issues," *Telegraph-Journal* (Saint John), (October 2, 2008), A1.

bibliography

GOVERNMENT PUBLICATIONS

Baldwin, John R. and W. Mark Brown. *Four Decades of Creative Destruction: Renewing Canada's Manufacturing Base from 1961-1999* (Catalogue no. 11-624-MIE). Ottawa: Statistics Canada, October 2004.

Begum, Nasima. "Characteristics of Short-Term and Long-Term Unemployment," *Labour Market Trends* (April 2004): 139–44.

Finnie, Ross, Ian Irvine, and Roger Sceviour. *Social Assistance Use in Canada: National and Provincial Trends in Incidence, Entry and Exit*, Analytical Studies Research Paper, no. 245. Catalogue no. F0019M1E. Ottawa: Statistics Canada, May 2005.

Finnie, Ross, Ian Irvine and Roger Sceviour. *Welfare Dynamics in Canada: The Role of Individual Attributes and Economic-Policy Variables*, Analytical Studies Research Paper Series, no. 231. Catalogue no. 11F0019-M1E. Ottawa: Statistics Canada, October 2004.

Finnie, Ross, and Roger Sceviour. "Social Assistance Use: Trends in Incidence, Entry and Exit Rates," *Canadian Economic Observer*. Catalogue no. 11-010, August 2004: 1–14.

Government of Canada. *Economic Adjustment in Canada*. Ottawa: Department of Finance, February 2006.

Government of Canada. *Public Accounts of Canada, Volume II: Details of Expenses and Revenues*. Ottawa: Public Works and Government Services Canada, 1988–2007.

Government of Canada. *Fairness at Work: Federal Labour Standards for the 21st Century*. Human Resources and Skills Development Canada: Ottawa, 2006.

Government of Canada. *The Economy of Quebec and Its Regions: Analysis of Trends*. Ottawa: Department of Industry, January 2003.

Hudon, Marie-Eve. *Official Languages in the Public Service: From 1973 to the Present*. Ottawa: Library of Parliament, August 2006.

James, Steven, Tim Sargent, Russell Barnett, and Claude Lavoie. *The Canadian Labour Force Participation Rate Revisited: Cohort and Wealth Effects Take Hold*. Ottawa: Department of Finance, January 2007.

Kieran, P. "Early Retirement Trends," *Perspectives on Labour and Income*, Vol. 2, No. 9, Catalogue no. 75-001-X1E. September 2001.

Lapointe, Mario, et al. *Looking Ahead: A 10-Year Outlook for the Canadian Labour Market, 2006–2015*. Catalogue no. SP-615-06E. Ottawa: Human Resources and Social Development Canada, October 2006.

Lord, Bernard. *Government of Canada Consultations on Linguistic Duality and Official Languages*. Ottawa: Canada Heritage, February 2008.

Madore, Odette. *The Transfer of Tax Points to Provinces under the Canada Health and Social Transfer*, Backgrounder BP-450E. Ottawa: Library of Parliament, October 1997: 1–17.

341

Marmen, Louise, and Jean-Pierre Corbeil. *New Canadian Perspectives: Languages in Canada, 1996 Census*. Ottawa: Public Works and Government Services Canada, 1999.

National Research Council Canada. *Looking Forward: S&T for the 21st Century; Global Context—Changing Demographics*. Ottawa: Minister of Industry, August 2005.

OECD. "Fundamental Reform of Corporate Income Tax," *OECD Tax Policy Series*, no. 16, ISBN 9264038116. November 2007: 1–174.

OECD. "Fundamental Reform of Personal Income Tax," *OECD Tax Policy Series*, no. 13, ISBN 9264025774. May 31, 2006: 1–144.

OECD. *Aging and Employment Policies: Canada*. ISBN-92-64-01244-3. Paris: OECD Publishing, 2005: 1–138.

Office of the Chief Actuary (OCA). *Actuarial Report (21st) on the Canada Pension Plan as at 31 December 2003*. Ottawa: Office of the Superintendent of Financial Institutions.

Parsley, Chris and David Halabisky. *Profile of Growth Firms: A Summary of Industry Canada Research*. Ottawa: Minister of Industry, March 2008.

Picot, Garnett and Feng Hou. *The Rise in Low-Income Rates among Immigrants in Canada* (Catalogue no. 11F0019MIE). Ottawa: Statistics Canada, June 2003.

Policy Research Initiative. *Population Aging and Life Course Flexibility: The Pivotal Role of Increased Choice in the Retirement Decision*. Ottawa: Government of Canada, March 2004.

Régie des rentes du Québec. *Actuarial Report of the Quebec Pension Plan as at 31 December 2006*. Québec City: Régie des rentes du Québec, December 2007.

Sawhill, Isabel. "Solutions to Poverty," Testimony before the Ways and Means Committee, Income Security and Family Support Subcommittee, U.S. House of Representatives, April 26, 2007.

Statistics Canada. *Financial Management System*. Ottawa: Minister of Industry, 2008.

Statistics Canada. *Provincial Economic Accounts*. Ottawa: Minister of Industry, 2008.

Statistics Canada. *Table CD1T46an—Labour Force Historical Review*. Catalogue no. 71F0004XCB. Ottawa: Statistics Canada, 2008.

Statistics Canada. *Induced Abortion Statistics, 2004*. Catalogue no. 82-223-XIE. Ottawa: Statistics Canada, July 2007.

Statistics Canada. *Health Statistics Division, Births*. Catalogue no. 84F0210X. Ottawa: Minister of Industry, 2006.

Statistics Canada. *Labour Force Historical Review 2007* (Table Cd1T46an). Ottawa, Statistics Canada, 2008.

Statistics Canada. *Population Projections for Canada, Provinces and Territories 2005–2031*. Catalogue no. 91-520-xie. Ottawa: Minister of Industry, 2006.

Statistics Canada. "The Changing Profile of Canada's Labour Force," *2001 Census: Analysis Series*. Ottawa: Minister of Industry, February 2003.

Statistics Canada. "Census of Population (Provinces, Census Divisions, Metropolitans)," *1966 Census*. Ottawa: Minister of Industry, 1967.

Statistics Canada. *Table 051-0001—Estimates of population, by age group and sex for July 1, Canada, provinces and territories, annual (persons unless otherwise noted)*, CANSIM (database), Using E-STAT (distributor).

Statistics Canada. *Table 051-0031—Components of population growth, census divisions and census metropolitan areas, 1981 census boundaries, annual (persons)* CANSIM (database).

Statistics Canada. *Table 051-0035—Components of population growth, census divisions and census metropolitan areas, 2001 Census boundaries, annual (persons)* CANSIM (database).

Statistics Canada. *Table 183-0002—Public sector employment, wages and salaries, annual (persons)*, CANSIM (database), using E-STAT (distributor).

Statistics Canada. *Table 276-0001—Employment Insurance Program, income beneficiaries by* province, type of income benefit and sex, computed annual average (persons), CANSIM (database), using E-STAT (distributor).

Statistics Canada. Table 051-0011—International migrants, by age group and sex, Canada, provinces, and territories, annual (persons), CANSIM (database), Using E-STAT (distributor).

Statistics Canada. Table 282-0012—Labour force survey estimates (LFS), employment by class of worker, North American Industry Classification System (NAICS) and sex, annual (persons).

Statistics Canada. Table 384-0004—Government sector revenue and expenditure, provincial economic accounts, annual (dollars), CANSIM (database), using E-STAT (distributor).

Statistics Canada. Table 384-0020—Government subsidies and capital transfers, provincial economic accounts, annual, CANSIM (database), using E-STAT (distributor).

Wood, Robert G., Brian Goseling, and Sarah Avellar. The Effects of Marriage on Health: A Synthesis of Recent Research Evidence. Washington, D.C.: Department of Health and Human Services, June 19, 2007: 1–68.

NEWSPAPERS AND MAGAZINES

"A slow-burning fuse: A special report on ageing populations," The Economist. June 27, 2009, p 5.

"A TILMA for all," Globe and Mail. January 15, 2009, A16.

Abama, Derek. "Canadian workers happy with jobs, says research group," Telegraph-Journal (Saint John). September 8, 2007, E1.

"The Absence of Fathers," Globe and Mail. July 31, 2007, A12.

"Against the Current," Globe and Mail. March 19, 2009, A12.

Agrell, Siri. "Harper not the only family man in this campaign," Globe and Mail. September 7, 2008, A4.

Anonymous. "Quebecers most stressed-out Canadians; Researchers urge study to probe root causes of high-anxiety levels of province's residents," Edmonton Journal. October 14, 2008, D6.

Anonymous. "AIG pelted with virtual tomatoes," Calgary Herald. March 24, 2009, D1.

"American Capitalism, R.I.P.," National Post. April 1, 2009, A10.

"A tale of two bellies; demography in America and Europe," The Economist, Vol. 364, Iss. 8287. August 22, 2002, 11.

Authier, Philip. "Quebec expects number of welfare households to fall; should be fewer cases because the economy is starting to pick up, minister says," Montreal Gazette. June 8, 1993, A6.

Bagnall, James. "1,300 Canadians lose jobs in March; but there's good news," Ottawa Citizen. April 10, 2009, A1.

Bagnall, Janet. "Quebec's saddest social challenge," Ottawa Citizen. February 28, 2008, A12.

"Bankrupt Canada?" Wall Street Journal (eastern edition). January 12, 1995, 14.

Bartlett, Bruce. "Large crowd turns out to hear pitch by Alta. company," Telegraph-Journal (Saint John). February 6, 2009, C4.

"The Battle for Brainpower," The Economist, Vol. 381, Iss. 8498. October 7, 2006, 9.

Beauchesne, Eric. "Skill shortage mounts; Canadian firms face labour 'tsunami,' Beatty says," Windsor Star. October 11, 2007, C1.

Becker, Gary, and Kevin Murphy. "Do not let the 'cure' destroy capitalism," Financial Times. March 20, 2009, 9.

Benham, Donald. "French issue won't go away for Pawley," Financial Post. March 29, 1986, 10.

Bertin, Oliver. "CN posts record results in '99," Globe and Mail. January 27, 2000, B5.

Bertin, Oliver. "CN chops 3,000 more jobs; railway has now cut half its staff since 1992; union chief condemns its 'greed,'" Globe and Mail. October 21, 1998, A1.

Blackwell, Tom. "MD uses lottery to cull patients," National Post. August 6, 2008, A1.

Boisvert, Yves. "L'autre secret sur le français," La Presse. January 25, 2008, A5.

"Briefing: China and the West, A time for muscle-flexing," The Economist. March 21, 2009, 27.

"Bulldozer Federalism," *Globe and Mail.* May 2, 1978, A6.

Burton, Brian. "Oilsands pace puts heat on pipeline builders," *National Post.* March 10, 2006, EJ11.

"Canada faces severe worker shortage; A time bomb has been created by demographics," *Times-Colonist* (Victoria). May 6, 2008, B2.

Canadian Press. "Quebec men more likely to commit suicide," *Sudbury Star.* May 5, 2004, 47.

Casey, Quentin. "Concern mounts over lack of next-generation fishermen," *Telegraph Journal* (Saint John). October 12, 2007, A1.

Cattaneo, Claudia. "Oilman bullish on Canada; 'Essential to grow oilsands,'" *National Post.* June 26, 2007, FP2.

Crowley, Brian Lee. "Equalization can be reformed: the Constitution is no excuse," *Chronicle Herald* (Saint John). April 21, 2004.

Dawe, Joseph. "Quebec pensions face crisis report; paper proposes lending some of the reserves of other Canadians' CPP to prop up ailing QPP," *Toronto Star.* January 17, 2008, B1.

Dufort, Daniel. "Le soliloque national," *Métropolitain,* Vol. I, No. 4. June 12, 2008, 8.

Elahi, Mahmood. "Satanic optimism of capitalism haunts us," *Ottawa Citizen.* March 30, 2009, A9.

Faiola, Anthony. "The end of American capitalism?" *Washington Post.* October 12, 2008, A1.

Faucher, Pascal. "Chauvins, les Québécois," *La Presse.* June 30, 2005, A2.

Ferretti, Lucia. "Histoire—Une Révolution tranquille très croyante," *Le Devoir.* April 12, 2008, F9.

Foot, Richard. "Despite recession, looming labour shortage big threat," Telegraph-Journal (Saint John). May 2, 2009, E4.

Foot, Richard. "Have-not no more: Canwest News Service Special Report," *Leader Post* (Regina). July 19, 2008, B8.

Friedman, Thomas L. "Greed, stupidity, dishonesty, and the market collapse," *Times-Colonist* (Victoria). December 1, 2008, A10.

Gagnon, Lysiane. "Quebec's Caisse of the blues," *Globe and Mail.* March 9, 2009, A13.

Gotlieb, Allan and Milos Barutciski. "Wanted: leadership on trade," *National Post.* February 7, 2009, A19.

Greenberg, Lee. "Ottawa to buck negative trend, report says; stable public-sector employment shields capital from downturn," *Ottawa Citizen.* April 1, 2009, D1.

Gunter, Lorne. "Court says no to sensible parenting; blatant state interference in father-daughter dispute sets dangerous precedent," *Edmonton Journal.* June 22, 2008, A14.

Gwyn, Richard. "Unchecked, unregulated greed breeds corruption," *Toronto Star.* March 20, 2009, A23.

Havemann, Judith. "Most find jobs after leaving welfare," *Washington Post.* May 27, 1999, A1.

Heinzel, Mark. "Economists watch Canada welfare reform," *Wall Street Journal.* July 31, 2000, A2.

Helliwell, John. "What makes people happy?" *Vancouver Sun.* October 30, 2007, B3.

Herbst, Moira. "Labor Shortages: Myth or Reality," *Business Week.* August 21, 2007.

Horrocks, Debbie. "Ottawa sides with Quebec to limit English education rights; Harper government supports Bill 104 restrictions before the Supreme Court," *Montreal Gazette.* December 11, 2008, A23.

Horn, Wade F. "There is no Substitute for Parents," *USA Today (Magazine).* Vol. 127, Iss. 2642 November 1, 1998: 34.

"Innovation Survey," *The Economist.* Vol. 385, Iss. 8550. October 13, 2007, 18.

Johnson, William. "A New Harmony?" *Globe and Mail.* May 23, 2008, A19.

Johnson, William. "The latest target: Anglophones," *Globe and Mail.* January 31, 2008, A17.

Johnson, William, Jeffrey Simpson, and Richard Cleroux. "Quebec angry but still undecided about federal sales tax reduction," *Globe and Mail.* April 12, 1978, A1.

Kelly-Gagnon, Michel. "Quebec Inc. must embrace globalization: Incestuous, government-supported model is outdated," *Montreal Gazette.* April 17, 2009, A17.

Kerr, Wendie. "Parizeau suggests a cooling of rhetoric," *Globe and Mail*. September 29, 1978, B1.

Klinkenberg, Marty. "Liberals' tax plan getting noticed," *Telegraph Journal* (Saint John). March 28, 2009, A1.

Lascelles, Eric. "The 'new normal'; when the recession ends, what will the economy look like? Likely an era of reduced GDP growth for North America," *National Post*. April 11, 2009, FP15.

Langlois, Simon. "Un portrait juste," *La Presse*. March 6, 2008, A27.

Lavoie, Gilbert. "Congrès des jeunes libéraux: Charest calme le jeu," *Le Soleil*. August 4, 2008, 4.

Lemieux, Pierre. "The (civil) servants rule," *Montreal Gazette*. March 11, 2002, D4.

Lerner, Sharon. "The motherhood experiment," *New York Times*. March 4, 2007, 20.

Marois, Pauline. "No to a bilingual Quebec," *La Tribune*. February 13, 2008, 15.

Marotte, Bertrand. "CN profit jumps 41% in first quarter," *Globe and Mail*. April 25, 2000, B10.

"Martinized," *The Province* (Vancouver). February 23, 1994, A28.

McMahon, Fred. "Welfare reform helps keep economy working," *National Post*. September 9, 1999, D5.

Meacham, Jon, and Evan Thomas. "We Are All Socialists Now (Cover story)," *Newsweek*, Vol. 153, No. 7. February 16, 2009: 22–24.

"Migration: A turning tide?" *The Economist*, Vol. 387, Iss. 8586. June 28, 2008, 32.

Migué, Jean-Luc. "Étatisme et déclin du Québec," *La Presse*. March 9, 1999, B3.

Mintz, Jack. "Tough, but right choices made: Blended tax important step for growth," *National Post*. March 27, 2009, A4.

Mintz, Jack. "Income splitting would help families," *National Post*. May 27, 2008, A12.

"No Replacing Traditional Families," *Globe and Mail*. September 13, 2007, A18.

Normand, François. "Larose est prêt à revoir le 'modèle québécois': 'Il faut décentraliser et débureaucratiser l'État,'" *Le Devoir*. May 13, 1999. A1.

"Oil Mergers. Well Matched," *The Economist*, March 28, 2009, 75.

Paillé, Michel. "Un progrès continu," *La Presse*. February 29, 2008, A17.

"The Price of Being Well," *The Economist*, Vol. 388, Iss. 8595. August 30, 2008, 60.

"Quebec after more francophones," *Montreal Gazette*. September 26, 1999, A4.

"Quebecers most stressed-out Canadians; researchers urge study to probe root causes of high-anxiety levels of province's residents," *Edmonton Journal*. October 14, 2008, D6.

"Quebec on the fast tract to self-rule: Parizeau," *Globe and Mail*. (December 1, 1990), A1.

"Quebec's quiet decline continues apace," *Montreal Gazette*. July 4, 2009, B6.

Radia, Andy. "Canada's birth-rate crisis," *Winnipeg Free Press*. March 2, 2009, A11.

Scott, Neil. "Western provinces talk of partnership," *Leader Post* (Regina). March 14, 2009, A9.

Scotton, Geoffrey. "The market works. The sky is not falling," *Calgary Herald*. August 30, 2006, A3.

Seguin, Rheal. "At gathering of leaders, Sarkozy to push for 'new form of capitalism,'" *Globe and Mail*. October 18, 2008, A16.

Seguin, Rheal. "Quebec pledges nearly $1-billion to boost work force," *Globe and Mail*, March 19, 2008, A11.

Seguin, Rheal. "Quebec yields to demands for probe of Caisse losses," *Globe and Mail*. March 13, 2009, A6.

Shingler, Ben. "Labor tops agenda; Meeting Premier Graham and his Quebec counterpart to discuss economic, social issues," *Telegraph-Journal* (Saint John). October 2, 2008, A1.

Silcoff, Sean. "Delivering a new Canada Post; is privatization the answer for an antiquated system using decades-old machinery?" *National Post*. September 17, 2007, FP1.

Simpson, Jeffrey. "Ottawa defies PQ with scheme for tax credits," *Globe and Mail*. May 16, 1978, A1.

"Society's great unspoken ill: The view from Montreal," *National Post*. June 6, 2006, A14.

Special Report. "Half a billion Americans?—Demography and the West," *The Economist*, Vol. 364, Iss. 8287. August 22, 2002, 22.

Saint-Pierre, Brigitte. "Fernand Dumont—Un grand penseur de notre époque," *Le Devoir*. May 3, 2008, G8.

Stastna, Kazi. "High suicide rate linked to Quiet Revolution," *Montreal Gazette*. February 6, 2007, A8.

Stastna, Kazi. "We're nicely educated but poor: Montrealers tops in getting payments from government," *Montreal Gazette*. February 10, 2004, A1.

Sturgeon, Jamie. "Jobs drought hits Ontario and Alberta; construction slump takes toll on former powers," *Financial Post*. March 13, 2009, FP6.

Swaine, Jon. "Three million families living in jobless households," *Daily Telegraph*. August 28, 2008, 4.

Thorpe, Jacqueline. "Economy risk real: Dodge, shrinking workforce must improve its productivity," *National Post*. June 14, 2007, A1.

Travers, James. "Public at tipping point on bailouts," *Toronto Star*. March 21, 2009, A10.

Veltman, Calvin. "De bonnes nouvelles," *La Presse*. February 11, 2008, A17.

Vieira, Paul. "Doha collapse to cost farmers $10M daily; Canada's position on supply management no help," *National Post*. July 31, 2008, FP3.

Vieira, Paul. "Ontario in decline; can Dalton McGuinty see the light and reverse the decay with his forthcoming budget?" *Financial Post*. March 21, 2009, FP1.

Wilkin, Martin. "Labour shortage is a myth: Companies can do more with less," *National Post*. July 5, 2006, WK. 7.

RESEARCH INSTITUTE REPORTS AND STUDIES

Alvarado, Angel, and Hugo J. Faria. "Government Size, Quality and Growth," *CESMA Working Paper*. April 2007.

Ambert, Anne-Marie. *Cohabitation and Marriage: How Are They Related*. Ottawa: Vanier Institute, September 2005.

Armstrong, Matthew. "Help Wanted: Long-term vacancies grow for Canada's entrepreneurs," *CFIB Research*. March 2007: 1-9.

Baker, Michael, Jonathon Gruber, and Kevin Milligan, "What Can We Learn from Quebec's Universal Childcare Program?" *C.D. Howe Institute E-Brief*. February 1, 2006: 1–5.

Banerjee, Robin and William Robson. *Faster and Younger? Not so much: Immigration's Impact on Canadian Workforce and Growth and Age Structure*. Toronto: C.D. Howe Institute, 2008.

Bibby, Reginald. *The Future Families Project: A Survey of Canadian Hopes and Dreams*. Ottawa: Vanier Institute of the Family, 2004.

Bish, Robert. "Organization and Opportunities: Local Government Services Production in Greater Saint John," *AIMS Urban Futures Series*, Paper no. 4. November 2004: 1–40.

Boyer, Marcel. "Quebec's Disappointing Economic Performance in the Last 25 Years," *MEI Economic Note*. May 2007: 1–4.

Boyle Torrey, Barbara, and Nicholas Eberstadt. "The Northern American Fertility Divide," *Policy Review*, No. 132. August and September 2005: 39–55.

Brooks, Arthur C. "I Love My Work," *American Magazine*, Vol. 1, Iss. 6. September/October 2007: 21–28.

Burniaux, Jean-Marc, Romain Duval and Florence Jaumotte. "Coping with Ageing: A Dynamic Approach to Quantify the Impact of Alternative Policy Options on Future Labour Supply in OECD Countries," OECD Economics Department Working Paper No. 371. 2004: 1-91.

Canadian Council on Learning. *Lessons in Learning: More Education, Less Employment: Immigrants and the Labor Market*. Ottawa: CCL, October 2008.

Canadian Restaurant and Foodservices Association. *Help Wanted: The Labour Shortage Crisis and Canada's Foodservice Industry*. Toronto: CRFA, June 2006: 1-9.

Canadian Taxpayers Federation. *On the Dole: Businesses, Lobbyists and Industry Canada's Subsidy Programs.* Ottawa: CTF, January 2007.

Canadian Taxpayers Federation. *La Belle Province: Same Ugly Story, A 12-Year Quantitative Analysis of Canada Economic Development for the Regions of Quebec.* Ottawa: CTF, June 2002.

Canadian Taxpayers Federation. *Peeling Back the Onion: A Taxpayers Audit of Technology Partnerships Canada.* Ottawa: CTF, February 2002.

Centre for Social Justice. *The State of the Nation Report: Fractured Families.* London: Centre for Social Justice, December 2006.

Chen, Duanjie, and Jack Mintz. "Limited Horizons: The 2008 Report on the Federal and Provincial Budgetary Tax Policies," *C.D. Howe Institute Commentary*, No. 270. July 2008: 1–20.

Clemens, Jason, and Niels Veldhuis. *Productivity, Prosperity and Business Taxes*: An Occasional Paper for the Centre for Budgetary Studies. Vancouver: Fraser Institute, January 2006: 1–46.

Clemens, Jason, Niels Veldhuis, and Amela Karabegovic. "Explaining Canada's High Unionization Rates," *Fraser Institute Alert.* August 2005: 1–7.

Crowley, Brian Lee, and Bobby O'Keefe. "The Flypaper Effect: Does Equalization Really Contribute to Better Public Services, or Does It Just 'Stick to' Politicians and Civil Servants?" *AIMS Commentary*, No. 2. June 2006: 1–11.

Daly, Kevin. *Gender Inequality, Growth and Global Aging*, Global Economics Paper No. 154. New York: Goldman Sachs, April 3, 2007.

Douglas, Roger Sir. *Short Term Pain for Long Term Gain.* Halifax: AIMS, 1995.

Dowbiggin, Ian. "Where Have All the Babies Gone? The 'Birth Dearth' and What to Do about It," A presentation at the IMFC Family Policy Conference. Ottawa: Institute for Marriage and Family Values Canada, September 26, 2006.

Drache, Daniel. "The Canada-U.S. Income Gap," *CSLS Research Reports.* June 2000: 1–6.

Elton, David, et al. *Where Are They Now? Assessing the Impact of Welfare Reform on Former Recipients, 1993–1996.* Calgary: Canada West Foundation, 1997.

Fagan, Patrick F., and Robert Rector. "The Effects of Divorce on America," *Heritage Backgrounder*, No. 1373. June 5, 2000: 1–34.

Fagan, Patrick. "The Real Root Causes of Violent Crime: The Breakdown of Marriage, Family and Community," *Heritage Backgrounder*, No. 1026. March 17, 1995: 1–50.

Focus on the Family Canada. *Canadian Attitudes on the Family*, A National Survey Conducted by the Strategic Counsel. Ottawa: Focus on the Family Canada, 2002.

Foot, David K. "Population Aging," in J. Leonard, C. Ragan, and F. St-Hilaire (eds.), *A Canadian Priorities Agenda: Policy Choices to Improve Economic and Social Well-Being.* Montreal: Institute for Research on Public Policy, 2007: 181–213.

Gholz, Eugene, and Daryl G. Press. *Energy Alarmism: The Myths That Make Americans Worry about Oil.* Washington, D.C., Cato Institute Policy Analysis no. 589, April 5, 2007.

Gresser, Edward. "Healthy Factories, Anxious Workers—Or, Why Lou Dobbs Is Wrong," *Policy Report.* February 2007: 1–12.

Horn, Wade F. "Wedding Bells Blues: Marriage and Welfare Reform," *Brookings Institution Note.* Summer 2001.

Howitt, Peter. "Innovation, Competition and Growth: A Schumpeterian Perspective on Canada's Economy," *C.D. Howe Institute Commentary*, No. 246. April 2007: 1–19.

Hymowitz, Kay S. "Child-Man in the Promised Land: Today's Single Young Men Hang out in a Hormonal Limbo between Adolescence and Adulthood," *City Journal.* Winter 2008.

Hymowitz, Kay S. "Marriage and Caste in America: Separate and Unequal Families in a Post-Marital Age," *City Journal.* Winter 2006.

Ikenson, Daniel. "Thriving in a Global Economy: The Truth about U.S. Manufacturing and Trade," *Trade Policy Analysis*, No. 35. August 28, 2007: 1–28.

Kelly-Gagnon, Michel. "Our Free Market Past," *FCPP Perspective*. Winnipeg: Frontier Centre for Public Policy, August 1, 2005.

Kirby, Jill. *Broken Hearts: Family Decline and the Consequences for Society*. London: Centre for Policy Studies, 2002.

Kozhaya, Norma. "The Retirement Age in Quebec: A Worrying Situation," *MEI Economic Note*. June 2007: 1–4.

Kozhaya, Norma. "Quebec's Relative Poverty," *MEI Economic Note*. May 2006: 1–4.

Kozhaya, Norma. "The Consequences of a Strong Union Presence in Quebec," *MEI Economic Note*. September 2005: 1–4.

Lawson, Robert, and Michel Kelly-Gagnon. "The Scope of Government and the Wealth of Quebecers," *MEI Economic Note*. February 2001: 1–5.

Lal, Deepak. *The Poverty of "Development Economics,"* 3rd ed. London: Institute of Economic Affairs, 2000.

Lerman, Robert I. *Marriage and the Economic Well-Being of Families with Children: A Review of the Literature*. Washington, D.C.: Urban Institute, July 2002: 1–38.

Loprest, Pamela. *Families Who Left Welfare: Who Are They and How Are They Doing?* Washington, D.C., Urban Institute, 1999.

Marcil, Jacques, and Owen Jung. *Against the Grain: Saskatchewan Economic Profile and Forecast*. Canada West Foundation, Calgary, 2009.

McMahon, Fred. *Road to Growth: How Lagging Economies Become Prosperous*. Halifax: AIMS, 2000.

McNiven, J., with Michael Foster. *The Developing Workforce Problem: Confronting Canadian Labour Shortages in the Coming Decades*. Halifax: Atlantic Institute for Market Studies, 2009.

Measuring Ontario's Prosperity: Developing and Economic Indicator System. Institute for Competitiveness & Prosperity Working Paper No. 2. August 2002: 1–48.

Migué, Jean-Luc. *Étatisme et déclin du Québec: Bilan de la révolution tranquille*. Montreal: Montreal Economic Institute, 1999.

Milligan, Kevin. "Quebec's Baby Bonus: Can Public Policy Raise Fertility?" *C.D. Howe Institute Backgrounder*. Toronto: C.D. Howe Institute, January 27, 2002: 1–9.

Milway, Jim, and Roger Martin. *Commercialization and the Canadian Business Environment: A Systems Perspective*, Comments on Public Policy Support for Innovation and Commercialization in Canada. Toronto: Institute for Competitiveness and Prosperity, July 2005.

Mueller, John D. *Family-Friendly Fiscal Policy to Weather "Demographic Winter."* Washington, D.C.: Ethics and Public Policy Center, May 2007.

Mulligan, Casey B. *Work Ethic and Family Background*. Washington: Employment Policy Institute, April 1997: 1–32.

Murray, David. "Marriage and Economic Liberty," *Acton Institute Religion and Liberty*. Vol. 5, No. 6. November/December 1995: 5–7.

Parke, Mary. "Are Married Parents Really Better for Children? What Research Says about the Effects of Family Structure on Child Well-Being," *Center for Law and Social Policy Brief*. May 2003: 1–13.

Popenoe, David. *Cohabitation, Marriage and Child Wellbeing: A Cross-National Perspective*, Rutgers State University of New Jersey: The National Marriage Project, June 2008: 1–26.

Popenoe, David, and Barbara Dafoe Whitehead, *The State of Our Unions: The Social Health of Marriage in America, 2007*. Rutgers State University of New Jersey: The National Marriage Project, 2007.

Popenoe, David, and Barbara Whitehead. *The State of Our Unions: The Social Health of Marriage in America, 2004*, Rutgers State University of New Jersey: The National Marriage Project, 2004.

Rector, Robert E., Patrick F. Fagan, and Kirk A. Robinson. "Marriage: Still the Safest Place for Women and Children," *Heritage Foundation Backgrounder*, No. 1732. March 9, 2004.

Rector, Robert E., and Patrick F. Fagan. "How Welfare Harms Kids," *Heritage Foundation Backgrounder*, No. 1084. June 5, 1996.

Richards, John. "Reducing Poverty: What Has Worked, and What Should Come Next," *C.D. Howe Institute Commentary*, No. 255. Toronto: C.D. Howe Institute, October 2007: 1–32.

Richards, John. "Now that the Coat fits the Cloth: Spending Wisely in a Trimmed-Down Age," *C.D. Howe Institute Commentary*, No. 143. June 2000: 1–60.

Robson, William B.P., and Yvan Guillemette. *No Elixir for Youth: Immigration Cannot Keep Canada Young*. Toronto: C.D. Howe Institute, September 2006: 1–21.

Schafer, Chris. "Welfare Reforms Jeopardized?" *Fraser Forum*. June 2002: 3–4.

Seymour, David. "Telecommunications Privatization, Services, and Provincial Well-being: A Comparison of Company Performance at SaskTel and MTS," *FCPP Policy Series*, No. 34. October 27: 1–14.

Smith, Iain Duncan. *Breakthrough Britain: Vol. 2, Economic Dependency and Worklessness*. London: Centre for Social Justice, July 2007.

Smith, Iain Duncan. *Breakthrough Britain: Vol. 1, Family Breakdown*. London: Centre for Social Justice, July 2007.

Stevenson, Betty, and Justin Wolfers. *The Paradox of Declining Female Happiness*. Philadelphia: Wharton School of Business, University of Pennsylvania, September 2007.

TD Financial Group. "Converting Quebec's Strength into Prosperity," *TD Economics Special Report*. April 10, 2007: 1–26.

Taylor, Amy, and Mark Anielski. *The Alberta GPI Accounts: Family Breakdown Report #13*. Drayton Valley, Alta.: Pembina Institute, 2001.

Taylor, John B. *Getting Off Track: How Government Actions and Interventions Caused, Prolonged and Worsened the Financial Crisis*. Stanford: Hoover Institution Press, 2009.

Taylor, Paul, Cary Funk, and April Clark. *From 1997 to 2007: Fewer Mothers Prefer Full-Time Work*. Washington D.C.: Pew Research Center, 2007.

Tomita, Toshiki. "The Need for Redefining Japan's Government Debt Management Policy," *NRI Papers*, No. 42. Tokyo: Normura Research Institute, February 2002: 1–16.

Wu, Zheng. "Recent Trends in Marriage Patterns in Canada," *Policy Options*, Vol. 19, No. 7. Montreal: IRPP, September 1998: 3–6.

Zweig, David and Chung Siu Fung. *Redefining the Brain Drain: China's Diaspora Options*, Working Paper No.1. Hong Kong: Center on China's Transnational Relations, 2005.

PERIODICALS

Akerlof, George A. "Men without Children," *Economic Journal*, Vol. 108, No. 447. March 1998: 287–309.

Allen, Douglas. "Welfare and the Family: The Canadian Experience," *Journal of Labour Economics*, Vol. 11, No. 1. January 1993: S201–S223.

Allen, Douglas., "An Inquiry in the State's Role in Marriage," *Journal of Economic Behavior and Organization*, Vol. 13. 1990: 171–91.

Becker, Gary. "On the Economics of the Family: Reply to a Skeptic," *American Economic Review*, Vol. 79, No. 3. June 1989: 514–18.

Becker, Gary. "Family Economics and Macro Behaviour," *American Economic Review*, Vol. 78, No. 1. March 1988: 1–13.

Becker, Gary. "Human Capital, Effort and the Sexual Division of Labor," *Journal of Labor Economics*, Vol. 3, No. 1. January 1985: S33–S58.

Becker, Gary, and Robert Barro. "A Reformulation of the Economic Theory of Fertility," *Quarterly Journal of Economics*, Vol. 102, No. 4. February 1988: 1–25.

Béland, Daniel, and André Lecours. "Sub-state Nationalism and the Welfare State: Quebec and Canadian Federalism," *Nations and Nationalism*, Vol. 12, No. 1. 2006: 77–96.

Blakey, T.A., S.C.D. Collings, and J. Atkinson, "Unemployment and Suicide: Evidence for a

Causal Association?," *Journal of Epidemiology and Community Health*, Vol. 57. 2003: 594–600.

Boycko, Maxim, et al. "A Theory of Privatisation," *Economic Journal*, Vol. 106, No. 435. March 1996: 309–19.

Bradbury, John. "State Corporations and Resource Based Development in Quebec, Canada: 1960–1980," *Economic Geography*, Vol. 82, No. 1. January 1982: 45–61.

Breton, Albert. "The Economics of Nationalism," *Journal of Political Economy*, Vol. 72, No. 4. August 1964: 376–86.

Brooks, Stephen. "The State as Financier: A Comparison of the Caisse de depot et placement du Quebec and Alberta Heritage Savings Trust Fund," *Canadian Public Policy*, Vol. 13, No. 3. September, 1987: 318–29.

Butterworth, Peter A., Kate Fairweather, Kaarin J. Anstey, and Timothy D. Windsor. "Hopelessness, Demoralization and Suicidal Behaviour: The Backdrop to Welfare Reform in Australia," *Australian and New Zealand Journal of Psychiatry*, Vol. 40, Iss. 8. August 2006: 648–56.

Caldwell, Gary, and Daniel Fournier. "The Quebec Question: A Matter of Population," *Canadian Journal of Sociology*, Vol. 12, No. 1/2. Spring 1987: 16–41.

Charron, Lucie. "Canada's Pension Predicament: The Widening Gap between Public and Private Sector Retirement Trends and Pension Plans," *CFIB Research*. January 2007: 1–13.

"Community without Politics," *Harvard Law Review*, Vol. 102, No. 4. February 1989: 913–19.

Congleton, Roger D. "Book Review of Vito Tanzi and Ludger Schuknecht, *Public Spending in the 20th Century a Global Perspective*," *Public Choice* No. 108, No. 1-2. July 2001: 197–200.

Courchene, Thomas J. "A Market Perspective on Regional Disparities," *Canadian Public Policy*, Vol. 7, No. 4. Autumn, 1981: 506–18.

Dawson, Deborah. "Family Structure and Children Health and Well-Being: Data from the 1988 National Health Interview Survey on Child Health," *Journal of Marriage and the Family*, Vol. 53, No. 3. August 1991: 573–84.

Di Tella, Rafael, and Robert MacCulloch. "Some Uses of Happiness Data in Economics," *Journal of Economic Perspectives*, Vol. 20, No. 1. Winter 2006: 25–46.

Dooley, Martin D. "The Evolution of Welfare Participation among Canadian Lone Mothers, 1973–1991," *Canadian Journal of Economics*, Vol. 32, No. 3. May 1999: 589–612.

Dooley, David, Ralph Catalano, and Georjeanna Wilson. "Depression and Unemployment: Panel Findings from the Epidemiologic Catchment Area Study," *American Journal of Community Psychology*, Vol. 22, No. 6. 1994: 745–65.

Duckworth, Angela L., and Martin E.P. Seligman. "Self-Discipline Outdoes IQ in Predicting Academic Performances of Adolescents," *Psychological Science*, Vol. 16, Iss. 12. December 2005: 939–44.

Easterlin, Richard. "Income and Happiness: Towards a Unified Theory," *Economic Journal*, Vol. 111. No. 473. July 2001, 465–84.

Easterlin, Richard. "Will Raising the Incomes of All Increase the Happiness of All?" *Journal of Economic Behavior and Organization*, Vol. 27, No. 1. June 1995, 35–48.

Ezrati, Milton. "Japan's Aging Economics," *Foreign Affairs*, May/June 1997: 96–106.

Finnie, Ross, and Arthur Sweetman. "Poverty Dynamics: Empirical Evidence for Canada," *Canadian Journal of Economics* Vol. 36, No 2. 2003: 291–325.

Fortin, Bernard, Guy Lacroix, and Jean-Francois Thibault. "The Interaction of UI and Welfare, and the Dynamics of Welfare Participation of Single Parents," *Canadian Public Policy*, Vol. 25. November 1999 S115–S132.

Gallagher, Maggie, and Joshua Baker. "Do Moms and Dads Matter? Evidence from the Social Sciences on Family Structure and the Best Interests of the Child," *Margins*, Vol. 4. 2004: 161–80.

George, M.V., F. Nault, and A. Romaniuc. "Effects of Fertility and International Migration on

Changing Age Composition in Canada," *Statistical Journal of the United Nations*, ECE Vol. 8, No. 1. 1991: 13–24.

Grenier, Gilles. "Earnings by Language Group in Quebec in 1980 and Emigration from Quebec between 1976 and 1981," *Canadian Journal of Economics*, Vol. 20, No. 4. November 1987: 774–91.

Gunderson, Morley. "Two Faces of Union Voice in the Public Sector," *Journal of Labor Research*, Vol. 26, No. 3. Summer 2005: 393–414.

Gunderson, Morley. "Earnings Differentials between the Public and Private Sectors," *Canadian Journal of Economics*, Vol. 12, No. 2. May 1979: 228–42.

Gwartney, James, Randall Holcombe, and Robert Lawson. "The Scope of Government and the Wealth of Nations," *Cato Journal*, Vol. 18, No. 2. 1998: 163–91.

Hill, Roderick. "Happiness in Canada Since World War II," *Social Indicators Research*, Vol. 65. 2004: 109–23.

Jin, Robert. "The Impact of Unemployment on Health: A Review of the Evidence," *Canadian Medical Association Journal*, Vol. 153, No. 5. September 1995: 529–540.

Kerr, Don. "Family Transformations and the Well-being of Children: Recent Evidence from Canadian Longitudinal Data," *Journal of Comparative Family Studies*, Vol. 35, Iss. 1. Winter 2004: 73–90.

Kerr, Don, and Roderic Beaujot. "Family Relations, Low Income, and Child Outcomes: A Comparison of Canadian Children in Intact-, Step-, and Lone-parent Families," *International Journal of Comparative Sociology*, Vol. 43. April 2002: 134–52.

King, Suzanne. "Unemployment and Mental Health in French Canada," *Journal of Counseling and Development*, Vol. 67, No. 6. February 1989: 358–60.

Klie, Shannon. "QPP Faces Crisis, CPP's Healthy Reserve Should Be Used to Cover Quebec's Shortfall: Report," *Canadian HR Reporter*. February 25, 2008: 1.

Korenman, Sander, and David Neumark. "Does Marriage Really Make Men More Productive?" *Journal of Human Resources*, Vol. 26, No. 2. Spring 1991: 282–307.

Kostov, Chris. "Canada-Quebec Immigration Agreements (1971-1991) and their Impact on Federalism," American Review of Canadian Studies, Vol. 38, Iss. 1. Spring 2008: 91-103.

Krieger, A.O. "The Political Economy of the Rent-Seeking Society," *American Economic Review* Vol. 64, 1974: 291–303.

Lemieux, Thomas, and Kevin Milligan. "Incentive Effects of Social Assistance: A Regression Discontinuity Approach," *Journal of Econometrics*. Vol. 142, 2008: 807–28.

Lichter, Daniel T., Diane K. McLaughlin, and David C. Ribar. "Welfare and the Rise in Female-Headed Families," *American Journal of Sociology*, Vol. 103, No. 1. July 1997: 112–43.

Lindbeck, Assar, and Sten Nyberg. "Raising Children to Work Hard: Altruism, Work Norms, and Social Insurance," *Quarterly Journal of Economics*, Vol. 121. November 2006: 1473–1503.

Lindbeck, Assar. "Hazardous Welfare-State Dynamics," *American Economic Review*, Vol. 85, No. 2. May 1995: 9–15.

Longman, Phillip. "The Return of Patriarchy," *Foreign Policy*, Iss. 153. March/April 2006: 56–65.

Madrick, Jeff. "Beyond Rubinomics (Cover story)," *Nation*. January 12, 2009: 14–18.

McCloskey, Deirdre. "Bourgeois Virtues?" *Cato Policy Report*, Vol. XXVIII, No. 3. May/June 2006: 6–11.

McMunn, Anne M., et al. "Children's Emotional and Behavioural Well-Being and the Family Environment: Findings from the Health Survey for England," *Social Sciences and Medicine*, Vol. 53, No. 4. August 2001: 423–40.

Milligan, Kevin. "Subsidizing the Stork: New Evidence on Tax Incentives and Fertility," *Review of Economics and Statistics*, Vol. 87, No. 3. August 2005: 539–55.

Morissette, Rene and Anick Johnson, "Are Good Jobs Disappearing in Canada?" *Economic Policy Review*, Vol. 11, Iss. 1. August 2005: 23-56.

Murphy, Michael. "The Evolution of Cohabitation in Britain, 1960–1995," *Population Studies*, Vol. 54, No. 1. March 2000: 43–56.

Norcliffe, Glen. "Regional Unemployment in Canada in the 1981–1984 Recession," *Canadian Geographer*, Vol. 31, No. 2, 1987: 150–59.

Palda, Filip. "Fiscal Churning and Political Efficiency," *Kyklos*, Vol. 50. 1997: 189–206.

Palley, Thomas, and Robert LaJeunesse. "Social Attitudes, Labor Law, and Union Organizing: Toward a New Economics of Union Density," *Journal of Economic Behavior & Organization*, Vol. 62. 2007: 237–54.

Picard, Derek. "A Comparison of Public-Sector and Private-Sector Wages," *CFIB Research*. October 2003: 1–19.

Picot, Garnett. "The Deteriorating Economic Welfare of Canadian Immigrants," *Canadian Journal of Urban Research*, Vol. 13, No. 1. Winter 2003: 25-45.

Pollard, Michael S., and Zheng Wu. "Divergence of Marriage Patterns in Quebec and Elsewhere in Canada." *Population and Development Review*, Vol. 24, No. 2. June 1998: 329–56.

PricewaterhouseCoopers. "Insights into staff retention for private companies," *Business Insights*. January 2007: 1-4.

Raisian, John. "Union Dues and Wage Premiums," *Journal of Labor Research*, Vol. IV, No. 1. Winter 1983: 1–18.

Rose, Joseph B., Gary N. Chaison, and Enrique de la Garza. "A Comparative Analysis of Public Sector Restructuring in the US, Canada, Mexico and the Caribbean," *Journal of Labor Research*, Vol. 21, No. 4. Fall 2000: 601–25.

Rouillard, Jacques. "La Revolution Tranquille, Rupture ou Tournant?," *Journal of Canadian Studies*. Vol. 32, No. 4. Winter, 1998: 23–51.

Ryten, Eva. "Physician-Workforce and Educational Planning in Canada: Has the Pendulum Swung too Far?" *Canadian Medical Journal Association*, Vol. 152, No. 9. May 1995: 1395–398.

Sahib, Padma Rao, and Xinhua Gu. "To Tie the Knot or Not: Cohabitation, Marriage, and Individuals' Attitudes to Risk," *Demographic Research*, Vol. 6. May 2002: 355–82.

Shapiro, Daniel, and Morton Stelcner. "Language and Earnings in Quebec: Trends over Twenty Years, 1970–1990," *Canadian Public Policy*, Vol. 23, No. 2. June 1997: 115–40.

Sharpe, Andrew. "Lessons for Canada from International Productivity Experience," *International Productivity Monitor*, No. 14. Spring 2007: 1–18.

Skogstad, Grace. "Canadian Federalism, Internationalization and Quebec Agriculture: Dis-Engagement, Re-Integration?" *Canadian Public Policy*, Vol. 24, No. 1. March, 1998: 27–48.

Starrels, Marjorie, et al. "The Feminization of Poverty in the United States: Gender, Race, Ethnicity, and Family Factors," *Journal of Family Issues*, Vol. 15, No. 4. December 1994: 590–607.

Strohschein, Lisa, Noralou Roos, and Marni Brownell. "Family Structure Histories and High School Completion: Evidence from a Population-based Registry," *Canadian Journal of Sociology*, Vol. 34, No, 1. 2009: 83–103.

Tanzi, Vito. "The Economic Role of the State in the Twenty-First Century," *Cato Journal*, Vol. 25, No. 3. Fall 2005: 617–39.

Tullock, Gordon. "Book Review of Niskanen's *Bureaucracy and Representative Government*," *Public Choice*, Vol. 12, Iss. 1. Spring 1972: 119–24.

Tullock, Gordon. "The Welfare Costs of Tariffs, Monopolies and Theft," *Western Economic Journal* Vol. 5. 1967: 224–32.

White, James M. "Work-Family Stage and Satisfaction with Work-Family Balance," *Journal of Comparative Family Studies*, Vol. 30, No. 2. Spring 1999: 163–76.

"World Congress of Families Reacts to UNFPA Leader Who Says Family Breakdown Is a 'Triumph' for Human Rights," *Mental Health Weekly Digest*. March 9, 2009, 298.

BOOKS AND PAMPHLETS

Ajzenstat, Janet. *The Canadian Founding*. Montreal and Kingston: McGill-Queen's University Press, 2007.

Ajzenstat, Janet. *Once and Future Canadian Democracy: An Essay in Political Thought*. Montreal and Kingston: McGill-Queen's University Press, 2003.

Ajzenstat, Janet, et al. (ed). *Canada's Founding Debates*. Toronto: Stoddart Publishing, 1999.

Arbour, Pierre. *Quebec Inc. and the Temptation of State Capitalism*. Montreal and Toronto: Robert Davies Publishing, 1993.

Arendt, Hannah. *The Human Condition*. Chicago: University of Chicago Press, 1958.

Armstrong Robert. *Structure and Change: An Economic History of Quebec*. Toronto: Gage Publishing Limited, 1984.

Baldwin, John and Peter Hanel. Innovation and Knowledge Creation in an Open Economy: Canadian Industry and International Implications. New York: Cambridge University Press, 2003.

Banting, Keith. *The Welfare State and Canadian Federalism*. Kingston: McGill-Queen's University Press, 1987.

Beaumont, P.B. "Public Sector Industrial Relations in Europe," in Dale Berman, Morley Gunderson, and Douglas Hyatt (eds.), *Public Sector Employment in a Time of Transition*. Madison, Wisc.: Industrial Relations Research Centre, 1996: 283–307.

Becker, Gary. *A Treatise on the Family*. Cambridge: Harvard University Press, 1981.

Behiels, Michael. "Quebec: Social Transformation and Ideological Renewal, 1940–1976," in Michael D. Behiels (ed.), *Quebec since 1945: Selected Readings*. Toronto: Copp Clark Pitman Limited, 1987: 21–45.

Behiels, Michael. *Prelude to the Quiet Revolution: Liberalism versus Neo-Nationalism, 1945–1960*. Kingston and Montreal: McGill-Queen's University Press, 1985.

Behrman, Jere R., Robert Pollack, and Paul Taubman. *From Parent to Child: Intrahousehold Allocations and Intergenerational Relations in the United States*. Chicago: University of Chicago Press, 1995.

Bercuson, David, and Barry Cooper. *Derailed: The Betrayal of the National Dream*. Toronto: Key Porter Books, 1994.

Berger, Carl. *The Sense of Power: Studies in the Ideas of Canadian Imperialism, 1867-1914*. University of Toronto Press. Toronto, 1970.

Berman, William C. *America's Right Turn: From Nixon to Clinton*. Baltimore: JHU Press, 1998.

Bernanke, Ben. *Essays on the Great Depression*. Princeton, N.J.: Princeton University Press, 2005.

Bhagwati, Jagdish. *In Defense of Globalization*. Washington D.C.: Oxford University Press, 2004.

Blankenhorn, David. *The Future of Marriage*. New York: Encounter Books, 2007.

Bliss, Michael. *Right Honourable Men: The Descent of Canadian Politics from Macdonald to Chrétien*. Toronto: HarperCollins Publishers, 2004.

Boessenkool, Kenneth J. *Back to Work: Learning from the Alberta Welfare Reform Experience*. Toronto: C.D. Howe Institute, April 1997.

Bothwell, Robert, Ian Drummond, and John English. *Canada since 1945: Power, Politics and Provincialism*. Toronto: University of Toronto Press, 1981.

Brinig, Margaret F. "The Effects of Divorce on Wives," in John Richards and Douglas Allen (eds.). *It Takes Two: The Family in Law and Finance*. Toronto: C.D. Howe Institute, 1999: 36–63.

Brody, Sylvia and Sidney Axelrad. *Mothers, Fathers and Children: Explorations in the Formation of Character in the First Seven Years*. New York: International University Press, 1978.

Brownlee, Eliot W. *Dynamics of Ascent: A History of the American Economy*. New York: Alfred A. Knopf, 1979.

Bruce, Harry. *The Pig that Flew: The Battle to Privatize Canadian National*. Vancouver: Douglas & McIntyre, 1997.

Bryden, P.E. *Planners and Politicians: Liberal Politics and Social Policy 1957–1968.* Montreal and Kingston: McGill-Queen's University Press, 1997.

Conway, John F. *The Canadian Family in Crisis,* 4th ed. Toronto: James Lorimer & Company, 2001.

Cook, Ramsay. *The Politics of John W. Dafoe and the Free Press.* Toronto: University of Toronto Press, 1963.

Courchene, Thomas (with Colin Telmer). *From Heartland to North American Region States: An Interpretative Essay on the Fiscal, Social and Federal Evolution of Ontario.* University of Toronto: Centre for Public Management, 1998.

Coyne, Andrew. "Social Spending, Taxes, and the Debt: Trudeau's Just Society," in Andrew Cohen and J.L. Granatstein (eds.), *Trudeau's Shadow: The Life and Legacy of Pierre Elliott Trudeau.* Toronto: Vintage Canada, 1999: 223–242.

Cronan, Shelia. "Marriage," Anne Koedt, Ellen Levine, and Anita Rapone (eds.) *Radical Feminism.* New York: Quadrangle Books, 1973: 213–21.

Crowley, Brian Lee, and Bruce Winchester. *The Mystery of the Missing Fiscal Imbalance.* Halifax: AIMS, 2005.

Cudd, E. *Analyzing Oppression.* New York: Oxford University Press, 2006.

Dalrymple, Theodore. *Our Culture, What's Left of It: The Mandarins and the Masses.* Chicago: Ivan R. Dee, 2005.

Dion, Léon. *The Unfinished Revolution.* Montreal and London: McGill-Queen's University Press, 1976.

Dubuc, Alain. *Éloge de la Richesse.* Québec City: Voix parallèles, 2006.

English, John. *The Worldly Years: The Life of Lester Pearson, 1949–1972.* Toronto: Alfred A. Knopf, 1992.

Erikson, Erik H. *Childhood and Society.* New York: W.W. Norton and Co., 1950.

Falardeau, Jean-Charles. *Étienne Parent, 1802–1874.* Montréal: Les Éditions La Presse Ltée, 1975.

Ferguson, Barry. *Remaking Liberalism: The Intellectual Legacy of Adam Shortt, O.D. Skelton, and W.A. Mackintosh, 1890–1925.* Montreal and Kingston: McGill-Queen's University Press, 1993.

Flaith, David. *The Japanese Economy,* 2nd ed. London: Oxford University Press, 2005.

Foot, David. "Population Aging," in J. Leonard, C. Ragan, and F. St-Hilaire (eds.), *A Canadian Priorities Agenda: Policy Choices to Improve Economic and Social Well-Being.* Montreal: Institute for Research on Public Policy, 2007.

Foot, David. *Boom, Bust and Echo: How to Profit from the Coming Demographic Shift.* Toronto: Macfarlane, Walter & Ross, 1996.

Fortin, Pierre. "The Baby Boomers' Tab: Already $40 Billion in 2020," in Rudyard Griffiths (ed.), *Canada in 2020: Twenty Leading Voices Imagine Canada's Future.* Toronto: Key Porter Books, 2008.

Fraser, Matthew. *Quebec Inc.: French-Canadian Entrepreneurs and the New Business Elite.* Toronto: Key Porter Books, 1987.

Friedan, Betty. *The Feminist Mystique.* New York: W.W. Norton & Company, 1963.

Friedman, Milton, and Anna Schwartz. *The Great Contraction, 1929–33.* Princeton, N.J.: Princeton University Press, 1965.

Friedman, Milton. *Capitalism and Freedom.* Chicago: University of Chicago Press, 1964.

Griffiths, Rudyard. *Who We Are: A Citizen's Manifesto.* Vancouver/Toronto: Douglas & McIntyre, 2009.

Guest, Denis. *The Emergence of Social Security in Canada.* Vancouver: University of British Columbia Press, 1985.

Gunderson, Morley. *Impact of Labour Market Institutions and Regulation.* Halifax: AIMS, forthcoming.

Gunderson, Morley. "The Public-Private Sector Compensation Controversy," in Gene Swimmer and Mark Thompson (eds.), *Conflict or Compromise: The Future of Public Sector Industrial Relations.* Montreal: Institute for Research on Public Policy, 1984: 1–44.

Harraway, Donna J. "Gender for a Marxist Dictionary: The Sexual Politics of a Word," in Richard Parker and Peter Aggleton (eds.), *Culture, Society, and Sexuality.* Philadelphia, Routledge, 1995: 76–96.

Heintzman, Ralph. *The Struggle for Life: The French Daily Press and the Problems of Economic Growth in the Age of Laurier, 1896–1929.* Ph.D. thesis, York University, 1977.

Hewlett, Sylvia Ann. *Creating a Life: Professional Women and the Quest for Children.* New York: Talk Miramax Books, 2002.

Hjertqvist, Johan. *Swedish Health Care in Transition: Markets and Competition Here to Stay.* AIMS, Halifax, 2001.

Holmes, Kim, Edward Feulner, and Mary Anastasia O'Grady. *2008 Index of Economic Freedom.* Washington D.C.: Heritage Foundation and *Wall Street Journal,* 2008.

Hymowitz, Kay. *Marriage and Caste in America: Separate and Unequal Families in a Post-Martial Age.* Chicago: Ivan R. Dee, 2007.

Inglehart, Ronald, Miguel Basañez, and Alejandro Moreno. *Human Values and Beliefs: A Cross-Cultural Source Book.* Ann Arbor: University of Michigan Press, 1998.

Isgut, Alberto, Lance Bialas, and James Milway. *Explaining Canada-U.S. Differences in Annual Hours Worked.* Toronto: Institute for Competitiveness and Prosperity, November 2006.

Leacock, Stephen. "The Proper Limitations of State Interference," *Empire Club of Canada Speeches 1924.* Toronto: Empire Club of Canada, 1924, 109–24.

Lindauer, David L. *The Size and Growth of Government Spending: A Background Paper for the 1998 World Development Report.* Washington D.C.: World Bank, September 1998.

Lipset, Martin Seymour. *The Paradox of American Unionism: Why Americans Like Unions More Than Canadians Do, but Join Much Less.* Ithaca, N.Y.: ILR Press, 2004.

Lipset, Martin Seymour. *Continental Divide: The Values and Institutions of the United States and Canada.* New York: Routledge, 1990.

MacDonald, Angus L. *The Speeches of Angus L. MacDonald.* Toronto: Longman's Green and Co., 1960.

Maté, Gabor, and Gordon Neufeld. *Hold on to Your Kids: Why Parents Need to Matter More Than Peers.* Toronto: Vintage Canada, 2005.

McCloskey, Deirdre. *The Bourgeois Virtues: Ethics for an Age of Commerce.* Chicago: University of Chicago Press, 2006.

McFetridge, Donald. *The Economics of Privatization.* Toronto: C.D. Howe Institute, 1997.

McMahon, Fred. *Retreat from Growth: Atlantic Canada and the Negative Sum Economy.* Halifax, AIMS, 2000.

McMahon, Fred. *Looking the Gift Horse in the Mouth: The Impact of Federal Spending on Atlantic Canada.* Halifax: AIMS, 1996.

McRoberts, Kenneth. *Quebec: Social Change and Political Crisis.* Toronto: McClelland & Stewart, 1980.

Meredith, David and Barrie Dyster. *Australia in the Global Economy: Continuity and Change.* New York: Cambridge University Press, 1999.

Milway, Jim, and Roger Martin. *Enhancing the Productivity of Small and Medium Enterprises through Greater Adoption of Information and Communication Technology.* Toronto: Institute for Competitiveness and Prosperity, May 2007.

Mintz, Jack. *Most Favored Nation: Building a Framework for Smart Economic Policy.* Toronto: C.D. Howe Institute, 2001.

Morgan, Nicole. *Implosion: An Analysis of the Growth of the Federal Public Service in Canada, 1945–1985.* Montreal: Institute for Research on Public Policy, 1986.

Morin, Claude. *Quebec versus Ottawa: The Struggle for Self-Government, 1960–1972*. Toronto: University of Toronto Press, 1976.

Murray, Charles. *Losing Ground: American Social Policy, 1950–1980*. New York: Basic Books Publishers, 1984.

Niskanen, William. *Bureaucracy and Representative Government*. Chicago: Adline-Atherton, 1979.

Owram, Douglas. *The Government Generation: Canadian Intellectuals and the State, 1900–1945*. Toronto: University of Toronto Press, 1986.

Paquet, Gilles. *What If There Had Been No Quiet Revolution in Quebec ...* Ottawa: University of Ottawa Press, March 1997.

Paul, Pamela. *The Starter Marriage and the Future of Matrimony*. New York: Random House, 2003.

Pereira, A., et al. *Moving in the Right Direction?: Labour Mobility, Labour Shortage and Canada's Human Potential*. Vancouver: Action Canada, June 2007.

Pontifical Council for Justice and Peace. *Compendium of the Social Doctrine of the Church*. Washington, D.C.: USCCB Publishing, March 2005.

Razin, Assaf. "Notes on Demographic Changes and the Welfare State," in Jane Sneddon Little and Robert K. Triest (eds.), *Seismic Shifts: The Economic Impact of Demographic Change*. Boston: Federal Reserve, 2002: 289–96.

Rauch, Jonathan. *Demosclerosis: The Silent Killer of American Government*. New York: Times Books/Random House, 1994.

Renaud, Marc. "Quebec's New Middle Class in Search of Social Hegemony: Causes and Political Consequences," in Michael D. Behiels (ed.), *Quebec since 1945: Selected Readings*. Toronto: Copp Clark Pitman, 1987: 48–79.

Richards, John, and Matthew Brzozowski. *Let's Walk before We Run: Advice on Childcare*. Toronto: C.D. Howe Institute, August 2006.

Richards, John, and Douglas Allen (eds.). *It Takes Two: The Family in Law and Finance*. Toronto: C.D. Howe Institute, 1999.

Riddell, Craig W. "Unionization in Canada and the United States: A Tale of Two Countries," in David Card and Richard B. Freeman (eds.), *Small Differences That Matter: Labour Markets and Income Maintenance in Canada and the United States*. Chicago: University of Chicago Press, 1993: 109–48.

Roberts, Lance W. (ed.) *Recent Social Trends in Canada, 1960-2000*. Montreal and Kingston: McGill-Queen's University Press, 2005.

Robin, Martin. *Radical Politics and Canadian Labour, 1880–1930*. Kingston: Industrial Relations Centre, Queen's University, 1968.

Roy, Fernande. *L'Histoire des idéologies au Québec aux XIXe et XXe siècles*. Montreal: Editions Boréal, 1993.

Roy, Fernande. *Progrès, harmonie, liberté: Le libéralisme des milieux d'affaires francophones de Montréal au tournant du siècle*. Montreal: Editions Boréal, 1988.

Sauvé, Roger. *Labour Crunch to 2021: National and Provincial Labour Force Projections*. Summerstown, Ont.: People Patterns Consulting, March 2007.

Scowen, Reed. *Time to Say Goodbye: Building a Better Canada without Quebec*, rev. ed. Toronto: McClelland and Stewart, 2007.

Scruton, Roger. *A Dictionary of Political Thought*, 3rd ed. London: Macmillan, April 2007.

Sharpe, Andrew, Jean-Francois Arsenault, and Daniel Ershov. *The Impact of Interprovincial Migration on Aggregate Output and Labour Productivity in Canada, 1987–2006*. Ottawa: Centre for the Study of Living Standards, November 2007.

Smith, James P., and Barry Edmonston (eds.). *The New Americans: Economic, Demographic and Fiscal Effects of Immigration*. Washington D.C.: National Academy Press, 1997.

Sneddon Little, Jane, and Robert K. Triest. "Seismic Shifts: The Economic Impact of Demographic Change: An Overview," in Jane Sneddon Little and Robert K. Triest (eds.), *Seismic Shifts: The Economic Impact of Demographic Change*. Boston: Federal Reserve, 2002: 1–29.

Speer, S.C. *Technocrats and Provincialists: The Rowell-Sirois Commission's Conception of Federalism, 1937–1940*. Unpublished Ph.D. paper, 2007.

Stanbury, W.T. "Government as Leviathan," in Thomas E. Kierans and W.T. Stanbury (eds.), *Papers on Privatization*. Montreal: IRPP, 1985: 243–74.

Stevenson, Garth. *Community Besieged: The Anglophone Minority and the Politics of Quebec*. Montreal and Kingston: McGill-Queen's University Press, 2003.

Stewart, Walter. *The Life and Political Times of Tommy Douglas*. Toronto: McArthur and Company, 2003.

Steyn, Mark. *America Alone: The End of the World as We Know It*. Washington, D.C.: Regnery Publishing, 2006.

Struthers, James. *No Fault of Their Own: Unemployment and the Canadian Welfare State, 1914–1941*. Toronto: University of Press, 1983.

Struthers, James. *Canadian Unemployment Policy in the 1930s*. Peterborough: Windy Pine Papers, 1984.

Tanzi, Vito, and Ludger Schuknecht. *Public Spending in the Twentieth Century: A Global Perspective*. Cambridge: Cambridge University Press, 2000.

Taylor, Charles. "Nationalism and the Political Intelligentsia: A Case Study," in Taylor, *Reconciling the Solitudes: Essays on Canadian Federalism and Nationalism*. Montreal and Kingston: McGill-Queen's University Press, 1993.

The Empire Club of Canada Speeches 1968-1969. Toronto: The Empire Club of Canada, 1969.

Vaillancourt, François, Dominique Lemay, and Luc Vaillancourt. *Laggards No More: The Changed Socioeconomic Status of Francophones in Quebec*. Toronto: C.D. Howe Institute, August 2007.

Vining, A.R. and R. Botterell, "An Overview of the Origins, Growth, Size, and Functions of Provincial Crown Corporations," in J. R. S. Pritchard (ed.) *Crown Corporations: The Calculus of Instrument Choice*, (Toronto: Butterworths, 1983): 303-368.

Waiser, Bill. *Saskatchewan: A New History*. Calgary: Fifth House, 2005.

Walkom, Thomas. *Rae Days: The Rise and Follies of the NDP*. Toronto: Key Porter Books, 1994.

Watson, William. *Globalization and the Meaning of Canadian Life*. Toronto: University of Toronto Press, 1998.

Watson, William, John Richards, and David Brown. *The Case for Change: Reinventing the Welfare State*. Toronto: C.D. Howe Institute, 1994.

Whelan, Robert. *Broken Homes and Battered Children: A Study of the Relationship between Child Abuse and Family Type*. London: Family Education Trust, 1993.

Wilson, James Q. *The Marriage Problem: How Our Culture Has Weakened Families*. New York: HarperCollins, 2002.

Watson Wyatt Worldwide. *A Report on the World Economic Forum Pension Readiness Initiative*. Davos, Switzerland: World Economic Forum, January 2004.

Yergin, Daniel, and Joseph Stanislaw. *The Commanding Heights: The Battle for the World Economy*. New York: Simon & Schuster, 2002.

Zimmerman, Carle C. *Family and Civilization*. Wilmington, Del.: ISI Books, 2008.

WEBSITES

Radio-Canada Archives: http://archives.radio-canada.ca/societe/religion_spiritualite/clips/6270

Castellanos, Alex. "The Tyranny of Good Intentions," *National Review Online*: http://article.nationalreview.com/?q=MWU2ODgzNzg2MmIyN2Y3ZWFjY2ZlODVmMTgzYjMwMjY=

Citizenship and Immigration Canada, *2006 Annual Report to Parliament on Immigration*: http://www.cic.gc.ca/english/DEPARTMENT/media/backgrounders/2006/2006-10-31.asp.

Sowell, Thomas. "Subprime Pols," *National Review Online*: http://article.nationalreview.com/?q=YjgwYzI4Njg3OWMxOGUzYmY0ZDMwYzY-wNzkzYjc1NDI=

CBC News: http://www.cbc.ca/news/yourview/2008/01/82of canadianswouldratherw.html

CBS News. *Love and Marriage: A CBS News Poll*. February 2001: http://www.cbsnews.com/stories/2001/02/25/opinion/main274410.shtml.

Sala-i-Martin, Xavier. *The World Distribution of Income*: http://www.columbia.edu/~xs23/papers/pdfs/World_Income_Distribution_QJE.pdf

Martel, Shelly. "New NS government program to benefit young fishermen," *Nova Scotia Business Journal*: http://www.dailybusinessbuzz.ca/?p=7938&utm_source=ConstantContact.com&utm_medium=email&utm_campaign=DailyBuzz_20090408

Economic Profile of Japan, *The Economist*: http://www.economist.com/Countries/Japan/profile.cfm?folder=Profile-Economic%20Data

JRank Family Library: http://family.jrank.org/pages/1578/Single-Parent-Families-Economics-Single-Parent-Family-Life.html

Crowley, Brian Lee. "Employment Insurance causes unemployment," *Chronicle Herald*. September 10, 2003: http://www.aims.ca/aimslibrary.asp?cmPageID=192&ft=4&id=102.

Department of Finance, Historical Federal Debt Figures: http://www.fin.gc.ca/frt-trf/2008/frt08_3-eng.asp.

Easterly, William. "Leaders Go Left, But Economists Get Back To Basics," *Forbes Magazine Online*: http://www.forbes.com/2009/01/29/davos-economic-basics-opinions-contributors_0130_william_easterly.html?partner=email

Greg Mankiw's blog: http://gregmankiw.blogspot.com/2009/02/news-flash-economists-agree.html

Ipsos Reid, *Press Release*, Poll on Work in Canada: http://www.ipsos-na.com/news/pressrelease.cfm?id=3896

Roback-Morse, Jennifer. *Prosperity Through Timeless Values*: http://www.jennifer-roback-morse.com/articles/cohabitation_fast_facts.pdf

Claire Joly's blog: http://www.leblogueduql.org/2005/10/le_mythe_de_la_.html

Andrew Coyne's blog: http://www2.macleans.ca/2008/05/14/mcguintonomics/

Loomis, Carol J. "A Conversation with Warren Buffet," *Fortune Magazine Online*: http://money.cnn.com/2006/06/25/magazines/fortune/charity2.fortune/index.htm

Sun Life Financial, *Press Release*, Poll on Retirement in Canada: http://www.sunlife.ca/canada/v/index.jsp?vgnextoid=1aaf570ea6d1f110VgnVCM100000bd2d09fRCRD&vgnLocale=en_CA&chnpath=%2FsunlifeCA

Transcript of speech by Prime Minister Stephen Harper: http://pm.gc.ca/eng/media.asp?category=2&id=2469

Statistics Canada, *Daily*: http://www.statcan.ca/Daily/English/061026/d061026b.htm.

Statistics Canada, *Daily*: http://www.statcan.ca/Daily/English/080721/d080721.pdf

"Ultramontanism in Canada," *Canadian Encyclopedia Online*: http://www.thecanadianencyclopedia.com/index.cfm?PgNm=TCE&Params=A1ARTA0008196

World Economic Forum, 2008 Summit on the Global Agenda: http://www.weforum.org/pdf/GAC/Reports/EconomicDevelopmentGrowth/EconomicGrowthandDevelopment.pdf

Oldaker, Randy A. "Some Tidbits on Ancient Athens," (accessed in November 2007): http://www.wvup.edu/Academics/humanisties/Oldaker/some_tidbits_on_ancient_athens.htm.

US Bureau of Labor Statistics. *Employment status of the civilian population, 1940 to date*: http://www.bls.gov/cps/cpsaat1.pdf

Rogusky, Derek and Mark Penninga. *Building a Healthy Nation: Policies to Encourage Strong Marriages and Stable Families.* Ottawa: Institute for Marriage and Family Canada: http://www.imfcanada.org/article_files/Building_a_healthy_nation.pdf

Leithner, Chris. "What on Earth Has Happened to Canada?" *Le Québécois Libre*, No. 131. October 25, 2003. http://www.quebecoislibre.org/031025-6.htm.